VULTURES' PICNIC

GREG PALAST spent two decades investigating corporate fraud and racketeering before he turned his skills to journalism. Author of the *New York Times*
bestsellers *Armed Madhouse* and *The Best Democracy Money Can Buy*, Palast's
reports appear on BBC's *Newsnight* and in Britain's *Guardian*. Born in Los
Angeles and a graduate of the University of Chicago, Palast lives in New York
City.

Praise for Greg Palast

"Palast's story—delivered in delightfully barbed tones—switches back and
forth between his many years spent digging up the dirt (figuratively and
otherwise) on money-guzzling oil companies . . . By taking his duties as an
investigative journalist to their logical conclusion, the result is a meaty
exposition of the real bad guys."   —*The National*

"Thrills like a spy novel but is even more exciting because it is TRUE."
                                                          —BookPleasures.com

"A cross between Seymour Hersh and Jack Kerouac."   —BuzzFlash.com

"The real Sam Spade."   —Jim Hightower, *The Nation*

"Palast upsets all the right people."   —Noam Chomsky

"We hate that sonovabitch."   —White House spokesman

"Book of the Year: Greg Palast's *Armed Madhouse*, incendiary . . . virtuosic . . .
had me cheering on my feet."   —*New Statesman*

"Great fun. Palast, detective style, provides . . . pieces of the secret puzzle."
                                                            —*The New Yorker*

ALSO BY GREG PALAST

The Best Democracy Money Can Buy

Armed Madhouse

VULTURES' PICNIC

In Pursuit of Petroleum Pigs, Power Pirates, and High-Finance Carnivores

A **Greg Palast** INVESTIGATION

» An oil rig explodes in the Gulf,

» Miss Badpenny slips into her leathers, and

» "the most important investigative journalist of our time" [*The Guardian*] goes on the hunt.

From the Arctic to the Islamic Republic of BP, from a burnt-out nuclear reactor in Japan to Mardi Gras in New Orleans, PALAST uncovers the story you won't get on CNN.

A PLUME BOOK

PLUME
Published by the Penguin Group
Penguin Group (USA) Inc., 375 Hudson Street, New York, New York 10014, U.S.A. •
Penguin Group (Canada), 90 Eglinton Avenue East, Suite 700, Toronto, Ontario, Canada
M4P 2Y3 (a division of Pearson Penguin Canada Inc.) • Penguin Books Ltd., 80 Strand,
London WC2R 0RL, England • Penguin Ireland, 25 St. Stephen's Green, Dublin 2, Ireland
(a division of Penguin Books Ltd.) • Penguin Group (Australia), 707 Collins Street,
Melbourne, Victoria 3008, Australia (a division of Pearson Australia Group Pty. Ltd.) •
Penguin Books India Pvt. Ltd., 11 Community Centre, Panchsheel Park, New Delhi – 110 017,
India • Penguin Group (NZ), 67 Apollo Drive, Rosedale, Auckland 0632, New Zealand
(a division of Pearson New Zealand Ltd.) • Penguin Books, Rosebank Office Park, 181 Jan
Smuts Avenue, Parktown North 2193, South Africa • Penguin China, B7 Jaiming Center,
27 East Third Ring Road North, Chaoyang District, Beijing 100020, China

Penguin Books Ltd., Registered Offices: 80 Strand, London WC2R 0RL, England

Published by Plume, a member of Penguin Group (USA) Inc. Previously published in a Dutton
edition.

First Plume Printing, September 2012
10   9   8   7   6   5   4   3   2   1

Copyright © Greg Palast, 2011
Art care of Matt Pascarella
Photos on pages 232, 242, 247 by James Macalpine
All rights reserved

℗ REGISTERED TRADEMARK—MARCA REGISTRADA

The Library of Congress has catalogued the Dutton edition as follows:

Palast, Greg.
Vultures' picnic : in pursuit of petroleum pigs, power pirates, and high-finance carnivores /
by Greg Palast.
p.   cm.
Includes bibliographical references and index.
ISBN 978-0-525-95207-7 (hc.)
ISBN 978-0-452-29864-4 (pbk.)
1. Petroleum industry and trade—Corrupt practices.   2. BP (Firm)—Moral and ethical
aspects.
3. Banks and banking, International—Moral and ethical aspects.   4. International
finance—Moral and ethical aspects.   I. Title
HD9560.5.P236   2011
338.7'6655—dc23   2011032687

Printed in the United States of America
Original hardcover design by Daniel Lagin

There's always an excuse to be a prick.

—C. Bukowski

There's a man by my side walkin'.

There's a voice within me talkin'.

There are words that need a-sayin'.

For Frank Rosen

United Electrical and Machine Workers' Union

Carry it on.

CONTENTS

1. Goldfinger 1

2. Lady Baba-Land: The Islamic Republic of BP 43

3. Pig in the Pipeline 95

4. The Coon-Ass Riviera 125

5. The Cheese Smelled Funny So We Threw It in the Jungle 167

6. The Wizard of Ooze 181

7. My Home Is Now a Strange Place 205

8. We Figured Out Who Murdered Jake 253

9. The Sorcerer's Stone 269

10. Fukushima, Texas 287

11. Mr. Fairness 313

12. The Generalissimo of Globalization 321

13. Vultures' Picnic 363

14. Lots of Fish 389

Contact the Palast Investigative Team 395

Read, Listen, Interact ... 397

Vultures' Picnic: An Investigative Comic Book Series 398

Watch This ... 399

Acknowledgments 400

Based on the reports for BBC Television *Newsnight,* for Channel 4 *Dispatches,* for ARTE, and for *Democracy Now!*

Portions of this story have appeared in SuicideGirls.com, *Hustler, Harper's Magazine,* BuzzFlash.com, *New Statesman, Rolling Stone, Dazed and Confused, Radar,* Truthout.com, The Raw Story, AlterNet, *The Guardian, The Shadow, Red Pepper, In These Times,* Top Shelf Comix, *The Observer* (London), and one story, forgive me, in *The New York Times.*

Everything that happens here, happened.

CHAPTER 1
Goldfinger

ROLLING HILLS, OUTSIDE NEW YORK CITY

It's all my fault, because I'm such a cheap bastard. I was told to rent a white van, something nondescript that painters or a handyman might use and wouldn't be noticed parked at dawn on a road where only BMWs and Carrera 95s play.

But I was afraid BBC wouldn't pay for the van rental (I was right about that) and so here I was in the Red Menace, my fourteen-year-old busted-up Honda with the *brakes* idiot light on.

Anyway, I won't move. *I can wait you out.*

Well, maybe I can. It's freezing insane cold and the Dunkin' Donuts coffee is cold, and I have to urinate out the last three cups I killed waiting on The Vulture to drive through his estate's electronic gate to his "work" so I can somehow tail him unseen in my ridiculous red car.

And now God is snowing on me. Thick, nasty, wet, heavy predawn snow, so everything turns white except my red beater. I might as well stick a flashing sign on the hood: I AM ON A STAKEOUT. I AM LOOKING FOR YOU.

We started at four A.M. It looks really glamorous on-screen when we broadcast these stories: the dramatic long-lens footage, then the jump and the confrontation. But after four horridly cold hours, there is nothing glamorous, just my bladder screaming at me.

Badpenny calls from our Toyota, staked out in front of Vulture's office building. Same issue—she and Jacquie have to pee. So now they could blow the whole story because *God forbid* they should just squat behind a tree and make some yellow snow. The women insist on porcelain and *have to* leave their post. All right, damn it, find a gas station but *don't let them see you.*

Ricardo is cuddling his camera. His baby. Ricardo is calm. Ricardo is *always* calm. He's just back from Iraq, where calm kept him alive. Ricardo is never hungry; Ricardo is never cold and *never* needs to urinate. Whatever drug he's on, I want it.

I tell Ricardo, "We stay." Why? If God doesn't give a rat's ass about The Vulture and what he does for a living, what he's done to Africa, why should I? Well, fuck God.

If I were a psychologist, I'd say I'm here because my father worked in a furniture store in the barrio in Los Angeles, selling pure crap on layaway to Mexicans; then later on, he sold fancier crap to fancier people in Beverly Hills and he *hated* furniture, and I hated the undeserving pricks and their trophy wives who bought it. I could smell their cash and the smell of the corpses they stole it from. They were *all* vultures, and the rest of us were just food.

So there you have it. My story, my motivation: resentment, envy, revolutionary fervor, whatever.

But I'm not a psychologist. I'm a reporter. And apparently one with a tiny, if fervent, international reputation: Just this morning I got a request from another young man, this one from Poland, who wants to join our investigative team. But instead of the usual résumé, Lukasz the wannabe journalist writes from Krakow that he walked away with my BBC press pass, my notebook, and my laptop, which he'd found at London's Heathrow Airport. Rather than money, he wants the job. It wasn't ransom: If I said no to the job, he'd return the pass and notebook anyway. But he'd already junked the computer after cracking my security codes.

I could use a guy like that.

But I don't ask why I'm here. I *know* why I'm here. It's because of what our Insider said on the tape about Vulture:

Eric's gone over to the Dark Side.

LAS VEGAS

The two-grand-a-night call girls are wandering lonely and disconsolate through the Wynn casino, victims of the recession. Badpenny, dressed full-on Bond Girl, is losing nickels in the slots and humming Elvis tunes.

Badpenny's assigned job here is to look good and get information. She's good at her job. A tipsy plaintiff's lawyer is telling her, "A woman as beautiful as you should be told she's beautiful every five minutes." His nose dips slowly toward her cleavage. I didn't know there were guys who still talked like that. Well, good. Take notes, Penny.

My own assignment is to hook up with Daniel Becnel. Becnel is just about the best trial lawyer in the United States. He doesn't have an office in Vegas or New York. He puts out his shingle at the ass end of Louisiana, at the far end of the bayous, where he defends Cajuns like himself, and that includes the wild-catters out on the Gulf Coast oil rigs.

I have just come back from the Amazon jungle, where I was tracking Chevron's operations. Chevron Petroleum monopolizes deepwater drilling in the Gulf of Mexico. Maybe Becnel and I could trade information. It's April 20, 2010. Hitler's birthday and my ex-wife's.

I found Becnel—far from the gaming tables and looking unpleasantly sober.

There was an explosion back home. A rig blew out and was burning. The Coast Guard called him. They want his permission to open an emergency safety capsule they'd found floating in the Gulf. The Guard assumed maybe a dozen of his clients who had been working on the Deepwater Horizon plat-form were inside, cooked alive.

The sound on the TV above the bar is off. The high, black rolls of smoke rising out of the BP oil rig remind me of my own office when it burned.

Something is *very* wrong in this picture. All I can see are a couple of fire-boats pointlessly shpritzing the methane-petroleum blaze with water. What the hell? Where are the Vikoma Ocean Packs and the RO-Boom? *Where is the Sea Devil?*

Because of my screwy career path, I happen to know a lot about oil spill containment. And I know a lot about bullshit. This isn't spill containment, this is bullshit.

Here is a skyscraper on fire, and the firemen show up with two bottles of seltzer.

How could they do this? How could British Petroleum, the oil company with the green gas stations, with the solar panels on the cover of their annual report, that kissed environmental groups full on the mouth by breaking ranks with Exxon to decry global warming . . . how could Green BP savage and slime our precious Gulf Coast?

The answer: *BP had lots of practice.*

By the next day, CNN's Anderson Cooper and an entire flock of reporters ran down to the Gulf to take close-ups of greased birds and to interview that mush-mouthed fraud, Louisiana Governor Bobby Jindal.

But I know something the other reporters don't know: The real story about the BP blowout is in the opposite direction, eight thousand miles north.

I have in my files a highly confidential four-volume investigation on the grounding of the *Exxon Valdez* in Alaska, written two decades ago. The report concluded,

> "Despite the name 'Exxon' on the ship, the real culprit in destroying the coastline of Alaska is British Petroleum."

I have a copy because I wrote it.

That was my last job. The job that defeated me: after years as a detective-economist, investigator of corporate fraud and racketeering, this was the case that ruined the game for me.

The important thing, the hidden story calling me north, is that the Deep-water Horizon disaster was born right there on the Alaska tanker route. Here's why: BP did the crime but didn't do the time. Exxon got away pretty cheap, sure, but BP walked away stone free, not one dime from its treasury, not one drop of oil blotting its green reputation. So I quit.

But for now, from the casino, Badpenny is booking me a flight on Alaska Airlines and calling around for a Cessna Apache to charter to the Tatitlek Village on Bligh Island. The network would have to trust me on this. I know that the key to exposing the cause of the Gulf spill is there in the Tatitlek Native Village. I need to speak with Chief Kompkoff.

SOMEWHERE OFF THE COAST OF AZERBAIJAN

Just after leaving Las Vegas, Badpenny received an e-mail marked "Re: Your Palast Donation," coming from, weirdly, a ship floating in the Caspian Sea near BP's Central Azeri oil drilling platform, that is, somewhere off the coast of Azerbaijan in Central Asia. It read,

be most honoured to help Greg out any way I could. As you
working on a [redacted] in the Caspian Sea for the past [redacted] years &
knowledge of how they operate day to day. I am currently on [redacted] &
weeks, would not be wise for me to communicate via [redacted] IT system, so

We replied, "Understood," and waited.

When the Deepwater Horizon well blew out in the Gulf, BP acted shocked. Just six months before the Gulf explosion, a BP vice president testified to Congress that the company had drilled offshore for fifty years without a major blowout. When the big well did blow in the Gulf, the company said that nothing like this had ever happened before. That is, nothing they reported.

Weeks after we received the first message from the ship in the Caspian Sea, we located our terrified source in a port town in Central Asia; and he told us BP's claim to Congress was a load of crap. He himself had witnessed another deepwater platform blowout. He seemed really nervous. And for good reason.

I didn't know where the hell I'd get the budget to get to Baku, the capital of Azerbaijan, but Badpenny booked it without asking. "I know you're going, so let's not discuss it."

ROLLING HILLS, NEW YORK

Cold coffee in a snowstorm wasn't what I had in mind. The original plan was not so screwed up. I'd enlisted that crazy bastard John McEnroe (really) to help us get consent to get onto The Vulture's property.

From satellite photos of Vulture's estate, we could pick out a tennis court not a hundred yards from his entranceway. To get cameras onto his property, we would show up in tennis whites with our smiling crew from the new reality show *So You Think You Can Play Tennis! Starring John McEnroe!* Would Vulture like to swing a racket with the champ?

But our timing went to hell. Tennis balls in a blizzard? Forget it.

Now London is calling on Ricardo's cell. BBC Television Centre. Trouble. Some flunky working for Dr. Eric Hermann aka The Vulture seems to have spotted a red car at the end of his driveway and called Dr. Hermann's PR firm in England, where it's already late morning. The Vulture's flak squawked at the BBC news desk, "Is Palast on a 'vulture hunt?'" Jones, my producer, says he told The Doctor's PR, *damn right.*

Jones adds, *"A farkin* red car!?" Forgive him, he's Welsh.

Cold, and now a bad, bad thought: *He's slipped us.* That's easy to do from a house bigger than the Vatican—twenty thousand square feet with nine bathrooms (we checked the tax records). Worse, the aerial photo revealed acres of woods on the blind side, which leads right to the back of the Doctor's office tower. And the profile said Dr. Hermann was a serious marathoner. This guy could merrily lope right across his private forest to his office, chuckling at the schmuck in the red car. Or maybe he could *apparate* there like a *Harry Potter* wizard.

Badpenny and Jacquie swore over the cell that they hadn't spotted one face from their photo sheet going into the building, but that could have been due to their inexcusable porcelain pit stop.

I drove the Red Menace too fast on the ice around the back roads to Hermann's office.

We already had the layout. Badpenny had done the recon a week earlier. She deliberately misaddressed an envelope, made a "delivery" to their office, acting like a confused ditz while mentally mapping the place. Now, as we're huddled against the snow, she tells Ricardo that if we could get by the distractible security guy with some BS, we could walk right into the fourth-floor office suites of The Vulture's company, FH International.

Inside the building—the security desk was oddly empty—Ricardo hopped the elevator, pulled his ultra-small digi-cam out of the sports bag and clicked on the microphone. A well-dressed woman riding up with us asked, "Surprise for someone?"

It was. But the surprise would be on us.

We hustled around the fourth floor with Badpenny's hand-drawn map, looking for the FH suite doors. Around and around the building halls we went, three times, comically lost. Then I noticed a huge white spot on the hallway wall: The big sculpted name plaque of FH International had been *unbolted from the wall*, the office number removed and the door locked.

Gone. In just *hours*. A billion-dollar group of international hedge funds . . . *pfft!*

I leaned against the door, just exhausted, just defeated.

Then I heard voices. Behind the doors. The Vulture had his employees *locked in*.

Now this was slapstick, this was the land of the weird: multimillionaires cowering under their desks in the dark, afraid of the guy in a red Honda. I was honored.

All this, the unbolted sign, the muffled millionaires, all to avoid answering this one question,

What, or who, is the Hamsah?

LIBERIA, WEST AFRICA

With The Vulture's crew still pretending they were invisible and building Security hustling us down the elevator, we knew the only way to get an answer to our question was to get inoculations and emergency visas and head out to Liberia. BBC was not happy about the cost of the airfare and I don't blame them, but I had to speak to the President herself.

Thirty-six hours after the stakeout in the snow, we were sweating at customs in Accra, in West Africa.

"WELCOME TO GHANA. WE DO NOT TOLERATE SEXUAL PERVERSIONS."

Well, as a national motto, that's a cut above *In God We Trust*.

It wasn't like the last time I tried to get a transfer into Liberia, during the civil war, in 1996, when the capital's airport was just a bunch of holes, bomb craters. Back then, the only flight in was chanced once a week by two Russians running contraband on an old Tupolev turboprop. I was told I could hitch a ride for two bottles of vodka. I asked if I could give them the vodka *after* we landed. *Nyet*.

Now I'm flying in on Ethiopian Airlines and taking the vodka for myself despite my promises to cut that shit out.

If you can't name the capital of Liberia, relax, this isn't a test. Most Americans don't learn the capitals of foreign lands until the 82nd Airborne lands there. Kabul. Mogadishu. Saigon.

Answer: It's Monrovia. The capital of Liberia is named after the U.S. President James Monroe, who helped former American slaves give birth to the longest-lived democracy in Africa, founded in 1847. Its democracy dropped dead when, in 1980, a Corporal Sam Doe marched every member of the elected president's cabinet out to the nearby beach, tied them to poles and shot them, TV cameras rolling. Ronald Reagan was elated and helped the killer dictator Sam Doe turn Liberia into a Cold War killing zone. One in ten Liberians would die.

Richard and I arrived in Liberia without two clues to rub together. But Ricardo had one. He had just learned some Arabic the hard way: As an involuntary guest of some bad guys in Basra, Iraq. He said, "You know, *Hamsah* in Arabic means 'Five.'"

Ah.

More significantly, a Hamsah looks like this:

The symbol is Lebanese. Of course.

MOTOWN

By the age of fifteen, Rick Rowley was doomed. Born in the middle of Nowhere, Michigan, a wasteland of rust and snow so awful we let autoworkers have it. As a kid, Rick would put his head down on the railroad track and wait for the rare vibration of a train on the move far away. He was fifteen years old on the day he got up and followed the hum down the track. He walked for over two hundred miles, surviving on peanut butter and Wonder Bread all the way to Motor City: Detroit.

Rick wasn't running away; his parents were OK. He was running *to* something; who knows what the hell it was.

Rick never made it back to Nowhere.

He listened. He looked. And he found that other people's stories were more important than his own.

Along the way, he picked up a small camera that listened and looked with him. He found more stories in Argentina inside the IMF riots, then six months in the Yucatan jungle, learning Spanish with the Zapatista guerillas, who named him Ricardo, then somewhere along the way a stretch at Princeton University, then several stints in Iraq, in Afghanistan, and in Lebanon, with Hezbollah.

He held the little thing, that digital camera, weirdly, cradled like an infant. The first time he filmed for BBC News, at my insistence, Jones said, "What's that? Some kind of toy camera?" No, it's my gun.

Ricardo doesn't like to talk about himself. It took three deadly potent drinks at a bar in West Africa to find out about the railroad track, Hezbollah, Princeton.

He's off now, un-embedded.

Ignoring Jones's advice, he made it back to Iraq to catch warlord Abu Musa's last arrogant words before Abu was blown into small wet pieces. Rick's a lucky guy. So far.

TATITLEK VILLAGE, BLIGH ISLAND, ALASKA

Chief Gary Kompkoff stood on the beach, watching the Very Large Crude Carrier VLCC *Exxon Valdez* bearing down on Bligh Reef. Kompkoff was wondering, *What the hell?*

It was near midnight, starlit and clear. As the ship's shadow loomed, the whole village joined him on the beach, wondering, *What the hell?*

Kompkoff told me he thought it was some kind of dumb-ass drill. Even a drunk couldn't miss the turning halogen warning beam lighting up their faces every nine seconds.

It wasn't a drill.

Now, don't get the idea that these were just a bunch of dumb Indians stunned by the appearance of the white man's supertanker. They didn't have televisions, but they did have training in oil spill containment.

Containing an oil spill on water isn't rocket science. Whether it's a busted tanker or a blown well, you do two things: First you put a rubber skirt around it. The skirt is called a "boom". Then you bring in a skimmer barge with a big sucker hose hanging off it and suck up the oil within the rubber corral; or you can sink it ("disperse" it with chemicals); or you tow it away and set it on fire. There are lunatic variants of course, most employed by BP. In 1967, the *Torrey Canyon*, in the English Channel, took a shortcut meant for fishing boats and broke up. It was the largest tanker spill ever. British Petroleum called in the Royal Air Force, which bombed the hell out of the slick as it floated across the Channel to France. The RAF was as effective on the floating oil as they are on the Taliban. Oil Slick: 1. RAF: 0.

Here's a dirt-simple illustration of how you contain an oil slick from a busted tanker.

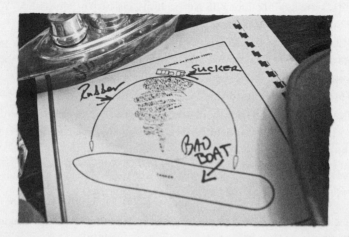

It's roughly the same for a well blowout. You see in this photo a small cartoon tug dragging the rubber skirt, called a Vikoma Ocean Pack, around the ship, while the other little boat, a Sea Devil skimmer, sucks up the blotch, the floating oil.

Here's the irony, or the crime, take your pick: I obtained this diagram from Alyeska, the company responsible for containing and cleaning up oil spills on Alaskan waters, no matter who owns the tanker. Alyeska is a combine of companies and the politically helpful cover name for its senior owner, British Petroleum. Exxon is junior. Some junior.

The tanker spill illustration is from the BP-Exxon official OSRP (Oil Spill Response Plan) for Prince William Sound, Alaska, published *two years before* the *Exxon Valdez* grounding at Bligh Island, Tatitlek. The oil companies' top executives swore to this plan under oath before Congress.

It was, I admit, a beautiful plan.

It had everything: suckers and rubbers all over the place, and round-the-clock emergency crews ready to roll.

Simple simple: Surround with rubber and suck. The Tatitlek Natives could have done that lickety-split and you would have never heard of the *Exxon Valdez*.

But *could have* are the two most heartbreaking words in the English language.

The Natives were the firemen with the equipment. It was right in the plan. They just stood there. *Why?*

During my investigation right after the *Exxon* spill, Henry Makarka ("Little Bird"), the Eyak elder, flew me over to the village of Nuciiq, abandoned now. He told me, "I had to watch an otter rip out its own eyes trying to get out the oil." Henry's a sweet guy, eighty now. But in case I missed the point, he added, "If I had a machine gun, I'd kill every one of them white sons of bitches."

He didn't say, "white." He used the unkind Alutiiq phrase, *isuwiq* something, *bleached seal*.

I needed him to tell me straight, no BS, what the hell happened in those meetings between the Chugach chiefs and the oil company chiefs twenty years earlier, to back up my suspicions, or to tell me I had hit another dead end. It was not a conversation he was happy to have, especially with a bleached seal investigator.

The Eyak, Tatitlek, and other Chugach Natives have lived in the Sound for three thousand years, maybe more, the very last Americans to live off what they could catch, gather, hunt. It was March 24, four minutes after midnight, 1989, when Kompkoff witnessed the moment when three thousand years of Chugach history came to an end, the moment when Satan collected his due for the Natives' complicity, especially Makarka's tribe.

LOS ANGELES, CALIFORNIA

Why am I flying all over hell? Why am I chasing down kooky potentates and cowering hedge fund speculators, then schlepping you up to the Arctic and down to the Amazon?

Why am I writing this all down, dragging you along with me?

My publisher wants me to write a neat little book on one simple topic, like "oil companies" or "banks" or "Recipes from *Sex and the City*." But the planet is not as simple as a quart of homogenized milk, all silky white.

It's a mess, it's a jumble. Get used to it.

That's how it is. That's how we work. I don't get to say, *Oh, please don't send me that smoking information this week*. And the weeks following the Deepwater Horizon disaster produced the heaviest shower of must-follow info in my career.

But, for the sake of clarity, and my sanity and yours, I will take you along with me, one investigative move at a time. Only in this first chapter, I want to show you how our work actually gets done, following down several tracks at once. Stumbling over each other, knocking our heads into walls (I get my best ideas that way).

I'm what Dr. Bruce, my high school science teacher, would call a honey dipper. Before Dr. Bruce earned his doctorate, he took one of the few jobs a Black child in the Deep South could grab to earn a few dollars, honey dipping. When someone dropped a wedding ring or a wallet down into the outhouse toilet, Dr. Bruce would dip into it with his bucket, pull up the stuff and go through it carefully. He got to enjoy it. So have I, dipping in, squeezing it through our investigative filters, finding the good stuff. There's not one topic, but there is only one story: I chase different turds around the planet, but it's all the same shit.

There is only one story: the story of Them versus Us.

THEY get homes bigger than Disneyland, WE get foreclosure notices.

THEY get private jets to private islands, WE get tar balls and lost futures, and pay their gambling debts with our pensions.

THEY get the third trophy wife and a tax break, WE get sub-primed.

THEY get two candidates on the ballot and WE are told to choose.

THEY get the gold mine, WE get the shaft.

Them versus Us: that's my career, my obsession—and my tombstone (*THEY* FINALLY GOT ME.).

This book, this journey, is a quest to unmask The Beast, the monstrous machine that works ceaselessly to take from Us to give to Them.

That's not answering the question, is it? The question of *why* I'm doing this.

I'm from Los Angeles, from the trough called The Valley, where the losers are tossed until there's a need for cheap labor and cheap soldiers when the *gusanos* don't supply enough.

I went back there, just once. When you drive over the Hollywood Hills and descend into The Valley, you don't see houses, you see a heaving smoggy soup that's a kind of puke-and-urine yellow. The female giving me a lift said, "I thought Southern California had climate. This is a *color.*"

I grew up and, fast as I could, got out of the urine soup. After failing at several unpromising jobs—ballroom dance instructor, sandwich-sign man, jazz drummer, sperm donor, ghost writer for term papers (*"an 'A' guaranteed!"*), I ended up an investigator. I did the big cases, involving hundreds of millions and billions of dollars. I got screwed around a lot. That is, my targets always seemed to slither away in time to catch the best table at Nobu.

So I quit. Now I'm an investigative reporter. I still get screwed around. But now, I can screw back.

THE GULF COAST, ALABAMA SHORES

The story I'd gotten from our scout Ronald Roberts was like some Grade B horror movie: Fish were drowning.

In weird places all over the Gulf, dead. I didn't even *know* a fish could drown. But then, what I don't know would be a book all by itself.

Ronald Roberts had gone to sniff the scene ahead of us and ask BP questions without raising questions himself. His real name isn't Ronald, it's Zachary: Zach Roberts the photojournalist. But if you Google "Ronald" Roberts, you get a photo of a Florida sex offender, deceased, as well as the author of the classic study *Fish Pathology.*

Despite the oil still barfing out of its Macondo hole, BP was in holocaust denial mode: *The fish were not dead.* And, BP said, if they were dead, BP didn't kill them.

Investigating fish murder isn't my game. So I would need an expert who wasn't full of shit and wasn't full of industry money. The field was narrow, so it's no surprise that without consulting each other, Ronald/Zachary and I settled on Dr. Rick Steiner. I knew Steiner as the Big Name in fish and oil contamination, the chairman of the biology department at the University of Alaska. Steiner literally jumped into the field two decades ago, wading into the *Exxon Valdez* muck engulfing his own boat.

Professor Steiner was not only beyond corruption, he was beyond telephones, somewhere in Africa. My research maven, Matty Pass, somehow tapping into our telepathic vibe, also went on the search for Dr. Steiner, locating him in that toxic toilet called Nigeria, playing with sludge left there by Shell Oil forty years earlier.

We lucked out because Steiner wanted to scoop up some of BP's dreck off the Mississippi coast for testing. The oil company wouldn't let Steiner come along with their rent-a-profs, so he arranged to visit the suspect water columns by submarine. No kidding.

The professor offered to take me down with him.

It was worth a flight to the Gulf Coast to do the Captain Nemo thing with Steiner so I could pick up some scientific clues to answer a question that just wouldn't let go of me: The wrecking of the Gulf Coast, the dead marshes and polluted wetlands shown on TV over and over . . . everyone agreed it was BP's oil. Was it really BP? I suspected not, and not without reason.

SEATTLE, WASHINGTON

Our floating inside witness, even out in the Caspian, knew he had to stay behind a cloak. He knew, and everyone in the industry knows: Bad things happen to people who drop a dime on BP.

Chuck Hamel could tell him. Hamel, an oilman, had partnered with BP and Exxon in Alaska. In 1986, he discovered that the Valdez terminal was a mess, a tanker accident waiting to happen. He was so shook up, he took the first Concorde he could find to London to tell BP's chairman, in person, they were in danger of a disaster.

BP's response was to hire a team of former CIA spooks to trail him. They tapped his phone. They broke into his house. They set honey traps, women lesser men would not pass up, but Hamel is unnaturally faithful to his wife. Then, when Hamel set up a meeting with a Congressman in Washington, BP's Alaska CEOs went nuts trying to figure out which whistle Hamel would blow. BP's black-bag crew ran a remote-controlled toy truck through hotel ventilation ducts and rigged the toy with wires for microphones to eavesdrop on Hamel. Unfortunately for the BP operatives, U.S. Navy Seals had set up a secret listening post in the hotel. The Navy's espionage team flipped out when they picked up the BP microphone, sure that the Russians were onto them. The Navy agents traced the signal, kicked in the hotel room door, and arrested BP's spies.

BP had to write a check to Hamel. But the industry was patient and got Hamel in the end. When Hamel first teamed up with Exxon, he was a wealthy oilman. He's no longer wealthy and has no more oil. I just spoke to him in Seattle, where he had moved after Exxon bankrupted him.

Hamel doesn't have a lot of good days now. He is ill, with not enough air to get through our conversations. But I needed his help.

I had braved through six hundred pages of BP's Oil Spill Response Plan for their Gulf deepwater operation. I didn't have to. It was pretty much a photocopy of the Alaska plan. Rubber boom, skimmer, emergency crews (and seal cleaning). That was the boom and skimmers I did *not* see around BP's burning, sinking Gulf rig when I caught it on the TV screens above the bar in Vegas. I can't say I was shocked.

The equipment wasn't there in Alaska and it wasn't there in the Gulf. Same company, same plan, same bullshit. The real question for me was, *How are they going to get away with it* this *time*? Hamel's good wife had had enough, and told him to stay low. But I figured Hamel might know someone who might know someone.

But whomever he could lead me to might not talk: after the job BP did on him and a half dozen others, not many industry or government insiders would poke their heads out, even to whisper to me off-the-record. Hamel gave me the number of Inspector Dan Lawn. BP's spies had tapped his phone too. But The Inspector, it seems, enjoyed the opportunity to educate his hidden audience of industry knuckle draggers.

KAZAKHSTAN

If I were a gumshoe on a divorce case, I'd look for the jilted partner. In investigating this multi-continental petroleum giant, I looked for the jilted partner.

Jack Grynberg was certainly jilted by BP, left standing at the Caspian Sea altar by John Browne, soon to be knighted Lord Baron Browne of Madingly and, until the Lord perjured himself in 2007, CEO of British Petroleum. In 1991, Grynberg Energy brought in BP as a partner in Grynberg's exclusive deal to drill the Kazakh side of the Caspian Sea.

Kazakhstan is the largest of those nations on the Central Asian Steppe shat out by Mother Russia in 1991, when she ejected her unwanted Muslims and Armenians, Uzbeks, Kazakhs, and Turkmen, pooping out new nations so fast that the "Kyrgyz Republic" received its unrequested independence from the Soviet Union in a surprise telegram, causing the party chiefs there to meet in emergency conference to ask, "How do we get mail? Do we need to print our own stamps?"

The Caspian Sea deal was the big score of Lord Browne's BP career. Then, in 2004, Browne screwed Grynberg out of, by my estimate, $180 million when BP sold the lease. Exactly how the Lord did the screwing—I'd have to get that from Grynberg.

I think Browne made a big mistake. Whatever, I figured it worthwhile to locate a bullheaded demi-billionaire oilman with a jones on for BP.

Grynberg owns more producing oil wells (672) than I have regrets, and that wealth doesn't include the massive payout he received through his dysfunctional financial marriage with BP PLC.

A former U.S. intelligence agent, Grynberg prefers to vanish when he is sought by the press. My crew left him messages and made calls to anyone and everyone who might get word to him. That got us a call from his cell from God knows where.

I offered to meet him in Denver, where he has 30,000 head of cattle, or London or Almaty, Kazakhstan.

Lucky for our bleeding budget, he had to make a quiet visit to New York during UN General Assembly week when he could meet discreetly with presidents, prime ministers, and dictators pretending to be presidents.

He had something for me to see. No, he would not fax it.

BAKU, MOSCOW, WASHINGTON

But there was the other half of the Caspian Sea that BP lusted for, under Azerbaijan's waters, off the ancient caravanserai of Baku. That's where the other BP rig blew, at least according to our floating tipster.

Azerbaijan is another ex-Soviet excretion. It became an Islamic republic, where the dictatorship requires all its citizens to pray five times a day to British Petroleum. I had to get in. But, you don't just show up in Azerbaijan with a film camera, asking questions.

Getting in was one thing. How to find the evidence, even about something as big as a giant blown-out oil platform, required expertise I was glad not to have.

I figured an oil spook like Grynberg could give me a hint about how to move through Baku's dark, ancient alleyways. Grynberg suggested I find a BP insider who worked with the oil company's XFI unit in Baku. He gave a name, but we would have to find his address and phone, which was somewhere in the Northern Hemisphere. Hint: XFI may stand for Exploration Frontiers International—or not. It may have existed—or not.

Well, Badpenny had something to start with.

Here's what we learned before attempting to meet him. Just minutes after the 'Stans were freed of Communist rule, BP's XFI team rushed in with offers to help the new nations develop their fallow resources. Or maybe to *help themselves* to the resources.

"The world runs on oil," a member of the Petroleum Club heading out there to the Wild East told me, "and oil runs on payoffs and pussy." It's not a sentiment you'd find on a Hallmark card, but then, the strongmen of the new Islamic republics don't get Hallmark cards. Britain's ambassador to Uzbekistan mentioned that Uzbek President Karimov boiled his opponents alive, not something you bring up at state dinners.

Absolutely no one was better at the P&P game than BP's XFI front man, Leslie Abrahams. The operator liked to boast to his buddies about how his envelopes of cash and his girls won the hearts of Baku's bureaucrats and their oil leases. In other words, this Abrahams was a professional creep. BP's creep. He passed the Azeri state oil company a "sweetener" of $30 million. The check was handed to him by Lord Browne, that is, the lord handed Leslie an old brown valise containing the check. The old bag was accompanied, appropriately, by Lady Margaret Thatcher.

But would Abrahams say this to me on tape, on camera? Getting him to talk was not so easy since he still conducted business in Baku, which requires his judicious use of contacts with an injudicious dictatorship. Furthermore, British intelligence, we were told, put a "D-1" notice on him. A "D-1" makes reporting what he says a crime in the UK.

Nevertheless, I hoped the BP bagman might be willing to shine a little light on some unpleasantness regarding BP's suspected involvement in overthrowing the elected President of Azerbaijan.

BP denied any role in that coup d'état, saying, "That's not part of our culture."

BP did lobby Tony Blair's government to release the greatest mass murderer ever convicted in a British court to help the company obtain drilling rights from Libya's dictator Muammar Gaddafi. That, apparently, is part of their culture.

I should note that, to BP's credit, the corporation refused a request for a half-billion-dollar bribe from Marat Manafov, a crony of Azerbaijan's strongman, to secure the Caspian drilling rights. Who sent Manafov to ask? Who knows? We can't ask Manafov. He was fired (that is, his body can't be found).

That left us Leslie the Bagman, the man from XFI, if he could be found and if XFI existed. It certainly is not on BP's Web site ("YOUR SEARCH 'XFI' DID NOT MATCH ANY DOCUMENTS"). But then, not every door has a handle.

Badpenny's exhausting planet-wide search found The Bagman where we should have looked first: at the Oriental Club, Westminster, London.

In today's legalistically prudish world, Abraham's little tasks for BP and Queen, a bit of bribery wrapped in vaginas, would be a jail-time offense. But until a mere decade ago, gentlemen weren't sent to prison. They were sent to the Oriental Club. Membership requires nomination by a diplomat, intelligence operative, or other bona fide claws on the arm of Empire's reach.

By phone, I explained to a coughing man with a plummy accent that our story was about oil.

The Bagman was game, but talk is talk: By any chance, did he have any, say, photographs? Chums from Baku days? The names of "Sirs" and "Ladies" flew from his memory—including John Scarlett, later chief of Britain's Secret Intelligence Service, MI6, who still signs his name as a single initial, *C*, in green.

Interesting, but our story is about BP.

Yes, he said, "About MI6."

He'd meet us in the Members' Bar.

Now, if you think the application of sex and cash is a form of corruption unique to Russia and Central Asia, take note that BP and other oil majors used the same technique with the U.S. Minerals Management Service to secure sweetheart drilling leases in the Gulf of Mexico. The difference is that the American apparatchiks were satisfied with much less cash and uglier women.

That's a fact: I've seen the photos. The Azeri prostitutes were just stunning—as one would expect of carefully selected Russian FSB agents.

———

How could I know if all this information from Kazakhstan and Baku was a bonanza or bullshit? I shot a note to our Web guru, Yuriy K——, whom we'd brought in from the old Soviet Union, to hook me up with someone who'd gotten inside the BP Azeri and Kazakh field operations as well as BP's partnership with Russia's "BP- TNK" oligarchs. The reply came back from Georgi Zaicek— George the Rabbit. Since when did Yuriy become Georgi?

Badpenny got him on the phone. *"Yuriy! Stop hyperventilating!"*

She calmed "Georgi" and handed me the phone. "Georgi's my other legal name. I can't use Yuriy K—— there. I hadn't told you, but I got myself in trouble, really big trouble." This struck me as a don't-ask-don't-tell moment.

More interesting was what "Georgi Rabbit" passed on to me from a third party with a phone number beginning +7-495-, that is, Moscow, for "Максим Шингаркин."

Badpenny has a passable knowledge of the Cyrillic alphabet and sounded it out: Maxim Shin-gar-kin.

Shingarkin? Google could find only one useful reference to "Shingarkin" in English, from the *San Francisco Chronicle:*

> Maxim Shingarkin, a former major in the Russian military's secretive 12th Department, which is in charge of strategic weapons, said suitcase nuclear bombs . . .

Sounds like a man we want.

I was told not to call Shingarkin directly but to call someone who would call someone who would then tell Shingarkin to take my call.

But first I called our "fixer" in London. How long would it take to get a journalist's visa for Russia and Azerbaijan? "You won't have time." Unless, of course, we went as "tourists" with a 5D. A Canon 5D Mark II is an ultra-high-resolution video camera that looks like a tourist point-and-shoot and can be fitted with a fearsome telephoto lens.

Matty Pass, our team's twenty-seven-year-old Wonder Boy, had just come back from Cuba with 5D footage of hijackers, political prisoners, and, for good measure, ooh-la-la photos of Che Guevara's comely granddaughter. Before boarding to leave Havana, the authorities threw him in isolation and grabbed all his printed literature, meaningless junk. They'd already stolen his laptop.

But they didn't realize that the still camera this tourist wore on his neck with benign photos of palm trees and rum parties had also collected disturbing videos. The good stuff, on memory chips, had already been spirited out via Costa Rica.

For the Caspian, the 5D it would be.

TEXAS AND TOKYO

By mid-May 2010, with his presidency floating facedown in the Gulf, Barack Obama had yet another crisis to deal with. Obama still had a couple of wars burning on the stove, and our troops needed, *right now,* "life-saving mine-resistant ambush-protected vehicles."

So the President sent an *emergency* funding bill to Congress. Defense Secretary Robert Gates marched to Capitol Hill and said Our Boys on the front lines would be blown to bits if they did not get $1.1 billion for the mine-proof vehicles, $137 million for new body armor, and $9 billion for two nuclear power plants.

Say what?

Actually, the Defense Secretary left that last one out of his testimony. I only know because an angel told me.

The angel is Harvey Wasserman of Columbus, Ohio. When God decides to smite this planet again, I know He will save Harvey from the waters, even though that means sparing Columbus.

Harvey is the Cassandra of Radioactivity. For three decades, he has stared unblinking into the menacing eyes of power industry evil and the bored eyes of news editors.

Harvey wanted me to sound the alarm, to bust open this billion-dollar nuclear boondoggle smuggled into the war bill inside the soldiers' body armor. And, said Harvey, there's a rock star who would make a donation to my investigations crew for writing it. But I don't take money for stories if someone has their jones in it. Harvey knows that.

And I have *no time.* I have to get to the Gulf of Mexico, the Caspian Sea, Alaska.

But this, said Harvey, is "*urgent.*"

Everything is urgent, Harvey.

But this is *urgent* urgent.

Not now, Harvey.

I admit, it was tantalizing. The $9 billion takedown was so brilliantly done. The billions were concealed as a small item, by military budget standards: only $180 million for "alternative energy," dumped in with some solar panels, appearing as part of the Army's plan to "go green." How some lobbyist wizards stuff $9 billion into a $180 million wrapper doesn't matter, just that they did it. The guys behind it really knew their game.

I smelled Houston.

The flimflam had that unmistakable aroma of the Houston Ship Channel where Exxon and BP dump their toxins from refining Venezuela's heavy crude. The city that gives pollution a bad name.

And the headquarters of NRG Corporation.

If there is some creepy, slithery way to tap into a free billion for some crack-brained and dangerous project, it would certainly attract NRG Corporation of Houston, Texas, and their entourage of bankers, contractors and muscled-up lobbyists.

"NRG is in," said Harvey, but not under the name NRG. NRG changes aliases like Lady Gaga changes the color of her whips. This time they named themselves Nuclear Innovation of North America. NINA: That's a good one. "Nina" beat out twenty big-name power companies, said Harvey, to win half the $9 billion in the war bill.

I know NRG well. And NRG claims they know me: They kept a file on my penis with supposed evidence it ended up inside a rising young politician close to then–Prime Minister Tony Blair. And I keep a file on *them*. So, for the moment, we're even.

But no one's giving NRG a dime, Harvey, let alone $4 billion, even if they change their name to Mother Teresa Nuclear Puppy Kisses. They've just come out of bankruptcy, so their investment grade rating is zorch; that means there's no way in hell they can get government financing. Furthermore, Texas regulators officially designated NRG an "imprudent" manager, government-speak for "incompetent," after squandering a billion dollars of their electricity customers' money on their older South Texas plants—"you *know* that, Harvey"—not to mention the serious safety violations at their nuclear plants and the company's record of massive fines for terrifying disregard for safety. Harvey, Harvey. This won't happen.

It will, he said. They've got a terrific "beard." They teamed up with Westinghouse Nuclear, and they're promising American jobs.

Harvey, there *is no* Westinghouse Nuclear anymore.

Yeah, there is. The Japanese bought the name.

And "Nuclear Innovation" has brought in Tokyo Electric Power to reassure the Department of Energy that they have "prudent" competent guys on top of the project because of Tokyo Electric's excellent record operating nukes in Japan. NRG is giving Tokyo a 20 percent slice; that's nearly a billion dollars out of the treasury subsidy.

I'm Googling while Harvey continues his begging. And there it is, the press release from "Innovation," dated May 10, 2010, not a week old:

> TEPCO [Tokyo Electric Power Company], acting as technical consultant, has provided the benefit of its experience achieved in developing, constructing, commissioning and operating the Advanced Boiling Water Reactors (ABWR) to the project. TEPCO also will continue to contribute to the essential task of training the highly skilled workforce.

So, Harvey, what you want me to do is tell my network and my editors to hold the presses because I have a story on how the White House is secretly funding a bunch of has-been operators to build nuclear plants in Texas with some Japanese guys with little hands who buy little girls' dirty panties from vending machines. I read that somewhere. Is it true?

"It's true."

I can't sell this one, Harvey.

Then Harvey decided to show me some leg. "Shaw is the A/E." He knew I'd stay on the line for that. "A/E" means Architect-Engineer, the firm that draws up and actually builds the plant, pours the cement, bolts the panels to the wall. Shaw, from Baton Rouge, Louisiana, is the latest corporate mask for another shape-shifter, Stone & Webster Engineering Company. In 1988, a jury found the company had deliberately falsified a nuclear plant's ability to withstand an earthquake.

Earthquake, shmearthquake. The company settled and the judge let them off the hook with a payment of $50,000. I'm sure they celebrated with a $60,000 lunch.

The investigator who uncovered the Stone & Webster fraud, Greg Palast, wasn't too happy about that. I don't hold grudges. I do hold files.

And here comes Stone again, dressed as Shaw.

Fascinating: How were a bunch of guys from Tokyo Electric, who sing the company song in the morning and can't hold their liquor, going to "train" a bunch of Houston rattlesnakes and Louisiana swamp rats?

"Still can't do it, Harvey."

But then, I did.

It was after I got The Brick through the door.

Three days after I guiltily put off Harvey, a package, no return address, no name on it, came from Houston. A pile thick as a cinder block.

I don't know who sent it. I don't ask. Whoever sent it took a hell of a risk to get it to me—career suicide, even imprisonment.

Sure I was tempted. But the Central Asia visa application can't be changed—getting one was already a dicey dance involving a cockamamie story for the Azerbaijan dictatorship's security ministry. You just don't show up in the Islamic republic like it's Club Med.

But that radioactive brick, the hot pile of documents from inside NRG, just sitting there in a rubber band, kept whispering, *Just take a look. Come on, you know you want to look.*

I looked.

Inside: lots and lots of paper, a crazy mix. Hand notes, financial spreadsheets, scribbles, filings to government, and most marked "confidential."

Now what? Maybe in Sam Spade movies or *Batman* or *Columbo*, the smoking gun smokes: the candlestick with the little bit of skull still stuck to it, the letter that screams "guilty guilty guilty."

That's not how it works, at least not in the big cases, the billion-dollar cons involving corporate chiefs with accountants and finance mavens who could dazzle Merlin. Incriminating info is chopped up like a jigsaw puzzle thrown on the floor, with most of the pieces missing; it's written in techno-Croatian, and if math is your problem, forget it. And it can take months or years to make it tell its story.

But this one went click, click, click. In a murder case, you look for fingerprints that match. In fraud, look for numbers that *don't* match. And here were two that didn't match—a lot.

After a day and a half I couldn't spare, I saw that "Innovation" had given the federal government what looked like their price for building the plant: $5 billion. In the crazy-ass world of nuclear, that's cheap, a winner.

Then there was another batch of numbers, some put down in private handwritten notes sent from Tokyo, which looked to me like the reactor builder's private estimate of the cost of the plant, what they would actually charge to build it. The note is marked over with *in confidence* and *proprietary*. And the numbers add up to *seven* billion dollars.

Call me crazy, but I just felt something wasn't straight.

Two numbers, two continents, off by $1.4 billion.

I'm sure there's an explanation. There's *always* an explanation.

I can't say no to Harvey Angel and sleep at night. What if I die and have to explain myself to the Lord and all I can do is mumble about deadline conflicts?

So, before I board for Central Asia, I slam down a story, *"Nuclear Option in War Bill—Smells Like Fraud,"* an exposé about Houston grifters, Japanese nuclear guys, and Louisiana tricksters. I've never had a spec story turned away in my entire career, which is why Harvey put the burden on me. "Never" came to an end. I got back a cheery e-mail ending with,

"It's an interesting story but doesn't quite fit for us."

What fit for them was a story titled "Lesbians Who Love Male Gay Porn." I kid you not.*

I shoved the Radioactive Brick to the corner of my sloppy desk, where it slept quietly for almost a year, until March 11, 2011. Then it went critical.

GENEVA

Badpenny is driving like a bat out of hell on the autobahn to Geneva. Something just doesn't make sense here. I see lots of cows. I see pretty chalets and fairy-tale castles and the Savoy Alps rising up like an angel's ice-cream cone and it doesn't make any sense. Per capita, Switzerland is the world's wealthiest industrial nation.

So where's the industry? All these flash Mercedes aren't paid for by cheese, chocolate, and cuckoo clocks.

"Drug dealers," says Badpenny, of the most powerful drug in the world: OPM. Other People's Money. She knew. She was born here. Escaped at eighteen.

Now she was showing me how to track some of that OPM. Months earlier, we'd found out that the President of Zambia had gone on a shopping spree here in Geneva with what we estimate was about $40 million in his pocket. We figured he deposited a chunk of it in an anonymous numbered account at Credit Suisse. Some call Credit Suisse a bank, some call it the world's most respectable Laundromat.

In one afternoon, Zambia's then-President Frederick Chiluba had, we heard, blown nearly a million dollars of his loot in one shop, Boutique Basile. Jones at BBC Television had asked Badpenny to see if she could somehow get in to film it.

Easy-peasy. She walked in, appropriately styled, with her cameraman, speaking in the local Alpine German dialect. Hearing the clerk speak French, she switched to *française* and announced herself as producer of yet another reality show: *Shopping with the Rich and Famous!* The clerk was thrilled. Yes,

---

* No, I'm not mentioning the name of the paper, because that would give you the impression that one U.S. news outlet is different from another. No American editor would choose a warning about nuclear plants over lesbian porn unless some plant actually burnt down.

of course, there were celebrities that came through all the time. He mentioned some Russian mafiosi which, given the gawd-awful clothes at insane prices, made perfect sense. And heads of state? Why certainly: the President of Zambia.

Camera rolling, Badpenny waltzed among the schmaltzy $8,000 leisure suits. Chiluba had apparently bought 200 shirts, 200 suits—each one costing more than a year's income of a typical Zambian village—and a tie, striped with rows of diamonds, for 125,000 Swiss francs (about $110,000 U.S.). And 100 pairs of elevator shoes (Chiluba was a bit on the short side).

Most important, we were certain that about $3 million of Chiluba's booty came from the man called Goldfinger.

WASHINGTON, DC

It was surprisingly difficult to find a guy whose business was protected by the President of the United States. I needed two detective agencies and a Badpenny all-nighter to find Goldfinger. But then, if your business is, as one UN diplomat put it, "killing babies" in Africa, you wouldn't expect him to list himself in the Yellow Pages.

It was assumed Goldfinger would keep himself, like most of his corporate shells, safely outside the country. But here he was at his mini-mansion near DC. No question this was our guy: a gold Cadillac with magnesium racing wheels out on the driveway for display. We knew about the mags from the Caddy aficionado's chat site, where he logged in as Goldfinger@DAI.com.

Goldfinger, née Michael Francis Sheehan, is Vulture Number 2.

Vultures are repo men. But unlike the scuzzy little guys who snatch your car for the bank when you don't make a payment on time, these are very big scuzzy guys who snatch entire nations that don't pay their sovereign debts on time.

I didn't give Vultures their name. Their own banks call them Vultures, the banks they enrich with the kills in their claws.

This is Goldfinger's story: The nation of Zambia bought some worthless tractors from Romania decades ago. When the world copper market went bust, Zambia went from dirt poor to desperately destitute. If you're forty years old in Zambia, you're a lucky guy: Life expectancy is thirty-nine—and dropping from the AIDS epidemic. The CIA profile of the country lists the typical weather of Zambia as "drought."

Romania, itself busted, told Zambia's finance ministry to pay just $4 million, a fragment of the $29.6 million owed for the tractors.

But somehow, Goldfinger jumped in and paid $4 million to Romania to get his hands on the right to collect the $29.6 million from Zambia.

Oddly, the government of Zambia, rather than pay $4 million to Romania to settle the debt, agreed to pay Goldfinger *four times* that much instead. Huh?

When Oxfam tipped me to this oddity, I suspected all was not kosher, and it didn't take us long to find an e-mail from Goldfinger to his hedge fund partner,

> As you will recall, we bought $29.6 million in, I believe, February of this year for about $4 million. . . . . The deal is going to get done for political reasons because we are going to discount a bunch of whatever to the President's favorite charity.

The President's "favorite charity," it seems, is the Boutique Basile. You don't need an MBA to figure this one out (though I have one). Pay to play. Baksheesh. Backhander. Bribe. Even the FBI, when they asked for a copy, didn't need translation. (We'll get to that.)

Hey, if everyone could pay $4 million and collect $15 million a couple of weeks later, we'd all do it. But would we all pay into the President's favorite charity? That's between you and your deity.

That's why we were out there before dawn near Washington, with a copy of the e-mail, for BBC London, to ask Mr. Goldfinger about his "charitable" donation.

Rich folk have their own police forces, the private security guys that patrol around looking for suspicious people like me. So, Ricardo and I kept our distance, with the camera covered up on the floor of the white rental car, while Badpenny, dressed in her Russian contessa gear, strolled up and down Goldfinger's street in the nasty cold, ready to give us a signal. Rent-a-cops stopped, and wanted to know why this elegant lady was loitering around at dawn in front of this gentleman's home, and we caught it on a remote microphone.

"I am looking for my poosy cat!" (I guess the cops didn't get the vaudeville pickup line. They were supposed to say, "Sorry, lady, we haven't seen your pussy." Badda-bing!)

Now, it's useless to collect a debt from Zambia if Zambia has nothing to collect. Even a vampire like Goldfinger can't suck blood from a stone.

But Zambia does have something: AIDS. About 25 percent of the adult population is HIV positive. So nations like the United States and Britain, responding to Bono's threat to sing "It's a Beautiful Day" over and over again, have agreed to provide aid. Goldfinger can't wait.

For Vultures, civil war, genocide, epidemics, drought, and Africa's pestilence of kleptocratic presidents are profit centers, opportunities to pick at an economic carcass others would walk away from with a shudder.

But how did Goldfinger get inside information on the Romanian debt? Goldfinger, we discovered, once worked with the World Bank, advising Zambia on its debt problems. Apparently, he was just casing the joint.

Zambia's finance minister could have put a halt to this game, but he had disappeared. Literally. The minister was employing witchcraft to make himself invisible. Minister Kalumba had good reason to vanish: $30 million was missing from government bank accounts. In the end, Kalumba was discovered hiding in a tree, believing himself invisible. However, the cops had outsmarted the minister: The Zambian police defeated his cloaking charm by removing their underpants. I can't make this up.

Once Kalumba was out, a new finance minister signed off to turn over, for no visible reason, the nation's treasury, the nation's fate, to Goldfinger's Caribbean shell company.

So, in the cold DC dawn, we waited, piecing together these mismatched puzzle pieces. And after four hours, the high, curved double doors opened and out came a dumpy little man with a limp, followed by a woman just as dumpy.

The mastermind of a cruel, brutal plan to seize an entire African nation and pocket for himself and his cronies the millions that should have gone for AIDS medicine. A man of such deep and untiring evil should look like Christopher Walken, like a proper villain.

But what walked past the pimped-out Caddie, the real Goldfinger, looked like a pathetic schmuck, slumping along in an old beige Eddie Bauer hunting jacket, goofy workman's cap, and worn-in Hush Puppies. This was a terrible letdown. Evil shouldn't be so dull. Evil should have a sense of style. Sharp-shouldered Nino Cerruti raw silk midnight-blue suits. Devils wear Prada, not JCPenney.

Nevertheless, Zambia bled, and someone had to confront this limping predator—and this morning, in the chilly air, it would be me.

I nodded at Ricardo and counted down, "Three, two, one, go!"

PARK AVENUE, NEW YORK

So this long blonde comes up to me after some forgettable book-hawking chat at Barnes & Noble and says, "I'd like to speak with you privately."

Of course you do.

"I need your help."

We all need help. What's your name?

She whispers, Patricia Cohen.

Means nothing to me.

She whispers, *Steven* Cohen's wife.

That means something. Steven *A.* Cohen?

A nod. "I have documents. Can you come to my apartment tomorrow?"

Sooner. The Energy-Finance Combine had just opened a door and said, *Come on in!*

Steven A. Cohen, SAC Capital.

Septa-billionaire ($7.4 billion net worth, give or take). Enough to be called a "philanthropist." The Genius "arbitrageur." In other words, he was trailed by just enough of a scent of criminality that the merely wealthy were happy to hand him their millions to play with, no questions asked. None answered.

The Sack knew which way a stock would move before God knew. He beat the knickers off Wall Street's best and brightest. He was Karnak the Magnificent, knowing which card the dealer would throw before he threw it—every time.

Using inside information? Heaven forbid! That would be *illegal*. "Research," his investors say, grinning. Why can't Badpenny come up with magical research like that?

Used wives are very attractive to me, as a journalist. They remain angry for years, and Patricia Cohen was very angry.

Now, when a lady of a certain age, even a blonde who could suck the air out of your soul, says she wants to tell the truth on her ex, she doesn't want to bring him to justice, she wants to bring him to his knees. First Wives want, first, the money; second, revenge; third, the money.

As I walked into her Park Avenue kitchen, I could smell vengeance burning. It was close enough to Mick Jagger's place to borrow a cup of sugar from him. Swanky, but hardly the digs of a billionairess. Obviously, ex–Mrs. Cohen was *very* ex'd.

———

"I think you're the man," she said, "I think only you have what it takes to do this investigation."

No good has ever come of those words, especially from a blonde.

I got out my pad. "Mind if I take notes?"

So why did she give up a guy who clearly had the game sussed? As always, it was another woman. The other woman was . . .

"His mother. He loved his mother."

I've heard of worse.

"Yeah, but he *really* loved his mother. He called her every day. Steven couldn't take a poopy without calling Mommy. Then we'd go to see her every week in Great Neck and have dinner with her, and she would say to him, 'All I know is, *money makes the monkey jump. Money makes the monkey jump.*'

"And we'd leave and half the time in the car he'd be in tears about his mommy humiliating him." Apparently, Steven's monkey hadn't jumped high enough.

ATHENS TO QUITO

Two weeks after the Deepwater Horizon caught fire and sank, Greece caught fire and sank.

On May 5, 2010, I open up the *Journal* and I could puke. There was this photo of a man on fire, just a bunch of flames with a leg sticking out. Two others burnt with him on a pretty spring day in Athens.

The question is, *Who did it?*

If you read the U.S. papers, the answer was obvious. A bunch of olive-pit-spitting, ouzo-guzzling, lazy-ass Greek workers who refused to put in a full day's work, retired while they were still teenagers on pensions fit for a pasha, had gone on a mad social services spending spree using borrowed money. Now that the bill came due and the Greeks had to pay with higher taxes and cuts in their big fat welfare state, they ran riot, screaming in the streets, busting windows, and burning banks with people inside.

Case closed.

I didn't buy it. It wasn't just a feeling in my gut, it was the document in my hand marked,

Well, it's my official duty as a journalist to disclose it. The firebombing, the mobs in the streets of Athens, one in seven workers marked for unemployment in a single week, the empty pension funds, and the angry despair that would sweep across Europe in 2010 began with a series of banking transactions crafted in the United States and Switzerland. The plan was eighteen years old, and here it was played out in the streets of Greece, then Spain and Portugal, and before that in Latin America and Asia. The riot was written right into it.

When I ask, *Who did it?* I don't mean the damaged fool who threw the Molotov cocktail into the crowded bank. I'm looking for the men in the shadows, the very big Monkey Jumpers who turned economies into explosive kindling, lit the fuse, then stood first in line at the fire sale.

I have their phone numbers.

The five phone numbers came from a message about "the end-game." The ominous note, also confidential, was written by Tim Geithner to Larry Summers. Over time, Summers and Geithner each would take a turn as United States Secretary of the Treasury. But in 1997, they had higher posts, as Masters of the Financial Universe. (I will explain later.) But, however valuable these notes, they were just a bunch of paper not worth bothering you nor anyone else with unless I could get confirmation they were legit. And that would require another expensive trip to Geneva.

Badpenny wanted me to bust the game. "So you're going to write about this, no?"

"No."

I had already talked a British TV network into ponying up for my BP hunt in Alaska and the Caspian. Plus, BBC and *The Guardian* had me looking for The Hamsah; Harvey the Angel was on my ass for the nuclear power investigation, and I had a Europe-based publisher who didn't care if Europe flew or farted—they just wanted 100,000 words to shove between two covers and sell sell sell. They'd been patient enough, and no one is going to pay us to traipse around the Alps like Julie Andrews in *The Sound of Music*.

So forget it.

Badpenny gave me that wicked grin and bought tickets for Switzerland, round trip from London.

―――

But first to Quito to go over this "RESTRICTED DISTRIBUTION" stuff with Ecuador's President.

That wouldn't be easy. President Rafael Correa swore he would never speak to American reporters, nor any Americans, really, after he was strip-searched in Miami while changing planes on his way back from an OPEC meeting in the Middle East.

Correa didn't take a lot of crap from the United States nor anybody, for that matter. Correa—"The Belt" in Spanish—ran campaign commercials using the Twisted Sister's anthem, "We're Not Gonna Take It."

He doesn't.

Ecuador was under siege by financial vultures. But unlike the Zambians and Liberians begging for a deal, Correa told the vultures to go to hell, he wouldn't pay. Fuck off. He simply would not pay ransom to speculators whose claims were just usurious horseshit.

Correa's flat-out refusal to pay caused an international freak-out in all the big banking centers. The IMF and World Bank brought down their hammers. They would cut off his nation's access to credit.

When Correa took office, his country was hurting. Despite its oil resources, despite the price of bananas doubling (yes, Ecuador really is the quintessential banana republic), the average Ecuadoran didn't have two peels to rub together. He'd won office not long after the two-mile-high capital was seized by angry Quechua-speaking women wearing bowlers and fedoras, banging empty food pots and setting cars on fire.

The hunger, the mass exodus of desperate Ecuadorans to the United States, Correa blamed on secret pacts with the World Bank and International Monetary Fund, which, he suspected, had been accepted by his predecessors (one certifiably insane, others certifiably corrupt).

His claim of secret agreements is nasty, wild, and 100 percent accurate. I had copies—and I thought he might like a look.

He did. So it was back to Ecuador with Ricardo, to the Presidential Palace.

GENEVA

By saying "Hands off our oil" and "Take your bonds and shove it," Correa broke the rules.

But whose rules are they? Who made them up?

Who said that the oil under the Amazon belongs to Occidental Petro-leum? That it's *turn over your resources to pay the vultures or else!* Who said that Greece had to let bankers seize pensions to pay other bankers?

When did we agree to live our lives on their game board, to let them tell us who is rich, who is poor, who runs the casino, who gets to load the dice?

The first guy to ask those questions died a bitter pauper, and worse, he nearly died in England. Jean-Jacques Rousseau hated the English. He was chased out of his native Geneva although he begged to stay and promised to live on an island in the middle of the lake, and write and speak no more. But Rousseau silent was still more dangerous than most men shouting. His house was stoned and the burgher bankers booted him across the Channel.

In the eighteenth century, when kings ruled by divine right and earthly whips, folks just took it and said OK. Then Rousseau wrote *Discourse on the Origin of Inequality Among Men.* He said the idea that a vulgar little hedge fund speculator like The Sack is worth $7 billion and you don't have health insur-ance (he cited the eighteenth-century equivalent) is because we've all agreed to *his* rules, *his* rules of property, ownership, and law. And why do we just go along with his rules? We don't know, because the rules go all the way back to when there were guys named Ugh and Thug. Thug had a big rock and put a fence around the best dirt for growing corn and left Ugh with just about noth-ing, and Thug said, "This is the rule and this is my big-ass rock. Get it?" And Ugh said, "OK."

So who holds the big rock today? Who made up this system and who enforces it for The Sack's benefit, for Goldfinger, for BP PLC?

We're told the Invisible Hand of the Marketplace holds the rock now, but it must attach to a very powerful arm. Whose? There were many candidates, several Thugs and their generals moving assets and reserves around the map. Undoubtedly, one of them sat within the high-walled compound rising up in front of Badpenny and me, the headquarters of the WTO, the World Trade Organization.

You see we had something more important to do on the shores of Lake Geneva than to follow Zambia's diminutive dictator on a shoe-buying binge.

We wanted to speak to an enforcer of the rules, the police chief of the Energy-Finance Combine eating Ecuador for breakfast, Greece for lunch, and still hungry for Brazil and dessert. Amazingly, we cadged a meeting with the Director-General of the WTO, Pascal Lamy, the Generalissimo of Globaliza-tion himself.

Lamy probably granted the interview on the basis of something kind I'd written about him when I was still drinking.

D-G Lamy came to the WTO from Le Crédit Lyonnais (LDL), the French megabank, where he also wore the epaulets of director-general. The fit and sparkly Frenchman, comfortable with himself and confident, dressed down for me, in a powder blue sweater vest. He was at ease but made sure I was not. He'd set our chat at his grand and dark conference table, a hollow room meant for folks more important than I will ever be.

So I spread my cards, my documents, on the table, fanned them out like a Texas poker player who'd drawn to an inside flush. Across the cover of the thick one on top was a clearly ineffective note:

Ensure this text is not made publicly available.

I knew I could make the General smile.

"The WTO is not some evil cabal of bankers," the banker insisted.

Maybe not. But the meeting notes of the non-cabal made for some pretty interesting reading.

It took an hour and a half to go over each, especially the one you could call the Magna Carta of Globalization. The Frenchman was amused, clearly delighted in the game. Their content and significance require their own chapter, and that will come.

PRINCE WILLIAM SOUND, ALASKA

What Exxon's oil didn't kill, Exxon's money did. I remember the grim prophecy of the Tatitlek President and Chief Kompkoff. (Kompkoff's daughter was—and forgive me for the stereotyped image—an eerily exact replica of Disney's cartoon Pocahontas, just that beautiful, and her husband a celluloid image of an Indian brave.) Sitting out under the Northern Lights with me, a year after the Exxon oil spill, Kompkoff was thinking out loud, troubled. "Lawyers say we might get maybe fifty thousand dollars each from Exxon. I tell you, we get that kind of money out here, well, man, I don't want to be here in the village. I mean, everyone's got a gun and drinking, you know; it could all go crazy, crazy."

For this new post–Deepwater Horizon investigation of BP, I planned to fly up to meet him to find out if the oil companies had finally set out the damn

Conex boxes of rubber boom they promised, and did they get the payout. It turns out, Tatitlek got their $50K checks, but Kompkoff failed to take his own advice to get out. I was having a hell of a time reaching him. Then I got an elder on the phone. She told me, "Oh, he's gone. Drank himself to death. It was after his daughter was murdered there by her husband. She died in her father's arms, you know."

I didn't know.

I told Matty to cancel the Cessna and instead charter a fishing boat to the village of Chenega, which was way out there in the middle of the Sound. I didn't want to chance flying in, lest they refuse me permission to land as they had done before.

Besides, Chenega's President still owes me $300.

It goes back to 1989. Chenega is the most remote village, the one that suffered the worst of the oil spill. Therefore, its President, Chuck Totemoff, was the man who would have to face down Exxon and BP's Alyeska consortium. I flew fourteen hours from New York to meet with him in Anchorage—but he never showed up, though the charter pilot swore he'd brought him in safely from the village.

Then, the next morning, while I was chugging down the sidewalk near the Captain Cook hotel on my cross-country skis, looking for breakfast, I saw Totemoff bent over a boilermaker at a local bar. You couldn't miss him. Chuck was as wide as he was tall, with an unmistakable topping of straight black hair. Chuck had been elected Chenega's President though he was barely in his twenties.

I sat down next to him. "What happened, Chuck? We missed you."

He looked pretty shattered. He'd been up all night at the Alaska Bush Club, a famous (or infamous) strip joint where women could be rented for private entertainment. He rented one, then another, then another, he told me. And now he didn't know how he could get back to the island as he'd spent the poor village's entire travel budget, which they'd given him in cash.

He wanted to explain. "Well, you know, did you ever have one of those nights when you just couldn't get enough pussy?"

I lent him three hundred dollars.

SOMEWHERE, USA

And then I got the e-mail. Badpenny was beside herself. "It's the Smart Pig!" she said.

She didn't mean the guy who sent the note. There's a pig in every pipeline, and not just the porky, bonus-bloated executive that gets sucked in once in a while. She meant the diagnostic machine that is supposed to pick up dangers. BP uses them, or is supposed to. They're kind of important. A gas pipe in California blew up, taking nine lives. Blame the pig. The pig should have caught the faulty welds that gave out.

The guy our files call Pig Man #1 had some devastating info on the Smart Pigs. Maybe they weren't so smart. But I'd have to meet him in person to get the skinny.

But, Pig Man #1 said, as they all say, "I only ask that you do not reveal my identity."

Of course it can't. You chose to work in an industry without mercy. They find you, they find out you squealed, they get you. A bullet to the back of the head of your career. They write NRB on your file—Not Required Back. Or the poison note about an affair is placed in the file (a BP special), or you're canned for "insubordination."

I promised Pig Man #1 we'd meet in Somewhere, USA, a location a couple hundred miles from both his base and mine of which we would keep no record; and when we filmed, we promised to show nothing more than the smoke he exhales.

I only ask that you do not reveal my identity - please keep me as an anonymous source on this matter.
I give you my name so you can discreetly verify my employment ⸻ ⸻ lds if you wish, so you car

FEDERAL DETENTION FACILITY, BUFFALO, NEW YORK

My week was going from absurd to insane. I received yet another package, this one from George Boley Jr., son of a political science professor at the State University of New York in Binghamton. I've heard lots about his dad, George Sr. On Professor Boley's vacations and time off from the university, he would return to his home in Liberia to lead his private army of children, some as young as eight years old, whom he drugged, starved, then whipped into a killing force armed with AK-47s. Boley ordered them to murder without mercy in the professor's war with another American academic, the economist, escaped convict, and (currently imprisoned) war criminal, Charles Taylor.

Boley Jr. claimed that his dad, the academic and/or warlord, had gotten a bad rap. It was a case of mistaken identity and mistaken motives. Nevertheless, the Department of Homeland Security was holding the poli sci professor as an unwilling guest at the Buffalo Federal Detention Facility on a visa violation. That is, he had failed to put down on his entry forms that he was a mass murderer.

The evidence, the enclosed government agent's affidavit, was based on the say-so of three unsworn witnesses, Mr. Sonny Swen aka Satan Baby, Mr. Garley Farley aka General Scarface, and Mr. Blano Tuan aka General Butt Naked (who went into battle thusly uniformed). During the Liberian civil war, my researcher Jim Ciment met with General Naked and found him credible and kind of charming for a man who executed his prisoners with a steak knife.

Homeland Security could have gotten it all wrong. They usually do, like when they charged me with violating the anti-terrorism laws. I swear I'm innocent. That's another story for another book.

But I hadn't traveled to Africa to investigate Boley or crimes against humanity. I was there to pick up what I could about The Vulture.

I wanted Boley Jr. to get me in to see his father in prison. I couldn't care less if Boley was a blood-crazed warlord or a shy professor (or both), but I was quite sure that Boley had some clue for me about the *Hamsah*.

LONDON

There comes a dark time in the career of every journalist known as The Meeting With The Network. To participate in this mystifying ritual, I was flown to London. It was a complete waste of my time and, I suppose, a waste of your time too, as I'm bothering to write about it. But this book is *reportage verité*, and I will conceal nothing from you, including scenes of painful annoyance.

I'd be doing my new oil investigation for Channel 4 *Dispatches*. Its weaker episodes play in the United States on PBS's *Frontline*.

I'm on a three-way call with my Russian from the 12th Department and going through the dump of documents I'm not supposed to see, when I get an e-mail from the network in London that they don't want me to wear my hat.

They had a meeting about it.

In Africa, a one-armed child hawks chewing gum; Muslim hookers in Azerbaijan wait grimly for the list of bureaucrats to service; black poison spews at 25,000 gallons a minute from the Devil's asshole at the bottom of the Gulf of Mexico; the Taliban plant roadside bombs, stone women, and have homosexual circle jerks while Obama holds in his gut a secret about Afghanistan that makes him feel like he's cheating his children even when he holds them.

And the network is thinking about my hat.

My director's thinking about my hat.

For four decades I've worn this fedora. When my nose went on television, I didn't realize my hat followed me because I never think about my hat. But Prime Minister Tony Blair noticed and his hounds told the press, "Don't trust a man in a hat." So, BBC said, "Wear the hat."

Now Channel 4, the rival network, decided that the hat was a BBC "icon." If my hat only knew its status! They didn't want a BBC icon. Worse, the hat was now a costume worn by Matt Drudge, a poseur pretending to be a journalist.

I can't have network executives writing e-mails in which they visualize dressing me and undressing me like a middle-aged Barbie doll.

I don't know about you, but I have much to do before the Devil's work is done.

To make sure Greg Palast doesn't run amok, The Network assigned a gung-ho Oxbridge boy, James B, to be my director, poor bastard. I checked his Web site. He'd also been to Liberia, and there is a clip of Director James in the bush, getting shot at while his mercenary bodyguard fires back, swearing. James continues filming from down in the grass, which evidences either extreme dedication to the story or complete insanity. I concluded it was both after he suggested we fly into Tomsk, Siberia, the coldest city on Earth, rent a helicopter, and fly over the Samotlor oil fields, which BP and its oligarch partners had turned into a toxic horror show. I pointed out that Samotlor is a Russian security zone, and according to Jane's Military catalogue, every MiG-21 carries two 30-mm cannons, a twin-barrel 23-mm gun, and a variety of heat-seeking air-to-air missiles. We, on the other hand, would carry our press passes and hand-lettered signs that read, *DON'T SHOOT! OUR MOTHERS STILL LOVE US!*

Helicopter canceled.

James did show his cautious side by going nowhere without his emergency surgical kit, including "heavy bleed anti-clot applicators, abdominal burn towels, quick-set fracture splints, a syringe sterilizer," and much more, hygienically sealed. Plus a satellite phone. Ricardo and I travel with Pepto-Bismol tablets, condoms, and mosquito spray, and me, out of habit, K-Y Jelly and a 3.4-ounce flask of Felipe II.

And my hat.

MANHATTAN, SECOND AVENUE, DOWNTOWN

The alarm at five A.M. wakes me up to one of those drippy mornings invented for suicide. What kind of sick fuck would make it rain before dawn? I have to do Amy Goodman's show, *Democracy Now!,* in a couple of hours. *Democracy Now!* is kind of a refugee camp for exiled journalists. Amy runs my BBC investigations when BBC's dear sister U.S. networks, the corporate capons, won't touch them.

My jet lag from the thirty-six-hour bounce to Britain is kicking me in the ass, and makeup call is 7:40 A.M. This shouldn't be happening: I spent my life doing everything humanly possible to avoid jobs where I have to punch the clock. Instead, I end up with jobs where the clock punches *me.*

Five thirty A.M. and still dirty light. I'd passed out on my official napping mattress and now, in the ugly early, I see Badpenny at her desk, her face lit by the laptop screen, working her vampire hours. She whips around, all sparkly and grinning, to tell me she has connected Montreux to Vulture Hermann. Oh, yeah, we still have the Vulture investigation boiling. Everything at once. Badpenny's excited, she's squirming in her leathers and pointing at the screen at abstruse SEC filings. "They're partners!" The Vulture is locked up as *owner* of Montreux with Straus, has been for years. "R—— will be *furious* because Hermann, straight to his face, denied any connection to Straus." I have every reason to believe this will make sense to me when I wake up.

She is beaming, as well she should, but I'm not up for this now and drag myself to the upstairs kitchenette.

Suddenly, Badpenny is thundering up the steps, shouting, *"OH NO YOU DON'T! YOU WILL NOT SABOTAGE YOUR ENTIRE DAY!"* and grabs my breakfast right out of my hand, splashing my Felipe II all over my wrist. (Two fingers of Felipe II in a coffee cup, no ice. Ice is disgusting in the morning. Or, in a rush, straight from the bottle.)

I pour another, but Badpenny grabs Felipe. She's nuts. She's *possessed*. I grab it back and she grabs it away again. I'm not going to let go. She's not going to let go. Now she's commanding me, like a tiny Stalin, *"I WILL NOT LET YOU DO THIS!"*

Let the fuck go, you crazy-ass . . .

The little thing is quite violent and she's *strong*. She's dragging me and Felipe to the top of the staircase and—*"SHIT NO!"*—we are all going to break our necks. I don't want to die like this. I try to slap her—this is no time to be a gallant—but holy shit, *she's fast*.

I thought she'd grabbed a steel rod, but it was just her fist. The blood, *my* blood, sprayed everywhere: walls, window, *ceiling*. The stairwell looked like the scene of a mafia hit. And by the time the blindness caused by the pain ceased, Badpenny had slipped away home.

I looked in the mirror. My face was getting bigger, swelling, and, my God, there was a hunk of my lip simply hanging down.

Amy Goodman's sweet Iranian makeup lady did her best to cover over my butterfly Band-Aids and the nasty gash. I told the camera guys to shoot only my left profile.

"And that was a special report from Liberia from BBC Television investigative reporter Greg Palast. So tell me, Greg Palast . . ."

Amy was saying something to me very, very sincere. She was asking me about Vultures. I was trying to stay mental. Amy kindly did not mention to the radio audience that her guest had a hunk of bleeding flesh hanging over his teeth. I'm sure Jeremy Scahill will get a fucking big laugh out of this.

Got back to the office and, just to get even with the arrogant little bitchlette, I lay down on the couch and killed three-fourths of the liter bottle. *"You should be told you're beautiful every five minutes."* Oh, *please!* A more sensible idea would be to kick your little ass every five minutes.

I'm lying there, working. That is, staring at a fly and puzzling the problem. *Vulture has a piece of Montreux?* How did I miss that? Here's how: Evil is healthy. Evil has running shoes. The Vulture gets up early. He jogs, he does marathons. That's a fact: Matty Pass looked it up.

Let us be honest: There are some people in this world who truly need a fist to the face. I'm one of them.

The next morning, I fired my co-author, Felipe II, and flushed my spare pint down the toilet. (Well, nearly did. I sucked down the one sip left, the one for the road, for the marathon.) The world is intoxicated and stumbling, which means I'd have to write this story, this book, stone sober.

For weeks, I wouldn't admit to Badpenny that I had stopped drinking. There is nothing worse than a woman who rags you and nags you. Especially when she's right.

JFK

By the end of this story, you'll find out whether Professor Boley armed children, killed children, ate children, or saved children; how Chuck Totemoff is well on his way to becoming the first Native American billionaire (with my $300); how Japan created its own slow-motion Hiroshima; and why Texas and Georgia are in a race to go next—and the location of BP's next horror show.

I'm not giving away the ending because I have *no idea* how this will all end. As I'm writing this, Badpenny is behind me, puzzling visas to Kazakhstan and Azerbaijan, and chartering float planes and jeeps for Alaska and hunting up a bayou fan-boat in the Delta. Right now, I am heading to JFK Airport with a parka and Bermuda shorts.

The question mark in place of a last chapter is driving my publisher crazy. But what drives *me* crazy is that, while I'm dead sure I can name four of them, the fifth man, the *Hamsah,* remains just past my fingertips.

CHAPTER 2

Lady Baba-Land: The Islamic Republic of BP

BAKU, AZERBAIJAN, 2010

I've just photographed every page of my notes with the pen-camera Badpenny slipped to me as I boarded the plane for Central Asia. I've ripped out the notebook's crucial pages and cleaned my iPad of everything but a folder marked *BP docs,* which now contains nothing but a colorfully illustrated edition of *Winnie-the-Pooh*. My son *loved* that book.

Director James calls our "outside safety" and says, *"We expect 'visitors' shortly. Take the souvenirs to the secure location we discussed."*

Secure the "souvenirs"??? They can't *possibly* figure *that* one out, James.

Now he's hiding our film under the mattress—*the first place they'll look! Oh, Jesus.*

But the film he placed there, he assures me, is meaningless junk. He is planting it for them to "discover"—and stop further hunting. Way to go, Jamie!

I'm alone now, waiting for the Ministry's police to knock on the door.

I get a call from that jack-off "managing" our investigation from London. "You have put the crew in danger. You are to stay off the streets and leave *forthwith*." Love to, sir. But the Ministry has already called the hotel clerks and had them lock up our passports and exit visas.

No one is leaving this place "forthwith"—not with the Three Stooges, our shadows, out there in the alleyway, the only possible exit. I see "Larry," the one with the fake leather jacket, and "Moe" in that heavy overcoat. It's dusk, but

I've got their photo. And what good will that do you, Palast? And where's "Curley Joe," number three?

I wonder if the Stooges know that Lady Baba is the Twelfth Sexiest Woman Alive? The First Lady of Azerbaijan. It's true. It's official. She won the title of Number 12 in a poll taken by *Esquire* magazine. I've put up this photo of her on my screen. I want to have something visible when they come in to soften their hearts, or at least, something for them to steal.

Esquire gushes, *"Azerbaijan's first lady Mehriban Aliyeva was granted this title because here's a Goodwill Ambassador that can do her job without saying anything."*

What exactly is her "job"? *Esquire* doesn't say.

Here she is standing next to her husband, Ilham Aliyev. He's only the third president of this new nation, which won its independence from the USSR in 1991. In its last decade as a Soviet Socialist Republic, Azerbaijan was ruled by a merciless KGB thug, Heydar Aliyev. Aliyev was replaced by a devout Muslim anti-Communist, the merciless President of the Azerbaijan Republic, Heydar Aliyev. Azeris pined for the days when Heydar was merely merciless.

I should say, "Baba" Aliyev. Grandpa. Aliyev wanted all Azeris to call him just Grandpa. And everybody did call him President Grandpa because he scared the shit out of them. Azerbaijan is a democracy. That is, they hold elections. Baba didn't win, but that's a detail. If you're not interested in details, you can skip ahead to the shoes.

So Baba's son is Baby Baba. What does Mehriban see in this guy? It's gotta be the mustache. She must have fallen for that mustache of his. And his Gulfstream G5 jet.

Or maybe it's his flagpole. I write, "President Aliyev has the tallest flagpole in the world." That's a fact. It cost his nation $30 million to "erect." *Palast, this is frat-boy stuff. You're losing it. Not a good time to lose it.*

Besides, it's got to be love, because the First Lady is already loaded. Quite a little entrepreneur she is. Mehriban Aliyeva and her family own Pasha Insurance, Pasha Construction, Pasha Travel, Pasha Bank, her own line of cosmetics and the Bentley dealership in the Old City.

How do I know? Because newspaper editor Elmar Huseynov began investigating the First Lady's assets. He's dead. But, a colleague of his gave me the run-down on what they found on Mehriban's balance sheet. Some other journalist tried to find out how Elmar ended up dead, and *he* ended up in prison. No one is trying to find out why journalist #2 is in prison.

Since the nation's wealth is balanced on the First Lady's stilettos, I've pulled up photos of eight pairs of hers. I thought the Ministry police would like to see what their beatings and BP have bought her.

Serious heels. These gray ones, they're Yves Saint Laurent's Tribute Pumps. About $900 for the off-the-shelf model. It took a while, but I got the price. I thought the Ministry visitors should know that their salary for three months could buy one. Not the pair. Just one.

The average worker's wage in Azerbaijan, since BP arrived, has fallen to about $90 a month. But that's not a fair measure, because nearly half the adult men don't have full-time work.

If they take me into custody again, I'll miss Hannukah with the kids.

I don't think they'll care.

I've learned that the President wears her heels while she spanks him, ordering him to "confess." *This is a complete fabrication.* But that's what I'll tell the Ministry. No, I won't, but I like to pretend I'm a tough guy, waiting for the police to knock on the door.

But I don't think they'll knock.

THE ORIENTAL CLUB, LONDON

The trouble began in London.

It was nearly Christmas, when the city is at its ugliest. Badpenny and I simply could not avoid this stop on my way to Central Asia. There was the matter of the $30 million check flown to Azerbaijan in the small brown valise aboard a private 727, fitted out with a hot tub *and the Iron Lady,* ex–Prime Minister Thatcher.

The check, the flight, the transfer of the valise from the jet to BP CEO Lord Browne and then into the hands of Azerbaijan's President had my attention. While Baroness Thatcher jabbered with Asian oil men over dinner drinks, Browne placed the bag and check into the hands of our Bagman Abrahams.

This occurred back in 1992. Yet, I just knew in my gut that to verify what Caspian Man had told us—that a BP offshore rig had suffered a blowout and the company covered it up—we needed to follow the money, follow the brown bag holding the $30 million. We needed this Leslie Abrahams, the Bagman.

In the London gray, Badpenny and I are looking for an unmarked building off Oxford Street with no number on the door. I choose the most grandiose entrance in the row of grandiose Georgian buildings and open it. Inside, a concierge with a thick Russian accent said, "Mr. Abrahams is expecting you, sir. In the Members' Bar."

We found it, just past the gilded elephants and the other embarrassing pirated detritus of the Raj, including one human-size Buddha shoplifted by the Brits from Burma while the Lord Buddha meditated on their follies.

The Members' Bar was darkened by four giant centuries-old oil paintings telling lies about history. *Colonel Philips Saving the Hostages* portrays a benevolent bewigged officer in a red waistcoat taking a child from the filthy hands of a turbaned sultan. *"Dedicated to HM George III."*

There is an overwhelming air of Casablanca about Leslie Abrahams, so I'm not surprised he is a member of the Oriental Club, a kind of rococo museum of the death of an empire. If Central Asia is "the Graveyard of Empires," the Oriental Club is where the corpses pour G&Ts, waiting for burial.

It was 11:30 A.M. and Abrahams was just finishing his breakfast, two fingers of Jameson's. Badpenny glared at me, so I requested "a tea, white, please." The crested china service arrived swiftly and quietly.

It was mad work finding Abrahams, but once reached, and despite his dreadful health, he was surprisingly eager to chat. The well-appointed Leslie rose, coughed a lot with a frightening rattle from his lungs, then dropped his substantial weight back into the deep leather chair, nudging a square brown diplomatic bag next to him, 1930s vintage. He had stories of the new oil Raj for us, of whiskeys shared with the former Prime Minister Thatcher in Baku. I wanted to know what else was in that bag Lord Browne had handed Abrahams for safekeeping.

"Just the cherub." The check. I guess a check for $30 million takes up a lot of space. Leslie said they called it a "royalty" on oil production, though there was no oil production. And the check would be handed to no one but the President, in private.

In 1992, when Lady Thatcher flew the bag to Azerbaijan, it was just a baby of a nation, only one year old. Thatcher had been wheeled out to say nice things about the brand-new democracy. However, the people of the nascent Islamic republic had, it seemed, misused their new democratic rights. They made a poor choice, Leslie explained, voting in a president who was "not very favorable to BP." The "unfavorable" President, Mr. Abülfez Elchibey, took the surprise check from Lord Browne's hand, but instead of sticking it into his pocket, he properly handed it to the state oil company. Then he gave BP the finger: The Caspian's oil would go to American Oil Company (AMOCO), not British Petroleum. Within a year, his mistake would be corrected. Elchibey would be kicked out in a military coup.

According to a report obtained from Turkish intelligence, the British (British Petroleum and British Government combined) supplied the guns for this regime change. That lesson was not lost on the man who overthrew the elected president. Upon seizing office, Heydar Aliyev, Baba, became *very* favorable to BP. Within four months of the coup he handed BP what the entire oil industry and Baba himself called "The Contract of the Century." BP won without bidding, offering nothing more than displays of friendship and affection, some of it supplied by Leslie Abrahams. For example, the Oil Minister needed his office redecorated, and the Minister of Communications needed a satellite phone (cost: $25,000 in cash), and they all needed hookers, procured by Leslie at certain late-night clubs in London for which the Azeris were jetted in on Lord Browne's own Gulfstream.

Anything else, I asked?

"I bribed them," Abrahams said, between coughing fits. "Envelopes of cash."

He had switched to coffee. I let him sip and recover, then asked for sums. He personally passed about "two or three million pounds" to Azeri officials—in addition to the $30 million check. A fastidious man, Abrahams always demanded receipts. The receipts don't say "bribe," of course, they say "telephone" or "cultural and educational support."

When Baba Aliyev dubbed the Caspian oil deal "The Contract of the Century," he wasn't kidding. For a meaningless promise of some oil-drilling infrastructure, BP nailed exclusive rights to the Azerbaijan section of the Caspian Sea. They figured it held oil reserves "roughly equal to those of Kuwait." So what was the $30 million check for?

"A little 'sweetener,'" said Leslie. Abraham's second empty whiskey glass was quietly removed.

A bribe? "I didn't ask." Leslie smiled. Gentlemen don't ask.

And what was in the attaché case he'd brought here to the Club? This time, no cherub, just old photos he laid out on the mahogany table: His younger self in Baku in front of the BP office, smiling, all in white, adorned with a Panama hat, and another one of Leslie holding a Kalashnikov. There were several of Abrahams with the British Ambassador. That was not unexpected: The British Embassy was a desk inside BP headquarters, in Leslie's office, in fact. A convenience.

One snap included Viscount Douglas Hogg of Her Majesty's Government's Privy Council; another at a nightclub with the striking Natasha, BP's Russian instructor who also provided affection as needed to seal a deal; and one photo, on which I lingered, with MP Harold Elletson (later outed as an MI6 agent) and Countess Lola Czerny.

The Countess, Leslie?

Ah, yes. She invited him upstairs for a private discussion. When he got to the room, she had a surprise for him. There was the British Ambassador, as

well as the President of BP-Azerbaijan, and John Scarlett, Head of Moscow Station for MI6.

To understand the gravamen of this little gathering, you need to know about one of those heartbreaking caesuras in history not reported on *Good Morning America*. The year was 1991, when, to celebrate their new freedom from Soviet rule, Muslim Azerbaijan and Christian Armenia went to war against each other. Armenia, backed by both Russia and the United States, kicked the Azeris back to Baku, allowing Armenians to complete the militarized ethnic cleansing of Nagorno-Karabakh in the South Caucasus.

A bit of history: When Stalin drew the maps of the USSR's Central Asian Republics, he created a Muslim island within Christian Armenia, Nagorno-Karabakh, and designated it Azeri territory just to keep the ethnic pot boiling.

Once upon a time, British Petroleum was an arm of British imperial power. Today, the British government is an arm of BP's imperial power. In this role as BP's little helper, Her Majesty's government added another "sweetener" to nail down the Contract of the Century for BP: a deal to re-arm Azerbaijan, a job necessarily done *sotto voce* to avoid pissing off the Americans and Russians.

However, it was important that BP, which was also seeking leases in Russia, to keep both sides of the killing happy. Abrahams could help. He had obtained official diplomatic status with the Azeri dictator's government, which gave him special access rights to cross through off-limits military zones to get to the oil fields.

The BP chief, Terry Adams, was in the confab in the Contessa's room. Adams made it clear that intelligence work was a required part of Abrahams's BP duties. As Leslie crossed the secure zones, he was to record the number of missiles and troop trains and any other Mil-Int. He would then drop the intelligence at the UK Embassy in Moscow on his travels out of Central Asia.

How did Abrahams feel about being a spy, a double agent as a matter of fact, a rook in the Great Game that cost the Muslim and Christian pawns so many tears and so much blood?

"It was exciting."

Who could back up his incredible tale? He suggested we speak with Princess Tamara Dragadze of the Georgian royal family, whom BP added to its payroll to open doors. The Princess was with Leslie when Lord Browne passed him the check, and she knew the whole game. But she ducked all my calls and messages—no surprise—which left our team no choice but to fly to Baku (not cheap) and hunt for Abrahams's former colleague, Fatima, who could find Zulfie, a guy who was also in on BP's pay-and-play business. And Zulfie, we hoped, could help us get to Natasha.

Abrahams knows his information will hit like a cluster bomb in the British Parliament and splash all over the papers in Azerbaijan. But he needn't fear arrest in Britain: The checks, cash, and purchased love traded hands when it was still legal for Brits to pay bribes. (Even today, Britons may pay bribes but only if the checks are written in Arabic.)

But reaction in Azerbaijan would definitely be a problem. While long separated from BP, Abrahams still operates a consulting firm in Baku. Presumably, spilling the beans will have unpleasant consequences, and not just for his businesses.

He acknowledged the risk. "It would not be wise for me to return to Azerbaijan. Ever." President Baby Baba remains a "good friend," he says, but Abrahams knows this won't necessarily help. Leslie related how one of Baby Baba's friends working in the Central Bank asked the wrong questions and received a quick answer—a bullet in the face. Not that Abrahams was suggesting any connection between the bullet and the presidential family.

So this was the end of Azerbaijan for him and for his new Azeri wife, and maybe, to be blunt, for Leslie himself. His recent, severe stroke had left it difficult for him to get through a sentence without the hacking that sounded like a death rattle. He even had to take a couple of vomit breaks during our chat.

Badpenny asked him, *"So why now?"* Why hand us the brown valise (which he put in our safekeeping)?

"The public interest," he said. But the public would have been interested long ago. He also hinted that he would not mind putting a bit of stick up the rear of that little shit Terry Adams, his former manager as President of BP-Azerbaijan, who'd promised to take care of Leslie but discarded him when BP and MI6 had all they wanted.

I think something else motivated him. As he gasped for air in the thick, baroque room, it seemed to me that Abrahams saw this as a last chance to have what he missed most from the Baku days in his Panama hat: being a very bad boy again. And that is damn exciting.

Stories of dungeons, bribery, and Natasha will follow below. But first history must speak up.

THE KHAZAR EMPIRE

Titusville, Pennsylvania, is damn proud to be the first place on Earth to produce crude oil. It's not true, but America just loves that story.

Fact is, as far back as the eighth century, Khazars, the vicious horsemen who once terrorized Central Asia, had a nice little business selling petroleum by exporting it from Baku—in one of life's ironies that makes history delicious—to the kingdoms of Arabia. (The Khazars built the only Jewish empire in history, something even Jews have long forgotten about, memorialized only in the Yiddish word *khazarei* or "a ridiculous mess.")

Here in Baku, a caravanserai on the Silk Road to China, the oil once bubbled up from the ground and into the Caspian Sea all by itself. It could be harvested like sturgeon.

Marco Polo, the great explorer of the thirteenth century, stopped at Baku to see for himself the blazes that magically lit the city through the night from the giant towers topped with turbans of flame. The Caucasian Muslims (the Stars of David long expunged from the land) had channeled methane gas into flaming pillars. This was the first culture to worship oil, but it wouldn't be the last.

Marco Polo recorded the trade in this extraordinary substance, petroleum, but wisely chose to stay clear of it, because, unlike olive oil, he noted, you could burn Baku oil but not eat it. Instead, he selected a Chinese invention, pasta, to bring home to Venice. Italians never regretted his choice. But Marco's picking pasta over petroleum haunted Mussolini and ENI, Italy's big petroleum corporation, leading both to make mistakes that would cost them dearly.

On July 22, 1912, Britain's young and frighteningly ambitious First Lord of the Admiralty, the Honorable Winston Churchill, sold His Majesty's Parliament on an astonishing new weapons system that would keep Britain master of the seas: liquid energy. Instead of bulky, balky coal or wind, petroleum oil would henceforth power the fleet's engines through internal combustion.

Britain had plenty of this liquid fuel. *The Daily Mirror* crowed about oil seepages in the English Midlands that indicated the British Isles had as much oil in the ground as Pennsylvania, Baku, and the Middle East, the only places on Earth then known to have large oil reserves.

Churchill, of course, knew *The Mirror* was as reliable then as it is now. And so, the young Naval chief knew the British Empire would need its own globe-girding oil supply. He eyed Persia and Iraq. But first, Churchill would have to invent Iraq, which he did, later, in 1919, with a razor blade, when he cut a "nation" out of the three Mesopotamian oil fields of the defeated Ottoman Empire.

In the meantime, the rubes and boobs were grabbing for the "Sound Investment" trumpeted on *The Mirror's* front page after Sir Winston's let-them-burn-oil speech.

> It is this pioneer characteristic which has made the British Nation the greatest commercial nation on the face of the earth. It is this same characteristic which will, in the very near future, give to far-seeing British Investors the paramount sway in the new Russian Oil Fields, where already much British Capital in the same locality is producing the most gratifying returns from its early investment.

Lenin would strike oil for the British investors. That is, the Bolshevik Revolution of 1917 freed the serfs of Russia and allowed the Islamic colonies on the Caspian to skitter away. The United States and Britain rushed in to recognize the independent nation of Azerbaijan, which, by that year, produced nearly half the world's petroleum and, it seems, half the whorehouses, casinos, and oversize mansions.

It took Lenin twenty-three months to realize his socialist revolution was running out of gas, literally. He ordered the 11th Red Army to invade and, killing only 20,000 Azeris, gave them the gift of petro-socialism.

Both Lenin and Churchill, keen anatomists of history, uniquely understood: Oil is liquid war.

And Churchill grasped it in his fist. "It" was Persia. Invasion was not necessary; Britain could just buy it. This ancient civilization, called Iran by its residents, was ruled by a Pasha with a big fruity hat and a big pile of debts that he'd piled up on a budget-busting trip to Europe. Churchill's drinking buddy (all Churchill's buddies drank), William Knox D'Arcy, picked Persia up for a song from the wastrel Pasha in 1901, then sold what would become British Petroleum, for a "gratifying return," to Her Majesty's government in 1914 at Churchill's insistence.

With Persia in its pocket, the British Empire left the Caspian Sea to the Soviets to abuse—and as a lure to successfully tempt the Axis to its doom. (Here's a photo of Hitler carving up a cake in the shape of the Caspian republics. The word *Baku* is on his slice. The Führer planned to carve up the Caspian by September 25, 1942, with Panzer divisions. They were sliced to pieces. It was an unusual case of eating your cake and having it eat you too.)

In 1989, The Wall fell and, in 1991, the Caspian republics gave independence another try.

The people voted in Abülfez Elchibey, a former dissident with a beard. His themes were Peace, Love, and Understanding. I think of him as President Hippie.

Armenia kept stealing bites out of Azerbaijan as if it were a warm cupcake. (I know that's hard to believe. Thomas Friedman has assured us that in the new world of globalized free markets, no two nations with a McDonalds will go to war. Here's a snap I took of a soda cup with the Golden Arches on it with Azeri writing. I understand that the dying words of several of the soldiers were, "Do you want fries with that?")

President Hippie's big idea was to run an oil pipeline straight through Armenia, as a way to grease enemy hearts, then dip the pipeline down through northern Iran to show solidarity with his Azeri brothers living across the border. From there, it would go up to the Russian Black Sea port of Novosibirsk, and thereby warm relations with one really pissed-off Russian Bear whose petroleum honey pot had been stolen away.

The Peace Pipe had something for everyone (Armenia, Iran, America, Russia, and Turkey) and therefore something for everyone to get angry about. Anyway, the Peace Pipe was snuffed—and so was Elchibey's presidency. The Azeri military couldn't beat Armenia, but they sure as heck could take out a hippie with a beard. Baba returned to power, no longer Party Secretary and KGB Chief but President and Grandfather.

It wasn't the Peace Pipe, or even losing chunks of the homeland to Armenia, that did in Elchibey. As Leslie the Bagman told us, "Elchibey was not favorable to BP."

No, he wasn't. Elchibey actually held something like an open bid for Azerbaijan's massive, barely touched Caspian Sea oil fields. AMOCO (American Oil Company) got most of it. Elchibey gave BP only a teeny-weeny sliver.

And so, as I have mentioned, four months after the coup, BP went from a dieter's skinny slice to the whole enchilada.

How?

BP sweetened the sweeteners. Besides the money that arrived with Lady Thatcher in the flying hot tub with Lord Browne, BP and its partners sweetened the accounts of the State Oil Company of Azerbaijan by up to half a billion dollars. I can't say the exact amount for sure. *No one can say* how much, except Baba and BP. And, I suppose, the chief of the State Oil Company, Ilham Aliyev, Baba's son, Baby Baba. And they ain't saying nothing.

Alas, millions don't buy immortality (lots of statues, however), and Grandpa knew he couldn't last forever. So, in August 2003, hearing wings of mortality, Baba chose a new Prime Minister, Ilham Aliyev, Baby Baba. Baby Baba was so good at the job of Prime Minister that just two months after Daddy made him Prime Minister, the public voted him President, replacing his father. He won with 76.84 percent of the vote.

But who's counting?

BP.

Those sweeteners in brown bags, YSL heels, and eleven men dead in the Gulf of Mexico: I was sure these were somehow connected, and I could find the connections only in Azerbaijan. That's how I ended up here, nervous, in a hotel in Baku.

So Badpenny's won and I hope she's happy. I say "won" because she'd been hounding me to go to the Caspian well before the Gulf blowout. Two years earlier, she tried to seduce me into a Caspian investigation by giving me, as a Hannukah gift, Robert Ebel's *Energy and Conflict in Central Asia and the Caucasus.* I even flew to DC to meet Ebel and can confirm he knows loads about the topic of energy and conflict because he *caused* a lot of it. He was head of the CIA's oil intelligence unit. (Maybe he still is. They don't say.)

I figured Ebel might know what happened to the half billion dollars in royalties and "sweeteners" paid to Azerbaijan. He calculates that, at the very minimum, the whereabouts of $140 million is "totally unknown." Or maybe the CIA *does* know. So let's amend that to "the whereabouts of $140 million cannot be revealed." That would be an awful lot of YSLs for First Lady Mehriban.

* * *

When Leslie the Bagman landed in Baku in 1992, he stepped off BP's Gulfstream with weaponry, wads of U.S. dollars sewn into his suit, and diplomatic status granted by the Azeri dictatorship.

In December 2010, when I arrived in Baku with my Director James, we flew economy class, armed only with Fatima's phone number from Leslie and a bogus invitation from some group promising we would not film the laughable "reelection" of Baby Baba. We had, though, arranged for "Fixers" to set us up to reach local BP workers on the Caspian drilling platforms who would know about the big blowout—but probably would not be thrilled to talk about it.

But first, could we somehow reach Caspian Man, our jittery source with information about the rig blowout?

I had to reach Caspian Man and convince him to speak to me here in Baku. Badpenny had left for Lucerne, Switzerland, with more important things to do, but I asked her to write an e-mail to her "boyfriend" from there. I dictated:

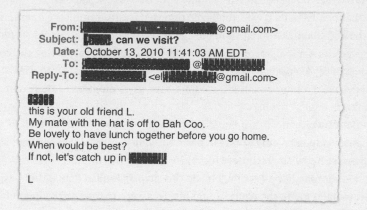

From: █████████ ██████@gmail.com>
Subject: █████, can we visit?
Date: October 13, 2010 11:41:03 AM EDT
To: █████████████████ @█████████
Reply-To: ████████ <el█████████@gmail.com>

██████
this is your old friend L.
My mate with the hat is off to Bah Coo.
Be lovely to have lunch together before you go home.
When would be best?
If not, let's catch up in ████████

L

Then another e-mail immediately after:

Subject: oooops sorry

Forgot to leave my new phone number 6xx 6xx 6xxx

;) -L

Badpenny was laughing. *"Bah Coo??? Oh, for Chrissakes, Palast, this is hardly the Enigma Code. It's Maxwell Smart!"*

So shoot me. My dear film director wanted to meet Caspian Man and *film him* in Baku, and demanded I send Caspian Man a missive through his official address on the Azeri e-mail servers. The fake adulterous invitation was just a way to avoid snooping search engines. I have to assume that BP and friends have raised their game since the disaster with the toy truck.

Badpenny couldn't resist asking, *"You gave him a U.S. number, but did you check the voice mail on your 'clean' line? Did you do a reverse search to see the name associated with it?"*

"Yeah, I was about to."

"Bullshit you were!"

Badpenny takes the opportunity to list the times I've lost the James Bond award.

"L" got a quick response from Caspian Man. "NO." Not a chance. He's so high up the official food chain, he'd be a cinch for BP or Baba's Ministry to identify even if he appeared in shadow with his voice scrambled.

Badpenny, in fact, was stone-cold opposed to attempting the interview in "Bah Coo" (Baku). Caspian Man, she feared, could lose his job; or worse. Baba's family runs Azerbaijan, and Azerbaijan runs on oil. Disrespecting the confidences of BP-Azerbaijan is disrespecting Baba. As one BP insider told me, "The Aliyevs have a long reach. Please don't ever say I mentioned their name." I won't.

And I won't meet Caspian Man while he's within Aliyev's reach, if only because Badpenny simply will not permit cavalier treatment of sources. She'll make sure he's visibly far away from us before we roll film.

Yet, despite her objection, I made this grossly foolish demand to Caspian Man to meet me in the Azeri capital just to assure the network I'm a reliable stooge capable of carrying out insane instructions.

IN THE DESERT, AZERBAIJAN

"Here in Azerbaijan we believe in human rights. . . ."

What a coincidence: I'm human.

". . . AND PLEASE GIVE US YOUR FILM."

Oh no no, not good. Not good at all.

My thumbs blindly text Matty Pass in Mexico City:

The enforcers here come in three colors: the military police still wearing their old Russian puke-green uniforms, the Ministry of National Security wear windbreakers without ID, and BP's own corporate police force sport black tunics, sashes, and those big Russian pillbox fur hats. They have little oil derricks embossed on their uniforms. They looked like the toy soldiers from the Nutcracker ballet, but they weren't dancing.

Our arrest, if you will allow me to pass the blame, is the fault of my Dear Director. James, back from endangering himself in Africa, decided that the best way to get information on BP's Caspian op was to make a direct assault off-road through the desert to Fortress BP itself, the giant pipeline terminus near Sangachal, like Rommel crossing the Sahara. It didn't end well for Rommel, either.

With the long lens on and in focus, we began filming BP's cancer-making machine, the steaming, flaming plant that sends the Azeri's Caspian Sea oil westward to light Europe's Christmas trees.

I showed BP's toy soldier our press credentials in both English and Azeri, neither of which he could read. (President Baba had suddenly changed the

Azeri alphabet, making most of the nation illiterate overnight.) Now it looked like I'd be spending the holidays in Baba's dungeon, licking rats for breakfast.

I said, "Look here: This paper says your so-called president is a weasel's patoot," which our "fixer" translated as: "This letter from the Foreign Ministry is authorization to make a documentary for British Television." James had switched the film in the camera to blank memory cards and told the military cop, "Hadn't begun filming yet, old bean."

We would now. I clicked on my hidden micro-cam in a pen, the one Badpenny had handed me as a gift as I boarded for Baku. And James, despite dramatically removing the film from our camera, rolled on unnoticed, recording to a second, unseen memory card.

A black SUV arrived on the remote desert track, unloading its impressive cargo, a colonel sprinkled with medals from the recent war Azerbaijan lost to Armenia. One of his hat holders said, by way of explanation, "British Petroleum drives this country." He thought that I, as a "British" journalist would be proud of that fact.

A shepherd on a horse no bigger than a carousel pony was caught up in the bust because his sheep had wandered across the pipeline.

Not knowing what to do with his flock and pony, they let him go. We moved under escort toward a sealed military base. James knew that once you've checked into Hotel Baba, it's not easy to check out. He insisted on pulling in to a gas station (not BP's) on this road to nowhere. It had a little truck-stop diner and we scampered over. When we walked in, the owner of the empty café thought he'd died and gone to heaven: a pack of rich foreigners with military brass!

"Do you want lunch?"

James said, "Of course not," but before his rejection could be translated, I shouted, *"BËLI!,"* one of five Azeri words I knew—*YES!*—which the proprietor took to mean I'd pop for a full-scale banquet for the whole gang. And that's exactly what I wanted. It's an *Islamic* republic. They can pull out your fingernails, but dissing a guest, rejecting hospitality, is a Koranic no-no.

The proprietor's wife (a third his age, I'd say) held up for my inspection a huge carp, still gasping, obviously just pulled from the chemical cesspool known as the Caspian Sea. *Bëli! Bëli!* Yogurts with spiced pomegranate? *Bëli!* Koutabs, Chorba, pitchers of Ovchala, Halvah for dessert? *Bëli! Bëli!** They

---

* Interactive editions will have the recipes.

had Ramush, the Caspian's Keith Richards (and just as ancient), rocking and cranked up high on a TV.

Then the festive air turned cold. The café door opened and a black, thick-sided—bulletproofed—Lexus pulled up right across the doorway. Two-hundred and seventy pounds of assassination meat walked in, a scar over his lip, stubble on his face, and two gold teeth. There was not one insignia, medal, epaulette, or uniform on the man. But everyone knew who he was. Everyone except me and James.

Does our dear director have an alibi about why we were filming at the pipeline, right *on top of it*, as it turned out, stomping on the Baba's Holy Pipe? James says he's "been trying to think up something" since the bust two hours earlier. That's good, James, you just keep trying to think.

We were in a game show now, like everyone else in this petro-police state, where meek contestants are questioned by an abusive clown and have to guess the answers the clown wants. There are no winners.

Mr. Murder grins and chuckles, and all colors of police and army chuckle with him, nervous. Then Murder sits down to tea. He chuckles with the colonel, and the colonel chuckles some more, sweating.

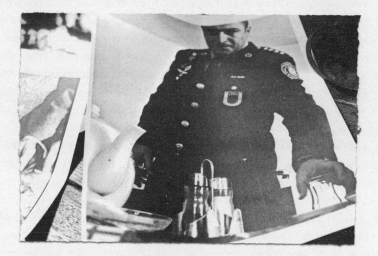

My fixer whispers: "MSN's Number Two." That is, he's the second in command of the Ministry of National Security, the secret police. They don't seem to bother with staying secret. I'm honored, but perplexed. Foreign TV crews are always under suspicion, under watch. There were the intermittent tailing cars (they had an inexplicable pattern: two black ones, then a white one). I even had my photo taken with one of my police shadows in the Old City. He smiled at the camera and gave a thumbs-up, in English, to "Channel 4!" But to take a top guy like #2 away from his busy schedule of brutality . . . why?

This is more than strange. The Ministry seems to know way more than they should. I intend to figure out how if only I can get the hell out of here.

Mr. Murder-meat pulled up a chair next to our translator. He knew our translator was also the presidential candidate of the Green Party of Azerbaijan. Go ahead and laugh. True, they don't hold a single seat in parliament, but no one does unless they express love for the Babas, especially the MP from Azizbeyov, Lady Mehriba.

By making Professor Green Party our translator (his name won't help you or him), we could also film him without raising a big hoo-hah.

Since the night before, Professor Green Party had been shining up his English, preparing to tell me on camera exactly what was going on: the coup d'état, the BP Contract of the Century, what money in whose bank account: Detailed corroboration of much of the Bagman's story.

Professor Green Party was a lion; he couldn't be bought or pushed around. He had balls of steel. He was going to lay out the whole shebang in a nation where even oblique mention of Baba or BP in less than glorious adjectives is risky business. I'd gotten a lesson about Baba's temperament just the night before, when I had dinner with a young video blogger. His popular site was dedicated to teaching Azeris how to hang, to talk, to dance—to party. Party Blogger told me, "We don't have a culture of getting together to party." I had already gathered that.

For fun, the Party Blogger put on a donkey suit and held a press conference. President Baby Baba saw the YouTube video of the event and suspected he was the ass. He was. He is. Whatever, the partying donkey got two and half years in prison.

It didn't help that the Party Blogger had blessed "the Father, the Son, and the Holy Pipeline."

The donkey's arrest was mentioned by the BBC World Service. Result: In 2009, BBC's Azeri broadcast was banned from the radio dial. America's Radio Liberty also broadcast the presidential ass and was booted off the air as well.

Murder-meat pulled his chair still closer to our translator and whispered to him in their lonely language. (Only the eight million residents of this oil kingdom speak Azeri.)

Even now, looking at the film from the pen, it chills me.

Green Party listened, turned white, mumbled, and nodded, then turned gray, aging in that instant. He looked as I imagined Jacob looked when he begged God and the angels not to let Esau beat him. *"Will you stay my brother's hand?"*

No sense asking me; nothing I can do.

Murder-meat grinned. He turned to the officers, chuckled, they chuckled back—and he signaled them to return our passports and press credentials. We were told we could now interview Professor Green Party, on camera. As our background, we had the giant grinning head of President Baba on the billboard in front of a chemical plant. A fresh gaggle of cops "escorted" us.

We rolled film. I asked the dissident Green Party candidate about what happened to the millions of dollars BP paid to Baba's oil company that no one can seem to find.

He responded, "Those who suggest there is corruption are only serving the purposes of Great Britain, the United States, and Israel!"

Israel??

Before my eyes, the brave Green Man was turning into an Islamic Republican; he was channeling Baba. And he was speaking in Azeri, so our uniformed hosts could hear he was being a good little foal, a good little donkey.

As Murder-meat's black sedan drove off, I could hear a couple of loose steel balls clinking in his pocket.

In fact, I had rehearsed this interview with Green Party the night before. That's unusual, but I needed him to practice his English for the on-camera version. So I thought I already knew his answers. But now, while he spoke, I wrote in my notebook for James to see,

He's backing down on everything

and underlined and circled it.

What had I expected? As the Party Blogger explained,

"IN AZERBAIJAN, POSSIBILITIES FOR DONKEYS ARE ENORMOUS. IF YOU ARE
DONKEY ENOUGH, YOU CAN SUCCEED IN PROBABLY ANYTHING."

Advice straight from the ass's mouth. Well, I too have munched a lot of
hay in my life, even without being shown the implements of torture.

TERMINAL TOWN

Our official cover story for filming in Baku was this: We would make a documentary about the "booming economy" of the Islamic republic. That the only
businesses booming are bribery and BP were details we left out of our application to the Ministry.

But still, we were more than willing to film the happy side of the oil boom.
So we drove out to Sangachal, Terminal Town, where BP's oil is stuffed into
the pipe for more deserving people in Western Europe. I expected to film the
Big Action, the usual oil boom-times berserker stuff; cash-rich oil workers
spending like lunatics. Except we couldn't find any of it.

We showed up in Terminal Town in the middle of the workday. Yet we saw
only listless men milling around in chattering groups.

At random, with our translator, I grabbed a loud, big one, Elmar Mamonov.

The tall, impressive man, a kind of Muslim Max von Sydow, was mildly wasted, probably on the local stuff that tastes like cough syrup and napalm, which gave him the temporary courage to say to me, on camera, "I will speak with you what has happened to us."

Walking along Terminal Town's main street with Mamonov was like doing the rounds in a cancer ward. "This one's daughter has breast cancer there; Rasul had a brain tumor. Cancers we had never seen. His funeral was last week. *Alev Salaam.* Azlan here—hey, Azlan!—had lung cancer and he paid to have one of his lungs cut out." And there was Shala Tageva, a schoolteacher, who has ovarian cancer. She needs treatment soon, but how, Mamonov can't imagine. Shala is Mamonov's wife.

Maybe that's why they call it Terminal Town.

Suddenly, Mamonov stopped himself.

"If I am arrested, you will help me, yes?"

Actually, I can't. But I leave out that detail. Am I going to be a complete shit and lie to him, or am I going to tell him the truth? *If they bust you, you're on your own.*

If big boys like BBC World Service got kicked, Mr. Mamonov, you will be kicked harder by Baby Baba's braying asses, right into some medieval hole. You will be forgotten, while my network sends a letter of apology to the regime for "accidentally" violating the conditions of our film permit.

I'm only half a shit. I told Mamonov, "We will do everything we can." At least I deliberately misspelled his name.

I applaud his unwitting courage.

* * *

At three A.M. on moonless nights, the air in Terminal Town gets funky, nasty. In Houston, near the Exxon refinery, they call it Sky Dumping. Toxins that should be sealed and buried—an expensive process—are instead loaded into furnaces and sent up the "flaring" stacks and belched into the sky. Hard to discover, harder to trace.

BP is not trying to choke poor Muslims to death. As the CEO of Shell USA once told me, "Oil companies have no ideology." BP has no religious prejudices. They Sky-Dump in Texas City too, and at their refinery on the Gulf, heavily Protestant; Exxon does it in Houston and in Cancer Alley, Louisiana, lots of Creole and Cajun Catholics.

I wandered around Terminal Town with James and his camera, pretending I can do something about all this. Now, if Mr. Azlan, the man who had a lung removed, were a seal or a snowy egret or a pelican covered in oil, I could get CNN and Anderson Cooper to come here in a flash. Or better, a whale: Then Azlan's plight would have a shot at the National Geographic channel.

But Azlan is just some Muslim schmuck at the end of BP's pipe. You could say he's one of the lucky ones—one of the few who got a job with BP. "But it cost me my lung! And they wouldn't pay to have it cut out! And then they fired me because I couldn't work hard enough!" What did you expect when you rejected Soviet occupation for BP occupation? You've got a lung left; how many do you need?

And frankly, what can I do about it? Mr. Azlan is not a very cute mammal, and he's not photogenically covered in crude. Here in Terminal Town, the oil residues enter their bodies and eat them alive from the inside out.

No one wants to see that.

I went into Mamonov's backyard, where he introduced me to his one chicken. At least the chicken is living large: It's got a huge coop all to itself. Mamonov told me he used to have twenty hens.

Out in the yard, keeping the chicken company, stood a piano, properly tuned. It is what remains from the Great Leap Backward. Elmar's family had fallen from a great height, and like all those who fall, they cling fiercely to one or two objects of the lost life. A homeless man keeps a television remote control, refugees will leave food behind yet haul a candelabra and broken candles, a chessboard, crushed silver Sabbath cups (my family), or, for the Mamonovs, the piano. It couldn't fit in their chicken coop of a house, but the classical instrument stayed with them, out in the desert air, kept for his daughter to play Azeri music of another time, the Shostakovich concerti often played by Rostropovich, a native son.

I remembered that a Rostropovich favorite was *Lady Macbeth of Mtsensk*. Lady Baba seems more comfortable with other tunes. I know that many consider her cruel, but at least Lady Baba did not force Elmar and his ill wife to attend the big Elton John concert. (Baby Baba spent millions on bringing the Liberace of the eighties to Baku.)

Mamonov's daughter made an appearance, shy, in a modest head scarf. She is about fourteen, a year older than my own daughter (who quit piano lessons, just lost interest, but I still have the keyboard packed away somewhere). I asked the young Miss Mamonova if she could play "Crocodile Rock."

His daughter also helps in his shoe shop. Elmar recalled selling a pair two years ago.

One other set of objects remains with Elmar the cobbler after The Fall: the shoe "lasts," the uppers without soles, nearly finished, and left so for a decade, fuzzed with dust. The workers of Terminal Town can no longer afford these work shoes because they have no work—nor need any for the same reason. If only Lady Baba would patronize his shop *just once* . . . but alas.

So the locals now wear sandals. Even Elmar, the shoemaker himself, wears cheap flip-flops as he falls backward with his nation into the fourteenth century. The tarmac on Terminal Town's Main Street is crumpling to dust; it is now just a medieval dirt track. The only thing missing is a camel.

CARACAS

What happened in Azerbaijan?

In Caracas they went crackers; in Alaska, locals tumbled ass over heels; in Africa, Britain, Kansas, and Rio, where Cariocas went cuckoo, everyone goes nuts when they strike it rich with oil. (Except for the Norwegians. They remain grimly temperate.) Oil gushes and the rich get richer, true, but the poor have a hell of a party. When elephants defecate, birds feast.

Everywhere I've traveled the oil trail, I've witnessed it. The explosive chain reaction of oil-heated shopping sprees boosts economies now geared to selling crap no one ever thought they needed before: a blender to make smoothies in the Arctic; life insurance, guns, porcelain Santas; smack, crack, and mouthwash; bagels and cream cheese flown in to go with the smoked salmon in Alaska (I appreciated that); toilets, DVD players, televisions (actually, televisions before toilets, always); Nobel Prize winners (the University of Texas bought several when gushers were found under its school properties); door locks, light-up crucifixes, lipstick (deep in the Amazon), fake weight-control pills, American toothpaste, cars that don't fit the roads, extra wars ("Oil will be our weapon to win back Karabakh!" said Baba until BP vetoed the idea); vacations, battery-operated toys, porn, scuba gear; and lots of shoes.

The jet fuel for such potlatches of quick riches are those hard-currency, easy-come-easy-go jobs like rig roustabouts, bellboys, air traffic controllers, copter pilots, hairdressers, pickpockets, and all the infrastructure operators and camp followers oil requires and acquires: to lay pipe, to sell sandwiches to the guys laying pipe, girls laying the guys laying the pipe, jobs jacking up the jack-up rigs, sky-dumping the sludge, and inevitably, loads of work cleaning up the spill.

It's a hell of a ride. It certainly happened here in Baku, in 1919 during the first Caspian oil boom.

Good times, crazy times, high-rolling times, the petroleum party that, inevitably, ends in a bust and hangovers. But here this time, the Azeris went straight to the hangover.

How could this happen? How could so many petrodollars escape without a couple pounds sterling falling out of BP's stuffed pockets?

What the hell went wrong? How could this nation with oil pouring out its eyeballs turn into economic roadkill?

What happened? BP happened. The Contract of the Century happened. Under the Hippie President's deal with American Oil Company (AMOCO), Azeris kept 30 percent of the oil to sell. But under Baba's Contract of the Century, Azerbaijan's share starts at just 10 percent. Looks like a pretty grim century ahead for the Azeris.

Let's do a calculation. BP has its long straw into a 5.4-billion-barrel reserve. At say, $100 a barrel, with a 90/10 split, that's half a trillion dollars for BP and peanut butter sandwiches for Azerbaijan.*

BP didn't even pay the contract's meager fee. A confidential U.S. State Department cable, retrieved by my good friend David Leigh at *The Guardian*, says Baba complained to BP that they cheated his treasury out of $10 billion. The split was supposed to change from 10 percent to 20 percent for Azeris years ago. When BP didn't pay, Baba threw a shit-fit, called in BP's local chief, and threatened to expose the company:

"[Aliyev] will make public that BP is stealing our oil."

BP's man grinned at Baba. He did not have to say, *Go ahead, Baba, let's have a public audit of the contract payments. The audit will have to go back to the $140 million and who knows what else that has disappeared. Feeling lucky, Baba?*

---

* To my fellow energy economists and amateur oil experts: I know this calculation is wild over-simplification. The SOCAR percentage under PSA rises, the amount that can be actually lifted from the reserve is lower, but the reserve itself will certainly get much higher and the per-barrel price is up to OPEC, the Almighty, and James Baker. I'm happy to get your calculations done with sharper pencils. Send to GregPalast.com/contact.

The autocrat obviously chose to toddle off into a corner and chew his pea-nut butter sandwich in moody silence. And he agreed to give BP an extension of its contract. (The United States later sweetened the pot with hints of weap-ons Baba's military could toy with.)

But peanut butter isn't nothing. The state still gets *some* of the oil. So then, why are these Azeris literally starving?

At least three sources gave me the answer, linking hunger and the nation's collapse to the Contract of the Century, the coup d'état, and the missing mil-lions. But like our Greenie at the diner, they panicked once I had the camera turned on. I'm not blaming them, I'm just saying I was a stuck duck.

That left me with only one option: the Crazy Lady.

BP WORKERS' HOUSING COMPOUND, BAKU

We found her in the oil workers' housing block in a dumpy part of Baku, in one of the tenement's top-floor rooms, like the Madwoman of Chaillot. The build-ings here are a mixture of Soviet grim and Third World decay. Nevertheless, 95 percent of the Azeri population would sell their children to live in these dumps.

"She's crazy," our translator told me.

Mirvari Gahramanli did not seem nuts to me. Schooled in several lan-guages and once the highest-ranking female in the state oil company, she headed an organization for the protection of oil workers' rights. That sounds like a union to me, but BP won't recognize, and Baba won't tolerate, real unions.

A union would not do much good. She pointed out that BP is actually *banned* from paying wages above the bread-and-water salaries earned in other parts of the so-called economy of Azerbaijan. It's right there in the Con-tract of the Century. She spoke with authority about how it went down: listing names and dates and the history of the Con Job of the Century.

That's why Mirvari's crazy. She'll say anything, even on camera. Even about the Twelfth Sexiest Woman in the World, who, she tells me, is seizing control of the social welfare money BP donates to help "the small people" (as BP's chairman calls us).

Before I left, I asked Mirvari about a photo on the shelf behind her desk. In it, she is standing in front of a line of policemen, a wall of riot shields and clubs. By herself, Mirvari is holding back the entire phalanx. It was like that man in Tianamen Square standing in front of the tanks.

What she didn't have on the shelf were the photos taken moments later. Mirvari opened a special file in her computer: There she is on the ground after the cops have beaten the shit out of her. Then she was jailed. Then she was beaten up again, then jailed twice more. So far.

Crazy.

But BP believes in love, not war. They offered Mirvari money. She said no. She said, "Pay your ill workers the money you owe them." BP said no.

But they did paint her hallway. BP painted it eco-green like their gas stations. That's the yin-yang of oil dictatorship. Baba does the beatings, BP does the paint-over.

And I thought: *Fuck global warming. This* is what will burn down our planet: placing cash and kisses in the hands of the petro-police state, while its other hand smacks down and jails a sweet lady like Mirvari; that makes oil rig workers accept a daily dance with death because to speak up is to starve; that makes you a prisoner in an unnumbered cell; that makes you look into the eyes of the ones you love and ask, *Will you turn me in?*

Did you know I'm writing this wearing a goddamn breathing mask? Asthma. Do I have to buy back the sky from BP and Exxon so I can breathe, so my kids can breath? Are we ready to choke while the military police ensure we sing Baba's anthem? Contract of the Century? *Who the hell gave BP the right to buy our century?*

Yes, Badpenny's right. I say *fuck* too much. But I look at this world and I don't know what else to say.

Back at the hotel we were greeted by Larry, Moe, and Curly, the three stooges the MSN had sent to watch us—and make sure we knew they were watching us ("Our fan club!" said our fixer). This forced me to wonder how long before Baba's boys would come 'round to "chat" with Mirvari about our visit. I thought about the Green candidate's goofy statement that telling the world the truth about corruption, coups, and crude would only be "serving the purposes of Israel."

The phrase came back to me now—and its ancient origin, Genesis 32, a favorite of us atheists. Did Professor Greenie know it?

If you've forgotten, here is the gist: Jacob was scared shitless that his brutal brother Esau, like the meaty messenger of the MSN, would beat him to death.

The Green professor looked to the safety of our British diplomatic power to protect him from his fellow Azeri, just as Jacob begged God to "stay my brother's hand." God, as usual, was silent.

In the Bible story, darkness falls and Jacob is suddenly attacked by a demon, a dark angel. They struggle all night. As dawn comes, Jacob, unvanquished, won't let the attacker go—until the dark spirit, the dark angel of Jacob's own fear and guilt and complicity, agrees to bless him. This was the blessing: The Angel told Jacob he wouldn't be Jacob anymore. From now on, his name would be Israel, that is, "He who has wrestled with God." Then Israel/Jacob crossed the sea to the land of Edom, to confront his brother without fear.

Mirvari told me, despite not winning a single round against BP, "I don't feel like a loser. If you don't fight, *then* you are a loser." She has wrestled her own dark angels and defeated them. She has crossed into Edom fearless; she is beyond their reach now. Mirvari has won her freedom within herself. Baba's goons cannot beat it out of her, nor BP buy it.

And they know it.

BAKU BEACH

Lady Baba's family owns the Bentley dealership. It's in the Old City. It's very old. No one knows how old, that's how old it is. How many other civilizations can claim to have been in continuous decline for more than eight centuries? Baku boasts the world's first sewage system. Time for a repair.

But the forgotten empires have left monuments that would knock your eyes out. The Maiden Tower, maybe fifteen stories of undulating stonework well over a thousand years old; ancient caravanserai housing outlets for Ermenegildo Zegna shoes and Prada accessories; vaulted catacombs turned into swanky restaurants and a Gucci boutique; medieval cobbled paths leading to the Bentley dealership and the showrooms for the Jags, Maseratis, and Rollers. It's Camelot Meets Rodeo Drive. Just fifteen minutes from Calcutta-on-the-Caspian.

The nation's per capita GDP has rocketed to over $10,100 per Azeri. Elmar of Terminal Town should be living large. But the typical wage, for those who can get it, is about $1,000 per *year*. The difference goes to BP and the lords atop the Old City pyramid, who put it to good use. Lady Baba's daughter Leyla spent £300,000 (about half a million dollars) on vintage Cristal Champagne at a dinner party for a dozen of her friends. Which raises the question, How does that lucky 1 percent fit all that cash into a low-slung Jag? Answer: They put it in the Bentley.

In an attempt to pretend there is an economy beyond indentured servitude to BP, Baba launched Baku into the tourism business. That is, Baba built casinos.

As part of the promotional effort, Lady Baba posed in her beach attire—a white evening gown—and then played lifeguard for the cameras, a rare bare-toed moment.

I took a walk on that beach at sunset. It had been given a big thumbs-up in *The New York Times* travel section. Why not? I did have my wet suit packed for surfing. I found a beachfront littered with vodka and Raki bottles. The shore was darkened by the shadows of massive, greasy platform rigs, big as chunky Eiffel Towers, sweating their unnameable ooze.

(I didn't see that in *The New York Times* feature. I should have known that they don't give you the straight story even about *sand*.)

I stopped for a piña colada at a thatched-roof bar surrounded by pastel chaise longues set out for sun-tanning, touched by the gentle breeze of odiferous carcinogens. Margaritaville in Hell.

There were no customers. There was no waiter, no bartender, no *nada*. But that's only because the casinos had suddenly closed—*bam!*—just like *that!*—on Baba's orders. The President remembered his nation was an Islamic republic, which would not tolerate such abominations. Or because, I'm told, Baby Baba had blown $2 million at the craps tables.

ALONG HEYDAR ALIYEV BOULEVARD

The intelligence report read:

> ". . . Lady Mehriban Aliyeva appears . . . unable to show a full range of facial expression."

The U.S. Intelligence officer assumes this is the result of "substantial cosmetic surgery."

Maybe. What expressions does she lack? Empathy? Self-awareness? The report does not say.

Kadija, on the other hand, has a full range of facial expressions. Just from her sensible shoes, flat black slip-ons, you could say Kadija is Azerbaijan's *last* lady. And proud of it.

We hired Kadija to shepherd us around Baku, which she did waving and grinning at our police shadows and translating when we were stopped by a "volunteer" in a black sedan. (He freely said, when she asked, that he would be paid for keeping an eye on us. On everyone.)

Kadija moved about with an air of almost comic impunity, as if laughing at the farce of a government would keep her free of its claws. She has a show on Radio Liberty, which, after the regime banned it from the radio dial, she broadcasts into empty ether. And she knows "what happened," why Elmar the shoemaker can't afford shoes, why half this oil-rich country is looking for work.

It goes back, she said, to the Contract of the Century. The original AMOCO deal with Baba's predecessor, President Elchibey, included the typical "local content" clause for equipment purchases. Baba let BP off the hook, however, and the clause vanished. BP did not have to use Baku-manufactured pipe or equipment.

That was weird, weird. This isn't Liberia. Baku had oil equipment factories. Correction: Baku, until recently, was the largest oil-equipment manufacturing center on Earth, supplying all of the Soviet Union. Now BP and Azerbaijan's own oil company have refused to buy virtually any of it.

The result: The biggest industry in Azerbaijan fell to pieces, with 90 percent of its workers dumped into the street. Starving oil workers in an oil boom. She drove me by the factories that Baby Baba says are back in operation. What operation means is that the busted-out windows of the empty buildings are covered over with six-story banners depicting the Baba family.

The oil industry's minister when the BP contract was signed, Rovshan Ismayilov, had arranged for Baku's factories to be upgraded to BP specs—but the state oil company still refused its own nation's equipment. In 1995, in a cabinet meeting chaired by Baba Aliyev, Ismayilov could remain silent no longer. He began shouting at the Oil Minister, at the whole cabinet, "YOU ARE SHOOTING FOR SHOPKAS RATHER THAN SERVING YOUR COUNTRY!"— then collapsed. A stroke hospitalized him for three months.

Shopkas, bribes.

At that time, President Baba hosted a kind of game show on national television. He would call up cabinet ministers before him on prime-time TV and dress them down for this failure or that. The chastised minister would beg forgiveness and promise to correct his ways under Baba's "far-seeing" guidance. (Baba demanded they use the phrase "far-seeing.")

After Ismayilov was released from the hospital, Baba hauled him before the cameras to explain why he had allowed 90 percent of the oil supply factories to close. The minister replied, "Because you, Mr. President, refused my continuing plea to return the local content clause into the contract with BP."

That evening's news announced that Ismayilov had been removed from the cabinet. His family, however, was not tossed out of the minister's mansion, because he had long ago refused to move into it.

Kadija knew the story well. Rovshan Ismayilov was her father. So, there was nothing more they could do to her, and she no longer cared if they did.

NIGERIA

Shopkas, bribes. Well, what do you expect in a place like that? Azerbaijan rates as the third-most corrupt nation on the planet, according to Transparency International.

However, Azeris don't have enough money to bribe each other. So who, dear reader, *is corrupting them?*

Well, who, in the end, supplied the pipe? Halliburton had a limo waiting when I arrived in Baku (not for me). Then, on my way to Terminal Town, I passed a huge office building marked BAKER-HUGHES, their Texas supplier.

Would Baker-Hughes pay a bribe? Well, yes, they even said so. The company pleaded guilty to bribing an oil minister to supply offshore drilling on the Kazakhstan side of the Caspian Sea. A *shopka* of $4 million.

Halliburton and its former chairman, a Mr. Dick Cheney, were charged by Nigeria with bribing their oil ministers, too, but the charges were dropped when Mr. Cheney became the Honorable Richard Cheney, Vice President of the United States of America.

When I went undercover in Britain in 1998, the fixers whom I was pretending to "hire" told me that U.S. executives always barged in with two questions: "Who do we reach? What do we pay?"

THE CATSKILL FOOTHILLS, UPSTATE NEW YORK

Lord Browne had scored the Contract of the Century. But BP did *not* take the oil. After all that MI6 skulduggery, the $30 million "cherub," hooker love, and a coup d'état, BP didn't want the oil. The Azeris were stunned. They had figured that techno-savvy BP would double and quintuple the dismal output of the Soviets. In fact, for the first years of BP operation, production *dropped* by 80 percent.

Huh? To understand why, forget everything you think you know about oil companies. They are not hunting for oil, they are hunting for profits. BP grabbed the Caspian Sea contract in 1994 when the price of oil was a joke, down as low as $15 a barrel. The Contract of the Century gave BP the right to drill the oil, but more important, the right *not* to drill it, to keep it off the market, to squeeze the world price higher. Capitalism's first commandment is: The lower the supply, the higher the price. And Baku was the perfect place to lower the supply. Baba could bitch, but BP had him by the *shopkas*.

Wars are fought over oil—not only to get it, a story you know well—but also to keep it from getting to market. And that is the story of Iraq 2003.

Badpenny was digging through the highly confidential *"Options for the Oil Industry of Iraq,"* which we had obtained through only the minimum amount of subterfuge and fibbing as the public interest required.

This *Options* plan was drafted in secret for the State Department by the oil industry. The Boys in Houston called for keeping Iraq in OPEC and therefore limiting Iraq's oil output. The plan would "enhance [Iraq's] relationship with OPEC" and keep the price of oil higher than the Washington Monument. It was the "Enhance OPEC" plan that rolled with the tanks into Baghdad. This wasn't a war of blood for oil. It was a war of blood for *no* oil, to limit the flow.*

---

* See "The Flow" in *Armed Madhouse*.

Transformation Activities

Decisions that are taken during the Rehabilitation and Transition phases will set Iraq's upstream oil sector toward one of the five scenarios identified in Figure 0.1. Whilst none of these decisions is irreversible in itself, changing direction and trying to make up for delays will become increasingly difficult as time goes by.

As was noted above, the four key questions regarding structure and process in Iraq's oil sector will all probably be addressed in one way or another during the Transition phase, namely:

Use or disclosure of the data contained on this page is
subject to the restrictions on the title page of this proposal.

Once Iraq's oil fields were capped and contained by war and OPEC, the price of oil bumped from $20 to $40 a barrel, then jumped to $100+ a barrel. Only then did BP open the spigot in the Caspian.

It was 2004 and I was in mortal combat with my latest book manuscript when the new volunteer, a Ms. Badpenny, came up to retrieve me from my brother-in-law's place in snow country. I'd gotten the hot doc about Iraq's oil fields and she'd been hunting down General Jay Garner, the viceroy Bush put in charge of Iraq, to verify it. There was blood in Baghdad and this young woman thought I should bust the story open on BBC Worldwide, the whole sick, secret oil company scheme. But going back to work for BBC would take me away from my crucial focus on blondes and brandy.

When she drove to my mountain writing hideout, I ignored her and told her I still had to break down the resistance of a couple of dull paragraphs. But then, I said, we could jump in the hot tub.

It was the only time I would ever see Badpenny shocked and horrified.

If looks were bullets, they would have had to draw a chalk circle around my dead body.

Jeez, OK, lady. Just being polite. I'd even changed the water after the blond copy editor left for the weekend.

Badpenny's accent now went full BBC World Service. "I've located General Garner and I need you to sign this letter. . . ."

What I saw now in her eyes was not virginal shock. It was a deep inward-looking sorrow.

I could see her tell herself, *I thought Greg Palast was different. I've fooled myself. He's just another dirty old groper.*

And now I felt like just another dirty old groper.

Years later, she would tell me that she was suddenly weighed down by a heavy disappointment and sadness, thinking she would have no choice but to quit the job she was born for.

From that moment, I kept a professional distance and respect for her years of fidelity waiting on her handsome young drummer boy away in Britain to make up his mind.

For some reason, I thought it important to let her know, "I'm a drummer too." She called BBC London and told Jones I was going back to work.

Who the hell was this kid?

R■■■■■■-Louisa von N■■■■■-Manzoni aka Velvet Vicious aka Ms. Badpenny is a train driver's daughter with a gift for languages, accents, mathematics, and fashionable disguise. Under the Alps, from her parents' bedroom window in the boxy workers' housing block, little Penny could see the peaks of Mount Pilatus above her, and below, Switzerland's bankers commuting to Zurich, where they counted and recounted the money they'd stolen from Hitler's victims and secreted for African warlords. It made her sick and crazy. "Switzerland is the only nation where the citizens are both prisoners and their own prison guards," wrote Switzerland's only Nobel Prize author, Max Frisch. She made her escape at fourteen on a stolen motorbike, got arrested, hauled back; took off again at fifteen, then at eighteen made it to London. In weeks she had learned enough English to write songs and front a punk band, which eventually grabbed the attention of the rock press. ■■■■■■ ■■■■■■■■■ ■■■■■■■■■■■■■■■ One marriage lasted long enough to get her a British passport.

Then, despite professing her fealty to the Queen, Badpenny took off for the States, jilted the drummer, landed in New York, where she'd found a professor of archaic French with little bony hands (she called them "griplets") and headed off. On Route 66, she declared she would not go one mile farther as an illegal alien. They turned off into the low-rider desert town of Fort Sumner, New Mexico, where two prison guards acted as witnesses to their marriage. By the time they hit Death Valley, she realized that Professor Griplets was too high a price for a green card.

November 2004. Stuck in New York to deal with crazy Immigration bureaucrats and her divorce, Badpenny killed time reading Churchill's six-volume history of World War II and, when that was done, used her bar tips to pick up a copy of Greg Palast's *The Best Democracy Money Can Buy*. Badpenny had been following his British Broadcasting reports on the Internet (she found American television news unbearable). While browsing GregPalast .com she found some fool had put in the office address—right across from the café where she waited tables. During her shift, she kept an eye on the second-story plate-glass window on Second Avenue, where Greg Palast and his team worked late, noting the time Palast would put on his fedora and leave. She wasn't stalking; she had decided to work for me and needed to find a way to inform me of her decision.

My research chief, Oliver Shykles, a genius with a rational dose of para-noia, hated working in front of that huge floor-to-ceiling window, especially after nearly one hundred threats of death and bodily harm that came after I published what *The Guardian* called my "robust" obituary of Ronald Reagan (*"Reagan: Killer, Coward, Con Man"*). Ollie had removed all signs visible from the street identifying our location.

I loved that office up the dirty stairs. Lots of sun for a downtown place and, at night, when it rained, the red blur of ambulance lights and the caffeine of their sirens.

It was midnight. I was walking the dog. It was cold and my brain was freezing.

Then, "Mr. Palast?"

Although lost in two huge winter coats, muffler and fur hat, I could make out it was a young lady—college age? I thought, after all the threats, *this is it. This is a Squeaky Fromme*, like that Manson chick who shot President Ford.

Then I looked at the eyes hidden in scarves: They were analytical, not murderous. *"Mr. Palast, I was wondering if you could use some help."*

No weapon! I was alive! My dog was alive! I had a rule: no rich kids and no one with a degree in journalism. And no groupies, not where I work.

So what kind of talents could "Squeaky" offer?

"I'm fluent in four languages and I do not need to sleep."

Perfect.

Within two weeks, it felt like jet fuel had been poured into the office engine. "Mr. Palast, might this be helpful?"

Well, no shit. She had somehow gotten her hands on the phone number of a pissed-off State Department diplomat in Kazakhstan who could authenti-cate the secret pre-invasion plan for Iraq's oil. I'm thinking, *Who the hell gave you singing lessons?*

(Note: Badpenny herself put the black marks in the manuscript over strategic letters of her full name and story. "Right now, I am un-Google-able." She's utterly horrified I'm writing about her at all.)

She could provide other help: Coats off, Badpenny's Bond Girl looks would be disturbing to most men—but, I should add, not to me. I'm not drawn to young women who were merely zygotes when John Kennedy was shot. I like to see a few miles on the odometer. I don't know why I'm telling you this.

THE CASPIAN SEA, 100 KILOMETERS OFFSHORE

Up until now, when Mother Nature goes homicidal, she gets away with it because some innocent corporation takes the rap. Like BP. At least that's what you learn by reading the company's press releases.

Let us remember what first drew me here to this bunghole called Baku. It wasn't the beaches. Or the Ermenegildo Zegna shoe store. It was the call from Caspian Man, the insider with his cryptic message sent from a vessel floating in the Caspian Sea. If his story checked out, we had the true, hidden cause of the Deepwater Horizon deaths. This was serious business. His info, if corroborated, changes the case of the Deepwater Horizon from tragedy to homicide.

IRAQ

Negligent homicide is an "if only" crime. As in: "*If only* my stupid cousin had taken the bullets out of the loaded gun before handing it to his violent and deranged brother, the poodle would be alive today."

If only BP had told us (Congress, safety inspectors, stockholders, the press, or anybody at all) that there had been a violent blow-out at their offshore rig in the Caspian Sea, then the eleven men on the Gulf of Mexico rig would be alive today. If only BP had confessed to the failure of its cheap-o cementing methods, ditto: These men would be alive.

If only.

Did our Caspian Man see this blowout himself, or was it just barroom rumor? The note to Badpenny put his entire career in jeopardy, so that gave his answer some weight. But what did he first see? We arranged a call, safe phone to safe phone. I heard bar noises in the background.

The voice said, "Orange boats in the water."

That's the phrase I wanted to hear. An eyewitness. An eyewitness who had been right there. I will never know, and hope I never will know, what it's like to have just a few minutes to live.

There was Caspian Man's story and there was BP's official story, written, I would guess, by someone who wasn't there to dance cheek to cheek with Death. It all happened on September 17, 2008.

The Official BP Story #1, released that day:

"A gas leak was discovered in the area of a Central Azeri platform this morning."

By this BP story, it was just Mother Nature farting away, how impolite of her. The gas release was at some rather safe distance from the oil rig.

Then, there was Official BP Story #2. It was tucked into an obscure environment assessment report in 2009:

"A gas release was detected around the CA [Central Azeri] platform in mid-September."

It was "in the area" in Story #1; now it's "around." With each BP story, the gas creeps nearer. Still, it is Mother Nature's gas, not from BP's well.

And so, it's no big deal, no danger. Nevertheless BP, ever concerned about its workers' safety, ordered an evacuation of the rig.

"As a precautionary measure we suspended all operations on the platform."

"Precautionary." In BP's story, because the leak was not under the platform itself, there was no real danger; but, what the heck, let's evacuate.

V. S. Naipaul, who won a Nobel Prize for Literature (and Bitterness), once wrote that imperial powers "don't lie, they elide." That is, they leave shit out. Caspian Man says BP left out that the gas was leaking from *under* the rig, and it was ready to blow sky high. Caspian Man, put it closer, *right under* the workers. He told me,

"... gas leaked outside the main riser, the platform was *engulfed in methane. HIGHLY explosive.*"

The orange lifeboats were thrown in the water in a panic. The crew was inside a "gas cloud." Evacuation wasn't a "precautionary" measure, it was a *"Holy shit, we're gonna die!"* measure. Caspian Man said,

"By the grace of God [Ins'Allah], the gas did not ignite so there was no explosion and no loss of life."

"Engulfed in methane," exactly the same as the Deepwater Horizon. A quick-thinking captain on Central Azeri ordered the platform to "go dark." So no lights, no sources of flame, not even a light switch flicked. On the Deepwater Horizon, it is believed that the platform blew when a worker, rather than jump off the rig as others did, began repeatedly to slam the "blowout preventer" switch to cut off the gas burst. A wise move—if the switch worked. It didn't, and the worker, for his act of heroism, was instantly vaporized.

All 211 workers on Central Azeri got off alive but with "some broken bones" (says Caspian Man) only because an emergency vessel conducted a miraculous escape in a record-setting hour and a half. Badpenny discovered that fact only because the owner of the evacuation ship received a special medal from Baby Baba himself for the lifesaving event—which, the autocrat seems to have forgotten, didn't occur.

Now we get to Official BP Story #3. Another one of Badpenny's all-night romps through Security Exchange Commission filings brought the gas leak still closer to the platform. The company (more American than British) is required by U.S. law to fess up to problems. The officers of the company sign the reports under penalty of perjury.

With the risk of prison eliciting something closer to truth, BP execs finally admit that the gas came up from under the platform.

"On 17 September 2008, a subsurface gas release occurred below the Central Azeri platform."

BP is inching closer to the truth. But it could still be the fault of that nasty hag Ma Nature passing gas right below BP's rig.

Remember the Naipaul dictum: They don't lie, they *elide*.

What did they leave out?

This, says Caspian Man: The blowout occurred right after . . .

". . . a nitrogen cement job."

Here's the smoking, exploding gun: Central Azeri blew because BP used an ultra-risky cement mix that sets quickly.

You've heard the phrase *as exciting as watching cement dry*. That's because it's so damn slow. Rigs cost a bundle per day to lease or operate—as much as a half million dollars a day. Time is money. So to speed up the Lord's own way of drying cement (evaporation), BP juices the cement with nitrogen. There's a risk, of course, but not to the guys ordering the quicky-tricky cement plug with nitrogen.

Who cares?

The Deepwater Horizon widows must care: This was the same cement mix that failed in the Gulf well, causing the Deepwater Horizon to fill with methane and blow itself to hell.

I smell "material omission." Maybe you can "elide" in London or Baku and the government doesn't give a damn, but in the United States, where the rule of law still holds on (if only by its fingernails), you can't just leave shit out that's important.

BP did not mention the nitrogen in the cement nor the evidence of its failure. Nor did BP mention that the Central Azeri rig filled with methane, and the crew of over two hundred souls were one Lucky Strike away from oblivion.

Is that omission "material"? If so, it could make BP liable for a charge of criminal negligence—or at least a good old horsewhipping. Doubtless, if regulators had learned of this near-deadly blowout using nitrogen-infused cement, the stuff, presumably, would have been banned or controlled. And BP itself would have been banned or controlled.

A lawyer might call it a "homicidal omission." But I'm not a lawyer, so I'll leave that conclusion to the suits. Maybe eleven corpses aren't enough; the law might require an even dozen to make it "material."

THE RIVIERA HOTEL, BAKU

I can see you've already rushed to judgment: BP's silence, its cover-up of the Caspian blowout, of the failure of the cheap crap cement, makes the company *guilty guilty guilty.* But BP is only guilty *if the blowout had actually occurred.*

Yes, Caspian Man told me so. One witness and I had to keep him under wraps. But what's the *proof*? And how the hell do you cover up a blowout that came within a matchstick of incinerating 211 rig workers *without it get-ting out?*

So was Caspian Man telling me a modern sea-monster story? Or describing a monstrous cover-up?

As my preacher friend Jesse Jackson says, *"I need a witness!"* Preferably two or more.

Please, Lord, give me one, just *one* of those 211 evacuees from BP's Central Azeri platform to agree to go on camera. We found a talkative rig worker but he . . . vanished. *Poof.* No way to reach him. Phones aren't answered. Friends can't locate him. *Something is happening here, Mr. Jones.* Something has warned the Ministry and BP to keep a lock on the lips of the offshore rig workers.

And something else: We contacted Fatima to contact someone who could contact Zulfie who could contact someone who could contact Natasha, Leslie's connection. But our fixer told us that Zulfie's contact said he suddenly had to leave the country on business and who knows when he'd return.

Nobody in Azerbaijan "suddenly" leaves. You need a special permit. You don't leave until Baby Baba says you leave. Someone had tipped the Baba cops and BP to our story. Some weaselly little Wicked Leaker. A leak could explain the special guest appearance of the security ministry's Number Two man at the truck-stop diner.

How the hell could they know . . . ?

So we did the only thing we could do. We loaded up our surfing gear bags and headed to the beach.

The idea hit me after our contacts found a second rig worker who con-firmed he had escaped from the methane cloud. Our Dear Director James had originally messaged the nervous rig worker to meet us at *our hotel* . . . to what? To be escorted up the stairs by Larry, Moe, and Curly? Why not just throw a noose around his neck?

That's when I thought of surfing. I'd seen a small hotel called The Riviera right on the seafront as we drove back from the desert. I suggested we get our fixer to rent a room for "her friends from Europe who need a place to dump their gear" and maybe crash for a night. The fixer would then return in two hours with us "surfer dudes" and our driver—Rig Worker #2. Our "driver" would help us bring up our surf gear—lights and cameras—so we could shoot him in shadow framed by the bright light of the blighted sea.

But our "driver" never showed. Calls, then checks by other contacts to his house, produced zero. Then someone answered Rig Worker #2's cell for him. "He has asked his company for permission to conduct this interview and is waiting for their response." In other words, he turned us in.

Dear Director was furious. "He shopped us, the fucker!" Yes, he did. And so would I, James. Obviously, they were onto the story *before* he gave us away. Rig Worker #2 was scared out of his shorts, and with reason. We're not in Kansas, Toto.

Then that call comes in from our Manager, the twat in London: "I've taken a decision." They really talk like that: *taken a decision*. We must get out "forthwith." We are "in danger."

Bullshit. We are Subjects of Her Majesty's Empire, and the secret police wouldn't touch a hair on my head even if I had hair. We are immune and that's why we're careless numbskulls.

We are not in danger but we are dangerous to those on the firing line here by our who-the-hell-cares attitude toward a dictator we consider an oaf and a joke, BP's tool and BP's fool. We can count on BP itself to keep us safe if only to avoid bad publicity. And then we fly away while some oil worker loses everything he has, and his kids are thrown out of the workers' housing block.

BP merely has to put three little letters next to his name: *NRB*—"Not Required Back" on the rig. Never, ever. On any rig ever. And Mirvari gets another beating. Or worse.

For us little Anglo-American boys with cameras, this is about as dangerous as Disneyland. But it's not Disney for the mice left behind when the mousetrap snaps shut and breaks their bones and lives. Yes, Lord Posh Twat of London, empire has its privileges and it makes me want to vomit.

STILL IN BAKU

But we're not leaving.

That's when we find out the Security Ministry called our hotel and told them to seize our passports. Our passports with the visa stamps that allowed us in and, more importantly, allow us out.

Not good, not good.

The Ministry police are on the way. "Routine," they tell us. I bet it is.

Who the hell turned us in? What wicked little creep said we were hunting for a BP blowout? Answer: *My own paper, The Guardian.* It was a one-in-a-thousand freak coincidence that began when they got this secret cable, boosted from the U.S. State Department:

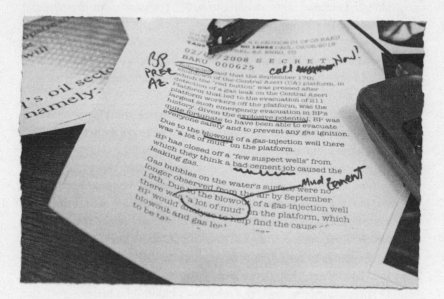

02/07/2008 S E C R E T BAKU 000625

The September 17th shutdown of the Central Azeri (CA) platform, the "red button" was pressed after detection of a gas leak on the Central Azeri Platform that led to the evacuation of 211 platform workers off the platform, was the largest such emergency evacuation in BP's history. Given the explosive potential, BP was quite fortunate to have been able to evacuate everyone safely and to prevent any gas ignition. . . . Due to the blowout of a gas-injection well there was "a lot of mud" on the platform . . . from which they think a bad cement job caused the leaking gas.

The leaked cables explain the honor of the appearance at the café of Murdermeat, Number Two of the secret police. Turns out, *The Guardian* told BP they were about to release the cables to get BP's response. BP knew I was on the case, and reasonably assumed I had a copy. Apparently, word went out from BP London, and the whip came down in Baku. But we were clueless about the cables, and, ended up filmless, with not one eyewitness on camera. I lose the James Bond Award again.

And, just to ice the cake, we had the wrong Natasha in our photo. Leslie the Bagman had *two* Natashas.

I blew the film, but not the story. The story isn't just about an exploding oil rig, though that's story enough. In Baku we learned that BP's money bought something as valuable as the oil itself: silence.

You can hide a terrifying blowout only in a police state. The Contract of the Century is enforced by the Beatings and Jailings and Censorship and Terror of the Century. The Silence of the Century.

Conspiracy is no fun without co-conspirators. To share costs, BP brought in Exxon and Chevron as partners in the Caspian. That is why the Embassy was writing to Washington. BP's U.S. partners were bitching about losing millions while the platform was closed to clear the explosive gas. They wanted President Bush to complain to the UK government, but quietly. The American companies could have sued BP for their losses. But the club clearly thought it prudent to keep silent. That silence is complicity.

The cable came from the U.S. Embassy in Baku. Who had the steel, the courage, the noblesse and fearlessness to bust this open to make this cold cable public?

No, not one of Baba's prisoners. He's one of President Obama's prisoners: Private Bradley Manning.

While I've been hunting the globe for evidence of oil industry killings, I've also been hunting for a much more difficult set of clues: to the source of human courage. Manning's is immeasurable.

Soldier Manning, in prison inside the Quantico Marine Base near Washington, DC, sleeps in nothing but his underpants. Not by choice. He's on sui-cide watch, even though no psychiatrist could be coaxed into saying Manning wants to kill himself. Like Jacob, he has crossed into Edom. He fears not, and certainly doesn't fear his own hand.

Democracy is more than voting; it's having the information to vote.

But before you start marching around your living room couch, singing "God Bless America," consider this: The U.S. Embassy cabled back to U.S. Sec-retary of State Condoleezza Rice about the Caspian blowout, about the lethal cement mix. Yet our Secretary of State never told us. Did you, Condi?

BP and its American partners concealed the dangerous blowout, and they powerful co-conspirator: the U.S. government.

So maybe we have to say that the United States is *almost* a democracy. And less so daily: Since September 11, 2001, the United States has been treat-ing information and informants by using Baba's system, not Jefferson's.

Well, at least we still choose our president by the ballot.

Correction: The Embassy cables were dated 2008, when George W. Bush was President. Baby Bush. He wasn't elected, either. At least not by the voters.

But that's another book, from another time.*

I'm killing nervous time looking up the price of Lady Baba's shoes. And pray-ing. Dear God: You made this mess, so get me the hell out of it.

And, what do you know, He answers! A voice in my head says, *If you have already checked out of the hotel, Palast, that is, if the hotel tells the Ministry police when they arrive that, sorry, the foreigners have packed up and left hours ago, then the desk clerks are off the hook.*

The clerks have figured this out too, so when we leg it down the stairs to request the bill to check out, there's a charge of $400 added for the use of a sauna and the services of a "masseuse." James wants to argue but I say, "PAY IT."

That's the most expensive massage ever that didn't have a happy ending.

James unrolls two thousand in Euro notes, and now we have our pass-ports and have checked out. We don't, however, actually leave the hotel.

I sleep in fits, fully clothed, the passport and visa in the front pocket of my pants.

---

* I've already written it. Click *here* in the interactive edition and I'll sell you a copy of *The Best Democracy Money Can Buy*.

AIRPORT AND OUT

Made it to the airport. It's named . . . no points for guessing . . . the Heydar Aliyev Airport. Baba International.

We're outta here! Only three X-ray machines and checkpoints stand in our way. No problem.

Then there is a problem.

I took James's suggestion to quickly move my "pen" from a pile of real pens to the middle of my checked luggage.

The cop at Checkpoint One signals me to come over. He shows me the X-ray monitor. Right in the middle, the thick metal camera-pen looks like a gun silencer against my briefs and socks. I pull it out and show that it writes my name. See!

He whispers to our fixer in Azeri: *"I know exactly what that is. And it's illegal."*

Here it comes. Hannukah with Baba, or at least his prison warden. The network won't help, the U.S. Embassy will just tsk-tsk: Carrying contraband, Mr. Palast? So sorry.

I hate me. Just for some cute film action, I get myself busted.

After this selfish walk down Me Street, I suddenly realized *Holy No God-damn* I have the "destroyed" notebook pages on there, a hit parade of our sources. I hate me even more.

Then the young cop *puts it back in my suitcase!* And he whispers to my translator, *"Get rid of this thing before Checkpoint Two because he'll never make it through."*

Thank the Lord not every grandson of Baba loves his grandpa's regime. They may carry his riot sticks, but they don't all want to kiss them.

Thank you thank you thank you thank you.

Now, rather than add a new stupidity to my current stupidity, I do *not* sneak into a corner to remove the pen—furtive action will be noticed. I kick my baggage over to the second security line . . . then frantically open the case, throw my clothes all over the floor, saying, "Where is it? WHERE IS IT?!"

James knows the routine and tells our translator to open her purse and drop it on the floor. *"Drop it?"* K asks. James, says, *"Right NOW!"*

She does and my socks and underpants and medicine kit fly out, piled all over her bag. I pull out my asthma inhaler, say, *"PRAISE GOD!"* and take a big hit from the empty medicine injector.

I can breath easy now, and carefully replace all my stuff in my bag.

Well, not all. A dirty sock has fallen into K's purse, which she's picked up while helping me repack. A dirty sock with a pen inside.

NEW YORK, DOWNTOWN, 2011

I'm sweating it: Where are my "pen" films with the ripped notebook pages, the evidence of the bust in the desert? And is someone with a soul more worthy than mine having my Austin Powers toy jammed into their privates to cover for me?

But all is well. I think. I just received a note from my *tovarish* in Central Asia:

> I sent the Christmas video to James via internet.

That will fool them: a Muslim sending a Jew a Christmas video. *Oy vey!*

* * *

I did not unpack my parka.

I was still certain the key to the Gulf blowout would be found in Alaska—as well as the key to the *next* blowout certain to come.

It was October. The Earth's axis was tilting toward its solstice. I had to get north before the Arctic night fell. My plan was to get to the Tatitlek village at Bligh Island and dig into the Natives' records. But my plans didn't mean much after I received an urgent communication from the Chief of Intelligence of the Universal Intelligence Agency of the Free Republic of the Arctic requesting I meet with the agency at Kaktovik, an island above the Arctic Circle.

I ignored this dumb-ass prank and waited for Matty Pass's next e-mail from one of Santa's elves.

Then the Chief of Intelligence sent a second, more urgent demand with copies of letters from Phil Dyer of Shell Oil Exploration and Production. Shell took "the Intelligence Agency" quite seriously. The oil company did not want to provoke a declaration of war.

The Chief of Intelligence, Eskimo Native Harry Lord, wished to meet with me so I could take a message—a warning actually—to "your Queen." I still thought it was too goofy to respond until the Agency said that the audience was requested by Etok, the legendary whale hunter and Inupiat leader.

I told Badpenny to find an air charter immediately, something heavy, like a Beaver, that could land on ice. Badpenny called an air cab operator and asked, "Is it possible to land at Kaktovik this time of year?"

"Can't say until we get there." We booked it.

SAN DIEGO, CALIFORNIA

But I couldn't go. Not yet. While packing, I got a call to get the first plane out to San Diego.

By the time I got to the hospital, Dad could only move his head, rasp a few words. But he left no doubt he was happy to see that my sister and I had made it in, happier that we don't sell furniture.

It was my mother's birthday, her eighty-ninth. My dad told us to get out of the hospital and have a blowout of a party. We did. It was a hell of a celebration.

What, then, is my inheritance?

In 1930, when my father was an eight-year-old kid in Chicago, he asked his older brother why people were outside in the cold snow waiting in a long line. His brother Harold said, "It's a bread line. They don't have anything to eat. They're hoping for bread."

My father ran to his mother's bedroom and grabbed my grandmother's diamond brooch, ran downstairs, and gave it to a man in the bread line.

The important thing is that, after my father gave away the jewels, no one in his family chastised him. Later, as the Depression rolled on, my grandfather lost everything. So Gil Palast was a failure early. Stayed a failure. He made sure of it.

I already told you what you need to know about my father: He hates furniture. But he sold furniture for thirty-five years. He sold it in Beverly Hills to trophy wives du jour.

When I turned eight, my father gave me some important jewelry: his medals from World War II. He wanted me to lose them, throw them away, anything. It was March 8, 1965. I remember the exact date because the day before, the U.S. Marines landed at Danang, Vietnam.

My father won the medals in the Pacific jungles for freeing the oppressed. Then, that day in 1965, that prick President Johnson had ordered my dad's army to return to the jungle to oppress the free. Johnson and Nixon and the rest of the gangsters had turned my dad's medals into garbage.

But life was not all garbage and Nixon and furniture. My parents danced— in fact, they were champs; they came in second in a tango contest when they were in their seventies.

And there was another kind of luck, if you were ready for it. I was thirteen. My dad was lying on the carpet in the living room of our dull tract house, killing a Saturday night hunting the radio for some Sinatra and stopped at the left side of the dial.

He called me over and said, "I want you to listen to this." It was 1965 and Martin Luther King was speaking about the three kinds of love as defined by the Greek philosophers. King's philosophy lesson was given in a church surrounded by angry white men who changed their white sheets for police uniforms and were prepared to burn down the church as they had done before.

King was on a march, and beaten while marching, from Selma, Alabama, to Montgomery.

My father told me, "You'll do that," meaning I'd go down South, I'd join the Freedom Riders, become a lawyer for King, a knight for justice in an unjust world.

But why didn't he go himself? Why didn't he join the march, join the fight? I know: kids, responsibility, furniture. Furniture didn't march. It sat there. It was sat upon. And the rich farted into the mattresses he sold them. The furniture store was locked from the inside by a poisonous fear of leaving life to chance.

So he put the burden of his quest on me. How screwed up is that? How staggeringly cruel.

On the fortieth anniversary of the Selma March, there was a big family-style dinner in Birmingham, Alabama, for the surviving giants of the Civil Rights movement. I couldn't resist going down to report on it. I got a seat at the back.

At the end of his solemn speech, Martin Luther King III, son of the martyr, said, "I'd like to acknowledge the presence of a heroic young man among us. I took his book to my father's grave and showed my father and I know he was pleased. Greg Palast, please rise." Then the giants around me stood up, and I accepted with grace a standing ovation from those more deserving than me.

I didn't bother to tell my dad.

By that time, he was a rotten old sonovabitch, bitter, bent over, incapable of accepting love even from his grandchildren.

I suppose that's how I'll end up. I don't see how I can avoid it. The river runs fast and the canyon walls are steep.

* * *

My mom had a gusher of stories to tell the crowd at the deli. I remember this one. Just a few weeks earlier, Mom and Dad had decided to have a nice day out. Mom needs oxygen to breathe, and my father, after his stroke, a walker frame to move. Mom dressed up in her goofy red, white, and blue patriotic garb, strapped on a canister of oxygen, and my father, limping a few inches at a time, made it to the local grocery store—to join the union picket line.

He was late, he was slow. But he was marching.

The party over, we headed back to the hospital, and the next day, as we expected, my father died.

His last words were to my mother. "Happy birthday."

At the memorial service, Badpenny could not stop giggling.

She was thinking about what my father did a few weeks before the end, around his eighty-ninth birthday. He was watching a Viagra commercial on TV. It ends with the warning, "If an erection persists for more than four hours, contact your doctor."

He called up his doctor and got the nurse. He'd taken some Viagra, he said, more than four hours ago and his erection still wouldn't go away.

"Mr. Palast, you shouldn't have done that! You'll have to get to the emergency room immediately."

"I can't go," he said. "I haven't shown all the neighbors yet."

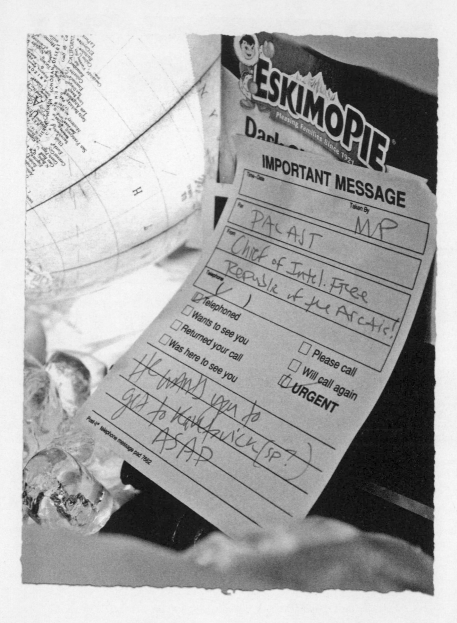

CHAPTER 3
Pig in the Pipeline

FREE REPUBLIC OF THE ARCTIC

There is a legend told among the Inupiat Alaskans who live above the Arctic Circle, *"Etok Tames the Green People."* It goes like this:

*I*n the Old Days, as today, the peoples on the edge of the Arctic Sea killed whales. It's just what they do. It's what they eat. But the Green People didn't like that, and so the Green People set out one day in their fancy-ass black powerboat to stop the people of the Arctic Sea from doing their whale killing thing.

It was a long, long time ago in 1979. The elders tell us how the Green People showed up outside the Inupiat Native village of Kaktovik in their black powerboat and set out their stores of vegetables on the beach. The Green People only ate green food. The Green People then set off in their black powerboat on their blubber-saving mission, with a plan to block the Eskimo's bidarka whaling ship. Quick as a Raven's wink, they got lost in a fog bank and stuck in the ice sheet. Prepared, committed, and resourceful, the Green People set out their pup tents on the ice floe and slept, hoping for the fog to lift in the morning.

But they were not lost. The Inupiat of the Arctic Sea knew exactly where the Green People were. Etok, the great whale hunter, told his villagers to accept the gift of the Green People and take all their vegetables. Etok then told his people to be patient, and, elders say, they lit up some excellent weed, put on Bob Dylan tapes, and waited.

During the summer the sun never sets in the Inupiat land. It just rolls around the sky in a Circle. And under the gyrating sun, the Greens' *expensive boat, being black, absorbed the radiant heat, melted the ice hold-ing it and drifted out into the endless Sea.*

By three A.M., the wait was over, and the patient Eskimo leader told his people to go and retrieve the lost black boat, call the Coast Guard, and claim it as abandoned property.

In the morning, the Green People awoke, still in fog, and did not see their boat, their boat with their emergency radio and food. The Green People drifted on their block of ice, lost and doomed. Etok told his people not to move, that the Green People must "cry themselves out" and obtain the wis-dom that comes with accepting your certain death by starvation, hypother-mia, or polar bear.

The Inupiat of the Arctic Sea waited an entire day. Then another day and another day.

On the fourth day, Etok figured the Green People were now wise enough, hungry enough, and thirsty enough. He ordered his people to rescue them. "They are vegetarians," the wise Etok explained to his people and ordered them to bring many buckets of mikiaq, fermented whale meat in congealed blood. The hungry Green People ate the whale, no longer giving a shit that it was some goddamned endangered species. The Inupiat told them it was not wise to enter the Native boats. The rescue party had brought along a filthy crude-oil barge for the frozen Green People to ride.

The Natives dumped the Green People at Dead Horse, where White Peo-ple take petroleum from Prudhoe Bay. The Green People, whose lesson had been taught to them without their knowing, thanked the Inupiat for saving their lives. And from that day forward, Greenpeace protected the Natives' right to kill whales as in the Old Days, and joined the Inupiat people in fight-ing their competitors, the commercial whalers or, as the Natives call them, "the fucking Japanese."

Etok is one bad-ass Eskimo.

THE SHOW GIRLS CLUB, FAIRBANKS, ALASKA, 2010

I didn't have any trouble picking him out, even in the pumping lights of the Fairbanks strip club where we were supposed to meet: the leather-dark face, a wolverine pelt sewn into his parka collar with its vicious fangs still attached, and, around his neck, five huge claws of the last polar bear killed by his father. Eskimo bling.

While I'd heard that Eskimos kiss by rubbing noses, the look in Etok's eyes suggested I wasn't going to get the nose rub.

"Mr. Palast, we are the last of the Pleistocene people," he told me. "It would be an honor to help you fuck up British Petroleum and fuck up your Queen, too."

It was entirely appropriate for Etok, as a head of state, to address his concerns through me, a reporter for British government television, to his diplomatic equal, the Monarch of Windsor; though, as Etok would point out, his realm was larger than Britain, with more resources. And unlike England, Etok's kingdom had never lost a war. I promised to carry his message back to Her Majesty.

In the fall of 2010, BP's oil was still sloshing around the Gulf of Mexico. Where would BP strike next?

I was tired of reporting on disasters after the body count, after the oil hits the beach, after pipes explode, and after kids get cancer. I wanted to film a disaster *before* it happened.

So I took Ricardo, his cameras, and my dear Director James to the North. Just above the Arctic Circle, where British Petroleum and Shell Oil are sharpening their drill bits, ready to bite into the receding ice of the Chukchi and Beaufort seas. For Big Oil, global warming is a profit center. The hole their hydrocarbons has punched in the ozone has opened up once ice-locked oil fields and tanker routes.

It's a global warming bonanza for BP if they can just skooch a few sea mammals out of the way. The Beaufort Sea is the part of the Arctic Ocean that meets Alaska's Arctic National Wildlife Refuge. The "Wildlife" of the Refuge includes the Inupiat-speaking Eskimos, the whale hunters. BP would have to move the polar bears, the whales, and the whale hunters. But that means the landlord has to approve. That's Etok. At least according to Etok.

Etok is at times the unofficial and at times the official sovereign of this polar territory, which is officially sovereign—except when it isn't. The confusion results from the historical oddity that the Eskimo never surrendered to "America" but America pretended they did. There was never a war, so there was never peace nor a peace treaty. For Etok, the Inupiat's Arctic remains a free republic under occupation—by the British. For the Eskimos of the oil-lush North Slope of Alaska, the BP and Shell logos are far more powerful than the American flag.

The first Eskimo movie star, Nanook of the North, died of starvation after he sold fur pelts for knives and candy to John Jacob Astor. Astor would resell them at Saks Fifth Avenue for thousands of dollars even in the 1920s. Etok has no sympathy for Nanook. Etok thinks Nanook used his knife on the wrong animals.

The Chief of Intelligence, Harry Lord, the one who sent me the invite to the Arctic, had given Etok my last book. The Leader, for whom preparation means survival, had highlights and notes on virtually every page.

Whether Etok trusted me or not, I don't know. He certainly decided he could make use of me to issue his ultimatum to BP and the Queen's ignorant subjects. Our television program, *Dispatches,* is carefully scanned by the UK's ruling elite. If he could get me into these closed-off zones, and in return, I could get his story out, well, we had a deal.

The Inupiat leader ordered nonalcoholic brews for us and took us to a corner of the empty barroom turned away from the stage. While a drugged blond giantess shook her stuff, Etok explained his purpose and his rules for our next day's travel to a Native-only town within his nation above the Arctic Circle. The big girl, feeling ignored, put on a long winter coat and sat down with us, nodding, as perplexed as we were.

ON THE LANDING STRIP AT KAKTOVIK

There was whale blubber everywhere, and whale bones big as taxicabs along the inexplicably long air strip, and huge blocks of whale fat in driveways and in backyards among busted ATVs and diesel-powered dogsleds. Giant hunks of whale meat were strewn in front of the stilt houses, with a dog tied up next to each pile. The dogs are tethered, kept out all day, in case a polar bear wanders in for a whale-meat snack. The dogs will bark long enough, before being eaten, to warn the families inside.

While bouncing in the back of the four-wheeler taking us from the "airport," James spotted a whale carcass. It was on a sand spit about a mile offshore. James was hot to film it. That sure would wow the network even if our London studios ended up getting picketed by untamed greenies.

Etok dropped us at the bunkhouse built for visiting white people. He took in James's request to visit the carcass and said we would be escorted there in Akootchook's boat. Akootchook is the local Deputy Chief. Akootchook, word came back, agreed to take us, but for now, the Chief was on a conference call with lawyers.

We had arrived right on the autumnal equinox, when endless day tips into endless night, and James fretted about losing the sunlight needed for filming. I knew enough to nap until further notice, and Rick quietly filmed lots of the icy emptiness.

James, seeing the precious daylight dying, asked Etok if he could tell the Chief to hurry up a bit.

Oh shit oh God no, James.

"LISTEN, YOU RUDE LITTLE IMPATIENT BRITISH PRICK. YOU WILL FOLLOW *PROTOCOL*, COCKSUCKER. THIS IS NOT YOUR FUCKING IMPERIAL COLONY."

Well, I figured James had to get a taming sometime, so at least that was now out of the way. James sat quietly, head down . . . while I listened with great care to Intelligence Chief Harry Lord and the tale of *"How Kaktovik Lost the Cold War."*

In 1947, the U.S. Air Force told the Inupiat of Kaktovik to get the fuck out. The U.S. military needed a big runway in case the Russians attacked America over the polar ice cap.

Kaktovik's island was an interesting choice. You can fly a hundred miles in any direction from Kaktovik and you'll find absolutely nothing. Nevertheless, the Air Force had to have that one single spot, the lone Eskimo village, within this vast emptiness. The Natives, by proving the location both geologically stable and weather-worthy, had placed a "steal me" sign on their homes.

Chief Akootchook, father of the current Chief Akootchook, sued to block the Natives' expulsion.

The military responded with a beach landing, a kind of mini D-Day on ice. The United States Marines came ashore on the skinny peninsula at the island's end. The invaders brought a bulldozer. Then, one by one, the GI's earthmover pushed each and every Inupiat house into the Arctic Sea. It must have taken quite some time. There were more than a hundred homes on that land spit.

Kaktovik was more than a village to the Inupiat. It was their metropolis, the closest thing Eskimos had to a shopping mall, where Inuit from Canada traded with Alaskan Natives. They called it Barter Island. The Air Force nodded its head to history by giving the military's new airport the identifying initials, BTI.

Akootchook still demanded a ruling from the courts. He got it. Unfortunately. The judge said the Natives of Kaktovik had to cease squatting on U.S. government property. It didn't matter that the Inupiat had lived there for a few thousand years before the United States or its government existed. Well, that's the fine print.

Some Natives remained, rebuilding, though on more treacherous shoreline. Then in 1954, the Air Force told the Natives to get off that land, too. America was building the world's most powerful radar network, the DEW Line, to watch for the Soviet surprise missile attack.

The bulldozer went to work again and the Eskimos moved up the shore until 1961, when the Air Force told the Natives they had to move yet again. The Natives, the Air Force determined, were a "security risk." The straggling crew of "security risks" picked up their whale guns and whalebone toys and moved again, for the last time, to the diminished little village I came to visit.

TO ALCATRAZ AND BACK

"The Americans," as Etok calls us, did not realize that the Battle of Kaktovik was far from over.

In 1969, four thousand miles to the south, in San Francisco Bay, the federal government owned another island, also beautiful and extraordinarily valuable.

Etok, with a group of a hundred Indians from the Lower 48, landed, heavily armed, on this bay isle, once the home of Alcatraz Penitentiary, and told the U.S. government to get off their property, Indian property. The Natives were prepared to die for it, but not alone. They made it clear that any American invaders would go with them.

How did the Eskimo Etok end up as a proud, if temporary, owner of Alcatraz Island?

He told me it started when, as a kid in the Arctic Slope town of Barrow, he would look out his window. He didn't like what he saw: the still-unburied bones of Eskimos who had died in the great influenza epidemic of 1918. The flu killed just about all the Eskimos of Alaska as it did most Alaska Natives, an ethnic cleansing by virus.

The boy Etok grew into a teenage hell-raiser, drug taker, and heavy drinker with a brain fast as a locomotive and as powerful.

By his twenties, the locomotive of his genius and anger outran the booze and took him to the Lower 48, where he learned what he could of what he called The White Man's Tools of Power, Crime, and Mystification: legislative lobbying, community organizing, international law, petroleum geology, political philosophy. As the original "chief of intelligence" for his Free Arctic Republic's Eskimo insurgency, Etok slyly hooked himself into the invading army's nervous system, from befriending the U.S. Senate's Appropriations Committee leadership to slipping his way into Harvard University and the Kennedy family circle.

Etok had to take temporary leave from the Native occupation army on Alcatraz Island because he had his teaching gig at the University of California Berkeley to complete. For a final exam, Etok required his students to show up on a designated dock on San Francisco Bay. When they arrived, Professor Etok ordered them aboard a pirate craft to take them all to reinforce the Indians at the island prison.

The university was discomfited by Etok's making a felony a required class assignment. The academic board also took issue with his failing any student who refused to board the ship and join the occupation. "I flunked every one of their racist asses," Etok told me. The university fired him. The occupation of Alcatraz ended in 1970 when Richard Nixon ordered its invasion at about the same time he invaded Cambodia. But Etok's group won, ending the U.S. policy of Termination and Relocation that had destroyed Kaktovik.

The ex'd professor returned to the North for the summer whale hunt and prepared for the next invaders: the British, who smelled oil at Prudhoe Bay. That same year, British Petroleum set out on a mission to grab control of the oil lying underneath the Natives, and to seize the pipeline route that would carry the oil through the Natives' land to Valdez.

Etok prepared himself for this trillion-dollar international chess match. Etok held the pipeline up for ransom. His uncle laid out several bear traps of lawsuits. They hired America's top "Jew lawyers," as he described them, including President Johnson's personal attorney. Etok won the backing of powerful senators, and launched his own corporate battleship, founding the Arctic Slope Regional Corporation. Etok was also savvy to the advice of the political philosopher Hannah Arendt: There is no power without state power. He created a new political entity, North Slope Borough County, the largest in the United States (and way larger than all of England). It was not quite national sovereignty, but it was a government recognized by the "Americans" under the comity clause of the U.S. Constitution,* with its own flag and power to make law.

Etok is still bitter over what he considered his meager winnings for the Eskimos in 1971: a deed to forty-four million acres of land, several billion dollars in no-bid contracts, oil royalties, and the multiplication of Eskimo power. A disappointment, but surely it must have been satisfying for Etok when the Inupiat of Kaktovik told the U.S. Air Force to get the hell off their Native property.

---

* Please don't ask me about "comity." That's Google's job.

Today, you cannot find any artifacts of the U.S. military occupation of Kaktovik. The Air Force had to remove all traces of their incursion except for the runway where the old village stood. Chief Akootchook needs the airfield to ship in goodies like Honda outboards for the whaleboat, high-speed Internet, and an easy way out and back for the Eskimos' vacations to Hawaii.

Nevertheless, one modern trinket is banned from the Arctic Republic. Etok has rejected twenty-first-century weapons for the whale hunts. The explosives and rocketry used by those pigs, the Japanese commercial whalers, "destroy too much of the meat," he told me. "You have to cut out all that toxic powder." So, Etok and villagers all along the Slope still use the nineteenth-century shoulder gun and the charge-tipped harpoon. Herman Melville and Queequeg would feel quite at home on Etok's hunting boat.

BEAUFORT SEA, ARCTIC OCEAN

Rick and a now-tamed James left the White Man's Bunkhouse, to follow Etok, Intelligence Chief Harry Lord, and me to Chief Akootchook's home on the shore of the Beaufort Sea, a fat appendage of the polar ocean. The Chief is an arctic Damien Hirst. When we got to the small stilt bungalow, we found his cellar full with a half dozen semi-frozen caribou and moose that he had chainsawed in half. "If you leave the skin on, it cooks up real fresh." I took his word for it.

I looked north into Nothing. This was the last house before the world comes to an end, my world, anyway. Akootchook's next-door neighbor to the north was in Norway, herding reindeer. Etok had made contact with the Norwegians in their "backyard," creating a circumpolar association of indigenous people. When Siberia's Governor tried to block Russian Natives from joining, Etok paid the Russian pol $25,000 in cash. Apparently, Etok speaks Russian.

Akootchook offered us some alcohol-free beer, which he asked Mrs. Akootchook, in a gentle, nearly inaudible Inupiat, to bring for us. He introduced her as "Daisy," her Bureau of Indian Affairs name, I assumed. But Etok, of course, wouldn't "Daisy" her. He called her "Mutti." Mutti had that small, round look of the cartoon Eskimo squaw, and I knew our director would be pleased with finding a recognizable stereotype. (Forgive us, Lord, for doing things the easy way.)

Daisy proudly showed me the artifacts she had gathered on the beach, the remains of the drowned houses of the old village. Junk that had been cluttering up sunken closets in the drowned homes had floated ashore, some of it a hundred or five hundred years old: arrow shafts, bone bracelets, and brass reindeer bells.

Reindeer like Santa? Yes, said Akootchook, three thousand head roamed here until the dynamite blasts for the seismic mapping for the oil chased them into the protection of the bigger, stronger herd of caribou. The caribou bulls humped all the female reindeer and put an end to the delicate lineage—the only known case of mammals screwed to extinction.

No one was going to fornicate a whale into extinction, but a little hydrocarbon in the water would chase them away. Whales don't like swimming in crude any more than you would, and they won't put up with it. If that happens, if the whales leave, kiss Kaktovik good-bye and about every Eskimo village on the North Slope.

This past year, the whaling sucked. Kaktovik caught only three. Etok's agreement with the whaling cops allows a catch of sixty whales a year on the North Slope, and this year they didn't get close. Still, three whales for Kaktovic is a lot of mucousy meat and blood.

Akootchook is nervous. For the Inupiat, whaling is not a Cultural Experience; it's an Eating Experience. They really, truly survive by taking whales, a few polar bears (only those, the chief assures me, who have attitude problems), seal, moose, and Rudolf the Red-nosed Caribou. They aren't fighting offshore drilling to preserve their lifestyle, but to preserve their *lives*.

If the whales, bears, and fish are scared off by Big Oil's filth machines, there will simply be no way for Etok's people to remain in the Arctic, at least not living as Inupiat. Some would stay on to man the port-a-potty concessions for the oil roustabout crews, or work the rigs themselves. Most would have to abandon their homes and go south, where they will get port-a-potty jobs in warmer climes.

They have no desire to don the BP suits with the little oil barrels on the badges I saw in Baku, to work the petroleum plantation. They don't want to end up as hired hands on their own land. The Inupiat don't need to be tamed.

Etok's message to the Queen to take BP's rigs and shove them has a price tag. The Eskimos are unique in having won oil royalty payments, so their choice to block the drilling will cost them easily a billion dollars, roughly a million per family.

I told Etok, "OK, *you* tell Her Royal Highness, on camera, what you think of BP's plan, but only if I get a bowl of *mikiaq*." Unfortunately, Mutti had just made some. Her face lit up with the opportunity to bring in a big plastic bucket of the greenish chewy whale meat hunks. It sits in a kind of mucous jelly and comes accompanied by a pan of congealed blood. Blood is unexpectedly sweet (vampires have a point), but whale—maybe the idea of it—nearly caused me to commit the social faux pas of vomiting on my hosts.

INSIDE LEVIATHAN

Look at me, I'm Jonah! Inside the carcass of a beast bigger than most New York apartments. I've never walked around inside my lunch before. This thing is impressive. And what is most impressive is the smell. But then, I can't imagine what I smell like inside.

Akootchook had taken us out by skiff to the pile of bones and blubber. And under the roof beams made by the rib cage, I attached wires to Etok for a formal on-camera interview inside the skeleton.

I was afraid that, like most people, once the camera is running, Etok would become a scaredy-cat, a weakling, all polite and *National Geographic*.

I opened the interview with what I thought was a reasonable question. "Etok, sir, I understand that you claim that drilling oil here endangers your tribe's lifestyle. But it seems that your lifestyle is, basically, just killing endangered species and eating them. Why should U.S. and British consumers support that?"

"LISTEN, YOU COCKSUCKING REDNECK COCKSUCKER, I DON'T CARE WHAT YOU FUCKING THINK OF OUR LIFE."

Whoa, there! No one had ever called me "redneck" before.

I tried it a different way.

"Sir, you claim that the Natives 'own' this property. I brought this up with Alaska Governor Hickel, who said, *'Just because your great-uncle chased a moose across some wilderness doesn't mean you own . . .'"*

"I DON'T CARE WHAT YOU AND THAT COCKSUCKER HICKEL THINK ABOUT MY UNCLES AND WHO THE HELL GAVE IT TO THOSE BP COCKSUCKERS. IT'S NOT YOURS. IT'S NOT YOUR COCKSUCKING BRITISH THIEVING PETROLEUM. COCKSUCKER."

Director James had his head below his knees. It had been a long, expensive journey to get completely unusable film. I asked Etok if he might repeat the last answer with a couple less *cocksuckers* in it.

I started again, "Hickel said, just because your daddy . . ."

"AND I DON'T CARE WHAT YOU AND FUCKING HICKEL AND YOU WHITE BASTARD KILLERS THINK. YOU NEVER OWNED THIS."

Rick's hands were freezing to the lens. He'd be leaving lots of skin on it, but he wouldn't complain. The sun was turning red-orange on the ice and the whale was smelling even worse.

British Petroleum and Royal Dutch Shell have already purchased the concession for the oil under these whale bones from the U.S. Department of the Interior. How would Etok get around that?

"WHO THE FUCK IS THE U.S. DEPARTMENT OF THE INTERIOR? YOU NEVER CONQUERED US, COCKSUCKER."

Oh yes we did—in court. Etok's uncle, claiming ownership of the minerals in Inupiat waters, sued the Department of the Interior in 1969. However, the federal government waved the sales receipt from the Russian Czar for all of Alaska. The judge bounced the Natives' case out on its ass. Etok's uncle then led a war party in a blockade of the Trans-Alaska Highway used in the pipeline's construction. The ice-road truckers simply drove around the Eskimo tollbooth.

The blood on the whale bones turned a darker red as the light dimmed. Etok expounded on Her Majesty's relationship to Alaska and British Petroleum. He noted that the Queen of England had knighted the Governor of Alaska, "that cocksucker [Tony] Knowles," after the Governor approved the BP seizure of half of the Prudhoe Bay oil field.

Ricardo, shooting from a distance as he strolled (and I slid) through the blubber, was gesturing to check if all was A-OK. Well, if our director's suicide is OK, then, yes. We got back into Akootchook's boat.

* * *

Alaska has always been about its energy resources. Whale oil, then coal, then crude oil. Abraham Lincoln's mean little Secretary of State Seward was no fool in buying "Seward's Folly." Seward recognized that Alaska represented liquid gold. To travel the Great Circle route to the Orient, U.S. warships and traders would need to re-provision along the way, filling whale-oil lamps against the Arctic night, and later, take on coal, then crude, for combustion-engine battle cruisers.

White people's need for whale oil far outlived Herman Melville. The first automobile transmissions required whale oil. Today, the best stuff, a liquid cut out of the brains and foreheads of sperm whales, is used for high-altitude components directing intercontinental ballistic missiles. Whale is used as a preservative for billionaire's trophy wives: blubber in high-fashion makeup, and ambergris in the most expensive perfumes.

It's interesting to note that when white people needed whale oil, no one gave a shit how many of these thoughtful mammals were hacked apart and melted.

> *Pity there was none. . . . He must die the death and be murdered, in order to light the gay bridals and other merry-makings of men, and also to illuminate the solemn churches that preach unconditional inoffensiveness by all to all.*

* * *

According to Chief Akootchook, the wildlife cops were radio-tagging and relocating the bears because they got in the way of drilling. Just like the Natives, the bears had to get the hell off the industry's real estate.

His line about the tagging might have been bullshit, so we decided to take a look for ourselves. Akootchook's seventeen-foot runabout had a 150-hp engine strong enough to rip through the thickening layer of ice to another sand spit. Inside the boat, the Native had stowed a rusted, antique Winchester, that really old type from the cowboy movies. You can't stop a bear with that, Chief.

"Don't have to. If a bear charges, I just have to stop *you*." The Jay Leno of the Arctic.

Rick, James, and I hopped to the sand spit with Akootchook to film two polar bears just jerking around in the water near the beach, hugging each other, rolling around on their backs. One got curious and walked out, strolling toward our camera fixed to a tripod, sniffing. Then he got *too* curious. Our host said emphatically, "Get back behind me *right now!*—but move *slow.*" The bear headed toward us. He did not seem menacing, but this fucker weighed more than all four of us combined.

Akootchook cocked the Winchester, just like Wyatt Earp, and fired. I don't like gunfire. Never have. The bear stopped, turned, and loped away, looking back at us like, "Hey, dudes, you should chill."

We moved quick to the boat. So did the bear. Oh, mama. This was not *National Geographic*. We scrambled into the skiff, and Akootchook backed it up as the bear came up and stared. Then Akootchook said those magic words, "I've lost steering."

I have a little boat just like this one. So I calmly (hysterically, actually) shouted, "Unbolt the cables from the helm and move the motor with your hands!" I grabbed and gunned the throttle while the Chief manhandled the outboard.

Obviously, we did not drift, dehydrate, and die in the Arctic Ocean; how doesn't matter. I came away from the incident with one happy thought: James had forgotten his satellite phone and hospital-in-a-bag. But I did turn on Ricardo, a man who has held his camera steady under fire in Iraq. "Shit, man, I'm disappointed in you, abandoning your camera. We can always get another cameraman, but not another shot like that."

Rick was (mildly) glum, "You can't be as disappointed with me as I am with myself."

DEAD HORSE

From Kaktovik, I flew with Etok into Dead Horse, whose prettified name, Prudhoe Bay, graces the BP/Exxon/Shell field, including the drilling rigs balanced on fake islands and the giant machinery that stuffs the crude into the pipeline for its ride to Valdez.

Etok looked down, his jaw clenched, and I could see history taking another bite of his heart. "A crime scene," he said.

In 1969, a New Mexico oilman and rancher, R. O. Anderson, discovered oil here and staked his claim. His "discovery" was quite some news to the North Slope Eskimos, who had been burning crude oil for centuries while the United States was still burning whales. Anderson's claim stake, in the name of his company, ARCO, also came as a surprise to the Natives, who already owned the land.

Now if it had been the other way around, if an Eskimo had "discovered" R.O.'s cows on R.O.'s ranch and decided to ship the meat to the Arctic, we'd call it cattle rustling, thievery. And we'd call his property a crime scene.

Etok's "Pleistocene" people had been digging oil for millennia, and since 1873, drilling for it. Etok's dad, from whom he inherited the Arctic's most experienced harpoon, was an engineer in the oil field during World War II, helping to pull up the Natives' crude for the U.S. Navy to fuel the defense against the expected invasion from Japan. The Navy never paid the $84 million it owes for this oil. (Etok, not surprisingly, vows to collect it.)

In 1970, not long after R.O.'s ARCO grabbed the North Slope drilling rights, the Arab oil embargo shot oil prices through the ceiling and made R. O. Anderson, "owner" of Prudhoe Bay, richer, by my estimate, than God. That wasn't enough. Anderson's "discovery" at Dead Horse would be worth even more if only he could get it to Japan.

Japan?

A geography lesson is required here.

In Mrs. Gordon's sixth-grade class, Alaska was that big-ass square in the upper left corner of the pull-down map of the United States hanging above the blackboard. Alaska had a strip of dots to the left of the square, the Aleutian Islands, the Ice Age stepping stones the Pleistocene hunters walked across from Russia. And there was a long thing hanging from it, a peninsula that looks like a hose dripping down to the Lower 48 states. You could almost see Alaska's succulent resources draining into our puny little states below Canada.

That's the deal, isn't it? We bought Alaska from the Russians and now we can suck on that fat straw, chug down the crude like a frat boy on his back getting wasted on a hose from a keg of beer.

But look at a globe, not a flat map. Turn it so that the Arctic, not the equator, is pointing at you. Think of the North Pole as the nipple, Alaska as whatever. What you'll see is that oil-starved Nagasaki is only two thousand miles from Alaska (that's why the Emperor chose it as the invasion route), a thousand miles closer than the refineries in California.

You'd have to be a complete pinhead to think Anderson and partners were going to ship their oil anywhere but to the Land of the Rising Sun.

Now turn the globe slightly upward and you see the cheapest way to move the oil to Japan would be to pipe it dead south to Valdez and carry it by tanker through the Pacific.

But 1970 also marked the first Earth Day. The day for Mother Nature was celebrated just three weeks before the largest mass demonstration in U.S. history: the two-million-strong march against Nixon's war in Vietnam.

Earth Day was a protest Nixon could join as a distraction from the national freak-out over the "draft," the Vietnam death lottery. Like a game show, 365 days of the calendar were picked out of a bowl. If your birthday was between 1 and 100, off you went (unless your name was Bush). A thousand Americans were dying each week alongside twenty thousand native Vietnamese.

Nixon painted himself as green as a BP gas station, with as much sincerity. Little did the mad, Red-baiting president know that the environmental movement, despite its hippie tree-hugger front, was carefully crafted and launched by the best of America's Leftist mass-mobilization organizers. It was centered around the brilliant biologists Paul Ehrlich and Barry Commoner, one of my mentors, who'd been trained by the Communist Party.

The guys in black jammies kicking the shit out of U.S. forces in Southeast Asia gave the tactically adept founders of the ecology movement the opportunity to widen the anti-war protests to include kicking the crap out of corporate polluters.

The militant biologist allied with a young lawyer Victor Yannacone who invented something he called "environmental law." Copying the tactics of the Civil Rights struggle, Yannacone politically militarized the birdwatchers of the Audubon Society and created a legal attack team for Audubon called the Environmental Defense Fund. Its first suit against a polluter was filed on behalf of their "client," plaintiff "Nature." Miss Nature won. (It would take at least a decade before corporate powers would purchase EDF's affection and destroy Yannacone. We'll get to that.)

The millions marching for peace were now ready to march against polluters. That was trouble for R. O. Anderson, ARCO, and British Petroleum. The water route to Japan was inherently dangerous. There could be a million-gallon spill. The Alaska Pipeline and water route would be one tough sell through a Democratic Congress. Yannacone's Environmental Defense Fund pushed for a less risky all-land route, a three-thousand-mile pipeline through Canada.

But R.O. wasn't going to let some caribou kissers get in the way of his dream of selling to Japan. So R.O. went to Washington, whistled, and President Nixon came right over to Anderson's quarters at the Watergate complex.

(While Nixon and R.O. met, I was serving my country in Washington, DC—in jail.*)

R.O.'s Plan A would be to wrap the shorter Prudhoe-to-Valdez pipeline in red, white, and blue. America must become Energy Independent! U.S. oil for the U.S.A.!

Nixon and R.O. must have had a chuckle as their pipeline to Valdez would keep the oil *out* of America. Not to mention that ARCO and partners had a quiet scheme to sell the Alaska Pipeline and oil fields to the British. BP had

---

* I'd been arrested under bullshit charges. Some cop, faking an arrest report, asked me, "Tell me what you were doing when you were arrested." Nothing. "Then why are you here in Washington, Gil?" "To overthrow the government." My father was happy I used his name. The ACLU got the charges against "Gil Palast" dropped.

signed a pact with Sohio, ARCO's partner, to buy out Sohio's Alaska assets. But BP knew it had to keep its Limey head hidden while the pipe to Valdez was wrapped in the American flag. BP's scheme was quite brilliant, I admit: The Brits would take formal ownership only after 450,000 barrels of oil had moved through the pipe.

Gamblers hope to improve their luck by having a good-looking woman blow on their dice before they roll them. Likewise, R.O. and Nixon needed Henry Kissinger to blow on their pipe. They knew Kissinger didn't believe in luck. The game had to be fixed, the dice loaded. Kissinger's solution was to use the environmental movement's power in Canada to raise objections to an oil pipeline across their pristine land.

It worked. Canadians balked at a pipeline from Alaska. So, as Congress prepared for a nail-biting vote on the pipeline authorization, the Canada land route pushed by environmentalists was simply closed off, at least publicly.

In fact, after its initial reservations, the Canadian government had sent a diplomatic missive to the State Department, saying Canada would remove its objection to the pipeline. Kissinger did not bother Congress with this information.

In March 1973 the United States Senate voted on the Valdez water route. It was a dead tie. Something almost never seen in American history. Few Americans know that the U.S. Constitution gives the Vice President of the United States the right to break a tie vote. In this rare constitutional maneuver, Vice President Spiro Agnew voted in R.O.'s favor. It was Agnew's farewell finger to America before his resignation and indictment on charges of bribery.

R.O. won his short, cheap pipe from Prudhoe to Valdez, but he lost the battle for Japan. He hadn't figured on Yvonne Brathwaite-Burke, the Congresswoman from Compton.

Compton is best known as the place where the competitive talking blues of former African slaves, called *signifying monkey*, was transformed into the less simian-sounding *rap*, then *hip-hop*. Compton, tucked into the armpit of Los Angeles, is the Baku of California. Brathwaite-Burke's district is home to filthy oil refineries and loads of poor folk. Filthy or not, oil to Compton meant jobs for her district.

At the last moments before the Pipeline vote in the House, this African American woman, usually ignored by the rulers, inserted an amendment into the pipeline bill requiring that every barrel of Alaska's piped oil must be shipped and refined in the United States. That is, Compton. She had called their bluff: If this was oil for America, then it had to stay in America. The stupid white men didn't know whether to shit or go blind. Her amendment passed.

Japan or not, R.O. now had his field and pipe, which he could then sell to BP for a queen's ransom. The Queen was willing to pay big bucks to give BP that magic 50.1 percent ownership of Alaska's oil.

* * *

Etok left us there at Dead Horse, after pointing out another crime scene, BP's Liberty "Island."

Just after the Deepwater Horizon exploded, President Obama halted all offshore drilling. BP Alaska just grinned. Rather than drill from a platform, it created a fake island, then drilled *sideways* for eight miles under the Arctic Ocean floor. Liberty is a Deepwater Horizon operation, but turned on its side. (These guys think Americans are stupid; but why is it necessary to prove it?)

Is BP operating more safely here than in the Gulf? When we landed, the Arctic Slope Regional Corporation (the one founded by Etok) was still cleaning up BP's huge spill from 2006, four years earlier. BP pled guilty to criminal violations of the Clean Water Act and was put on three years' probation.

The company was still on probation when it blew out the Macondo well in the Gulf. Now, if you steal a bike and break probation, you go to jail. If a corporation breaks probation, they go to . . . what? BP did not even lose its Gulf lease or its right to operate the Pipeline. Apparently, Power and Mystification overbalances Crime.

The company paid a $20 million fine for failing to inspect the Alaska Pipeline for corrosion. Think of the $20 million as a cheap permit to delay a half billion dollars in pipe replacements.

What's $20 million? BP's Alyeska consortium has moved half a *trillion* dollars' worth of liquid through that pipe. But I didn't fly to Dead Horse to sightsee at a fake island. I am looking for an "old friend" I've never met.

A couple of years back, I received an extraordinary note from a guy who couldn't be better placed. The message was like manna from Heaven, or if I were Inupiat, a whale falling from the sky.

From ████████████████████████████████████
Subject: *Insider scared.*
Date: 20 October 2010 09:57:09 EDT
To: Greg Palast ◀█████████@█████████com▶

How can I confidentially contact Greg Palast)
Alyeska Pipeline and helped with their pipeli

How can I confidentially contact Greg Palast? I am an ex-employee of BP and I can tell you all about the safety issues on the Pipeline.

"Ex-employee" is one way of putting it. I confirmed who we had. Calling himself an ex-employee is like calling a shark an "ex-minnow." He had been a big fish at BP-Alaska, BP-Azerbaijan, BP-Colombia. I was hoping to find him still in Prudhoe, and talk face-to-face.

But his e-mail address had changed. I didn't like that. I liked it even less when, after searching all night, Badpenny located his new office number—in Houston. I gave him a ring through his office switchboard and heard his friendly Southern drawl:

"Doncha ever ever EVER call me here. Or call me anywhere. Ever *EVER*. I work inside this . . . well, can't talk can't talk."

I took it he didn't want to talk.

I work inside this . . . This Leviathan. Swallowed whole.

DELTA JUNCTION

Rick and I skulked around the off-limits part of the Dead Horse Prudhoe encampment, Etok's buddies on security detail winking us through. I didn't know what I was looking for, but I found it anyway: A huge airplane hangar–size building marked *PIG*. It wasn't BP's Lord Browne's old office. It was another crime scene. The BP/Alyeska pipeline was dripping and ripping. In five years, it had dumped a quarter-million gallons of crude into the tundra. BP's pipeline is an *Exxon Valdez* in slow motion.

Based on the cancers I'd seen in Ecuador, I knew what would happen if this oozing continued. But this is America, not Ecuador, and we don't let these things happen. So how come it is happening?

I only trusted one man to tell me the truth: Inspector Dan Lawn.

When we found the Inspector, he told me I couldn't understand spam if I didn't go immediately to Pump Station #9 on Delta Junction, which, according to a map, was a couple hundred miles from nowhere. He offered to take us by Jeep. Including his drive from Anchorage, that meant a thousand-mile trip for him without sleep.

I should say "Inspector Lawn, retired." Now that he no longer has to spend his days monitoring oil transport, he spends his days monitoring oil transport. He's a walking Wikipedia of pipes and petroleum; and I love to stand in the warm shower of his gushing spray of facts, figures, and documents. For me, the hundreds of miles by Jeep alongside the pipeline was a techno-treat.

Just months earlier, on May 24, 2010, Pump Station #9 had cracked open and barfed up 100,000 gallons of crude. A 100,000-gallon spill used to be news. But you didn't read about it because the Macondo hole in the Gulf was spewing that much in four hours. Add 100,000 gallons to the 200,000 gallons at Prudhoe. Those are warning spurts of BP's next disaster.

Why is the pipe going to hell? I asked the Inspector for just the facts.

"They haven't pigged it." That is, they didn't run the Pipeline Inspection Gauge, the PIG, the robot that runs inside the pipe. If they had, the Smart PIG (one with sensor-feelers) would have squealed at every crack and rusty chunk of the tube.

Sure enough, the records show that 400 miles of the Pipe hadn't seen a PIG in eight years. Why? It costs up to a million dollars a mile to operate. Four hundred miles, $400 million. BP must have realized it's cheaper to pay a fine.

After endless government scoldings, the company merely threw coins on the ground for the fines and laughed until Pump Station #9 caught fire and spewed oil, then laughed some more. The Inspector filled me up with another book's worth of scary info, then dropped us in Fairbanks and began his second sleepless night of driving. Badpenny, worried, stayed up past dawn chatting with him by cell every hour to keep him awake and safe. If you need a guardian angel, you could do worse.

But here's what bugged me. There was one time when the Smart PIG *did* squeal. And its timing was brilliant.

In 2006, BP's Trans-Alaska Pipeline suffered a remarkably timed accident. They ran the PIGs and found that the pipes converging on Prudhoe were cracking, eaten up by corrosion. The BP consortium, thinking about safety first, shut down the pipeline. It was an *emergency*. And it was August.

How could they suddenly discover massive corrosion that had been there for years? Inspector Lawn had written jeremiads about the corrosion *seventeen years earlier*. And his umpteenth warning was published just five months before the panicked shutdown.

Besides, BP should have known about the problem years before that, if only because they had tapped the Inspector's home phone. (BP was caught spying on the Inspector, had to pay him a bundle, and he used it all to create a foundation for oil transport safety. In other words, the man is a Passion Play in a parka.)

They missed the corrosion for seventeen years until August *2006*. So why did a PIG suddenly oink?

That was some smart pig. The business pages of the August 8 *Washington Post* might give us a clue:

PIPELINE CLOSURE SENDS OIL HIGHER

BP TO HALT PRODUCTION OF 400,000
BARRELS A DAY IN ALASKA

————

News that BP would have to suspend production equal to 8 percent of U.S. petroleum output for an indefinite period helped push the price of crude oil up by 3 percent yesterday, to $76.98 a barrel on the New York Mercantile Exchange. The price jump underlined the fragility of world oil markets, already anxious about the thin cushion between global supply and demand and potential threats to flows from Iran, Nigeria, Iraq and the hurricane-prone Gulf of Mexico.

BP sold eight million barrels a day. In just a few days, the windfall would more than pay that $20 million fine.

Am I saying that BP *chose* to shut the Pipe at that exact moment when they could squeeze the world market? Would BP lie and manipulate the market like that? *I am saying nothing.* I shall, however, note that six weeks before the shutdown, a BP executive pleaded guilty to criminal manipulation of the U.S. propane gas market.

OK, we have motive. But opportunity? Something was very odd about BP's PIGs. The Inspector said they weren't run. But now we knew that when they were run, they didn't see a thing for years. Then suddenly, they did.

Something about these PIGs isn't kosher.*

First clue: When BP shut down the pipeline, National Public Radio ran a gushing report about the brilliant PIGs used by the industry. But PIGs aren't perfect, a pipeline consultant told NPR. The reporter agreed, adding, "There have been cases where a pig said a pipe was okay, then it later ruptured." Then, an industry guy said, "Someone might misinterpret the pig's data."

WHAT!!??!!

QUESTION ONE: Must U.S. reporters submit to hypnosis before interviews? Lobotomy? Or are they just drugged by careerism and lazy-fuckism?

————

* Yes, I have written this entire chapter just to use that terrible, terrible pun.

QUESTION TWO: What if these pigs weren't dumb at all but instead were astonishingly clever? What if pig data was *deliberately* misinterpreted, or *deliberately controlled* to miss trouble?

To shut a pipe for corrosion and replace it costs millions and millions. If the pig could be calibrated to be less sensitive, millions could be saved. Billions even.

So I asked myself: The oil companies use smart pigs, which they pay millions for, but then the pigs turn out to be kind of dim-witted. They miss stuff. Pipes explode. People fry. Nevertheless, the companies *don't sue the PIG maker?*

A human you silence with threats. A robot you silence with computer code.

Badpenny went back to a note that gave us the closest thing to a journalistic orgasm: it was from someone who *knew* the program had been jacked, fiddled, faked. The software used to analyze the data made the PIGS dangerously, deliberately stupid. How did this guy know? He *wrote* the program.

Now came the hard part: Bringing him in from the cold and corroborating this information. "Pig Man #1" said, "Forget it." His career would be toast. He could get sued, blackballed.

Then, suddenly, Pig Man #1, after an extraordinary turn of events, changed his mind. He would not remain silent. His decision wasn't an easy one.

SOMEWHERE, USA

"They threatened me. Last night I got a call and they threatened me. If I talked."

Oh shit oh no oh my God *how did they find out* damn it but *please please tell me you're still getting on the plane.*

"But I'm still getting on the plane."

Dear Lord, I take back everything I've said about You this week.

It was Pig Man #1. We met somewhere in the USA. I forget where.

In a darkened room—not a hotel, no receipts to track—Rick wired him up, put a blinding light behind him to leave his face only a talking shadow with nervous hands.

"Wow," said Pig Man. "I feel like I'm in the CIA." Rick said, not thinking, "The last guy I filmed was CIA. In Afghanistan."

Pig Man asked, "What happened to him?"

We changed the topic to the lighting.

Pig Man wanted to take a souvenir photo of me on his own cell phone, nothing that will transmit via computer. Director James said, "Absolutely no!" We went through the motions of ultra-security although the company knows who he is, knows who I am, and we know they know it. But we didn't like to think about that.

Pig Man told me again about the marvelous machine, the Pipeline Inspection Gauge, the way it could chug through a pipeline, leashed to a GPS, sending out beeps and boops. An elaborate and expensive software program translated PIG-ese into colored charts that marked spots of dangerous corrosion, bad cracks, or other dangers. The law requires it, so BP bought the software, and uses it.

Or *maybe* BP used it. But if BP did run the PIG through the Alaska Pipeline, shouldn't it have caught the corrosion that led to the 2006 explosion, to the Prudhoe Bay spill disaster? Yes, he said, absolutely. The PIG would have caught it in advance.

But only, he added, if errors in the program were corrected.

Was it corrected?

"My team corrected it. I was part of a team, corrected the error."

His team even did it on their own time. They were very proud that they had found the problem and did the difficult reprogramming to conform the software to the sensitivities required by federal law. I know Americans love to hate bureaucrats with their thick rule books, but if you lived on top of a pipeline (and several million of you do), all I can say is, *the thicker the better*.

Up until his team's fix, BP's robo-pigs were fugitives from the law. Now he could make them law-abiding porkers, conformed to the rules. The geeks proudly showed the correction to their supervisor.

They were fired.

Not immediately, though. First, the supervisor tried to explain the difficulties of the fix: "The exact phrase that he used was, 'This is not going to make a lot of people happy.'"

Why?

"He said that if we release the software with the fix that we could potentially lose sales."

The company would lose sales if their customers found out their software actually worked?

Exactly.

The oil and gas companies, BP among them, preferred the error to remain in the program, in violation of the law?

"The consequence of fixing the software would be that the client using the software would now have additional costs. . . . That pipeline operator would need to apply fixes to a greater number of pipeline segments, they would have to do more re-routes, which are expensive."

Expensive is an understatement. Each ten-mile re-route could easily cost $100 million, $200 million.

The company told Pig Man's crew, "The people we are selling the software to, pipeline operators, BP, if they were to see that, overnight, they have more problems to deal with, they have larger segments, they have segments that are now classified as higher risk, they would not be so inclined to purchase the software. So they made a business decision."

Their fix to the software would never leave that office. And the guys who did the fix, only three months into a one-year contract, were terminated.

Were you told not to make it public?

"Yes."

He'd been a little nervous to this point, now he was *big* nervous.

"We had to sign nondisclosure agreements."

They were required to conceal "any problems of this sort or the nature of the software we worked." It could not "be made public at all. Under threat of lawsuit." Nice.

But maybe the company was just kidding, and the nondisclosure agreement was just a formality. Maybe he had nothing to fear.

No. He got a call.

"People who worked at the company, they informed me that if I were to speak publicly about this, I would be sued."

The question was, how did they know he was talking to me? I had the answer: It was my fault.

Good little reporter that I am, I simply could not accept Pig Man's word without corroboration. Literally millions of dollars hung in the balance and, we soon learned, some burnt corpses to account for.

So I approached one of his coworkers, who verified everything and even agreed to go on camera. But a couple of weeks later, Pig Man #2 panicked and ran. It was just after September 9, 2010, when a pipeline blew in California; eight dead. Some people blew apart instantly, some burnt slowly. I know: I've been there, years back, when I was an investigator. I discovered that the giant energy corporation called Peoples Gas that moved natural gas from the Gulf of Mexico into Chicago had been warned by engineers to fix a dangerous pipeline design. The company decided it was cheaper to wait and pay for the coffins. After eighteen people burnt up, they apologized. They paid out a few bucks, including my fee.

The September 9 pipeline explosion meant the stakes were getting higher. To protect himself and his own career, Pig Man #2 ratted out Pig Man #1.

"I was threatened," Pig Man #1 repeated on tape, speaking calmly now, with a resignation to the consequences. "A person can be—can be made silent, can be made bankrupt by this power that they hold. Any person that speaks out against the pipeline companies puts a lot at risk, puts a lot . . ."

He trailed off, talking about what could befall "someone." Needless to say, the "someone" was him.

My only justification for printing and filming his story, and jeopardizing this good man further, beyond the feeble thread of "the public interest," is that I can offer Pig Man a bit of protection. *Dear Pig Man employer: I have a much bigger file than I am spilling here. Any company that dares to go after Pig Man #1 will have much to lose. Capisce? If Pig Man is touched: I know who you are, I know where you operate, and I know what you've done.*

You notice I have not named BP's software provider—because it's not about a bad apple, it's about an industry rotten from branch to root.

And BP itself? They have plausible deniability. The oil giant could say, like Mr. Gambino, "I didn't know that Big Louie off'd Jimmy the Skunk."

But deniability isn't plausible—because, as Holmes would say, "the dog didn't bark." When the pipe busted in 2006, why didn't BP bark, bite, and sue its software designers? After all, the failure to find the corrosion problem cost the oil company tens of millions.

Here's why: Because the software firm could turn around, "discover" their "accidental" error, and hand it to BP: The total cost of repairs and reroutes to the industry would run into *tens of billions* of dollars.

Or the software maker could ask BP when the pig was run. Was it run at all? Where's the data? It costs a million dollars a mile to run a diagnostic pig test. Cheaper to keep them locked in that giant metal PIG-pen in Prudhoe, eh, BP?

Omerta, then, is the wise course both in The Mob and in the Oil Patch.

But now I was curious: Why Pig Man #1? Why now? How come he didn't run away squealing in fear like Pig Man #2?

He sent the note that got us all hot after he read my story about BP's Prudhoe pipe burst. Before that, he thought of the coding episode as a professional disagreement, the bottom-line guys stomping on the expert. But reading the Prudhoe story, he realized, that, "This stuff had real-world consequences."

Before that, Pig Man #1 stayed *schtum* for years. Still, when I first approached him, he said "no way" to filming, even in shadow. Something then changed his mind, made him volunteer to put his ass on the line. It was the California pipeline blowup. The eight dead. It finally struck him: "People die."

> "I was very disconnected from the real impact that such work has on the general public and people. And so when seeing the explosion . . . it made a direct link between inaccuracies in software that *result in death. . . .*"

His corporate mask had slipped when the photo of the burnt houses hit the front pages.

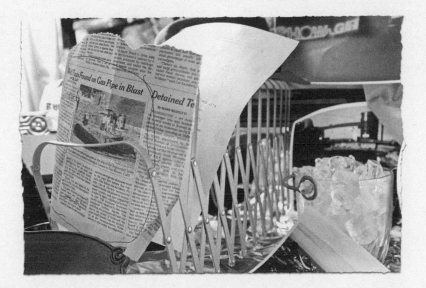

It turns out, the California company whose pipes blew, PG&E, had bad welds holding together a thirty-inch-diameter pipe that wasn't supposed to have welds at all. A PIG, honestly programmed, could have picked that up easily.

Pig Man #2 saw the same photos, and it caused him to run away. So, what pushed #1 to be a fool to courage?

I took a guess and asked him about the genesis of his soul. "Tell me about your dad."

His father, he said, was one of the first people in the industry to use computers to analyze pipeline flow and conditions. His dad was one of the men who *invented* the Smart PIG.

"I talked to my father before I came down here." Of course he did.

"He thought I'm doing the right thing."

Of course he did.

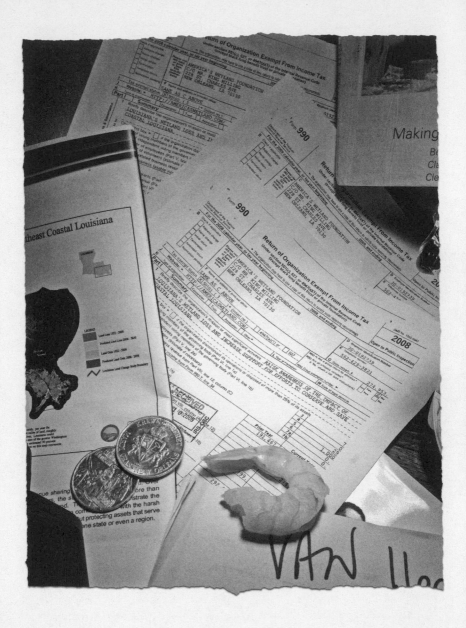

CHAPTER 4
The Coon-Ass Riviera

A RUBBER DINGHY OFF THE GULF COAST, MISSISSIPPI, OCTOBER 2010

This was my first investigation of fish homicide, so I figured Rick and I needed a boat because Professor Steiner's submarine had just cleared the Panama Canal and wouldn't arrive in time for our filming.

However, Badpenny couldn't hook up a canoe, let alone a skiff, because BP had put every Coon-Ass captain on its payroll for the oil clean-up, which mostly involved floating around looking busy when CNN showed up. BP would have to OK our taking one of their indentured boats, and BP never said OK unless they controlled the fish story.

But it is my experience with the human animal that cold cash can make people forget about their contracts (and their marriage vows, the Ten Commandments, and all sense of self-respect). Still, the boatmen told Badpenny, "*Non, cheri.*" BP's string of cash was longer than mine and that wouldn't change anytime soon.

Dr. Steiner told us to meet him at a particular dock behind a casino hotel in Biloxi. So we flew into New Orleans and drove to the coast town whose only claim to fame is that it's three hundred miles due south of the birthplace of Elvis Presley.

Just after sun-up, and without enough coffee, Ricky Ricardo Rowley and I headed through the casino past the exhausted, straggling gamblers who refused to leave until the last of their cash was taken from them.

Beyond the slots, a door led out to a dock, where the resourceful Professor Steiner and his crew were waiting for us in a Zodiac, a rubber-hull dinghy bolted to two screaming 150-hp outboards, which could shoot us to the crime scene like a rocket.

The biologist aimed for a barrier island a mile offshore, then, a hundred yards from the beach, killed the engine and told Rick and me to jump out. Who was I to question the man? I stepped off, fully clothed, sank right up to my sack, and headed through the yuck to the beach, like MacArthur returning to Bataan.

Rick followed, his baby, his precious camera over his head, still filming, followed by Steiner, who reached the beach and began with a religious invocation: *"Holy Christ! Smell that!"* I really didn't need to schlep along a PhD to tell me I was on the edge of throwing up my breakfast.

Black *ick*, crude oil. The professor's stunned look, though, surprised me. This man had seen it all: dogs drowning in oil slicks in China, the Caspian cesspool off Baku, Alaska's dead beaches (where he lives and literally breathed the *Exxon Valdez* spill), and the oil smear in Africa known as the Niger Delta, where Steiner had been only two days before on some UN mission.

He'd seen it all, but not this. He did not expect viscous tar mats the size of sofas and hardened oil slicks like driveways to nowhere half a year after the blowout and a hundred miles away from the well head.

Steiner picked up what looked like a large bovine bowel movement and dumped it into my hands. It was a glop of BP's spume with, he explained, "hydrogen sulphide in it, heavy metals but, also, the polycylic aromatic hydrocarbons. . . ."

Those are my favorites!

". . . And, you know, things like benzopyrene and benzofluoranthene and such like . . ."

Fish hated the stuff because it killed their children and their children's children.

". . . Very highly toxic, they're carcinogenic . . ."

But humans just *love* the stuff, if you look at the news footage. Right after the Deepwater Horizon blew up, fifty thousand grinning volunteers hit the Gulf Coast beaches and—*God Bless America!*—picked up the stuff bare-handed, or scooped it with beer buckets, garden rakes, picnic coolers, whatever.

". . . It doesn't kill immediately but lasts, you know, things like nerve damage, physiological injury, behavioral changes, reproductive changes . . ."

I dropped the tar ball.

". . . leukemia."

* * *

But this *just can't be!* Fully two months earlier, in August 2010, Dr. Terry Hazen of the University of California's prestigious Lawrence Livermore Laboratory announced in *The Washington Post*:

> We've gone out to the sites, and we don't find any oil.

They didn't? No oil plumes in the water? How do you miss a floating oil turd bigger than a quarter horse? If the tar ponies are riding up the beach, they had to be swimming in the water column. As the biologist Yogi Berra once said, "It's amazing what you can see when you're looking."

Two months before we got there, Zach Roberts (our man working under the name "Ronald" Roberts, fish expert) said this gunk was all over the place. So how had these biologists missed this?

Badpenny and I discovered the problem: In February 2007, there had been an oil spill in Dr. Hazen's lab: British Petroleum had squirted half a billion dollars into his laboratory to pay for studies of the biology of oil spills.

That's billion, with a *b*.

Hazen couldn't keep it all. He was tasked with spreading BP's easy-squeezy throughout the academic community. As a result, by the time Deepwater Horizon blew, nearly every biologist from China to Chattanooga had their gonads in a jar on Lord Browne's old desk in London.

Hazen's can't-see-no-oil-plumes study was signed by thirty-two scientists and printed in *Science* magazine. Drill deep down in the footnotes (we did), and you'll find that thirty-one of the thirty-two co-authors were suckling at the laboratory's BP money teat. Therein lies your problem, professors. No need to panic, you're not blind! You have BP's dollars taped over your eyes.

This reminded me of Nirvana's *Nevermind* album cover: a baby underwater reaching for a dollar bill.

But how come no one laughed the rent-a-scientists right out of the journals? Answer: Independent biologists were locked out.

While walking the smeared beach, Dr. Steiner told me he had asked to go along on BP boats to take samples with their scientists and look at their raw data. In other words, to keep the science honest.

Forget it. No way. They weren't going to let Steiner and his sampling bags anywhere *near* the test sites. Rogue scientists, not to mention reporters, are banned from these beaches, supposedly for our own safety. It's locked off like Area 51. Now I understood why Steiner had us invade from the sea, unannounced, and walk the plank.

If BP's scientists didn't find oil plumes, what did they find? "We don't find any oil, but we do find the bacteria," said Hazen. They found germs. Magical germs.

From the *Science* monograph:

> Our results show the potential exists for intrinsic bioremediation of the oil plume in the deepwater column without substantial oxygen drawdown.

"Intrinsic bioremediation" means that oil spills can clean themselves up. Bacteria in the ocean will simply eat up the oil. Yum. And so, virtually all the oil that spewed out of the well just . . . vanished!

Discover magazine gushed, "Hazen's results suggest that the deep ocean has its own janitorial crew that is standing by to mop up the threat of oil contamination."

Thus, the science from BP is this: There's no problem with drilling the hell out of the Gulf's deepwater. If a well blows, you just let the Good Lord's bacteria chow down. It's not true, but hey, it's true enough for U.S. reporters. I found the stories of the microbes who just love oil spills on CBS, NBC, CNN, and, of course, National Petroleum Radio.

NPR broadcast a long interview with Hazen on a program called *Science Friday.* It should be called *Science Payday,* a reliable mattress for corporate rent-a-profs. No researcher with an actual beaker of goo was invited to reply, and BP's funding of Hazen was not mentioned. (Nor was BP's funding of NPR, for that matter.)

From my time in Alaska, I know all about the oil-eating bugs. Two decades ago, Exxon had news crews film the dumping of boatloads of waxy, marble-size miracle germ balls all over the beaches. It didn't work, but by the time the failure was evident—and little Native kids began swallowing the balls—the cameras had long since departed.

Now, without shame, BP and the Interior Department are using this same "Bugs Ate the Oil" stunt in the Gulf. They added a twist. Maybe it didn't work perfectly in cold Alaska, but bacteria just love Mississippi.

This Mississippi island was impressively oiled, but I wasn't impressed. Something was missing.

Habeus corpus picis? Where are the fish corpses, Professor?

In the water, Steiner explained. While we would see a couple of oil-packed fish carcasses on the beach, the big slaughter is actually going on way out there, in the fishing grounds and beyond.

The killer: BP, that is, Bacterial Plumes.

Steiner told me that bacteria were indeed eating up some of the hydrocarbon from the blowout, "but mostly the methane, not the heavy crude." Bacteria certainly munch on some of it (good), which encourages bacteria to make bacterium babies by the trillions (bad). As the bacteria feast, said Steiner, they breathe, as all creatures do. The result: not much oxygen left in the water for fish. The fish can't breathe and they drown.

In the third grade, my science teacher, Mrs. Schneider, told us that oil floats on water. Oil industry scientists have yet to graduate beyond third grade semi-facts. In fact, microscopic droplets stay deep rather than pop to the surface. The plumes of berserk bacteria, tall as the Empire State Building and wide as Manhattan, are creeping around under the surface, a roving fish holocaust.

After BP's thirty-two scientists said they could not find these oil and bacteria plumes, Steiner's submarine arrived. BP wasn't expecting that. He found the killer plumes as distant as three hundred miles from the well head.

* * *

Far down at the island's tip, Ricardo's telephoto lens picked up Black men, about two dozen of them, bobbing up and down, up and down. We waded back to the dinghy, approached, and jumped off once again.

The sun was up and murderous. It didn't burn away my bald scalp only by the grace of the network chief in London who *personally* authorized me to put my hat on my head. (And you thought TV executives had no excuse for their existence.)

We waded in.

The Black men went up and down. Up and down.

It was clear now we'd found a BP clean-up crew. In rhythm, they dipped down to stick their long clean-up tools into the sand and lifted up the stuff to pour into buckets. They inched forward in the vicious sun, shoulder to shoulder. Bend, shovel, lift; bend, shovel, lift.

At any minute, I expected them to start singing:

"Breaking up tar balls on the chain gang, HA!
Breaking balls and serving my time, YAH!"

Down the shore, we found the work gang's supervisors in the shade of a green tent: three white guys, college age, sitting on folding chairs. BP's young, shaded Caucasians gave us little yellow booties so we could safely walk across the poisonous black tar to observe the African Americans at work.

Alaskan Natives have long ago learned you never handle decaying oil without wearing head-to-toe Hazmat spaceman suits complete with hooded respirators. Here, the African Americans were dressed for picking cotton: shirtless or raggedly covered in the brutal sun. BP didn't allow the yellow safety suits—they looked bad on TV.

Bend, shovel, lift.

The work gang wielded some new piece of equipment I hadn't seen on

the Alaska clean-up. When we reached them, I saw that the specialized instruments were pooper scoopers—the ones you buy at K-Mart to clean out your kitty litter box—duct-taped to broom handles.

I approached one scooper man, who gave his name as Raphael Gill.

How deep can you get with that "equipment"?

"A *quarter* inch. They want you to do it like this. Skim the top."* Gill and his coworker showed me the required dainty skimming move. Meanwhile, Steiner walked down, out of the sight of the laid-back supervisors, motioned me over, took out a utility knife, and dug maybe eight inches before he hit a layer of oozing crude. This ooze layer runs, Steiner said, "for about six hundred miles." That's the official underestimate.

Gill said, "The deeper you dig, the more you find." But he didn't dare dig. They catch you digging, he said, and you lose your job. And there are no other jobs.

"They *really* don't want you digging."

They don't? OK, Steiner, if they're not digging out the oil, then what exactly is the pooper scooper crew *doing?*

"The term," said the professor, "'is Clean-up Theater.'" Politicians and news crews fly over or float by on BP media tours and it looks pretty impressive.

The BP crew had completed about two hundred yards of beach. The island is four miles long. They had been skimming that same two hundred yards for "a week or so," said the overseers in the tent. "A month or so," said Gill. Every storm repaved the two hundred yards, so they had to start again.

Two hundred yards a month. Let's do the math. Six hundred miles of crud carpet all the way to Steinhatchee, Florida. That's 3.168 million feet at 600 feet (200 yards) per month or task completed in September 2450, that is, in a little over four centuries. By that time, BP biotechnicians will have created life forms that enjoy tanning on crude-smeared beaches.

Bend, skim, lift. Bend, skim, lift.

In the 147 years since the Emancipation Proclamation, Mississippi's population of color has gone from picking cotton balls to picking tar balls.

Observing this scene, I knew my old science teacher, Dr. Bruce, with his honey-dipping expertise, would have been here on the line if he hadn't somehow emancipated himself.

---

* To see Mr. Gill do the bend-shovel-lift and the author playing with tar balls, click on the photo (if you have the enhanced edition) or go to GregPalast.com/VulturesPicnic.

BP had learned much from the Exxon spill twenty years earlier. What they learned was that you don't have to pay $26 an hour as they had done in Alaska. These men got $14.

For $14 an hour, they were instructed not to talk, not even to each other. But Gill gave me the lowdown anyway, while never ceasing to bend-skim-lift. He would not give the straw bosses any excuse to dismiss him.

"I don't care if they fire me for telling the truth, because I want to work seven days and they won't let me. I lost everything due to the oil spill."

He used to work in a casino, but he was laid off when Coast tourism drowned in BP's oil. For Gill, that was blow #2, after Katrina.

"I ain't got no way to be here no more. No car, they don't want to pay me, help me get no car. I don't know what to do. I give up. That's what's brought me out here. I got my bread and my bologna in the refrigerator. That's it. A couple of hot dogs."

And what about your kids? He said he has three.

"Well, they—I don't eat sometimes. It's all right."

President Obama offered to provide unemployment compensation to Mississippi, completely funded by the Federal Treasury. But Republican Governor Haley Barbour turned it down, as did the Governor of Louisiana, Bobby Jindal. They wanted to show off their anti-Obama macho to fellow Republicans.

Why are there only baloney-sandwich jobs here, craps tables or pooper scooping? Decades ago, when I was here on a murder-and-accounting investigation, Gill's choices would not have been so limited. The Gulf Coast from Louisiana to Biloxi had been a strip of commercial fishermen's sheds, busted docks, really bad housing, really bad deep-fried food served in newspapers from shacks, dis-repaired A.M.E. churches, and Waffle Houses. The beachfront, such as it was, was home to the typical citizens thrown off the good Delta farmland: Black folk, Cajuns, and what genteel members of Mississippi society called "White Trash." But the trash—white, Black, French—at least had their homes, their little boats and little shops. They had *something*.

Then, in 2005, giant casinos fell on their houses and crushed them. Really. Let me explain: Mississippi, a very pious Christian state, did not allow gambling. But it did allow casinos, as long as they were not actually on Mississippi land proper, but offshore, floating in the Gulf on large pontoons.

In 2005, Hurricane Katrina lifted up these huge floating hotel-casino hulks and threw them right on top of the fried chicken shacks, boat sheds, homes, and churches of the locals.

The religious people of Mississippi called it an Act of God. God clearly wanted casinos, not homes and churches, on the beachfront, which was now prime real estate, and henceforward, Mississippi allowed casinos on dry land. Governor Barbour obtained over half a billion dollars in federal hurricane recovery aid to repair the damage to homes and shops. Somehow, the money ended up rebuilding the casino hotels on the plots of the little homes that were smashed or washed away.

The Coast's flooded-out poor were exiled, joining the ranks of America's Katrina refugees, dispersed to Texas and Florida. The few that remained were put to work manning the craps tables, parking the cars, wearing the g-strings, and guarding the slot machines in the new Green Felt Plantations.

Five years later, when the well blew, the beaches in front of these casinos were put at the top of BP's list for clean-up. The skim job looks good, but you wouldn't want to swim in the water. That doesn't matter: There is no such thing as a gambler who swims, and their bored wives tan by the pool.

The thirty Waffle Houses strung out along the coast, built of brick and stout as military pillboxes, stood their ground through the hurricane. As a result, Biloxi is today a gleaming city of mostly-empty twenty-story gambling cathedrals separated by Waffle Houses. In the one next to the Hyatt, I met the Pink Poodle waitress. She dyes her hair pink and curls it to look like a toy poodle. She told me she's worked the Waffle for thirty years. Best job in town, she told me.

I believe it.

*   *   *

There are damn good reasons why BP grabbed science by the balls and kept independent experts like Steiner off this beach, barred from the crime scene.

After the *Exxon Valdez* crack-up, the government put professor Steiner and a bunch of other PhDs on a team to investigate the oil's harm to Alaska's ecosystem. Their research put a harpoon through the oil companies' nonsense excuses and tiny hearts. It cost the BP-Alyeska consortium plenty for the safety upgrades on the Alaska tanker route Steiner's team recommended: double hulls, escorts, all that. In other words, Science was not Big Oil's buddy, that is, untamed science was not.

In the 1989 Exxon case, the government chose the scientists for the official investigation. This time, the feds allowed BP to choose half the experts to investigate the company. "That's like the Mafia having half the seats on the FBI directorate," Dr. Steiner said.

Before sundown, he sped us back to the casino dock so he could grab a plane home to Anchorage, I assumed so he could start the semester at the University of Alaska.

I assumed wrong. I asked when classes start. He said, "I'm not teaching anymore. I was fired."

What?

Steiner had taught there for *three decades*. He had *tenure*. He is an international star. How do you fire a tenured professor? Was he caught with an undergraduate under the Bunsen burners?

Worse. He testified before Congress against offshore drilling. He told the Congressmen not to trust BP. Nor Shell nor Chevron nor Exxon.

He shouldn't have done that. An internal memorandum revealed that George Bush's Commerce Department displayed displeasure with the professor's foolish act of reckless honesty. The university charged Steiner with unacademic "advocacy" for using the words *tragedy* and *disaster* to describe the tragic *Exxon Valdez* disaster.

The politicians thought up a way to get rid of Steiner: You can't fire a tenured professor, but you don't have to *pay* him. The feds cut off his funding, the university just smiled, and Steiner and his sample bags were forced out on the street.

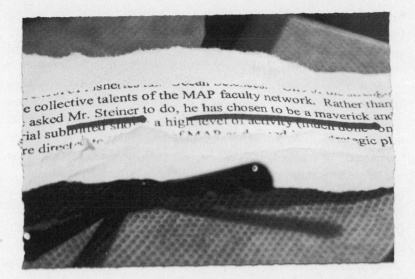

"Rather than working within this [Administration's] network as I have asked Mr. Steiner to do, he has chosen to be a maverick."

There was no appeal to Alaska's Governor over the issue of the sanctity of independent scientific thought at the state university. Why? Because Governor Sarah Palin knew that Steiner was going to Hell. Palin, a fundamentalist Christian, insists that the Earth was created five thousand years ago, and anyone who doesn't say so is going to burn for Eternity.

Furthermore, the idea of "extinction of species" just doesn't go with God having created all the animals on the Fifth Day of the Creation Week, that is, a Thursday. Only God can snuff his own stuff.

For Palin and the creationists, "environmentalism" and "Satanism" are only seven letters apart.* The Earth, in Palin World, is a disposable model. At five thousand years old, it's practically brand new and can be remade from scratch (or Chaos) in just six days. And furthermore, the Earth and all its creatures are going to be wiped out anyway in the Apocalypse, which is right around the corner, well before the 2050 global warming doomsday date. The

* Remove Satanism from Environmentalism and you get an anagram of "evil ore." But you knew that.

Apocalypse is followed by the Rapture, when antiabortion Republicans will rise into the Lord's heavenly hotel-casino in the sky.

But the Lord was not made wroth by Steiner; rather, the professor had pissed off Shell and BP and so Governor Palin.

Steiner noted, "Alaska politicians can't get elected unless they swear they drink a cup of crude oil each morning with breakfast." A month after Steiner was fired, Palin guzzled petroleum on the floor of the Republican Convention, where she accepted the party's nomination for Vice President. The party faithful chanted, "Drill, Baby, Drill!" Palin promised that, if elected, she'd let Exxon and BP and Shell punch more holes in Alaska and the Gulf of Mexico.

Sarah says she's a Christian, but she practices Saks Fifth Avenue, and that ain't cheap. The Governor and her hubby, Todd, and the rest of the Wasilla Hillbillies went to town at Saks on a GOP credit card when she grabbed those Jimmy Choo knee-high "Hallie" boots with the four-inch heels *to die for:* $1,195. The credit card bill was paid for by GOP donors. The party's new #1 corporate donor is Koch Industries, which recently joined BP's Alyeska consortium. Now as well shod as a thoroughbred, Palin ran her race as Big Oil's Drill Babe.

Dr. Steiner once had a second career for income. In Alaska, herring has always been more valuable than education, so the biologist and some friends bought a commercial fishing boat for $370,000. It was 1988, a year before the *Exxon Valdez* hit the reef. Since then, for two decades now, no one has caught a herring in Prince William Sound. Steiner's partnership went belly-up with the fish.

So there I am on the filthy Mississippi beach with the fired professor and failed fisherman, who dresses like an Eddie Bauer catalogue fell on his head (wearing steel-toe Gortex-lined Vibram-soled Timberland boots). Steiner was doomed. In this world *and* the next.

But the professor went down knowing this: He was right. When he warned against BP drilling Alaska's Arctic and the Gulf of Mexico, he was a damned prophet. And because he was right, they hated him even more.

I like Steiner and assured him I'd be honored to keep him company in Hell. And besides, since Palin's going to Heaven, I'd rather not.

* * *

Nota Bene. No, I'm not a shoe fetishist, I'm a journalist. A reporter has to get behind the mask. You can put on a phony smile, but you can't put on phony shoes. Nevertheless, there's a limit to this line of investigation. Right now, Bad-penny's steaming.

"*I'M DONE. I'M DONE WITH THIS STUFF. I will* not *look at another fucking pair of Versace fucking buckle-toe pumps!*" ($750, Neiman Marcus). She's only eight feet away, but she's sent an email: "THIS WHOLE THING IS SHITE! A VERY DESPERATE WAY OF BRINGING SARAH PALIN INTO IT."

Desperate, yes. But I'm a desperate man. These are desperate times. "Shite"? She's writing in her British accent. Not a good sign.

WASHINGTON, DC

Meanwhile the media was all a-twitter with news that the Gulf would be saved by JFK himself, or at least the man who played him in the movies, Kevin Costner.

Costner had ridden on the *Exxon Valdez* (in the movie *Waterworld* at least) and could clean the Gulf, no problem.

Some sharpies had convinced the aging actor, then sliding from A-list to B, to invest $20 million in perfecting a canister, kind of like one of those Orec vacuum cleaners they sell on late-night TV, but bigger, that could suck up 210,000 gallons of oil-polluted water a day and spit it back out clean. Wow!

Congressmen held hearings, fawning on the celebrity; news reporters, looking for something sexier than an oily pelican, scooped it up.

OK, let's do the math. If the Costner machine scrubs 210,000 gallons of water a day, that's 16,000 cubic feet of H_2O (one cubic mile) of polluted water in 9,120 days. That would mean a Costner machine would have the job done in slightly less than 25,000 years.

Nevertheless, BP and Big Oil *loved* it. If the public could be convinced that oil spills could go away with an abracadabra Costner machine, so much the better for the oil industry's offshore drilling plans. Well, no one ever went broke underestimating the mathematical skills of the American public.

BP bought thirty-two Costner sucking machines. By using several at once, BP cut the time needed to clean-up the Gulf to less than eight centuries.

WAFFLE HOUSE, GULFPORT, MISSISSIPPI

I looked at BP's oil slathered across the shoreline and I thought about my favorite secret beach on St. George's Island, and the Flora-Bama Bar and Grill on the state line. The Flora-Bama had an enormous sign on the roof, big as the building under it: BREAKFAST 6AM BEER BISCUITS AND GRAVY. They serve that fine fare, which looks something like a big blob of mucous, to the seine-net fishermen who want to get a little buzz on before heading out. The evening special at the Flora-Bama was always deep-fried grouper throat.

After the oil spill, this Southern-fried culture, at least as they've known it, will be no more. Of course, a case could be made that that wouldn't be so bad. I looked it up: One-third of Deep South adults are obese. Well, a third of New Yorkers are in therapy. How do you choose?

Ricardo and I scored plush digs cheap in a nearly deserted casino hotel, and after midnight, Rick left his camera and decided to try his luck at black jack. He went alone: I have no luck to try. Later, Rick told me he played a hand sitting next to a young guy in a little vinyl vest, black shirt, and clip-on tie, one of the crew who parks cars. The parking lot kid was burning up his break-time losing the tips he'd earned since his previous break.

Ricardo folded and left. He looked at the parking lot guy and couldn't imagine anything more tragic, that is, more tragic than leaving your camera up in the room when you have a chance to film pure heartbreak.

I went to see Poodle Lady.

* * *

It's late. Poodle Lady pours me cup number four. If Matty Pass were here, he would order the pecan waffles, the vegan freak. I like these Waffle House mugs. Poodle tells me to just take one with me when I go out for a "smoke" and don't bring it back in. Poodle knows I'll leave a big tip.

As I sat there working on my coffee, I laid out the facts: The Delta coastline is poisoned and dying and BP is to blame.

Everyone knows that. Everyone can *see* that, right on TV. Here are the bodies—the Gulf Coast, the fisheries, the wetlands—and right there was the smoking, *exploding* gun, BP's Deepwater Horizon platform.

Two hundred news crews have come ashore at Grande Isle, Louisiana, and filmed the black greasy crud slathered along the beachfront and the stinky gunk infiltrating the swamplands that barfed out of BP's Macondo well. They filed stories about the precious Coast, its wetlands filled with pelicans and Cajuns, smeared and wounded by BP's runaway well.

But I had a problem with this. Any time NPR and *The Washington Post* agree, I figure it can't be true. Everyone goes along with the official story. BP, those Brit bastards, assassinated the Gulf Coast: It was the "lone gunman, single-bullet theory" everyone accepted. I didn't buy it, but my only evidence was my memory. And what I remembered was this: Grande Isle was *always* a shit-hole.

I know. I was there long before BP's oil sludged up. Twenty-five years ago, while on another nasty investigation for the city of New Orleans, I'd taken my wife for a weekend down here to the Coon-Ass Riviera, what Cajun locals call this Gulf Coast shoreline at the end of the Delta.

For twenty dollars to a guy who spoke an English I couldn't understand, I rented this old whitewashed bungalow between the beach and a bayou. It stank of cockroach powder and mildew. It was night already. I don't know why, but in the quiet, in the flare light, I was suddenly, violently happy. I even wanted to make love to my wife. But for her, the idea of placing naked skin against dank, yellowed sheets gave her the creeps. She passed out exhausted, fully clothed.

I took a walk on the beach, which was a litter heap of empty lubricant containers, with weird brown foam at the water's edge. On the horizon, the flames of the derricks flared gas, burning like candles on a birthday cake in Hell.

And I loved it.

"Oil is a wild animal," one of my law professors taught us, which no border nor property line nor corporate logo can contain. And that night, under the Creole moon, dark enough to hide the flotsam and garbage, I thought about a civilization that took thousands of years to advance from hunting wild animals to hunting wild black tar. The liquid beast was certainly more ferocious, and here, on Grande Isle, the beast would, at predictable intervals, go mad.

* * *

The official story didn't add up. When the *Exxon Valdez* struck Bligh Reef, everyone blamed Exxon, while the real culprit, BP, skulked away without a scratch. And here we go again. Now was it BP's turn to take the rap for a crime they didn't commit? Who would tell me the facts, with no BS?

The file cabinet in my head opened to a confidential memo from my Hurricane Katrina investigation:

"Where is the cyanide pill?"

The cyanide was meant—jokingly, I assume—for the man known as "Professor Hurricane." There's no question, some powerful gentlemen had to make Professor Hurricane go silent, somehow.

Years back, Professor Ivor "Hurricane" van Heerden of Louisiana State University, like Steiner, staked everything on the truth—and lost. In America, losers are suspect. Government, industry guys, environmentalists, everyone told me to stay clear; so I figured I better get to him right away before he sailed away, literally.

A guy who would rather eat cyanide than bullshit: I figured that made him an expert I could trust not to jerk me around on a tough question: *Did BP do it?*

1,500 FEET ABOVE THE MISSISSIPPI DELTA

I found Professor Hurricane working down in the Delta. We scooped him up from the airstrip at Houma, the dirty navel of Louisiana oil country.

Ricardo asked to have the Cessna's doors removed. The pilot said no. I liked that pilot.

I had told Rick to get some cool film while flying over the oil damage.

We didn't see any. From the moment we lifted off toward the rising sun, we saw only gorgeous nature all the way to the horizon, stunning tufts of green isles carved by canals and veined by bayous, a water wonderland.

Damn. We needed film of *ugly*. I shouted and mimed, frustrated, "SO WHERE'S THE DAMAGE??"

If ignorance is bliss, I must surely have been the happiest man in the air that morning. By cranking up the volume on my noise-enhancing headset to high-pain level, I was able to get an education from Professor van Heerden over the engine's grind.

Damage? I was looking at it.

Until a few decades ago, this was one of the great cattle ranching areas of America, the Coastal Prairie, where cowboys never heard a discouraging word. "Fifty years ago, the wetlands would have just been a blanket. In fact, they called them prairie marshes because they looked like prairie. You know, they grazed cattle on them."

Then, bad luck, oil was discovered just about anywhere in the prairie where you could punch a hole. And they punched lots of holes. The cheapest way to get out the oil was to drag drilling rigs through the natural bayous, then cut huge gashes into the grassland, which floats on a soft delta substrate. Unlike the Rockies, where you can see the ugly scars of big equipment, the rig trails in Louisiana simply filled with seawater from the Gulf. That salty water increased the grass kill.

It's very pretty.

To get the black gold up to the Exxon refinery at Baton Rouge and else-where, the crude and gas had to be sucked out with 10,000 miles of pipes. And then barge-ways. "This beautiful carpet, we starved it to death, and then we cut it up; we dissected it with ten thousand miles of canals."

Each mile of canal and pipe was a slice out of the land. And so the prairie swooned and sank from a million cuts and turned into swampland ("wet-lands" if you're a member of the Sierra Club). At least shrimp moved in—they'll eat anything—and 'gaters and trash fish.

But they're going now too, and fast. The saltwater tides chew up the remaining land and the Gulf of Mexico marches *a quarter mile a year* toward New Orleans. Louisiana is simply vanishing, five hundred square acres a *week*. And so shrimping and fishing are sinking to their doom as well. After Hurri-cane Katrina, the rest of America was wondering why the dumb-ass folk in New Orleans built a city below sea level so close to the sea. Well, when the city was founded, it wasn't anywhere close to the Gulf.

Sucking the oil out from under the soft land also speeds the sinking. And so the Gulf creeps to New Orleans.

But sometimes it sprints. Cypress groves, now poisoned by salt, gutted by canals, once provided an impenetrable mat of natural nails too painful for any hurricane surge to cross. "A cypress grove can reduce the surge by six feet within a mile." Now the cypress are nearly gone, an open invitation to New Orleans for any mean-minded storm. That's Ecology Rule #1: When you shit all over Mother Nature, She shits it back on you.

So what I was admiring was, in fact, a poisoned, diseased, dying land. I was enjoying the beauty of the scars of chronic leprosy. What looked like a natural Venice was just the intermediary illness on a land that will soon drown and disappear into the sea. All for its oil.

"The slicing up and the exploration and mining of oil and gas has created most of the wetland loss," Dr. van Heerden told me. They'd ripped up and lost twenty-five miles of wetlands.

Well, one man's catastrophe is another man's profit center. We flew over former ranch-hands' bunkhouses converted by the oil industry into mid-water accommodations for rig workers.

Then the professor wanted to show me the *bad* news. The pilot assumed we wanted to get a fly-over shot of the BP Macondo well, gravesite of the Deep-water Horizon. CNN flew out there and back. Everybody did.

I gave the pilot a thumbs-down. At the professor's request, the pilot turned hard east and dropped us down to three hundred feet. We buzzed the tops of the jack-up rigs and their burn-off flares and skimmed by a platform surrounded by that telltale bloom of shine: an oil leak that no U.S. network would bother showing you, right in the heart of the Delta land.

It was everywhere, sheen and chocolate liquid glopping out near the white markers where over three thousand wells have been abandoned. BP safely capped six hundred of them, at least so they claim, but the hydrocarbons found floating now in the most sensitive areas don't have a Deepwater Horizon chemical tag. Shell and Chevron abandoned even more than BP. The worst leakers were wells of unknown ownership or owners dead, lost, forgotten, van Heerden told me. Years ago, they had sold their crude to Standard Oil, now Exxon, but Exxon washes its hands of responsibility for the leftover flow of toxins.

The smoking gun is oil, all right. Oil is murdering the Gulf Coast, but it's an inside job: wells and pipes and canals and the killer poisons and slashing the cypress and the crap these guys dump straight off the rigs. When drilling and pumping is done, they sink the greasy platforms (they call it a "redneck reef") or just leave them there to defecate from inside the Delta itself.

So *who done it*? The killers have their fingerprints all over the state's records. The number of wetlands acres simply removed by each company:

ConocoPhillips	3.3 million acres
ChevronTexaco	2.7 million
ExxonMobil	2.1 million
Shell Oil	1.3 million

And what about Big Bad BP? A meager 234,000 acres, 0.2 million, a number so low it nearly qualifies for Sierra Club membership.

These numbers are crazy sick, yet this is only the acreage of wetlands *removed with the permission of the state.* The narrow cuts authorized by an oil-maddened bureaucracy become, as the tides gouge through them, wide scars. Eventually, the skinny bits of remaining land give up and give in to the sea.

Bottom line, Professor?

"Well, the total land loss in Louisiana averages twenty-five thousand acres a year."

If, like me, you don't own a farm, 25,000 acres translates into *40 square miles* of Louisiana disappearing each year. And the BP spill? "We ended up with oil on about five hundred fifty acres of marsh."

Cold calc: If you measure disaster by the death of Delta wetland, there's a Deepwater Horizon *every week.* But it's not on TV. It's just not photogenic.

Compared to this wetlands kill rate, the bit of oil that floated in from BP's deepwater eruption is a cold sore on a cancer, "mostly caught safely by the coastal reeds," van Heerden says.

BP is *innocent?* I'm not up to this. The London piggies who killed the coast of Alaska then skulked away Scot-free are now taking the blame, throwing their executives into volcanoes, writing checks to Governor Jindal, and confessing to a crime *they didn't commit*? The petroleum chessboard, rotating in seven dimensions now, is getting curioser and curioser. And van Heerden's tour had barely begun.

Now, from the air, we could see big-ass dredgers. They looked like those humongous Ewok war machines from Star Wars. They were piling up sand into what looked like the world's biggest kitty litter box. It was, kind of.

The Professor pointed to the growing pile of sand and shouted over the engine, "A BERM," whatever that is.

The Ewoks had scooped up a million or so tons of Delta bottom and made a big pile.

The pile, the "berm," was already forty miles long, van Heerden shouted. It would capture the BP oil floating into the wetlands.

I'm thinking, *No it won't.*

"IT CAN'T. CAN'T PICK UP OIL," said van Heerden.

Sand? Walls in the water made of sand?

"IT'S DESIGNED TO WASH AWAY."

"???"

Cost?

"THREE HUNDRED SIXTY MILLION."

Shaw? It's Shaw?

"YOU'LL HAVE TO LOOK UP THE CONTRACT."

No, I didn't. It was the Shaw Group. Had to be. But van Heerden would not repeat the name. It would be like a Harry Potter character shouting "Voldemort."

Apt comparison. While there were better-known bastards in the heavy construction business—Bechtel, Halliburton, for example—Shaw Group was heavy metal's Dark Lord, deep in the shadows.

Sometimes a flicker of light illuminates them. One of their hired Economic Hit Men, after much meditation and mushrooms in the Andes, wrote a *Confession*. Dr. John Perkins spilled his soul about the coup d'états, threats, and high-finance flimflam that made Shaw and partners roll. Perkins, once an economist with Gucci loafers and a briefcase full of numerical bullshit, had been my nemesis. I was the investigating economist for the environmental groups trying to stop his frighteningly incompetent engineering company client from building nuclear plants. I got used to being the bubble gum stuck to the bottom of his loafers.

But since Perkins came out of the cold with his *Confessions of an Economic Hit Man,* he's now my BFF. I am forever grateful he pulled down the pants of Shaw's Stone & Webster unit. This is the company I had the government charge with civil racketeering, the company that lost control of a nuclear reactor project, letting the costs rise 1,000 percent, then covered it up with fraud.

Now, skimming low on the coastline, I was looking down on their parent company's multimillion-dollar sandbox, guaranteed to wash away.

I scribbled: *SANDBOX>SHAW?*

After flying another hour along the coastline, the Professor told the pilot, "Here!" and we turned hard to the north, running straight at New Orleans, entering what looked like a secret shortcut through the Delta to the city, a kind of man-made Mississippi. That's exactly what it was. And van Heerden's career had drowned in it.

Van Heerden's career dive began with something he said in July 2005 on a British television documentary about New Orleans:

"In a month this city could be underwater."

And it was. Thirty days after his warning, every resident was told to get the hell out of the city by car or by pony. At least two thousand left the hard way—floating facedown, a vision that makes me ill and furious to this day.

You'd think the Professor would get a medal for being right, tragically right. But Louisiana burghers thought squirting poison into his cornflakes more fitting.

Van Heerden is not some kind of clairvoyant weirdo. Rather, he was deputy head of the Louisiana State University Hurricane Center, one of America's top experts on hurricanes, a soft-spoken, thoughtful technician who can be a serious pain in the ass. And when he isn't a pain in the ass, he is a serious threat to the Establishment.

Van Heerden not only predicted New Orleans would drown, he could name the guilty party. And it was not Katrina. The hurricane *never touched*

New Orleans: "Katrina swung wide east of the city," van Heerden told me. "Katrina missed the city by thirty-five miles." So don't blame the Lady.

The killer goes by the name of "Mr. Go" and he was right under us as we flew north toward New Orleans.

MR-GO, the Mississippi River-Gulf Outlet, is undoubtedly the most bone-headed, deadly insane project ever built by the Army Corps of Engineers. It is a seventy-six-mile-long canal, straight as a gun barrel, running right up from the Gulf of Mexico to the heart of New Orleans. I've made a little map for you.

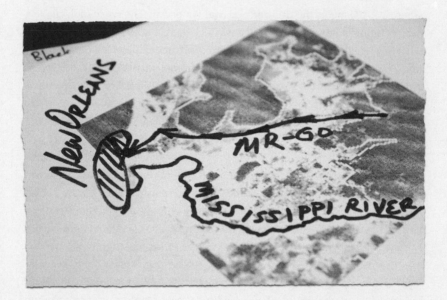

MR-GO was Katrina's welcome mat to the city. Van Heerden calls it "the Hurricane Highway."

Until the Army Corps made this crazy gash in the Mississippi Delta fifty years ago, that green wreath of cypress and mangrove protected New Orleans. MR-GO was designed to allow tankers to avoid the Mississippi's twists and turns and shoot right into New Orleans from the Gulf. It also allowed hurricane waves to shoot in as well.

Van Heerden explained that if the Corps and industry had left a natural cypress barrier of just three miles around the city, the surge caused by Katrina's wind would have gotten lost in the trees, reduced to next to nothing. "Katrina would have been a storm of no note."

New Orleans would have stayed dry and alive.

After flying about fifteen miles up the canal, van Heerden said, "Down there, ahead, that's the government's admission of guilt." It was a gigantic plug that closed up the canal. President Obama had ordered a half million tons of rocks dumped in to prevent another Katrina. It was the government's confession written in stones.

Van Heerden then asked the pilot to make a tight, blood-draining circle where MR-GO meets the Gulf Intracoastal Waterway. The two canals make a perfect funnel pointing to the city. It was sickening, because you can visualize what happened. Two storm surges squeezed into one channel heading straight into New Orleans's Ninth Ward. The two eight-foot surges then became combined into a sixteen-foot wave. The wall of water moved faster than a locomotive. But this time, the tsunami was man-made.

And the federal government, Big Shovel, and Big Oil knew it and knew it before it happened. Van Heerden said his whole department, "the LSU Hurricane Center, had been warning them for a number of years about this Funnel, the Hurricane Highway," the tsunami maker, where MR-GO and the Intracoastal Canal meet, and that the levees were too short to hold it back. "Them" included just about every government agency with a listed phone, from city hall, to the Governor, all the way up to George W. Bush's White House senior staff, whose counsel spoke directly with van Heerden, then ignored him.

The MR-GO slash job on the Delta caused the government's own hydrologists to raise alarms from Day One of construction. One internal Army Corps report I've seen warned of "the possibility of catastrophic damage to urban areas by a hurricane surge coming up this waterway."

However, the Corps' engineers were barred from challenging the Big-Oil/Big-Shovel combine's sales pitch to Congress.

"So, basically, the port industry, oil and gas and the big construction companies, the civil engineering companies that benefit from all of the Corps of Engineers projects," sold MR-GO, van Heerden explained.

But again, Mother Nature took the rap for destroying New Orleans when the real culprit was the surge up MR-GO and the missing marshes. The drowning of New Orleans was not an Act of God. It was an Act of Lobbyists. An Act of Engineering Contractors. An Act of Chevron. An Act of Exxon.

LOWER NINTH WARD, NEW ORLEANS

We landed at a small airfield at the end of the MR-GO gun barrel so van Heerden could show us where the Gulf exploded into the city. The Lower Ninth Ward once had the highest concentration of African-American home owner-ship in the United States. Now it has the highest concentration of African-American-owned rubble.

It has been five years since the flood and it still looks like Berlin 1946. Half the houses gone and half the remainder empty, each with a big X and some code painted on them.

I walked with van Heerden to a vacant house with 1 DEAD DOG spray-painted on it, and next to the X sign, 1 CAT, the number 2, and 9/6 partly covered by a bank's foreclosure sale notice. The Professor broke the code for me. The house contained one dead dog, one live cat, and two corpses.

The 9/6 meant rescuers couldn't get to it for a week, so the bodies must have been quite bloated with gases, floating around the living room on top of the Mississippi water. The couple must have paddled with the family pets until the water pushed them into the ceiling and they suffocated.

Van Heerden had tried to prevent this tragedy. I knew that from my first meeting with van Heerden, at the Hurricane Center in 2006.

It was one year after the hurricane and I was in Baton Rouge, Louisiana's capital, investigating a company, Innovative Emergency Management, which had the contract for planning the evacuation of New Orleans. Some plan. I dropped into Innovative's local headquarters for a copy of it. They said they didn't have the plan. They had a plan, all right: get in your car and drive like hell. But not everybody has a car. But then, Innovative didn't have a lot of experience in emergency evacuation planning. They're experience was in Republican Party funding. They knew it. I knew it. And, rather than explain how they got the contract, they thought it best to try and grab our camera and call in the anti-terrorism police. (Bush had put evacuation planning in the hands of Homeland Security.)

We bolted, jumped into the van Matty Pass had idling in the parking lot, and shot over to LSU to find out what the hell was going on.

Dr. van Heerden, at the time the Hurricane Center's Deputy Director, knocked me over with a revelation. His department, knowing of the goofy IEM plan, developed a real plan for no charge. Bush and the State rejected it.

Good story. But I could see he had something troubling his mind, and I kept filming. Van Heerden showed us on his computer monitor a full-color graphics film re-creating the flood: the levees giving out, 80 percent of the city underwater. Only it wasn't a re-creation: It was designed years *before* Katrina.

(The city's emergency evacuation boss had written across a map of this plan: *KYAGB*—"Kiss Your Ass Good-Bye.")

Hence, the calls with the White House. But the professors, like modern Noahs, were ignored by officialdom, especially because they suggested the oil and gas industry should stop savaging the protective wetlands.

We put the story on air, which did not exactly boost van Heerden's standing with LSU. The university's response to van Heerden's revelations was to take away the professor's computer. Then they took away his chalk, barring him from teaching where he might infect students with curiosity.

When homeless survivors of Katrina sued the Army Corps over MR-GO, van Heerden offered his expert testimony. The university said if he testified, they would fire his ass. He got the info to the lawyers anyway, and in November 2009, Federal Judge Stanwood Duval ruled that the Corps' plugging its ears to the warnings was nothing less than

"negligence, insouciance, myopia and shortsightedness [that] resulted in a catastrophic loss of human life and property in unprecedented proportions."

The judge ordered the federal government to compensate victims and rebuild their homes, mostly just cheap shotgun bungalows.

When the seawalls failed in Westhampton Dunes, Long Island, in 1992, Congress voted for funds to rebuild every destroyed mansion (average value $3.4 million), even going so far as to haul in hundreds of truckloads of sand to make sure the Wall Street debt vultures did not lose a minute of tanning time on their private beaches. But this was the Ninth Ward, New Orleans. Congress would have to authorize payment ordered by the judge. That wasn't about to happen.

New Orleans calls itself "The City That Care Forgot." In fact, it's the city that *everyone* forgot.

Out of Washington came a memo, found in university files, demanding to know why van Heerden's "irresponsible behavior is tolerated." That's when

LSU's Robert Twilley made his little cyanide joke. As an established and well-respected expert in hurricanes, the university couldn't just fire van Heerden. Instead, they pulled a "Steiner" on him: pulled the funding for his post. However, as Professor Twilley wrote, the entire Hurricane Center was a nest of experts run amok. Van Heerden was just one of the "crazies." So they "Steinered" the entire Hurricane Center: They shut it down.

Let me repeat that: Louisiana shut down its hurricane center. After Katrina.

FRENCH QUARTER, NEW ORLEANS

When we got back to our hotel from our grim tour with Professor Hurricane, Ricardo took off for the French Quarter to "vacuum up B-roll." He brought back film of sloshed white girls showing the camera their tits, trannie hookers wobbling on high heels, and some tourists pretending to have a good time covered with Mardi Gras beads though it wasn't Mardi Gras. The whole carnival of American decay on parade.

I didn't need to look at any of it. I stayed back in the room, with my notes to keep me company.

The LSU Hurricane Center had been closed because of "budget constraints." Really? A quick search found that just three months after van Heerden was axed, there was, suddenly, no budget constraint.

The university had received a big check for $300,000, but instead of funding the hurricane center, the money was tagged for a new "Wetlands Center." When I say "big check" I mean that literally; it was one of those big poster checks, huge as a desk, used for newspaper photo ops so the donor gets big publicity.

And here it is:

The guy with the beard, holding the check, is the new center's director, Robert Twilley—Dr. Cyanide. With him is the leader of the civic charity whose name is on the check, an environmental organization, America's Wetland.

Who?

I am a terrible man. I assume that any charity that combines patriotic *America* with green *Wetland* must be a front. But for whom?

America's Wetland promoted "climate sustainability." A quick check revealed its Climate Sustainability Sponsor is Chevron. Its World Sponsor is Shell Oil, and its backers are the American Petroleum Institute, ExxonMobil, BP, and topped, like everything else in Louisiana, by Tabasco Pepper Sauce.

America's Wetland (AW) wouldn't say if it got money from big oil or how much, though Shell wasn't shy, trumpeting its $3 million payment to its front. I noted that, besides oil and hot sauce, America's Wetland had another sponsor, Shaw Construction.

Matty Pass dialed up tax experts who got us AW's Form 990, the government filing required of all registered charities. The $300,000 payment couldn't be identified. Check for yourself.*

Despite the name America's Wetland on the photo-display check, the university had to admit to me that, yes, the money came from Chevron, 100 percent of it. AW was the wet green cover. Three hundred grand from Chevron seems like a nice way for the oil company to say "thank you" to the school for axing van Heerden and friends.

This led me back to my note: *SANDBOX>SHAW?*

The top layer was easy to excavate. Anyone could do it with a pooper scooper: The Big Sandbox was a Bobby Jindal Special. With Anderson Cooper and CNN giving him a soapbox, Governor Jindal stamped and shrieked that the Mississippi Delta needed "protection *right now*"—he held up a vacuum cleaner on CNN, Jindal the Cleaner-Upper—and declared that he was seizing the BP fund for spill victims, and . . .

> . . . dammit, going to build a wall of sand to protect the precious wetland, right now, whatever it takes, whatever it costs. And that I, Bobby Jindal, won't let no goddamn pointy-headed environmentalist bureaucrat from some goddamn paper-shuffling office in Washington and some foot-dragging, prissy metrosexual President Obama tell the good folk of Louisiana to wait on some goddamn "enviry-mental impact statement" by some greenie who wants to have gay marriages in the military, stop me, Governor Bobby Jindal, from saving these Precious Wetlands from the tide of oil threatening our Way of Life.

Or words to that effect.

The rednecks, the tea-baggers, and the screw-them-tree-hugging-bureaucrats-in-Washington crowd and Fox and CNN just *ate it up,* despite the uncomfortable truth on which every expert, bar none, from the Environmental Protection Agency to Greenpeace to the pinhead professors could agree: Jindal was nuts, and his dissolving sandbox was either a hoax or a horror.

What was the Big Sandbox's big oil capture? One thousand barrels. *That's*

---

* For a copy of these documents themselves and my flight over MR-GO with Professor Hurricane, click on the images (in enhanced edition), or go to GregPalast.com/VulturesPicnic/.

it? I pulled out my calculator: 1,000 barrels is 1/5 of 1 percent of 1 percent of 1 percent of the spilled oil. For a third of a billion dollars.

I thought: Jindal's a *genius*. A Hindu who found Jesus in time to run for office. The born-again Republican may sound like Baton Rouge, but there's more Bangalore smarts in that good ol' boy than he'll admit.

Here's a guy who had *zero, nada, no plan at all* to prepare his oil state for a big oil blowout. Compare Jindal's Louisiana to the State of Alaska. Post–*Exxon Valdez,* Alaska forced the oil industry to spend billions on spill response, but Jindal's state, moving more than *ten times* the amount of oil as Alaska, demanded nothing. Still doesn't.

But, with his Big Berm sandbox, Mr. Do Nothing was now Mr. I'm Taking Charge, Mr. Get The Greenies Out Of The Way. And with Anderson Cooper there in the canoe with him, picking up oily birds (I can't make this stuff up), Jindal's national recognition numbers made him a presidential contender.

(How do they do it? The voters must take some responsibility. I pulled out my calculator again, and just as I suspected, if Lincoln had simply let Louisiana and Mississippi secede, America's average IQ would rise by 0.3 percent.*)

But why a sandbox? For $360 million?

The question isn't *why?* but *who?* The Shaw Group was the shovel. It was indeed their Ewoks machines scooping up sand from the Delta bottom and making piles. But we guessed that. And who was the biggest contributor to Jindal's campaign for Governor? Shaw Construction. We could have guessed that, too.

There are lots of other wasteful projects Jindal and Shaw could use to diddle each other. Why this particular goofy boondoggle? Why this bogus affection to save the wetlands that Jindal would happily slash with drilling rigs? Why big berms?

The Answer: America's Wetland. America's Wetland was the lone environmental group in the state to back the berms. Back in New York, Badpenny dug in and found out that America's Wetland had been pushing hard for constructing the great sand pyramids long *before* the spill. In other words, all this crazy spending had nothing—*nothing*—to do with stopping BP's oil from floating into the Delta.Not many environmental groups love big shovels; and, even if they do, they wouldn't have the clout to move the State of Louisiana to

---

* Mississippi has the lowest average Intelligence Quotient in the United States. At 85, way down the Bell curve, no one is close, except Louisiana at 90.

blow a third of a billion on their say-so. Something was missing, and it wasn't the Tabasco Sauce. Yes, oil companies use green beards, but America's Wetland was the key to something bigger. I went back to basics: Don't follow the oil, follow the *money*.

And the money led me to Whitney Bank, the JP Morgan of the Gulf Coast.

Whitney Bank was not a wild guess, because holding up the check with Dr. Cyanide was a fit, tall man of royal bearing, a gray-maned banker from Central Casting, R. King Milling, former President of Whitney Bank.

R. King Milling, Governor of the Atlanta Federal Reserve Bank.

R. King Milling of Milling, Benson and Woodward, the big oil industry law firm founded by R. King's granddaddy in the nineteenth century.

R. King Milling, Chairman of Governor Jindal's Coastal Protection and Restoration Authority. That's the crew that wrote the official demand to President Obama to build the berm.

No surprise it was King Milling: I knew it had to be one really big Fat Cat that needed a third-of-a-billion dollar litter box.

The King and America's Wetland were on a crusade: to have the federal government fix the wounded wetlands, a laudable goal, no?

No. If you burn down my house, and you get caught, you pay. I don't ask the taxpayers to cover your bill. America's Wetland wanted America, not Big Oil, to pay to clean up Big Oil's mess.

The oil industry was in full-on panic mode. The Louisiana Supreme Court, by just one vote, four to three, absolved the oil companies from paying for the damage they had wrought on the wetland. That is pretty thin insurance against a liability of several billion dollars. With the Deepwater Horizon blowout, an angry Louisiana public could easily force amendment of the law.

America's Wetland won't say where it gets its money, but Shell Oil is not so bashful, crowing that it gave this "environmental" group $3 million.

With Shell's $3 million behind it and more, America's Wetland launched an impassioned campaign to have 100 percent of the U.S. taxpayer's share of oil royalties given back to the oil companies or to their contractors—like Shaw—for "restoration" work to save the Delta. Even the government of Azerbaijan wouldn't take that deal, no matter how many shoes you bought Lady Baba.

Big Oil faced new threats after the Deepwater Horizon. Green groups not sponsored by Shell, like the Gulf Restoration Network, called for a moratorium on deepwater drilling and for tighter regulation of the industry, beginning with an end to the oil industry's slash jobs on the coast. To save the wetlands, you could start by not digging out more of it.

But that wouldn't do. According to a powerful defender of the Gulf industry called America's Energy Coast (whose Chairman is R. King Milling), all these regulations are simply strangling the economy of the Gulf and the United States of America.

Milling's Wetland group agrees with Milling's Energy group. Rather than regulate industry, Milling's "environmental" groups call on government to "unlock barriers to increasing the resilience of industry e.g., electric utility and oil and gas sectors."

And Milling's bank agrees. Whitney Bank had been chewing its corporate fingernails down to the cuticles over new drilling regulations that threaten its core business. And Eddie the Eagle agrees with Milling's bank. Eddie is the cartoon and comic book character America's Wetland created for schoolkids (through a generous gift from Chevron).

Besides, how do we know that the oil companies caused the damage to the wetlands? Anyone with eyes could see that the guilty party is that destructive she-wolf, Mother Nature.

That is, anyone with eyes watching television. The local tube was blanketed by ads from what is easily the most powerful civic organization in the state, Women of the Storm, formed immediately after New Orleans drowned.

These were not women *in* the storm; rather, Women of the Storm is comprised of that circle of genteel rich white ladies who, after the flood, came out of their plantation houses to wipe the brows of the fleeing Black folk. The Women got awards and praise from Congress but never spent a night sleeping in a FEMA trailer.

Am I being unnecessarily nasty about ladies doing their best to be helpful? Maybe it's because *Stephen* of the Storm never got his award from Congress. Stephen Smith, a young Black man I met, can't swim, but he paddled a floating mattress from attic window to attic window and pulled half a dozen people to safety. He then brought them to a bridge on Highway 10 and watched helicopters pass over for four days. An elderly man with him, who'd given his last bottle of fresh water to his grandkids, died of dehydration, waiting. Stephen closed the lids on the eyes of the corpse. After they were finally picked up, Stephen was herded onto a bus, driven hundreds of miles to an unknown destination, and dumped off. It was Houston. His kids were bused to Baton

Rouge. The French Quarter Marriott Hotel fired him and he remains in Texas, working for minimum wage, unable to afford to bring over his family.

But I digress.

The Women of the Storm ran these slick, slick, slick ads. I want you to take a look at one.

It opens with Mother Nature, that harpy, ripping up the coastline. The winds howl. The trees bend and waves crash while a voice tells us, "Crippling storms . . . hurricanes . . ."

The ad continues: These storms and hurricanes are not threatening birds or fish but . . . *"our energy security."* It's that beast Nature against the defenseless . . . oil industry. An odd message for a charity. But it's done so slickly, you really have to watch twice, and slowly, to know you've been greased. The actress Sandra Bullock even lent her voice to one.

The Nature-did-this-to-us campaign has expanded. Women of the Storm boasts a new deal that will put its "public service announcements" on over six thousand movie screens.

The women storm troopers are calling for 80 percent of the fines levied against BP to go to "restoration."

This was easily a million-dollar campaign. But who could afford to pay for these spots?

The trail of clues led, not to BP London, as I expected, but to this penthouse office atop the Whitney Bank building on Poydras Street in New Orleans.

I could see the web, I could see the spider. What Creole conjury gave R. King Milling eight long legs?

I puzzled this through as Ricardo and I kicked along the riverbank, trying to decipher the vibrations of *gris-gris,* the amulets of dove's blood and sap used here by those with a grudge and an enemy. And everyone has a grudge and at least one enemy.

My cell rang and I assumed it was Badpenny, hoping she had found a way to get us in to the Poydras penthouse. But the voice on the line had a chocolaty Ninth Ward drawl.

"Palast, now listen. This is everything you need to know about King Milling. *Milling is the Rex.*"

CAFÉ DU MONDE, ON THE MISSISSIPPI

I've worked investigations in New Orleans for two decades and still can't break the code. But for the price of a chicory coffee and beignet smothered in powdered sugar, I could always get no-shit guidance from the poet, trial lawyer, and one-time city councilman Brod Bagert. There isn't anybody from the Quarter to Bayou LaFourche who doesn't know the Bullfrog of the Café Du Monde.

Here's some background:

The fall of the Confederacy in 1865 spawned the rise of the Mystical Order of the Knights of the Ku Klux Klan, whose white-sheeted pogroms against the freed Black population effectively undid their emancipation and restored the Old Order. In Louisiana, the target was Catholics, the "French."

So, the elite of New Orleans, including the Frenchmen, had to create their own orders. By 1872, the secret societies, the Mystick Krewes of Comus and Rex, begun before the Civil War, took on a new mandate: to designate the exclusive rulership of the city and name its King.

For more than a century, membership has remained secret, kept behind masks during Mardi Gras, except for the Rex of the Rex, the King of Carnival, who is announced and, arriving by riverboat, given the key to the city by the

Mayor. In 1993, crown and key were given to R. King Milling. His wife's brother was named the other honored Rex, of Krewe Comus.

Tourists are charmed by the Rex floats, gawk at the Krewe's exclusive masked ball attended in Louis XIV costumery and at the truly royal robes and jewels of King and his debutante Queen. What outsiders cannot see is that the naming of the Rex is a deadly serious ritual here. It acknowledges an authority that reaches quietly and deeply into Louisiana society.

"So Mrs. Milling is Queen *and* Queen-in-Law?"

"King's wife, Anne, is the most important female in New Orleans society, founder of Women of the Storm."

No businessman, no financier, no priest, and certainly no politician would cross a couple so crowned.

WHITNEY BANK BUILDING, TOP FLOOR

King Milling has a conference table longer than my kitchen and red Honda combined. Imagine a mahogany runway for a small plane in a banqueting room of dark-stained hardwood, with cathedral windows high overhead, sparing Milling the views of the ruins of the drowned city.

I grabbed a rich, deep leather chair, much like the one Les Abrahams set himself into at the Oriental Club. I could barely believe I was asking royalty,

King Rex Milling, if he could pour me a coffee. Milling could not believe it either.

Not that many Americans know me, but he knew exactly. He is paid to know. And I enjoyed his terse look toward the nitwit PR flak who was bamboozled into granting me the interview.

(*"Good work, Penny!"* James gushed. Her poshest English accent "from London" had pulled off this bank job, plus an oily note from Matty Pass, who kept my name out of it.)

The Rex went to work. Unrequested, Milling launched into the much-practiced Terrible Tale of the Disappearing Delta. It dazzled. The King on his float, but instead of Rex's coveted gold doubloons he tosses on Fat Tuesday, he threw me coins of wisdom, poetry, and fact—he tossed "45 percent of the nation's saltwater marsh . . . the lineal land on which we live . . . engineering failure . . . Katrina . . ." And Mother Nature, heartless, unrelenting, insatiably devouring the Delta, "continues to subside under its own weight."

Then to the finale line: ". . . 90 percent of the offshore production to this country. Period."

I asked, "So how much of the damage is attributable to the oil companies?" Milling stopped. I felt as if I'd just farted at a debutante ball.

He recovered and called on Science.

"Scientists that I've talked to . . . and these are the ones that the state is using and that we've brought in from all over the country . . . they believe that root causes of this issue is this, is this *river. And but for that river we cannot fix it."*

Aha! It's Old Man River done it.

But why did he have to bring in scientists for the State of Louisiana when Louisiana State University has the most renowned experts in the field?

"Nobody," he averred, "can sit down and figure out who did what to whom."

Oh, but they have.

I did not think it polite to mention the U.S. Geological Survey's official *Process Classification of Coastal Landloss in the Mississippi Delta* had, in fact, made that calculation. If you're curious: oil and gas drilling, 36.06 percent of the loss; with related infrastructure and industry, 70.74 percent. Old Man River's water-logging and waves responsible for 29.26 percent.

How about the calculations of Dr. van Heerden, Mr. Milling?

A smile. "I know Ivor very well!"

But then a sorrowful look. "I'm not sure what his science position is. . . ." (He's been fired. It's in the papers.)

And, Milling helpfully cautioned me, "Quite frankly, you'd have to go check what his credentials are."

Then, I felt compelled to ask, *"Should the oil industry repair the damage they created?"*

The King was stunned by the idea, as if he'd never heard such a thought. "I know no reason to make them do it."

Who then, how then, stop the wounds that are chopping up the Delta and dumping it into the sea?

Here's where the genius of America's Wetland, of America's Energy Coast, of Eddie the Eagle, of King Milling and the several shapes into which he transmigrifies shone from his throne: We're all to blame! We *have all sinned.* Chevron bulldozers, true, but *fishing boats* create damage when they float through the canals.

> "We know that every fishing lugger and every dock and every boat that goes through this causes a degree of deterioration."

Those damn shrimpers.

Now his Southern drawl crescendoed:

> "It's a HOLISTIC issue. You have to have EVERYBODY AT THE TABLE because EVERYBODY is going to [be] impacted and EVERYBODY'S going to lose everything if we don't GET THEM ALL AT THE TABLE to try to SOLVE THE PROBLEM. The 501(c)3s [charities, like Women of the Storm], and the ENVIRONMENTAL GROUPS like the Environmental Defense Fund, Nature Conservancy . . ."

Oil companies should not pay for damage?

> "Talk to the Environmental Defense Fund. Talk to all the ones that we participate with. They're all with us!"

Togetherness was what it was all about. His heart was in ending conflict and putting our shoulders to the wheel and pulling together and getting beyond the blame and all that. His groups had been formed at the Governor's request. The oil-state senators were at the table too. "All the environmentalists" in the room with industry and government focused on the Common Goal, saving ourselves, our children, from the loss of our Precious Wetland.

Of course the Environmental Defense Fund and the Nature Conservancy bellied up to Milling's table, with their spoons out. Those two understand the value of cooperation. They even kept mattresses tied to their backs so their industry "partners" can take their pleasure wherever and whenever needed.

Milling takes no chances. He spent a pile on focus groups around the country to choose the exact phrases that would resonate, that would sell. *Swamp* and *Cajun* are out. So is *oil*. Toxic oil became think-positive *"energy!"*

And inhibiting words—like *regulation* or *rules* or *fines* or *limits*—were banned from the vocabulary.

At the core of this apotheosis: the carefully constructed Myth of Milling. The banker who became crusader for the environment! Even that Yankee liberal PBS-er Bill Moyers gave Milling a gushing profile. The new progressive businessman! *The Times-Picayune* awarded King the city's "Loving Cup."

Love is everywhere.

Shell and King's client Chevron have come into the tent and found green religion. And they tithe.

It's all about *solutions,* about *saving our Energy Coast.* BP painted its stations green, but Milling went further, turning Chevron, with *voodoo and gris-gris,* into a crusader for the environment! The Sustainable Climate Sponsor.

Everyone was at the table. *Milling's* table.

The man is the maestro. He has figured out how to completely control the terms of the debate.

What do "scientists" think? Ask Milling's scientists. Ask Dr. Cyanide at his Wetland Center.

Government? Ask Milling, Chairman of the Coastal Protection and Restoration Authority.

Business? Ask Milling of America's Energy Coast.

Finance and insurance, New Orleans society? All at Milling's table.

Anyone not on the America's Wetland/Women of the Storm/Energy Coast/Coastal Protection and Restoration Authority/Federal Reserve Board team is simply out of the picture. Disappeared. All the oxygen has been sucked out of the water; there is no room left in the debate. The debate is over. The forty-six groups affiliated with the Gulf Action Network, from Greenpeace to

Sierra Club, well, they get no press, no loving cup, no door to policymakers, no government appointments or professorships—they are fish drowned in water. The residents in the FEMA trailers, the Black men with the pooper scoopers? No table manners. That is, no *conference table* manners. Not invited.

But BP and Bush and Obama and Jindal and EDF and Shaw the Shovel and rich Stormy Ladies and the Army Corps and LSU are all together, cheek-to-cheek in full costume at Rex's ball.

And doubloons are tossed everywhere, $360 million for the kitty litter, billions for this project, and billions pouring from the U.S. treasury like crude from a Bayou blowout.

An Energy-Finance cluster-fuck in a sandbox.

OUT ON POYDRAS STREET

Then we were out on the street. My fault.

I had to ask where America's Wetland got its money.

Hadn't Leslie taught me anything? Gentlemen don't ask gentlemen such questions.

King refused, with hauteur, telling me to "look it up" in his tax forms.

Well, as a matter of fact, I happened to have America's Wetland IRS tax filing with me. But something was missing from the filing: Schedule B, the list of donors. Might he provide it?

His Majesty was not used to such impertinence.

"NO NO GODDAMN IT NO I'M NOT GOING TO DO IT *BECAUSE I'VE HAD IT WITH YOU.*"

King has something in common with my executive producer.

Could he give me maybe just a peek?

"STOP! GODDAMN IT! STOP! PICK THIS UP"—whereupon, he smashed our microphone on his defenseless conference table—"*AND GET OUT OF HERE.*"

I took it the interview was over.

FORMER SITE OF THE LAFITTE HOMES

In 2006, a year after the great flood, Patricia Thomas took me to her beautiful home.

I helped her break into it through the metal seals. I met her when I saw her neighbor, her cousin, standing with her two children in front of it, crying. Night was falling and the police told her if she attempted to take her two children back into their house, they would be arrested.

Their homes were scheduled for demolition with their possessions still inside.

"Where'm I going to go, mister?" she asked me. "That's what I'd like to know; where'm I going to go?"

We broke in, but we had little time before the cops would bust us. In the kitchen, the skin-and-bones, toothless Black woman suddenly started shouting, *"Katrina didn't do this! Man did this! Katrina didn't take away my home! Man! Man did this!"*

True. An insider at the Housing Authority of New Orleans (HANO) told me they'd been trying to get those poor people out of there for decades. This was prime real estate between the French Quarter and finance district.

I was the insider. HANO was my client.

"This wonderful property between the Quarter and business district," says a brochure from the group that tore down her house, will be rebuilt using hurricane repair funds, low-income tax credits, and financing from JP Morgan and Whitney Bank.

The Lower Ninth Ward remains a ruin, but Obama's U.S. Secretary of Housing came down to praise this plan for the renaissance of New Orleans, the demolition of LaFitte homes, crafted by the nonprofit group Neighborhood Housing Services of New Orleans, R. King Milling, Chairman.

NATAL

The Rex's toadies and stooges, Dr. Cyanide and other industry tools, should have done their homework before they decided to lean on Dr. van Heerden.

Silencing this Louisiana State University professor, with the quiet voice and strange Afrikaans accent, must have seemed easier than crushing a Girl Scout with a bus.

They should have checked how van Heerden arrived at LSU from South Africa: by a boat he built himself, the *Ex-Natalia*.

They should have asked the courage question: *Who's your daddy?* Milling's daddy was another oil company consiglieri. Van Heerden's family members were imprisoned for fighting the apartheid dictatorship.

Ivor built his boat and sailed half the world from Natal, South Africa, to escape the deadly secret police of the old regime. After standing up to South African thugs and killers, van Heerden was hardly likely to bend a knee to oil companies and their banker.

I asked the prophet if the city was ready for another Katrina.

"No," van Heerden said softly. "Definitely not. If anything, it's worse than when Katrina hit. A section of the flood wall itself has sunk about nine inches." The homicide that is about to happen.

There is nothing new under the sun.

וַיַּרְא יְהוָה, כִּי רַבָּה רָעַת הָאָדָם בָּאָרֶץ, וְכָל-
יֵצֶר מַחְשְׁבֹת לִבּוֹ, רַק רַע כָּל-הַיּוֹם.

"Man is corrupted in the Earth," the Lord said to Noah.

Nothing has changed since Genesis 6. It is greed and arrogance and deception, not water, that drowns us.

And van Heerden? His ark is in his yard. He never dismantled the *Ex-Natalia*. South Africans have defeated apartheid, so now, he says, he'll sail away home to the Land of the Freed, escaping from this benighted oil colony, Louisiana U.S.A.

CHAPTER 5
The Cheese Smelled Funny So We Threw It in the Jungle

When BP's Gulf well blew, Chevron began to shit bricks, as it watched its stock drop 10 percent. The stock market feared a deepwater drilling ban, because Chevron, not BP, is the big boy in the Gulf's deep waters.

So Chevron's chief did the honorable thing: He stabbed BP in the back, badmouthed the Brit executives, blamed them for being slovenly incompetents who don't know which end of a drill is up. Chevron CEO John Watson told the *Wall Street Journal*, "This incident was preventable." Furthermore, Chevron, unlike BP, has a "robust" oil spill response system.

Well, hold on there, my dear Watson. Your plan *is* BP's plan. All the companies have *one* plan together for a Gulf blowout. Same plan, same equipment, share and share alike.

So it wasn't the BP plan that screwed up. It was the BP-Chevron-Shell-Exxon-Conoco plan that fell to pieces. And, Mr. Watson, as lead driller, *you*, buddy, were in charge, not BP.

Watching that TV screen in Vegas, I could not believe these guys had no rubber boom, no sucker ships, no crews, no nothing. It was Son of *Exxon Valdez*. In my career, I've seen corporate pigs snort and wallow, but this was a special return performance.

In all fairness, I should note that Chevron, Shell, and Exxon quickly responded to the Gulf blowout with full-page ads promising to spend a billon dollars on oil spill response equipment. From the Chevron press release:

"The new system will be engineered to be used in deepwater depths up
to 10,000 feet. . . . Dedicated crews will ensure regular maintenance,
inspection and readiness. . . ."

Thanks! But, Mr. Watson, that stuff was required *before* the BP blowout.
Well, that's just a little white "elision." (I especially like the part about "dedicated crews," straight from the 1969 Alaska plan.)

How come we don't know that Chevron and Exxon and the gang are as
responsible as BP for the Gulf disaster? Let me put it another way: Why would
BP take the blame in the Gulf and let its consortium partners off the hook?
Answer: for the same reason Exxon took the hit for BP and the consortium in
Alaska.

The reason is that the industry keeps its eyes on the prize: the right to
keep drilling, to open new offshore sites, to slither out of costly new regulations, and bust any moratorium on drilling.

The consortium understands: It's not who wins this particular game, it's
about keeping the game going.

When something goes wrong, the industry gives the public someone to
spank. BP, bend over.

I imagine the oil boys passing around the fright mask—Exxon saying,
"Your turn, BP!"—and laughing.

"I do not agree that this is an industry-wide problem," Exxon's CEO told
the press without a hint of a chuckle.

To sell this whopper, the boys needed a tag line that would put the blame
on one company only and limit even that to human foibles, just as they had
done with the *Exxon Valdez*, blaming it on poor Captain Hazelwood, the drunk.
So the industry settled on the tag line *BP's culture*. Bad culture: like failing to
wear gloves at the opera, or mixing the salad fork with the paté knife.

The Drunk Skipper of 1989 became the Bad Culture of 2010. New century, same jive.

But who would buy this "BP culture" con? Well, it depends on who they
can fund to sell it.

A COTTAGE IN THE WOODS,
OUTSIDE NEW YORK, OCTOBER 2010

Pluto and I don't watch TV, so this was something really special. The Public Broadcasting System was about to broadcast *The Spill,* its investigation into BP.

We watched.

PBS, after working on the story over the six months since the spill, disclosed that . . . BP had neglected safety!

Well, no shit, Sherlock.

Pluto rolled over on the rug and looked at me as if to say, *Don't we already know this?*

Retrievers are cynical by nature. I told him to hold judgment and watch more.

Patience paid. PBS then revealed that . . . *BP had neglected safety warnings for years!*

That's true. But then, so has PBS. The Petroleum Broadcast System has turned a blind eye to BP perfidy for decades.

If the broadcast on BP had come six months *before* the Gulf blowout, or exposed BP for their crimes in the Exxon spill; or, any time over the years of BP safety violations that flashed DANGER-DANGER, I would say, "Damn, that PBS sure is courageous." But six months *after* the blowout, PBS has shown us it only has the courage to shoot the wounded.

But hey, at least PBS is now on the case.

Or is it? Despite the press release hoo-hah that this PBS *Frontline* investigation would break news from a deep-digging inquiry, what we got was "Investigation by Google," old stuff from old papers that PBS forgot to report the first time around. Well, that's OK. It's not like I was expecting Edward R. Murrow.

Well, something's better than nothing, right?

No, not in this case. Through the entire hour, PBS told us again and again and again, the problem was BP alone, and BP's *culture* alone. BP's culture is unlike cultures of Chevron and Shell who have turned Ecuador and Nigeria into toxic cesspools, unlike ExxonMobil's culture of bribing the President of Kazakhstan.

How could PBS have missed the story?

Remember the Naipaul Rule: They don't lie; they elide.

And here's the Big Elide:

Go to the top of the PBS *NewsHour* Web site, the older, now-hidden views of the site. You'll find this:

Note the logo of PBS's prime corporate sponsor: Chevron Petroleum. Chevron is still top corporate sponsor, but its logo seems to have vanished, the way Exxon removed its name from the Valdez tanker.

I told Pluto to keep watching. And sure enough . . .

The PBS "investigative" report admiringly featured the comments of Rex Tillerson, CEO of ExxonMobil, Marvin Odum, President of Shell, and of course, John Watson, CEO of Chevron.

These gentlemen endorsed the PBS conclusion that, as its narrator intoned, "BP did not operate to industry standards."

Really? Did PBS investigate these oil CEO claims or just run their sponsors' assertions?

Perhaps the oil executives are right: The oil industry's "standards" typically involve mass poisoning, outrageous bribery, and the use of mercenary death squads to silence media and activists.

So what's this all about? Well, Pluto, it's like this:

As the oil from BP's well belched into the Gulf of Mexico, Big Oil understood that it had to control the message.

This is their message: Chevron culture *good!* ExxonMobil culture *good!* Shell culture *good! BP culture bad bad bad!*

PBS repeated what they were told. Instead of asking questions, the network asked for money. But hey.

Earlier that evening, Chevron/PBS *NewsHour* ran a "tease" of the *Frontline* report and worked in the BP "culture" shtick twice in six minutes.

BP is "bad" and so the industry is off the hook, and therefore there's no pressure to stop crazy-ass deepwater drilling. The Big Oil destruction machine can stay in high gear.

Even BP loves to hear that rotten-culture fairy tale. It's their path to easy redemption. Watch: The company will soon find deliverance by adopting a new "culture" under its new managers and, I assume, restore the PBS sponsorships BP had so foolishly dropped.

Why am I picking on poor little PBS? I'll be the first to tell you they are the best you're going to get on the U.S. boob tube.

But the Public Broadcast System takes our tax money. It owes us something, no? If we can't get the real story about Big Oil, at least we deserve an apology.

I was waiting for the PBS *Frontline* reporter to say, "BP has kept the truth locked in its files for years—and so have we at PBS. *AND WE ARE ASHAMED.* Send us back your Ken Burns DVDs for a refund."

But no, they didn't apologize; they asked for more money! And we will send it, leveraging Chevron's and ExxonMobil's payola.

As P. T. Barnum once said, there's a PBS donor born every minute.

* * *

In 1998, a hot-shot producer and BBC Television in the UK decided to film an investigation of BP and blow open the company's record of recklessness, centered on its screw job in Alaska.

But Alaska is far from London and costs a bundle to film, so BBC begged PBS and *Frontline* to throw in a couple of bucks. No way. So the BBC investigation died for lack of a U.S. partner. Instead, *Frontline*'s producer, television station WGBH, spent several million dollars on *The Commanding Heights,* a six-hour hosanna to the wonders of privatizing the energy industry. Oil company consultant Daniel Yergin removed his lips from the industry's wallet just long enough to write it. When the CEO of the program's sponsor, Enron, was arrested, new cash was provided by that newly privatized commander of the heights, British Petroleum.

YES, I'M JEALOUS.

Squished sour grapes are pouring down my chin and onto my Suicide Girls T-shirt. *Why isn't it me pontificating on PBS, pretending to report a story in a deep, serious voice, getting a Poke award or whatever they call it? Yes, it was my investigation of BP that PBS turned down twelve years ago because, after I folded my detective biz, I thought, maybe, MAYBE some U.S. reporters would like to look at my files; and U.S. TV's response was to drop-kick me across the Atlantic to England, where I've been reporting from exile ever since on a beer-and-pretzels budget in Baku because British Broadcasting Company cannot take money from British Petroleum. IS THERE NO JUSTICE? IS THERE NO GOD?*

Apparently, there is, and He has one of those PBS coffee mugs.*

Since PBS was bent over getting sponsored by Chevron and therefore in no position to investigate the oil company, I did it for them.

AMAZONIA, ECUADOR, 2009

Ricardo and I were dumped off at the end of a jeep track on a riverbank in a downpour to wait for our riverboat, which I assumed would be something like the steamer Humphrey Bogart piloted down the Ulanga River in *The African Queen.* The day before, I had received a message that the Cofan Natives of the Amazon forest would have a boat waiting to take us across an Amazon tributary to their village.

Our driver pointed to a canoe, a dug-out log with a hand-carved paddle, deep in mud, tied to a tree. "*Su barco.*" "Your boat," he said.

Rick remained calm—I hate that in him—as we sank in the muck to untie

---

* To balance things out, PBS agreed to broadcast a brilliant one-hour film by renowned docu-journalists Danny Schechter and Charmayne Hunter-Gault on the unpleasantries of globalization. The dissenting show was funded by cookie sales, and PBS ran it opposite the Academy Awards.

it. I did my clown-on-a-tight-rope walk to the back of the canoe. I made it, but Rick's $500 microphone didn't: I'd dumped it in the gray rushing river. Rick remained calm.

And I kept thinking, Anderson Cooper wouldn't do this. How could they get his makeup guy into the canoe?

We got lucky. A Cofan came out of the forest, and having mercy on these dumb-ass white guys, untied the log canoe and paddled off alone into the rapids to the village, returning half an hour later in another, longer canoe, this one with a little outboard motor.

I was on the hunt for Emergildo Criollo, a con man, a trickster, perpetrator of "the biggest fraud in history." That's how a Chevron Oil Corporation lawyer described him to me.

As a fraud investigator, I couldn't resist meeting this master flimflam artist, the Chief of the Cofan Indians. Even in the twenty-first century, meeting him was not so easy. The Cofan are way the hell in the middle of Ecuador's rain forest.

Once again on land, or on mud, we were led through the dripping trees and vines to a couple dozen homes on low stilts. I just kind of barged in on a few folks. In one stilt house, a man about my age was making a necklace of seedpods, which he gave to me. Didn't catch the name, not that I could pronounce it anyway.

How the hell do you live out here? "Yucca, corn, little animals we hunt," he said in Spanish. A lot of villagers speak Spanish, not just their odd tongue. He said, "In the old days, we hunted with blowpipes." He nodded to the one that hung on his wall. But now, he said, they use shotguns. He laughed and smiled, maybe because he knew what we knew, that the shotguns had been used by some Cofan on the oil drillers. Nothing fatal, just educational.

Inviting ourselves to join in their communal meal of yucca and chicken, we got in line with the village elders and a couple of curious monkeys. Until a few years ago, they were *on* the menu.

Then the Chief appeared, Criollo, the big-time fraudster, wearing the same ragged farmer's clothes as everyone else.

I said, "*Señor*, we need to talk. Alone." We walked to the big chief's house. It looked a lot like everyone else's. Something's missing. *Everything's* missing. Maybe it's the perfect con.

The Chief has claimed for years that his people were getting sick, dying from Chevron's oil. Chevron tagged Criollo as a shakedown artist. The Natives may be "primitive," but even cavemen know oil companies have deep pockets.

I got down to it: Anyone die out here?

He introduced me to a wrinkled woman, tiny as a mouse, Cecilia Q'nama. She spoke only Cofan, and the Chief translated. She told me about relatives of hers getting strange diseases. Miscarriages, deformed kids, dead kids, only since the drilling started.

Maybe it was bullshit. Maybe she was in on the shakedown with Chief Criollo. I had an epidemiologists' report back at my hotel. It said there was a sudden epidemic of childhood leukemia in the oil-production zone. Maybe the epidemiologists were in on the con too. The oil company said so.

Around us were puddles and rain forest sinkholes, with that telltale rainbow of oil sheen, drilling residue pumped and dumped in holding pools left to drain into the water. The miles of slithering contamination here in the Amazon made the Gulf Coast look like Kew Gardens.

I ended up out here in the rain forest half by accident. I had some confidential papers from the World Bank I intended to give to Ecuador's President Correa. But, going through the confidential documents, it was clear that there was no way to understand Ecuador, which had just rejoined OPEC, without first following the oil. And following the oil back to ChevronTexaco (Chevron

bought Texaco in 2001) meant going into the oil fields in the jungle and grill-
ing the Natives about their claims of illnesses and deaths.

Maybe it was all a hoax concocted by Indians and greedy lawyers. Don't
kid yourself, such things happen. I had to look for myself.

Criollo gave us a lift in another motorized log out to some farmland. Or,
more accurately, tar land. At one little farm, the oil residues were squooshing
up under the house. Everywhere we walked. *Flupth. Flupth*. The farmer Man-
uel Salinas, his wife, and his kids were covered with these suppurating pustules. But they couldn't leave. There was nowhere to go, and no money to go
there.

Why the hell was everyone out here so raggedy-ass busted?

I asked Criollo about the Cofan's deal with Texaco, three decades ago.

"They came in helicopters. They gave us cheese and diesel fuel and knives.
The cheese smelled funny, so we threw it in the jungle."

I asked the Chief if the men from the oil company explained that they
were taking the Native's oil.

"We couldn't understand. They were talking in Spanish." At the time,
Cofan spoke only Cofan. It was 1973, the same year BP and partners, nine
thousand miles north, got the rights to Valdez from the Chugach Natives.
Whatever, the Cofan got the cheese and Texaco got the oil.

Four billion barrels of it.

After they sucked up the crude, Chevron's Texaco unit bugged out, leaving
no assets in Ecuador. Not even a rubber band, not a thank-you note. Very
smart, very clever. If a court ever came down on the oil company, Chevron
could stick out its tongue and say, "Nyah Nyah Nyah," because there would be
nothing in the country to impound to pay for any judgment, medical care, or
clean-up.

Of course, this farm family, this Salinas guy, might have been in on the
con with the Chief and the epidemiologists. Despite Chevron's claim it was
all a gigantic fraud, I just could not bring myself to scrape off one of Salinas's
pus-filled scabs to see if they were real or just the Halloween stuff used when
white guys came around with a camera.

The Cofan knew that to survive in the jungle, you needed lawyers. One young
local farmer, Pablo Fajardo, apprenticed himself to an oil-town lawyer and got

a certificate just so he could file a suit. Joining up with the Cofan, the farmers sued Texaco over the dead kids and the skin pustules.

The day after we arrived in the Amazon, Ricardo and I followed Chief Criollo into town, where he announced he would file a renewed claim against Chevron. This was serious stuff. Instead of his saggy farming clothes, the Chief was decked out in ritual scarves and a kind of cape. He had painted his face with war stripes and led a small band from his village by boat, then by jeep, then by foot to the roustabout town of Lago Agrio ("sour lake"). The place looks like a movie set from an old Western.

In this nowhere town in the middle of the jungle, we followed the Chief as he marched to the courthouse, then up the steps, always looking straight ahead, not acknowledging the smirks of bureaucrats. On the top floor, with a slow, regal motion, he handed a clerk his latest demand in his $27 billion claim against Chevron.

With the feathers and war paint, it could have been a Peter Sellers comedy, except no one was laughing. The look in the Chief's eyes was as determined and regal as I could imagine of Henry V before the battlefield of Agincourt. Here was no Mardi Gras King, no voodoo impostor.

But in the end, this was the jungle and he was guy with paint on his face,

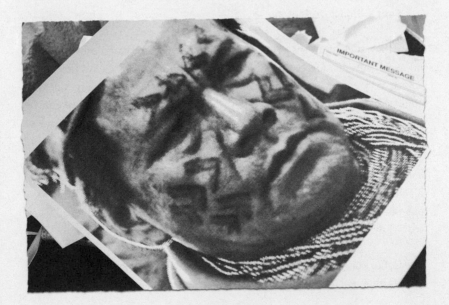

dropping off a petition typed for him by a farmer lawyer to tell a multinational oil company to write a check for several billion dollars. Good luck.

In my experience, I find that flimflam artists can't stop themselves from grinning. Criollo didn't grin. Maybe the Chief was just better at it than most. Criollo's eyes were stern but deeply sad.

I still had a job to do. I asked him, Did he himself have any experience with the oil poisonings or was this just secondhand stuff he was peddling?

"My three-year-old went swimming," he started in Spanish, "and began to vomit blood." The kid died quickly. His other son died slowly, of cancer.

QUITO, THE CAPITAL

"And it's the only case of cancer in the world? How many cases of children with cancer do you have in the States?"

Texaco's lawyer, Rodrigo Perez, was chuckling and snorting.*

"Scientifically, nobody has proved that crude causes cancer."

OK, then. But what about the epidemiological study about children with cancer in the Amazon traced to hydrocarbons?

The parents of the dead kids, he said, would have some big hurdles in court: *"If there is somebody with cancer there, they must prove it is caused by crude or by the petroleum industry. And, second, they have to prove that it is OUR crude."*

Perez leaned over with a huge grin.

"Which is absolutely impossible."

He grinned even harder.

Maybe some guy eating monkeys in the jungle can't prove it. And maybe that's because the evidence of oil dumping was destroyed.

Deliberately, by Chevron.

I passed the ChevronTexaco legal duo a document from their files labeled *"Personaly confidential."* They read in silence. They stayed silent quite a while.

Jaime Varela, Chevron's lawyer, was wearing his tan golf pants and white

---

* I couldn't make these guys up. I suggest—I *insist*—that you read and watch the film of the lawyers' defense of their oil company, by clicking here in the interactive editions, or going to GregPalast.com/VulturesPicnic/. You can also read there the Texaco "destroy" memo in full, in English and Spanish.

shoes, an open shirt and bespoke blue blazer. He had a blow-dried bouffant hairdo much favored by the ruling elite of Latin America and skin whiter than mine, a color also favored by the elite.

Jaime had been grinning too. He read the memo. He stopped grinning. The key part says,

> gulatorias, o a aquellos que usted juzgue
>
> dado, y todos los informes previos
> · las del campo, y ser destruidos.

"Todos los informes previos deben ser sacados de las oficinas principales y las del campo, y ser destruidos."

". . . Reports . . . are to be removed from the division and field offices and be destroyed."

It came from the company boss in the States, "R. C. Shields, Presidente de la Junta."

Removed and destroyed. That smells an awful lot like an order to destroy evidence, which in this case means evidence of abandoned pits of deadly drilling residue. Destroying evidence that is part of a court action constitutes fraud.

In the United States, that would be a crime, a jail-time crime. OK, gents, you want to tell me about this document?

"Can we have a copy of this?" Varela asked me, pretending he'd never seen it before in his life.

I'll pretend with them, if that gets me information. "Sure. You've never seen this?"

The ritual of innocence continued as they asked a secretary to make copies. "We're sure there's an explanation," Varela said. I'm sure there is. "We'll get back to you as soon as we find out what it is."

I'm still waiting.

CHAPTER 6
The Wizard of Ooze

HELSINKI STATION

Jack Grynberg said, *How did you find me?*

I looked under G.

The old spook was a hunter, not used to being hunted.

I'm not Sam Spade: Grynberg only gets found when he *wants* to be found. Besides, the question wasn't *how,* but *why.*

If we wanted to get the real story of how BP got away with covering up the rig blowout horror shows, I had to follow the money, not the bubbles.

Lord Browne had cranked up BP from the oil industry's little sister into Big Oil Giant #1 by finding huge new fields in the former Soviet Islamic republics. The big question: Did m'lord Browne have a magic nose that could smell oil, or just a snout for sniffing creeps likely to take a payoff?

I was counting on Browne's jilted partner, Jack Grynberg, to show me how Browne pulled petroleum rabbits out of a hat, to explain the "cherub," and to take me backstage to see how the levers were pulled.

* * *

Matty Pass got the call. An address on Central Park South. Ricardo and I cabbed it uptown, showed the doorman our IDs, and shuttled up to meet the tycoon in a dinky apartment he'd borrowed, a claustrophobic studio loaded with someone else's junk. Grynberg said there were no hotel rooms in New York, which was bullshit (I checked), but then what do I know about the kooky habits of the ultra-rich.

At least there were gorgeous views of Central Park until Jack snapped the metal blinds closed tight. But I got my wish: The Wizard of Oz of oil had invited me behind the curtain.

We squeezed in and saw, laid out on the queen-size bed, a real beauty, a gigantic seismic map, unfolded and flopping over onto an Oriental rug. It was covered with a zillion jagged lines. It looked like a photocopier had had a heart attack, the phrenology of oil and gas under the Earth's skull. Behind the lines, I could see the outlines of Cyprus, Lebanon, Israel, and the Egyptian Nile. It was General Grynberg's battlefield map, and Jack let me take it in.

Grynberg made himself comfortable in an old upholstered chair, and I made myself uncomfortable on a stool. I began with the obvious.

Question: *How does some professor of geology (Grynberg's preferred identity) get a piece of the Caspian Sea worth a billion or three?*

It started, he told me, in 1989, just as the Soviet Union was falling apart. The Communist Party General Secretary of the Soviet Socialist Republic of Kazakhstan, USSR, Nursultan Nazarbayev, visited Canada and, according to the Grynberg tale, made a spur-of-the-moment request to the U.S. State Department to visit a successful cattle rancher who could speak Russian. Grynberg, as a side business to oil, kept 30,000 head of cattle. Nazarbayev liked cows. While checking out the herd, The Communist chieftain asked Grynberg, a geologist, if he'd like to look at some seismic maps Nazarbayev had back in Kazakhstan. Jack flew there, looked, saw lots of oil, called Lord Browne in London, who immediately agreed to sign on with Grynberg Energy to drill the world's largest oil strike in a decade.

Jack, Jack, never bullshit a bullshitter. Nevertheless, I let him load me up with this cow-pie fairy tale.

Now let me re-tell this tale with facts a wee more plausible. During the Cold War, Grynberg headed the Defense Department's intelligence unit that analyzed Soviet resource information stolen by "our very able spy network." The unit operated out of the U.S. Embassy in Finland, the CIA's Helsinki Station.

Geologist Jack interpreted the intelligence for the CIA, the Defense Department—and Jack. Undoubtedly, Grynberg would have seen clues about the seismological profile of the Caspian Sea and, in the back of his head, must have kept a mental copy of this, the most valuable secret treasure map of modern times.

Now, I don't know if Grynberg is a religious man, but any doubts he had philosophically or geologically would have been laid aside after reading dispatches of a scene straight from the third book of the Torah, from Exodus. It was 1985. The Russians were trying their hand at drilling in the Caspian waters and quickly struck oil—way too much of it. They had disturbed a giant who released methane of unbelievable pressure. Maybe a Russian lit a cigarette, I don't know. But I do know the fireball rose seventy stories in the air and, *mirabile dictu,* the seven-hundred-foot column of fire burned for an entire year.

Grynberg, like Moses, must have heard the tower of flame calling to him, "Jack, Jack, *here* is the Promised Land."

(I suspect that Moses confused the Caspian Sea with Canaan Land, which are, after all, in the same northerly direction pointed out by the Mighty Outstretched Arm of the Lord. I seriously doubt the Holy One, Praised Be He, would have chosen Israel for His Chosen, which sits on nothing but sand. He must have meant Azerbaijan, above the sweetest crude oil deposit on the planet.)

Anyway, the foolish Soviet pharaohs, having been literally burnt by their attempt, pretty much abandoned their Caspian mother lode.

Jack, with Caspian seismics in his head, had a lot to dream about and, as the Cold War slogged on, a lot of time to dream it.

Then, in 1989, his dreams came true. The Berlin Wall fell, Soviet Premier Gorbachev lost control of the Warsaw Pact, and to little public notice, the Soviets lost control of the internal empire, the "Stans" (as in Uzbekistan, Kyrgyzstan, Turkmenistan, Azerbaijan, and Kazakhstan).

But James Baker III noticed. James, George H. W. Bush's Secretary of State, was counsel to Exxon and nearly every other member of the Houston oil cartel both before and after his Bush work. It was Baker's team at State who contacted Grynberg about hosting the "unplanned" visit to the United States by Nazarbayev to talk about "cattle." In those days, Nazarbayev and Baker had to be cautious about how they spoke. In 1989, the Soviet Union and KGB still existed and would have been carefully monitoring the man from Kazakhstan. Soviet intelligence did not trust their own, even the Naz, especially in that year, when Russia's soldiers were running for their lives out of Afghanistan. Moscow was beginning to lose its grip on Kazakhstan and the other Soviet Islamic states. Soon, Gorbachev wouldn't be able to order a pizza from Kazakhstan, let alone order around Nazarbayev.

Nazarbayev, yearning to be freed from Soviet central planners, wasn't dreaming of cows, he was dreaming of becoming the oil sheik of Central Asia, *insh'Allah.*

Secretary of State Baker shared that dream. He saw a once-in-a-century chance for the West to finally win the Great Game, grabbing the resources of the 'Stans away from Russia. Baker's boys called Grynberg. Nazarbayev, former head of the Kazakh KGB, would have known all about Jack, who was his U.S. counterpart from Helsinki Station, or quickly learned it: geologist, oilman, spy. Nazarbayev's kind of guy. *Yes!* Nazarbayev told State, he would be pleased to take a side trip to play cowboy in Colorado.

Once on the ranch, Nazarbayev got to it: "I have maps. In Kazakhstan. Want to look at them?" He could have said, "How much gold can you carry in your arms?"

After their meeting, Jack flew to Kazakhstan, and his eyes were popping from holding in his hands the treasure maps that had lain secreted in his memory chest for decades. Grynberg swiftly got Nazarbayev to sign a deal giving Jack the exclusive rights to put together a drilling consortium that would throw down the billions needed to suck out the liquid gold.

Jack couldn't wait to call his buddy John Browne, then exploration chief for BP. Years earlier, Jack and John had become an item, businesswise, when Browne agreed to back Grynberg's quirky offshore drilling project at the Nile Delta near Israel. However, their timing was crap. It was 1973. In October, on Yom Kippur, Egypt attacked Israel (that didn't bother Britain much), and Egypt seized both banks of the Suez Canal (that *did* bother Britain much). The result: The Bank of England scuttled the BP-Grynberg deal.

In 1991, Browne, hearing Grynberg's voice from Kazakhstan, insisted Jack get to BP HQ London immediately. Grynberg hustled there and went straight to the CEO's office. Browne locked the door and wouldn't open it until they had divided the Caspian between them.

Then shit happened. Grynberg took his new best friend, President Naz, to Venezuela to meet the oil club boys. I asked for a photo of this improbable event, and Jack showed me a snapshot of the Kazakh President with him in Caracas, playing tennis. (Grynberg won, of course, though after much debate with himself.) Nazarbayev "fell in love" with a pair shoes and Jack popped for them.

"What's Nazarbayev's shoe size?" I asked.

"Nine and a half."

Grynberg's intelligence habits remain sharp.

There followed a side trip to the Alaskan Arctic to admire BP's sideways offshore drilling trick. It was there that another of Jack's guests, Kazakh Prime Minister Nurlan Balgimbayev, mentioned that the French oil company Total "put down a $5 million cashier check." Grynberg: "And he says, 'Jack, why don't you do the same?'" For Grynberg, $5 million was lunch money; but he chose to lecture the Kazakh potentate on the U.S. Foreign Corrupt Practices Act.

The Kazakhs thought Jack just didn't get it. So, President Nazarbayev invited Grynberg to his vacation *dacha*, where the President thanked Jack for the shoes, then hinted that something a little more substantial could help Jack win the game. In case Jack didn't get his drift, Nazarbayev showed Grynberg some useless seismic info Nazarbayev had received from this guy named James Giffen. Grynberg knew Giffen as a small-change oil pipe salesman, but clearly, Giffen was moving in on Grynberg's signed deal by a willingness to grease the pony.

Jack told the President, *"I don't bribe."* Good on you, Jack! Very admirable, but costly. Nazarbayev handed Giffen, the pipe salesman, the contract to create the consortium for the Kachaganarak and Kashagan offshore fields. And so James Giffen snatched the billion-dollar baby right out of Grynberg's arms.

* * *

The following information you can read for yourself in *United States of America v. James H. Giffen*, filed in 2003 after Giffen was handcuffed at New York's JFK Airport.

Just an excerpt:

> On July 28, 1995, by KO-1 [Kazakhstan Official-1], Mobil agreed to pay to Mercator [Giffen's firm], on behalf of Kazakhstan, Mercator's fee for consulting services to Kazakhstan. . . . On or about May 3, 1996, Mobil closed its purchase of a 25% interest in the Tengiz oil field for approximately $1.05 billion. . . . Accordingly, Mobil on May 17, 1996, wired the balance of Mercator's fee, $41 million, to Mercator's account at Citibank in New York.

Giffen's $41 million in "consulting services" appeared to require no more than locating Mobil Oil. Personally, if I were Nazarbayev, I would have used a phone book. He had reason not to.

Then, the indictment states, after a long journey of the funds through . . .

. . . an account in Switzerland in the name of Havelon Trading S.A., a British Virgin Islands corporation . . . On February 6, 1997, JAMES A. GIFFEN, the defendant, caused Havelon to wire $20.5 million to KO-2's Orel account.

Did you follow the money? Mobil Oil to Giffen's shell company Mercator to KO-2. A stone-cold bribe, a whale of a bribe.

Everyone and their cousin knows that "KO-2" is President Nazarbayev. KO-1, by the way, is his greasy little Prime Minister, the one who hit up Jack for the $5 million.

By the time all oil company booty arrived in the Swiss bank accounts, the easy-squeezy topped $100 million. To celebrate their haul, Prime Minister KO-1 told Giffen to send a Donzi speedboat to President KO-2, plus two snow-mobiles and then a fur coat for Mrs. KO-2.

But someone dropped a dime on Giffen. So the multimillionaire player Giffen was frog-marched to a jail cell, not a common sight in the United States. His consulting firm was charged with bribery under the Foreign Corrupt Prac-tices Act and tax violations. (He did not declare the bribes on his income tax forms. For *shame*.)

With Giffen 'cuffed, his coconspirators in the oil industry were forced to pick a fall guy, someone to toss into the volcano with Giffen. J. Brian Williams, Mobil's top man in the Caspian, ended up with the short straw. He pleaded guilty and was sentenced to three years. Giffen faced twenty years in prison or more.

Bad guys in the clink. Justice done.

Not quite.

Mobil's partner, AMOCO, soon to be absorbed by BP, also paid money into Giffen's Swiss bank accounts. So did Texaco (later of ChevronTexaco). So did Phillips Petroleum.

Yet AMOCO, Phillips, and Texaco executives got bonuses, not prison time.

Giffen bargained for a plea and offered to give up his Swiss bank account with $84 million in it.

That's quite a penalty, at first glance. But the numbers don't add up. Liter-ally. Giffen's Bribes-R-Us operation collected, by my calculation from the indictment, no less than $105 million. But $84 million is not $105 million. Since when is a felon allowed to keep $21 million of looted booty?

And why was Giffen charged only with corrupting the deals on the Tengiz onshore field? What about the offshore fields, BP's big scores, Kashagan and Karachaganak, owned with Grynberg?

And this is truly weird: Plea agreements in such cases usually require the defendant to tell the truth, the whole truth, and nothing but the truth about their crimes: names, dates, places, everything. But not Giffen; he was not required to rat out anyone. The Justice Department did not demand he name a single oil company, a single source of his $84 million nor his $105 million, nor, crucially, any Kazakh president.

The truth might have set Kazakhstan free. The line that the collapse of the Soviet Union liberated its citizens does not ring true to the journalists in Kazakhstan dungeons. Nazarbayev, once a brutal Soviet KGB chief, found religion and became the brutal Islamic chief. His gendarmes arrested anyone who so much as breathed a word that the President has taken millions in bribes from Western oilmen. By the cutesy gimmick of naming Nazarbayev as KO-2, there is no "proof" that the President gorged on the bribe money from Giffen.

Reporting the identities of KO-1 or KO-2 risks imprisonment for defaming the Great Leader. Of course, imprisonment is for the lucky. The unlucky find themselves in fatal traffic accidents or "committing suicide." If the Justice

Department forced Giffen to make public the names of KO-1 and -2, to finger these guys who sold out their country's oil for a few silver coins and a speedboat, the KOs might be knocked out of power and the game would be up.

So, what looked like Justice triumphant in the Giffen-Mobil case was in fact a shambolic trial, a flimflam, a cover-up, with one executive thrown to the wolves, one fixer thrown to the kittens, and Big Oil laughing all the way to the Caspian.

This brought to mind the Zambian finance minister who used a voodoo charm to make himself invisible from the police. Did BP and Exxon and Chevron-Texaco and Phillips (now of ConocoPhillips) have some kind of magical fairy dust that made them invisible to the Justice Department?

It seemed so. And I think I know the names of some of the fairies.

Most were in the "P-group," a slough of top politicos, a lobbying power team headed by Ronald Reagan's former chief of staff, Michael Deaver, former Attorney General Dick Thornburgh, and former Justice Department lawyer Reid Weingarten. Reid told Thornburgh's successors in the Bush Jr. Administration that naming Nazarbayev in the indictment would mean the axe for U.S. oil companies, an odd legal defense but extraordinarily effective.

There was fairy dust everywhere. On September 6, 2005, while Justice pondered indicting Nazarbayev and his Big Oil funders, Canadian financier Frank Giustra flew out of Almaty, Kazakhstan, in his private jet. His cargo: former President Bill Clinton. In Giustra's pocket was a big piece of Kazakhstan's uranium. (There's no hint that Clinton squeezed the Naz to turn over the ore to Giustra. That's not how gentlemen do it.) Following his Kazakh uranium strike, Giustra made a secret $31 million donation to former President Bubba's foundation.

Another chubby cherub of a fairy, Clinton's former Secretary of Energy, Bill Richardson, wrote a gushing valentine to the Kazakh kleptocrats called *"Crazy for Kazakhstan!"* in *The Washington Times*. Why? I don't have a clue except that a month before writing the article, that crazy Richardson joined Kissinger & Associates whose clients have been up to their asses in Kazakh and Caspian machinations.

I was left asking this most important question: Every oil company is at least *mentioned* in the Justice Department criminal complaint, even if unindicted, except one: BP. *So how did BP, in the midst of this baksheesh bacchanal, end up the big winner in the Caspian without joining in Giffen's payoff party?*

I needed someone who could tell me if BP was either innocent as Snow White or the wily Godfather in this ring of racketeers. I needed an insider in the conspiracy who might tell me its tales. I needed a member of the gang on the outs, steamed about it, who could not be bullied—and who had balls of steel. That's why I had sought out Jack Grynberg.

But first, I had to ask myself a question Jack wouldn't: *Who sent Giffen?* Giffen was a nothing, an oil pipe hawker, a plumbing supplier, and suddenly he was wheeling and dealing with the big boys of Houston, London, and the Caspian. Who gave him Nursultan's phone number?

Remember: It was James Baker's State Department that set up the meet between Jack and Nazarbayev. Grynberg's prissy refusal to pay and play threatened to blow the entire geopolitical coup that the State Department and oil giants lusted for. Jack had gone screwy on them, all play-by-the-rule-book. The U.S. government would need a tool, someone who needed the cash and would leave his rule book at home.

I have this question: Could Giffen have possibly sidled up to Nazarbayev without U.S. diplomatic and intelligence encouragement or approval, without the connivance of Baker, Bush Sr., and then Bill Clinton?

Indeed, Giffen, in chains, swore under oath that he paid the money *as an agent of the U.S. government, as an agent of the CIA, National Security Agency, and State Department.*

Grynberg waved that away. Giffen was no agent. He, Grynberg, was an intelligence professional; Giffen is a weasel, a nutcase shyster with a whacky alibi.

Maybe. I'll check that out myself, Jack.

For a nothing weasel, Giffen seemed to have some serious inside mojo. In 1992, Baker's State Department used Giffen, not the Kazakh diplomats, as the go-between to Nazarbayev in arranging the strongman's meeting with President Bush Sr. The Bush-Nazarbayev meeting, by the way, occurred after seven key events:

1. On December 20, 1991, U.S. Secretary of State Baker joins Nazarbayev in his sauna at the dacha near the Kazakh capital, where they discuss oil and gas.

2. Five days later, the United States becomes the first nation to recognize Kazakhstan's secession from the Soviet Union and hails its new President, Nazarbayev.

3. Chevron, which bought the Tengiz oil field from the Soviets just before the secession, wants Nazarbayev to recognize its rights.

4. Giffen is named Nazarbayev's "Counselor" and Chevron's chief, Dick Matzke, complains to Jack about being asked to pay $20 million through Giffen to play in Tengiz. Chevron refuses.

5. Baker's law firm's client, Mobil, hires Giffen as consultant and ponies up $50 million. Mobil gets a slice of Chevron's Tengiz field.

6. Chevron gets the message and agrees to pay 75 cents a barrel to the state oil company by way of Swiss bank accounts.

7. Texaco, Phillips, and others hire Giffen. He had a terrific sales pitch, reportedly telling one reluctant exec, "There's a lot of guns in Kazakhstan and bad things can happen."

Despite Jack refusing to pay the bribe, BP (and therefore BP's shadow partner, Grynberg) got the lion's share of the Karachaganak and Kashagan fields from the Kazakh government; and Jack began to wonder how BP got so lucky—and begins to look this gift horse in the mouth—most particularly after BP and his supposed buddy, Lord Browne, shaved a bit off Jack's share.

Jack was leading me to ask about another puzzler, that $84 million in Giffen's Swiss account. It did not come from the $105 million pile given to him by Mobil and partners. It doesn't match a single number in the indictment for the Tengiz payoffs. So I asked, Where did Giffen's $84 million come from?

Jack said it was *his* money; at least, he was billed his share of it by BP. It was for Kashagan. Jack was furious that BP made the payoff, though frankly, he was a lot wealthier for it.

Kashagan? The $100 billion offshore field wasn't even mentioned in the Giffen indictment.

Who else was in with BP on the payoffs? Jack took me through the math: "What's interesting about $84 million is that the consortium in Kashagan had seven partners, and $84 million is very easily divided by seven, meaning $12 million each."

How did he know BP used Giffen as a bagman for this deal?

"BP charged me for it." He pulled out the accounts from BP's files. It was a detail that BP hid from Grynberg by burying it in their invoice for shared costs.

This is what I had come for, this piece of paper, this rock-hard evidence of payment to the bagman, which neither BP nor Giffen could deny and which Jack would give me only by hand, not by mail.

There it was: at the bottom, a list of payments including $500,000 to Giffen under "Administrative charges." *

But, Jack, how do you know it's a bribe?

"Because it never says 'bribe.'"

For fun, Jack told me, he had asked BP what Giffen was "administering." Rather than answer, they gave Grynberg his money back.

But that was just bribe *administration*. What about the bribes themselves? He told me that the going price for a piece of Kazakhstan was $40 million. BP had billed Jack for his percentage of BP's $26.4 million payment. ($26.4 million is two-thirds of $40 million. BP owns two-thirds of the Caspian site.)

What does a bill for a multimillion-dollar bribe look like? Jack had audited

---

* The public interest requires the release of this restricted document. I offered BP to keep it confidential if the company or Lord Browne could credibly explain its legitimate purpose. They have declined to do so.

BP's partnership accounts and discovered the $26.4 million under the heading "production sharing" royalties.

Ah, "production sharing." That's how Leslie the Bagman described the $30 million payment in Baku.

Frankly, Jack, "Production Sharing" sounds legitimate to me.

Jack smiled.

"THERE WAS NO PRODUCTION."

The light began to shine on the contents of the brown valise Lord Browne handed to Abrahams in Baku. That too, the Bagman told me, was for "production sharing." And again, there was no production.

Production sharing, Grynberg explained, doesn't begin under the Kazakh contract until 2014. "So you can't have production sharing, so that was a stupid way by a BP accountant to hide a bribe. There [it] was: two-thirds of $40 million."

Not so stupid, really. While that Mobil executive was pinned to the bars in Joliet Penitentiary, getting serviced by a three-hundred-pound mouth breather who calls himself Christine, Lord Browne was getting his knighthood from the Queen.

While Rick did his best to photograph the confidential documents in the darkened apartment, I was tempted to ask, *"So, Jack, any idea who dropped the dime to the Swiss authorities about Giffen's $84 million account?"*

I knew the answer, so why ask? Instead, I asked Jack why he was such a pain in the ass. After all, as one arbitrator noted, BP's bribes *made him rich* (or richer).

"I think bribery is absolutely the worst thing in the Free World that ever happened."

Come on, Jack, *you* went through the worst that ever happened, the Holocaust.

"That's money that belongs to the people!" Meaning it's the people of Kazakhstan, or of Azerbaijan, or of Louisiana who get screwed by payoffs. Mobil paid $50 million to KO-1 and KO-2 and picked up Tengiz for spit, just $1.05 billion for a 25 percent interest in seven billion barrels of oil and condensates. Do the math: Mobil paid up front just *60 cents a barrel (or a penny and a half per gallon). Fill'er up!* Plus, Mobil picked up a fourth of the 14-trillion-cubic-foot gas reserve, worth, oh, a few billion more, thrown in for nothing. A

fair price for the Kazakh people would have been several times what Mobil (now ExxonMobil) got away with.

Crime pays. But Jack was sick of it. Grynberg knew damn well what happens when the guys with the guns get together with the guys with the money. In 1995 while Mobil was stuffing Nazarbayev's Swiss accounts, the average wage in Kazakhstan was $61 a month. Then, wages dropped further, and in the middle of an oil boom, mass starvation knocked on Kazakhstan's door.

* * *

No question, Jack was insanely altruistic. But not *all* altruistic.

Now the squiggles on the map on the bed had a meaning.

He explained how BP screwed four nations with a single screwdriver. Follow this:

In July 2002, BP sold its interest in Kashagan to the French company Total for $612 million.

Two days later, Total sold BP half its Nile Delta field off Egypt's shore for spit, for a ridiculously low $10 million.

The stink of sulfur rose from the combination of these two deals. Right after BP sold its Kashagan share for $612 million, British Gas sold the same size share and received three times as much, $1.8 billion. Is BP stupid?

And the $10 million for the Nile? Lord Browne should have remembered that Grynberg, his old partner on the failed Egypt venture in 1973, *still had the seismic info* and knew the Nile Delta was worth billions, not $10 million, a joke. Is Total also that stupid?

So BP is stupid and Total is stupid—but two stupids make one brilliant scam. By slashing the sticker prices on what was effectively a trade, Grynberg explained,

—"[BP] cheated Kazakhstan because they paid tax on $612 million, not $1.8 billion."

—"Total cheated Egypt and the people of Egypt out of taxes because they sold property worth billions for $10 million."

The British and French treasuries would have been ripped off on taxes as well. So why is BP's partner, Grynberg, telling me this? Because BP paid Jack's family their share (reported as 15 percent) on the $612 million fake-o price, not the $1.8 billion real value. "THEY CHEATED THE GRYNBERG FAMILY."

I did some quick calcs in the margins of my notepad. Out of the $612 million, BP handed Jack a lousy $92 million and shafted him out of $184 million more! Personally, I don't know what it feels like to get burgled for $184 million, especially when you just got a check for $92 million.

The Grynbergs sued BP. It was 2008, after Jack cracked the BP-Total reservoir swap game. Grynberg doesn't need the extra $184 million (not many people can say that), but the hell if he was going to let Browne prance around as the genius knight of the petroleum world when it was Jack who won the Caspian by finding it and seizing it, while Browne got it by stealing it from Jack.

"Browne bribes," Grynberg told me, with disgust in his voice for a contemptible method of doing "business" in which thievery parades as entrepreneurship.

Jack insists a higher justice must be served, with a soupcon of vengeance. Grynberg uses some of his millions to dog Browne and BP anywhere in the world they try to cheat the locals who don't have resources to defend themselves from the petroleum Goliath. Grynberg paid the legal bills of the Ute Indians who sued BP after the company was caught skimming gas from Ute Reservation wells. Grynberg handled the investigation himself, going through BP's drilling records.

On top of that, Jack spent $20 million to file lawsuits against BP on behalf of the U.S. taxpayers. U.S. law has a strange and wonderful provision allowing anyone to sue a company that cheats the U.S. Treasury. He says BP is manipulating royalty sums owed the United States. (So far, the courts have said No.)

In the battle for reputation, money, and control, only Grynberg or Browne could survive. The smart money should have been on Grynberg. Browne is now bloodied and broken, after he was caught lying to a court about renting his boyfriend from Boots & Suits, the unofficial provisioner to the House of Lords. So now Jack refers to m'Lord Browne as "the felon," though no charges were brought against the lord.

Our information is that someone near Browne believes Grynberg was behind opening the closet containing the lord and his boyfriend, exposing them. Did Grynberg do that? Gentlemen don't ask. I'm not a gentleman, but I didn't ask.

* * *

What about Giffen's reported sales pitch to those who won't join his team, about guns and "bad things happen." And crossing Nazarbeyev can get your life insurance cancelled. Grynberg was no reckless amateur. Recently, he wore a bulletproof vest in Paris when he testified against the thuggish President of the Central African Republic and his demand for payola. But Grynberg simply brushed off Giffen as a bigmouth, a leech, a go-fer who'd seen too many grade-B gangster films.

But there are indeed a lot of guns in Kazakhstan and bad things *do* happen. A Kazakh reporter begins investigating his President for bribery and "commits suicide," shooting himself in the head and the stomach three times. Some reporters still don't get the message. And suddenly, buses are accidentally rolling over them, and their children are found hanged. Something was pushing Jack into real danger and it wasn't the money. The few hundred million wasn't worth it.

* * *

I imagine Grynberg originally trusted John Browne on the Caspian deal because of their parallel lives. Like Grynberg, John Browne is Jewish, which is rare in an industry of tooled-boot cowboys from Houston and royal grandees of the Raj in London.

Sharing the commonality of the mistrusted, Grynberg and Browne would help each other on their parallel paths. But the path, though close, was separated by an uncrossable chasm.

In Poland, during the war, Jack joined the anti-Nazi resistance, a little guerrilla, twelve years old, surviving on stolen potatoes and carrying homemade explosives. Jack refused to talk about it, but I knew.

At twelve, little John Browne was earning honors at the boarding academy at Ely, which was already six hundred years old when Henry VIII renamed it King's School. John's mother survived the Auschwitz concentration camp, but after the war, she married into Anglo-Persian Oil Company royalty.

The future Lord Browne lived with his mother until her death, even taking his mommy to management strategy sessions and board meetings. Paula Wesz, Mrs. Browne, spent her life surrounding John with defenses against a vicious world, encouraging him to become as powerful and as wealthy and as un-Jewish as possible so no one could hurt him as she was hurt. Assimilate. Pass. Hide. Hide his circumcised *schmeckel* and its nasty lust for other little boys. In the protective cocoon she wove, the lord's mother created a domineering and monstrous weakling, an emotional and moral cripple, a manipulative martinet. A lionized but frightened fraud.

Grynberg, orphaned and hunted by the Nazis, was a child soldier who raised himself unprotected but armed, hungry, and deadly from an early age. Jack never has, and never will, drop his weapons, always a guerrilla, always taking on a tank with his Molotov cocktail or its equivalent in lawyers.

*   *   *

Rocks and Russia made Grynberg rich. I didn't have to ask him how he learned to speak Russian. I spoke with one of his compatriots in the Jewish Resistance on the Polish-Byelorussian border, Chaim Ajzen from the *shtetl* Hrubieszów. The young resistance fighters, said Ajzen, were taken into the regular Red Army as the Soviets rolled west for the assault on Berlin. War won, the Russians immediately arrested the Polish and Jewish guerillas, hauling them deep into the gulag, on the reasonable grounds that, in the new Soviet workers' paradise, it was not a good idea to let free a bunch of guys who dissented by taking to the hills and blowing up bridges.

To escape from the camps and survive across war-shocked Russia would have required learning some Russian.

But Grynberg, like almost all the Resistance survivors, would not speak of this painful time. Fleeing into the hills to save himself, little Jack, like Chaim Ajzen, must have left his mother and father and sisters and brothers to die, probably shot in the family basement, one or two dragged off to be gassed. Ajzen's own parents, hearing the Nazis were coming, told him, "It isn't right for a son to see his parents killed," and told him to run to the forest.

And the others? I asked Ajzen. His uncle Solomon, "Sollie," was a special case. As the rancher who supplied the Polish cavalry with the horses that charged the German panzer tanks, Sollie was taken to the town square, where all the residents were ordered to attend. The Germans shot Sollie in the head, to the horror of some, to the cheers of others. An old man who as a boy tended horses for Sollie, and revered him, drew a picture of Sollie for me, from memory.

And the others? "Hitler killed them all. Hitler killed them all," my grandmother Anna repeated several times. She'd left Hrubieszów safely in 1921. Chaim Ajzen, Yiddish for "Life of Steel," her cousin, is my great-uncle.

* * *

I walked out into a nasty New York rain. I forgot to ask Grynberg, *Say, Jack, whatever happened to "Cows for Kazakhstan"?*

And then it hit me: I'm stupid! I'm an amateur, a schmuck! The air-conditioning!

Jack had chosen a private building that was none too fancy but was locked tight, unlike a hotel, where you could rent a room nearby, bribe clerks, or fool the maid service. It was unobtrusive and secure, out of prying sight lines. BP couldn't run one of its microphone-carrying toy trucks through the vents like they did to Hamel or break into a room like they did to Inspector Lawn or do whatever else they do these days. An old-school spook and underground sabo-teur who had earned tens of millions of dollars in a shark tank of KGB murder-crats, Grynberg was one of the few oilmen who knew what "safe house" meant and had the brains to use one.

Clearly, Grynberg plays on a complex chessboard I can't even see, let alone know where the pieces move. And I have no doubt I am now one of Jack's pieces. He's the one who tipped me to the Bagman with No Address. And now he has sent me off to London to ask questions he himself is not allowed close enough to ask of BP and his lanceman, the Lord of Madingly.

Well, why not? There is no God, but there is Grynberg. I'll take what I can get.

CULLODEN BAY, TRINIDAD & TOBAGO

Christmas coming, for some. Another urgent message arrived from the Chief of Intelligence of the Free Arctic Republic. We were needed up there again. The temperature in Kaktovik: -20°F. That's the *high* temperature during the day's one hour of sunlight.

So, Badpenny books a flight to the new BP drilling site . . . off Culloden Bay, Tobago (89°F, water temperature 82°F). She's brought nothing but the iPad and a thin wrap to wear over that 'kini with the strawberries. I've noted that when those strawberries bounce, men go mad, the blood drops from their brains to their boxers, they become idiots.

Not me. I don't get my meat where I get my bread.

The stopover in Port of Spain is unavoidable. PoS, capital of Trinidad, is a bit of a toilet. And I have deep respect for that, the down-at-the-heels government buildings, the Third World crappiness of it. Not every oil capital has to be a Baku, a bribery bacchanal of imitation Dubai, an economy that balances on the First Lady's stilettos.

The huge dollops of loot from the oil and gas wedged between Trinidad and Venezuela have been passed around to the Trini citizens.

Offshore, just beyond the horizon, BP's platforms are sucking up Tobago's hydrocarbon, so I've been conducting an extensive investigation of the environment. By snorkel. I've been staring at angel fish and they've been staring at me. Unlike Baku, unlike Biloxi, nothing is floating that I can burn with a lighter.

Compared to central Baku, it sucks: not one Bentley, not one Lamborghini, and the biggest shop is the Penny Saver, where you can get plastic sandals. The footwear here is a joke. Ferragamo would commit suicide in a place like this.

Now we come to the critical part of the investigation. Under the palm tree, Badpenny is playing Scrabble in English on her iPhone. Krishna is pouring me, despite my stern protest, a second snifter of El Dorado 15, even more delicious than Angostura brandy. I have a new love.

Krishna Persad is the Grynberg of Trinidad. I figure Dr. P, as everyone calls him, can fill in the numbers for my investigation of BP.

Here are the numbers:

	Azerbaijan	Trinidad & Tobago
State cut of oil	10%	55%
Minimum drilling required	None	Lots
"Profit" Oil for govt	After 5 years	From Day One

In Trinidad, BP gets a slice. In Azerbaijan, BP gets the pie. And in the USA, we get Baku'd.

COURTROOM 11, MOYNIHAN FEDERAL COURTHOUSE
SOUTHERN DISTRICT OF NEW YORK, MANHATTAN

Jim Giffen looks damn good. He's tanned, he's fit. Looks like he played a few holes this morning before his sentencing. Giffen lives right on the fairway at the famous Winged Foot Golf Club. Nice house—I'd filmed it by accident while looking for his neighbor, Hermann the Vulture.

And I suppose, at the end of play, Giffen, the guy with the "people here have guns" motto crushed a few balls just to stay in practice.

Courtroom 11 looks a bit like an exclusive gentlemen's club, which it is, with marble and rich leathers and mahogany. Here, gentlemen are sentenced for gentlemen's crimes. No "boosters" from the Bronx here. Right now, the place is crowded with old white guys from Winged Foot, all with the same leathered faces and thick white razor-cut hair, in Brooks Brothers blues and shoes, plus some of their trophies garnished with pearls.

The judge is running late, and Giffen and his lawyers (I counted eight, at an average of, say, $600 an hour) were joshing each other and giggling and having a fine old time. There's the big-shot *consigliere* Bill Schwartz and some young pudgy-faced blond boy to hold his briefcase and a matching female blonde to hold *his* briefcase. Under her gray suit, you could see the outline of thighs muscled from hours on the treadmill at the New York Health and Racquet Club. (I obviously had time to kill.)

"All rise!"

Judge William Pauley III sat down, we followed, and His Honor asked his buddy Schwartz if he had something to say about Giffen before handing down sentence.

U.S. v. Giffen is called "the granddaddy of bribery cases" because of the sum, over $100 million, its recipients "KO-1 and KO-2," and Giffen's client list, which looks like a birthday party at the Houston Petroleum Club: Exxon-Mobil, ConocoPhillips, and (still unknown to the government) BP.

For all the millions that flowed through his hands, and the millions that stuck there, Giffen was just a glorified delivery boy, a bagman, a mule. But unlike some poor sucker from Ecuador who carried baggies of cocaine in his stomach, Giffen carried Swiss bank account numbers in his BlackBerry.

Caught holding the bag for Mobil and company, Giffen would finally go down.

The night before, I got ahold of the cell phone number of a high-level Justice Department insider, who agreed to talk to me on *"deep, deep background."* (The scrapbook of this investigation would make an odd photo album: no faces, no names, except for those strange few with more courage than common sense.) Mr. Deep-Inside said, *"Justice caved in. Just caved in. They had the documents, it's all documents, hard evidence. Giffen's been allowed to plead tax code violations, no personal admission of bribery."* It was a sick crawl-down, but still, Deep Insider says Giffen has agreed to a year in the slammer, felony rap, plus probation, and fines in the millions. A slap on the wrist. But with a bit of a sting.

The Granddaddy of bribery cases had stalled all through the Bush years. Giffen's defense that he was a secret U.S. government agent, a big laugh, had delayed the case for six years while George Bush defended the CIA's new powers to say fuck off to any snooping court inquiry.

With Obama in, Giffen would finally face Justice. But not KO-2, The Naz, President Nazarbayev. Another source via Russia told me that Hillary Clinton had sent her Deputy Secretary of State to Kazakhstan, just before Justice offered Giffen a plea, to reassure bribe taker KO-2 that neither he nor his creepy little Prime Minister, KO-1, would be named in a U.S. court.

This was a sweet little deal for Giffen: The bagman was not required to reveal any payment from BP, nor cough up the sources, nor the seven names that so easily divide into $84 million. The government didn't ask for names—and prays nightly that Giffen will never say them. Giffen held the government hostage: If his Swiss hidey-holes were traced to the Seven Sisters, then the oil companies would have to be indicted with him. Then, under international law, *these contracts could be voided.*

Contracts that are the fruit of crime cannot be enforced. BP, France's Total, ConocoPhillips, Texaco, Italy's ENI, and the rest of the gang, if indicted, would be out of the Caspian on their *keisters*. China, giggling on the sidelines, would end up with the whole caboodle.

A huge scrum of reporters is down the hall, covering a blonde in the Bernie Madoff trial. I am the only reporter covering the Bribery Case of the Century. Lucky me.

Now, Schwartz stands. Giffen's mouthpiece is about to earn his $600 an hour. At a dark-wood lectern, tall and dramatic, the attorney says that his client had merely "failed to tick a box on a tax form"—that was his only crime, to which he now confessed. He'd given up an $84 million bank account. Giffen had, in fact, already suffered as if under sentence for years, a virtual prisoner in his own home! (Home on the links, Alcatraz for the Affluent, Rikers for the Rich.)

The judge is asking if "the Government would like to comment." There are two guys in cheap suits I hadn't noticed before, looking uncomfortable, like they'd just been called on by the teacher and they hadn't done their homework. Barely audible, one said, "Uh, no."

There's a pause. Suspense. I wonder if they're going to drop their pants, grab their ankles, and say, "All yours, Mr. Giffen!"

The Judge says gently, "Will the Defendant rise for sentencing."

His Honor, from the Nassau County Republican machine, had a soft look in his eyes. He says Giffen is a "great patriot" who acted "for the best interests of the United States."

Huh?

I hope I'm getting this exactly:

"I have read an extraordinary amount of the classified material." The Judge couldn't reveal details—he smiled—but, *"Suffice it to say, Mr. Giffen was a sig-*

nificant source of information to the U.S. government and a conduit of secret information from the Soviet Union during the Cold War."

Holy shit, Giffen really was an agent.

"For years, Mr. Giffen was a source able to work his way into the highest level of the Soviet government, an invaluable conduit for our agencies and interests. He was instrumental in the release and freedom for Soviet Jews."

My God, it's *Schindler's List, Part 2!* I was reminded of all the Nazis who grabbed some starving Jew after the war and claimed they had saved them.

"And then, after the end of the Soviet Union, Mr. Giffen used his connections with the President of Kazakhstan to work with the U.S. government in advancing our nations strategic and business interests."

So it's true. Poor Jack Grynberg. Giffen wasn't "some pipe salesman," as Grynberg thought. The State Department had set up Jack to rope in Nazarbayev, pay him what had to be paid, and get the oil away from the Russians and Chinese. But Jack went rogue and started up his one-man holy war on bribery. The Agencies sent in a replacement, Giffen, to take care of KO-2 and KO-1 and take Jack out. Well, Jack, "bad things can happen."

The Judge is working himself into a patriotic froth. Giffen "was one of the only Americans with sustained access to" the Kazakh kleptocrats. "These relationships, built up over a lifetime"—the Judge stared sternly at the two cheap suits—"were lost the day of his arrest."

In other words, you Justice guys with your dimwit FBI screwed this up bad, burning an intelligence asset. Schmucks.

I'm listening as the Judge apologizes for the FBI interrupting Giffen's transfers of cash.

He agrees with Giffen's mouthpiece. *"This ordeal must end!"*

Ordeal? At the Winged Foot Country Club? Maybe I'm in the wrong business.

"How does Mr. Giffen reclaim his good name? This court begins that process by acknowledging his service. We all owe Mr. Giffen our thanks."

Oh my god, is the Judge going to make us all stand up and say *Thank you, Mr. Giffen?*

Now sentence is pronounced. Giffen has pleaded guilty, but his record will show him only as making a paperwork error on a tax form, a misdemeanor far less severe than a DWI.

As bribery had been confessed, the felony will be charged against Giffen's corporation, which, as far as I can tell, exists mainly on paper. *Bad, bad piece of paper!* Even the piece of paper gets off lightly: the only "bribery" the Judge will put on record is *"a Christmas gift of two snowmobiles, only $16,000, gifts which are a common part of local culture."* (I don't remember snowmobiles in Terminal Town. A chicken, yes.) The law requires the Judge to charge the piece of paper a $32,000 fine, an amount Giffen has in change between his sofa cushions.

And Giffen himself? The Judge *apologized* to Giffen for his arrest and one night in the pokey. That would be his prison sentence, "time served," that one night. The Justice Department? They asked that Giffen should, at least, be given probation.

The Judge ruled, "There will be *no probation*." Giffen has suffered enough.

However, because Giffen pleaded guilty, there must be punishment, a fine.

"I must fine Mr. Giffen the required $25."

* * *

I worked my way into the elevator with the laughing, backslapping party on its way out for drinks. On the courthouse steps, I shook Giffen's hand and congratulated him. But I wouldn't let go. A cheap trick, that. Grinning at him while my grip turned his wrist subtly, I maneuvered Giffen into range for Rick's telephoto lens. Matty Pass, who'd slipped into the pack of his gleeful crowd, handed me a microphone from under my legs. I put it in Giffen's face.

"BP-Kazakhstan paid you half a million. What was *that* for?"

Giffen, who'd turned his head to take more congratulations, suddenly snapped around at me, "I never got paid by BP. There's no document to prove it." Matty handed me the document. The invoice mailed by BP to Grynberg.

The moment I showed it to him, Giffen shouted in my face, "Sleaze!" And just as I asked, "What did you pay Nazarbayev for BP?"—I got one hard-slamming body check from my blind side, nearly throwing me down the courthouse steps. From the scrum around Giffen, the muscular blonde locked eyes with me. If she did it, she earned her $600.

I deserved it, this slam, this final blow to any silly schoolboy hope that a teensy-weensy bit of justice remained in the system. I felt like I should offer to pay CIA agent Giffen's $25 fine. Here was an education worth paying for.

CHAPTER 7

My Home Is Now a Strange Place

ALASKA, BEFORE THE BEGINNING

Raven, that lying little bastard, came to Chenega Island, where the people slept and slept because there was only darkness. From His kayak, Raven gave them a box filled with Daylight, and in return, He demanded and they gave Him a wife, Qaleratalik, "Weasel in a Summer Dress." He fed Qaleratalik only moss from His beak, which she could not eat.

One day, when Raven was hungry, He told His grandchildren, "I have captured a huge seal just around the point." And when His grandchildren left their fire to look, Raven ate all their food. They returned, and Raven, laughing, asked them if they found the seal although He knew that there was no seal. And so, His grandchildren died of disappointment.

Uncounted millennia later, Russians arrived on Chenega Island. They told Chief Axuna about an Old Deceiver, Satan, who lives on this Earth; and Axuna, whose name meant "Cowardly Otter Anus," was christened and re-named Makarichemovitsky, which means "Little Bird." Then they took Little Bird's furs and whale oil.

The Orthodox priests in dark caftans christened another family, naming them Totemoff after the fancy sticks they worshipped, which the Russians burnt. Then, on Nuciiq Island, the priests baptized their cousins Kvasnikoff ("Whiskey-children"), kidnapped them, and abandoned them on the isolated end of an impenetrable glacier surrounded by the Gulf of Alaska. If the Whiskey-children didn't die, Russia would gain a supply depot and whaling station conveniently located at the entrance to Prince William Sound.

Axuna already knew all about the Old Deceiver; and Axuna knew Raven, the lying bastard, wasn't what he pretended to be, that Raven used charcoal and sorcery to appear handsomely black. For a thousand years, the Chugachmiut warned each generation that underneath, Raven is white, ugly like ice.

Mudqnò. That is all. There is no more.

In 1867, Abraham Lincoln's nasty little Secretary of State William Seward bought Alaska from the Imperial Czar for two and a half cents an acre. Of course, the Czar never actually owned it. Our young, troubled nation and Lincoln's successor, who despised Seward and especially his "polar bear garden," were happy to forget about Chenega village and the Chugachmiut Natives until Good Friday, 1964, two days too late to warn them . . . .

CHENEGA VILLAGE, PRINCE WILLIAM SOUND

Natives of Chenega tell the story of how the ice peaks of Montague Island jumped twice a man's height and just minutes later crashed back down.

Good Friday, March 27, 1964. At 5:36 P.M., seismologists' machines worldwide recorded a monster shake, 9.2 on the Richter scale, shimmying down Alaska's coast. Tsunami waves big as battleships were sure to follow. Warnings went out to coastal towns from Anchorage down to Malibu. But no message was sent to the shortwave at the Chugach Native village of Chenega in Prince William Sound near the quake's epicenter.

Seal hunter Nicholas Kompkoff, Chenega's chief, saw the ocean simply disappear in front of his stilt house. He knew right away the water had been sucked into a wave beyond the horizon and it would return with a vengeance.

Kompkoff shepherded his four daughters up the gravel slope toward the church on the high ground, pushing them to run as fast as possible on little legs. But not fast enough. Just as the wave hit, Nicholas reached out, grabbed the two girls closest to him and ran with one under each arm. His two other daughters were seized by the water and dragged out into the frozen Sound. One came back. Days later, Nicholas found her body stuck in the high branches of a pine tree.

Satellite telemetry indicates the Natives had way underestimated the mountain's leap. The snow peaks of Montague Island rose thirty-three feet, then fell, sending a wave measuring eighty-nine feet seven inches over Chenega village.

Nicholas's younger brother, Don, told me he was lifted by the wave but managed to grab the cross at the top of the church steeple, holding on to his life there, the only verifiable instance in which Jesus saved.

Two days after the quake, a postal plane flew over to drop the village's mail out its window but could not find Chenega—because it wasn't there. Of the dozens of stilt homes, every one of them was swept away—with a third of the residents still in them or fleeing. The pilot, Jimmy Firth, on a hunch and a second flyover, spotted a few wrecked pieces of the blue church roof.

Nicholas and those of his people who survived were boarded onto a rescue boat, divided up, and dumped in Anchorage, on Tatitlek Island, and at the Eyak village in Cordova.

Over the next few years, Nicholas became both a drunk and an Orthodox priest. In 1968, Father Nicholas put a gun under his chin and pulled the trigger. The bullet shattered his jaw but missed his brain. The church's embarrassed bishops defrocked him.

Still, each and every year on Good Friday, Nicholas and a few die-hard Chenegans would make the chilly pilgrimage by boat to the old village, to gather washed-up bones, leave one cross on the beach, and repeat an increasingly pathetic vow to return to the Sound and rebuild their homes.

Do miracles happen? I like to think so.

In March 1969, a helicopter descended from the heavens over Cordova, and a man from Humble Oil came looking for Father Nick with an offer to solve Chenega's problems. The biggest problem of all was that Raven had given Chenegans the sun and moon but failed to give them a signed deed for the real estate. No one in the village had a piece of paper saying, "We own this." Until they could get that piece of paper, Chenegans could not return.

The Humble man would fix that, using the powers of his company in Washington to get them the title to their island homeland. The company with the gentle name of Humble was the Alaskan subsidiary of something far less humble, Standard Oil Company, which would rename itself Exxon Corporation three years later.

"Mr. Humble" wanted only one thing in return from Nicholas: for him to sell Humble and its partners the old Chugach village of Valdez.

Valdez is a sacred place for the oil industry. The shaky geology of Alaska ("tsunamigenic subducting continental plates") made Valdez the only spot on the whole of the state's 44,000-mile-long coast that could handle a mammoth oil tanker port. Therefore, the Valdez property was worth, say, a couple of billion or so.

How much would the oil giants pay the Natives for Valdez? They offered Father Nicholas one dollar.

* * *

Maybe Nicholas Kompkoff was a "dumb, drunk Injun." Maybe not. I write this at Nicholas's grave on Evans Island, at the New Chenega village. Over here you can see the Arch Priest Nicholas Kompkoff Clinic and sobriety center and the little church with the blue cupola completed in time for Nicholas to lead his last prayers, and the two dozen little bungalows for the returned Natives, almost every one a millionaire.

Let us pause and pretend this is the happy ending. No sense jumping ahead to the tragic conclusion just yet.

* * *

Humble Oil and its less Humble parent, Exxon, came through, lobbying Congress to give Chenegans ownership of both the old village and the new one on Evans Island chosen by geologists as safe from tsunamis. On the twenty-fifth anniversary of the Great Earthquake, the families of New Chenega sailed to the old village to lay crosses among the ruins. Then, they sailed back to bless their new homes. It was Good Friday, 1989.

That night, at four minutes past midnight, the *Exxon Valdez* ran aground and spilled more than eleven million gallons of oil. The black wave soon engulfed the old village, then the new one, and then its fishing grounds, blinding and burning every seal in their rookery, smothering all shellfish, killing a million birds, slathering contaminants across one thousand miles of waterfront, and leaving New Chenega isolated in a poisoned sea. The three thousand years of Chugachmiut life subsisting off the Sound's waters had come to its end.

Mudqnò. That is all. There is no more.

WORLD TRADE CENTER, NEW YORK

Until March 24, 1989, the morning of the spill, no one cared if a Chugach Native dropped dead, which they did, often and young.

But, beginning four minutes past midnight, these Natives, for the lucky lawyers who caught one, became a summer house in the Hamptons, a Mercedes with all the trimmings, Rod Stewart singing you "Happy Birthday," a younger mistress, *and* a new trophy wife.

One Chugach was worth—I don't want to exaggerate—maybe a fifth of their weight in golden legal fees. Each Native was redeemable, like coupons, for all these things, Rod Stewart included, if only you could get yourself a Chugach.

The silver-haired attorney Melvin Belli was accosted by a fellow passenger on the first flight from San Francisco to Anchorage. "I see, Mr. Belli, you are chasing ambulances again." Belli replied, "Madame, I get there *before* the ambulance."

This would be a legal turkey shoot for plaintiffs' lawyers. Within days of the tanker grounding, Exxon said it would pay for all the damage. The Exxon man said so on TV. Exxon would do, "whatever it takes to keep you whole."

No risk, then: Get yourself a Native, sue, and take your slice. Quick, easy, lucrative. On the other side of the table, oil company lawyers did not just dream of Mercedes. They ordered them the day the tanker grounded: From four minutes after midnight, they began billing a Malibu beach house a week—and they would get it, win or lose.

I was trying to wake up the guy who slept in the box in front of my office door on Second Avenue. My neighbor hadn't yet swept up the crack vials (she made them into art objects). I had coffee in one hand, a bagel with scallion cream cheese in the other, and I could hear my phone ringing and ringing upstairs. I paid the guy in the box his toll (fifty cents), ran up the flight *(Doesn't anyone sweep these steps?)*, and got the message to get to the World Trade Center *"right now, Palast."*

Hill, Betts and Nash is one of those quiet white-shoe firms that provide discreet representation for Her Majesty and the Lloyd's list on matters of Admiralty Law. They made certain Britannia ruled the waves, including handling the last little mess BP made in the *Torrey Canyon* crack-up. These gentlemen would not rush off to Prince William Sound to grab themselves an Indian. But Hill, Betts could count on the Native-napping lawyers to call on them to actually handle matters of the law of the sea.

Lawyers need facts (now and again) on which to argue the case and calculate the damages and thereby their fees. So when I saw Exxon's tanker on the front page that morning, I figured I'd get a call. As a detective, I specialized in the work most sober people would find numbingly dull, requiring the creation (or destruction) of proprietary computer algorithms, but mostly, deep dives into tens of thousands of pages of corporate documents and account books, decades old and covered with dust and bullshit. It was worth millions, even billions, to my clients, and in return, they paid for my bagels.

I took the message, ran downstairs, jumped the box (I only paid going in, not out), and cabbed it to World Trade Tower One, where Hill, Betts commandeered the entire fifty-second floor. I walked past the stares at reception (I dressed like a slob), down a discreet, carpeted hall lined with models of clippers, steamers, cruise liners, and the portraits of the mustachioed founders of the firm, to the office of the Senior Partner. It always knocked me out: the view of the Statue of Liberty when I worked there into the night and, when I bothered to look down, the pretty lights of the jam-up on the West Side Highway.

"You'll *love* this one, Palast. It's got everything for you: a big bad oil company, trees and birds covered in oil—and poor little Indians." Greg O'Neill enjoyed making fun of bleeding-heart liberals like me.

At the reception desk, I had picked up an envelope with a Delta ticket to Anchorage.

"Palast"—O'Neill grinned some more—"I'm telling you: This will be your Vietnam." Well, at least the ticket was first class.

* * *

The first thing our new Chugach clients ordered our gold-plated legal team to do was sue to prevent the *Exxon Valdez* from returning to their Alaskan waters. Not any other tanker, just the *Exxon Valdez*.

The Natives hoped to ward off the return of the Tanker of Death, the vessel of the Deceiver, the Raven, the one who had killed his grandchildren with broken promises.

You can call it goofy, you can call it superstitious. But the U.S. Congress did not find the Natives' demand to bar the Devil Ship as insane as you might find it. In 1990, Congress voted the ban into law. But then, insanity has never deterred Congress.

Ultimately, Exxon did patch up the supertanker, rechristening it with a name suggested by thoughtful PR consultants: VLCC *SeaRiver Mediterranean*. But the Natives weren't fooled. They were wise enough to demand the ship's banishment from Alaska no matter what name Exxon painted on its bow.

By winning passage of the "Tanker of Death" law, the Natives had suc-
ceeded in keeping the cursed *Exxon Valdez/SeaRiver* away from Alaska. The
problem is that the Natives' satanic blackbird god is a trickster, never wearing
the same mask twice. "Careful," my late Eyak friend Laughing Eagle told me,
"Satan is a beautiful woman, the most beautiful woman." The Devil never
appears in the form you are expecting.

In May 1996, after the ban on the devil ship went into effect, Exxon's
Mobil unit launched a new tanker for the Alaska run. I called the company, but
no one could tell me why they named the new tanker the VLCC *Raven*.

* * *

It was the most expensive tanker launch ever. Never in the history of ship-
building has a buyer spent so many millions on publicizing a new ship that
didn't take passengers.

The oil giant ran double-page ads in papers across America trumpeting
the vessel they cutely called "*two of the safest ships ever built,*" meaning that
there was one tanker inside another, a "double-hull" ship. If the outer hull col-
lides with a reef, the oil remains safely inside the second, inner hull. It would
have prevented "most of history's collision-caused spills," the ads told us.

The oil company's big ads were headlined, "QUOTH THE RAVEN: NEVER-
MORE." But then, that's what Raven *always* says. Once again, we encounter
V. S. Naipaul's axiom about imperial chiefs: They don't lie, they *elide*.

Here's what the oily eliders left out:

In 1971, eighteen years before the *Exxon Valdez* hit Bligh Reef, the Alaska
State Legislature passed a very un-insane law requiring the use of double-
hulled tankers on the Valdez oil route. But Chevron, Exxon and Mobil sued to
block the double-hull law. They won. In other words, had the oil companies
not killed the law, the *Exxon Valdez* would have had two hulls and the spill
would never have occurred.

Mobil built its much-ballyhooed double-hull tanker in 1996 simply
because the company had no choice. Double hulls were written into federal
law right after the *Exxon Valdez* disaster.

Back in 1971, British Petroleum was still the baby sister of the oil giants.
New on the scene, BP dutifully built three double-hull tankers to operate from
Valdez in accordance with the Alaska law. But when their oil company sib-
lings sued and won the right to go one-hull naked, BP spent several million

dollars rerouting the ship's pipes to fill in the safety gap between the two hulls. This marked the first time in history that an oil corporation made a major investment in deliberately making their ships less safe.

PRINCE WILLIAM SOUND, ALASKA, 1989

State Inspector Dan Lawn, grabbing a fast launch from Valdez, was the first to reach the shipwrecked tanker, risking the ride through the sickening fumes and fountains of crude that could explode with the touch of a match. In the tower, Captain Joseph Hazelwood, three sheets to the wind, greeted the Inspector. Everyone knew The Inspector. "Hell of a way to end a career, huh, Dan? What should I do?"

Inspector Lawn said, "Joe, I'd start by putting out that cigarette."

* * *

That's it? Some drunk at the wheel of a tanker drives it up on a reef and ruins a thousand miles of coastline? Just one of those *ooops . . .* sorry! moments. Human error.

The newspapers, TV stations, government, everyone bought the human-error story. Exxon was culpable, but only because they let a known alky take the wheel.

I didn't buy it. It was too easy, too perfect.

The smoking gun is just left there, right next to the body, oily fingerprints all over the place: "DRUNK SKIPPER HITS REEF."

We had the perp (Captain Hazelwood) and the weapon (the VLCC *Exxon Valdez*). Hazelwood was drunk and the drunk driver drove the ship onto the rocks just like your dumb cousin Louie who killed two six-packs and ran his pickup right through the garage door. Simple. Too simple.

And something else was suspicious. Exxon *didn't deny it*. Exxon really seemed to like the story: Yep, we had a drunk at the wheel; he cracked up the boat; wasn't our fault he was drunk but, boy, are we sorry; and we'll pay for the mess he made. Case closed.

Why was the biggest corporation on the planet so ready to take the blame for its captain? Why were they so ready to say, "We did it—that is, our guy did it—and we'll pay."

Did Exxon have a heart? A soul? A sense of guilt and honor?

And was I just some cynical sonovabitch who only thinks the worst of the corporate animal?

Hazelwood was charged and found guilty of operating a boat while intoxicated (a conviction later overturned on a technicality). He paid a fine, lost his license, did penance in a soup kitchen. His employer was guilty of leaving a drunk driver in charge and paid a fine of nearly a billion dollars, no complaint. Why couldn't I just drop it there?

Whether Exxon had a heart, I couldn't say, not having had the pleasure of doing an autopsy. But I knew it had a *scheme*. And, in the shadows, another company on my own list of suspects, British Petroleum, had, I was sure, an even *schemier* scheme.

CORDOVA, PRINCE WILLIAM SOUND, 1989

Four plane changes in twenty hours got me to the Alaska Bar in Cordova. Not to drink—I myself wasn't yet a drunk. (I hated alcohol except for cherry wine at Passover.) I started there because that's where most things start in Alaska, in a tavern, whether shipwrecks or homewrecks.

At this bar across from the docks, I found Cliff Olsen, an Eyak Native, one of my clients, getting a light buzz on. A navigation map showing the tanker channel was nailed up near the end of the wooden counter. Cliff ran a finger down the map from Valdez to the sea. "Hell, I've taken boats through the Narrows stone drunk and never hit a damn reef."

Really?

After leaving the bar, I called the World Trade Center and spoke with Gordon Arnott, a ship's navigator turned lawyer. Many of the lawyers at the Admiralty firm had experience in the salt, and Arnott had steered tankers through the Sound. "That's right," he said. "We *always* left Valdez after some 'pops.'"

And something else: Hazelwood wasn't driving the *Exxon Valdez* drunk. *Because he wasn't driving.* He was nowhere near the helm. He was passed out below-decks, snoozing off the boozing.

Now we're cookin'.

OLD CHENEGA, KNIGHT ISLAND

Exxon and its industry partners paid Father Nicholas a dollar for the inestimably valuable Valdez. But Nick's signature alone wasn't enough. For the oil combine to lock down Valdez, Nicholas would have to divide his dollar with other Chugach village chiefs and get their signatures, too.

Their first target: Tatitlek's chief, George Gordaoff. In 1989, I found him in his log bungalow in the Eyak Natives' Old Village, located in deep forest, miles from Cordova. George, age showing, was on the couch, not well. His wife, Mary, who'd taken over as Chief, had kept the papers from those meetings with the oil men decades earlier. She got angrier and angrier as she unfolded each document and map.

In 1969, Gordaoff, then a commercial fisherman, knew any tanker leaving Valdez would have to steer clear of Bligh Reef, a hazard right off their village island. Gordaoff worried that if oil hit Bligh or nearby fisheries, it would be the end.

So when the oil company honchos came around for his signature, Gordaoff told them, before he'd take their dollar bill, they would have to agree to use the latest in radar, or forget it. The lawyers for Humble Oil told him to put his radar plan in writing. That must have given them a chuckle. They knew Gordaoff was illiterate.

But Mary encouraged him to dictate his detailed plans, including what he knew of Loran-C radar and radio tower placement. So the oil companies were stuck, and the demand for radar was typed into the deal for Valdez. That was Promise #1: radar.

Gordaoff also demanded escorts. He said there would be no deal unless the tankers had escort boats to guide them around the reef. The Natives knew it like the backs of their hands, so they offered to pilot the guide tugs. The oil companies added Promise #2: escorts with experienced pilots.

The company lawyers then ran off with the Natives' signatures to a Democrat-controlled Congress that was about to vote down the Pipeline. Congress favored an all-land route for North Slope oil, safer than tankers from Valdez but a heck of a lot more expensive to construct. But now that the Natives, the ancient stewards of the land, were A-OK with shipping oil—sprinkled with radar and stuff—who the hell is the Sierra Club to say it's unsafe?

The oil companies who would own the Pipeline, a consortium including Exxon, ARCO, Shell, and Sohio (British Petroleum's American cover), put the radar, equipment, and pilot promises into their congressional testimony and into pledges to the Department of the Interior. That gave the oil companies' promises to the Natives the force of law. The oil company executives swore in their permit filing,

> "Sophisticated navigation equipment and highly trained ship personnel should eliminate any probability of groundings in the Prince William Sound."

On the night of March 24, 1989, the *Exxon Valdez* did indeed have the most sophisticated radar you could buy, the Raycas Fairways system, the first GPS. Today you could buy it for maybe two hundred bucks, but back then, it cost millions to install and required special training to operate. So Exxon had it turned off.

Another seaman turned lawyer, Terry Gargan at Hill, Betts, figured that one out. The radar had been busted since the ship's maiden voyage two years earlier. The company decided, hey, why blow money on a system the crew didn't know how to use anyway. The "highly trained personnel" were clueless about working the Raycas system.

With radar equipment out of business, the ship was not legally fit to sail. Exxon knew it, but the ship sailed anyway. The oil industry did live up to its promise to sail the Sound escorted by an emergency pilot tug—twenty years after they made the promise, *after* the *Exxon* spill, and then, only under threat of legal sanctions.

*   *   *

With the documents Chief Mary and George handed me, we now had the oil company promises in writing. But so what?

A promise made by one oil corporation to another oil corporation is a contract. A promise made to a Native is a *what*? A treaty? A statement of goodwill you can wipe your ass with?

I knew what it was: *a crime*. The crime was racketeering. RICO: The federal crime named after Johnny Rico, the movieland mobster played by Edward G. Robinson, the Racketeer Influenced and Corrupt Organizations Act. I had to

convince a judge and jury, as well as our own lawyers, that Exxon and its partners were a mob equivalent to the Cosa Nostra, to the Mafia, against which the
RICO law was aimed.

There is a difference of course. Unlike the Mafia, Exxon and partners had
a huge advertising budget and a Texas oilman named Herbert Walker Bush in
the White House.

But I had this: Exxon and its partners had suckered the Natives into giving
away something valuable in return for a lie. That smelled an awful lot like
"fraudulent inducement," the first "predicate act" needed to bring a RICO case.

I had these scraps of paper from a Native woman in the woods. To charge
the world's biggest corporations as gangsters, I would need a whole lot more:
It required reviewing thousands of pages of supporting documents we'd have
to somehow uncover. And it would require my best and soberest years.

STEINHATCHEE, FLORIDA

We also needed witnesses. I needed insiders who would spill to outsiders. To
find them, I needed a hound dog. I needed a blonde.

I needed Lenora Stewart.

Lenora is a Southern belle, very blond, with a light, lilting accent and the
gentility of an alligator with indigestion, the gnarliest PI you'd ever want to
avoid. If I ask Lenora to hunt down a deer, she'll come back with just a bloody
leg, burping with satisfaction.

She grew up on the bad side of Steinhatchee, Florida (I'm not sure there
was a good side), where drag races are still run on the hard beach sand.

I needed Lenora to put her lovely claws on and dig. Her new assignment
would be to convince people to put their careers, reputations, and fortunes on
the firing line.

SEATTLE, WASHINGTON

But before heading to the far north, Lenora stopped in Washington State to
meet with a man who could not chance setting foot in Alaska, Captain James
Woodle, once Alyeska's Marine Superintendent for the Port of Valdez.

Years before the *Exxon Valdez* crack-up, in no-BS memos, Captain Woodle
warned the Alyeska chiefs that spill containment equipment was missing,
busted, inadequate, a frightening joke. He was told to zip it. He didn't.

Alyeska waited, and watched. Then, on an icy day in February 1984, he went into colleague Henrietta Fuller's office to use the copy machine, and closed the door to keep out the cold. He was in her office "from 0820 to 0840," someone noted with military precision. This information, including a notation that Fuller later borrowed the Captain's sweater, went all the way up to George Nelson, BP's President of the Alaska oil consortium. And the order came down: Alyeska could now fire Woodle without fear he'll squawk.

The Captain's immediate Alyeska supervisor waved the file at him: the absurd evidence of his twenty-minute "affair" and the threat that Woodle, a married man, could be smeared with it. The Captain wouldn't back down: He insisted BP and Exxon were not prepared for an oil spill. The Captain was then relieved of his keys, his badge, fired for "insubordination," and escorted from the docks.

Woodle told his wife of the phonied-up "affair" file. But Alyeska held another card: The Captain was told that unless he kept his memos from the eyes of public and regulators, he would lose severance benefits. Furthermore, the Captain would have to agree, in writing, to leave Valdez, where he'd been a City Councilman, forever. Under the threat of financial ruin, he signed.

But then, after the tanker hit, the Captain decided it was time to speak to us about the cover-ups and the threats.

So, crucial equipment was missing. That's stupidity, carelessness, negligence. But knowing it and concealing it, that's fraud, a second "predicate act" necessary to bring a case under the RICO racketeering law.

How do we know it was deliberate concealment? We talked to those ordered to do the concealing.

TANKER PORT, VALDEZ

There were lots of oils spills in Alaska waters before the *Exxon Valdez* cracked. Smaller, true, but it would have signaled the system had gone to hell. BP's Alyeska's water samples would have picked up the traces of spilled oil. Lenora found Erlene Blake, a technician in the Alyeska testing lab. Erlene told us that Alyeska kept a bucket of oil-free seawater in the lab. If they found evidence of hydrocarbon in the Sound's waters, they were directed to dump it down the sink and refill the sample vials from the bucket of clean water. They called it the Miracle Barrel.

What else?

The Chugach agreement to sign away Valdez imposed a requirement on the companies:

> "BE IT FURTHER RESOLVED that the several oil companies employ the latest chemical and other anti-pollution methods for protection of the fisheries, wild life and migratory birds at all times."

The state rules required it anyway, so the oil men agreed. You want equipment? *Hey, we got it!* The key piece of equipment would be state-of-the-art "containment barges" loaded with the best and newest Vikoma Ocean Packs, miles of rubber to hold in the oil and skimmers to suck up the oil caught by the rubber corral.

In May 1977, as the first tankers left from Valdez, oil consortium honchos reassured worried State of Alaska environmental officials by promising two containment barges, one of them

> ". . . to be located near Bligh Island, which could double as a pilot station."

With these containment and skimmer vessels at "strategic locations along the coasts," they assured the state, they could pick up all but a fraction of the biggest spill. The BP-Alyeska plan was, I admit, pretty good-looking. On paper. But you can't pick up much oil with a couple sheets of paper.

The *Exxon Valdez* crashed right there at Bligh.

Think about that. First off, if they'd put up the pilot station, there is no way on Earth that the tanker would have sailed right into it. Even a stone-drunk pilot would notice a supertanker bearing down on his kitchen. The ship would have been warned off. And if the equipment had been there, as I've told you, no one would remember the *Exxon Valdez* today. The rubber and the skimmers and suckers could have been set out in minutes, not days as happened. It would have been like a fire started across the street from a fire department.

So where were the wondrous containment vessels? One of them *simply didn't exist*. The other was out of business for repairs, locked up in dry dock at Valdez, its equipment stored away in warehouses or locked in ice (this is Alaska).

You could say that was dumb, the barges that weren't there. But stupid is not fraud. Deliberate fibs are.

To nail the racketeering charges, I had Lenora hunt through the state files looking for something that wasn't there, "the dog that didn't bark." She confirmed: there was no record of a Notification of Nonreadiness per rule 18 AAC 75.340 *and* 75.350.

We are supposed to hate all those nasty little regulations with strings of numbers and dots. But we have them because corporate powers can't be trusted unless they are hog-tied in red tape. Unfortunately, the law assumes that oil companies are honest as nuns and would confess to not having working equipment and will voluntarily fill out a Notice of Nonreadiness and then shut down the entire pipeline system.

No tanker can move from Valdez if the containment vessels are out of business, "Nonreadiness." That is just plain common sense—and it's the law. But it's also expensive. A typical VLCC is hauling $50 million in crude. Ten ships backed up means half a billion dollars just sitting on its ass and waiting. BP and the gang could not let that happen. So they lied. That is, they elided. They didn't fill out the Nonreadiness form, and they let the *Exxon Valdez* sail.

Even when the ship was bleeding oil, Alyeska kept up the con. From the ship, Inspector Lawn radioed Alyeska, wanting to know when the heck the containment vessel would arrive. Alyeska's Bill Shier radioed back, "It's on its way, Dan. On its way."

The truth was, it hadn't left the dock. It finally showed up fourteen hours after the grounding. By that time, the slick was spread over a hundred square miles of water and was on the move. There wasn't enough rubber boom in the world to corral it.

PRINCE WILLIAM SOUND, ALASKA

You can't run supertankers through danger zones without a team of first responders ready to jump if stuff happens. It's like a fire department for oil shipping. Congress demanded it, the regulators required it, and the oil companies promised it. Humble Exxon and ARCO, to sucker in the Natives out of their property, promised the Chugach all the response team jobs as the "good consideration" in the purchase contract for Valdez where the price is stated as, "One dollar and other good consideration."

BP's Alyeska came through on this promise. They trained the Natives to drop from helicopters, lay protective boom, run skimmers, and be ready to roll 24/7.

It wasn't seal hunting, but it was money.

And then BP fired them all. After seven years, once the Natives helped the company break the Teamsters Union, the Natives were dumped, and for more than a decade the full-time spill response crews required by contract and law were manned by ghosts. Alyeska just grabbed some names off its payroll and dubbed them "oil spill response" crew. A few were given enough training and a minimum of equipment for "showtime"—inspections.

Covering up of the elimination of the Native emergency response crews was not easy. How do you make Natives simply disappear? How do you shut down the fire department without someone noticing? Someone did notice: Inspector Lawn. The man is fueled by suspicion, a walking accusation machine—and always correct. Always. Based on his detective's sense of smell, the Inspector wrote a memo dated May 1, 1984, wondering if the BP consortium had secretly eliminated its "dedicated force" for spills. A surprise inspection was needed.

But Alyeska doesn't like surprises. BP's oil group insisted that it be given notice of the "surprise" reviews. On November 4, 1986, Alyeska informed the government:

> "This is written to provide information to use in planning the un-- announced spill drill. . . . November 19 would be the best day. . . ."

BP kindly suggested a couple other days and times when, with sufficient notice, they would allow a surprise inspection.

But Inspector Lawn, on his own, showed up unannounced for an unannounced inspection. BP, caught with its corporate pants down, screamed to its political friends in the government. Lawn was demoted, no longer an inspector, locked to a desk and hung out the window by his heels as a warning to other inspectors who dreamed of surprises.

A union complaint got Lawn's badge back. But Alyeska wasn't done with him. They tapped his phone. British Petroleum's chief in the United States hired Wackenhut Corporation to listen in on The Inspector just doing his job. (I'd investigated these Wackenhut guys, now operating under the alias "Geo," for negligent homicide, child rape, and espionage.* Nice guys.) They were trying to get something on The Inspector to stop him from talking to Congress. They got nothing. Brutal doesn't mean competent. And luckily, they were incompetent enough to get caught. I don't think BP minded that: The word went forth that these Brits didn't hold their teacups with their pinkies in the air.

Another state inspector wrote a memo moaning that "I would like to see an unannounced spill drill scheduled for, say, ten P.M. January 2."

But he didn't dare, lest he got BP's Inspector Lawn treatment.

```
      Bob Martin
      Deputy Director
      EQO, Anchorage                          FILE NO.

Thru:Bill Lamoreaux                           TELEPHONE NO.
      District Office Coordinator
      SCRO                                     SUBJECT.

From:Dan Lawn
      District Office Supervisor
      PWSDO, Valdez


      Over the past several months, there has taken
      the Alyeska Valdez Marine Terminal operational

      Not only have there been severe personnel cut:
      tine maintenance have been reduced drasticall
```

---

* For more on Wackenhut, espionage, child rape, and homicide, visit GregPalast.com/Vul turesPicnic.

On the night the *Exxon Valdez* hit their reef, the oil spill response team at Gary Kompkoff's village, stripped of their jobs, authority, and equipment, just watched hemorrhaging crude flow by, helpless.

Now I was up to four frauds committed upon the Natives, not to mention the con job on regulators:

PROMISE #1: State-of-the-art radar. Missing, and non-operation concealed.

PROMISE #2: Oil spill equipment. Missing, and absence concealed.

PROMISE #3: Spill containment barges. Not operating, not loaded, condition concealed.

PROMISE #4: Work on the spill response teams. The jobs were terminated, and danger concealed.

So, in giving up Valdez, the Natives, as my dad would say, were "screwed, blued, and tattooed." So were Congress, the regulators, and the public.

However, screwing the public is not a crime. But racketeering is. For racketeering charges to stick, I needed a conspiracy.

Let me stop here and talk about conspiracies. "Conspiracy" has gotten a bad rap of late. When I'm on American TV, I can assume I'll be called "a conspiracy nut." It always gets a laugh—from the conspirators.

I'm not a conspiracy nut but a conspiracy *expert*. "Conspiracy" as I'd describe it in a courtroom is nothing more than an agreement between two or more parties, acting in secret, acting in concert, who know their scheme is going to hurt someone.

To file a RICO claim, I'd need a conspiracy. With these guys, it was like picking one chocolate from a big candy heart.

This one would do. . . .

PHOENIX, ARIZONA

August 1988. Seven months before the spill.

The Boys are having a meeting, doors closed. The chieftains of British Petroleum, Exxon, Mobil, ARCO, Hess, Unocal, and Phillips Petroleum have gathered to discuss their pipeline.

As far as the oilmen in the room were concerned, Theo Polasek, that pain in the ass, and their other Valdez managers, had gone up to Alaska and "gone native," bitching and moaning for equipment in case of a tanker grounding. Did they think the Alyeska consortium is made out of money? (It is, but that's a detail.)

In the old days when competing corporate big shots met, it was called an illegal cartel, market fixing, monopoly:

> "People of the same trade seldom meet together, even for merriment and diversion, but the conversation ends in a conspiracy against the public, or in some contrivance to raise prices."

That's Adam Smith, another conspiracy nut. But no one asked his opinion. Adam Smith burned *whale* oil, so what the hell did he know about getting crude out from under the caribou?

Anyway, it wasn't a cartel, it was a *"consortium,"* a perfectly legal entity. And it had a really smiley-face name: Al-*YES!*-ka.

The Alyeska Boys (and they are always boys) owned the pipeline together, but the leader was the new kid on the petroleum block, British Petroleum. The pipeline, the shipping lanes, and the containment and clean-up of a spill fell to BP. The British had the biggest slice, so Alyeska was their baby and it was their job, BP-Alyeska's alone, to make sure of two things: no explosions, no spills.

There were explosions and there were spills. That should have provided several lessons for their future operations in the Gulf of Mexico. But what was the lesson?

BP was in charge but it couldn't spend a dime without an OK from a majority of the consortium members, and that meant taking coins from the tight pockets of the Exxon Texans. To them, BP's fool of a manager in Valdez wanted to spend millions and millions on an oil spill that had not happened.

The Port Superintendent, Theo Polasek, complained to them that, with the meager bit of equipment he had in Alaska, containing a spill "at the mid-point of the Prince William Sound is not possible" in case a tanker grounded there. The companies promised twice, in writing, to the state, that they would put out the equipment at Bligh Island. But it wasn't there. Not having it there meant jacking the regulators.

So what happened? When BP suggested spending at least a couple of shekels to make good on the consortium's written commitment, a nod to the line drawn by the law, the Exxon rep spat. His company didn't intend to give good Yankee dollars to some pussies from England to blow on protecting seals and avoiding icebergs.

ARCO's chief, Stanley Factor, wrote to a BP Senior Vice President that he better not spend a dime until ARCO and Exxon said he could—and that was that. No equipment for Bligh Island.

In fact, if an Exxon tanker bumped an iceberg, Exxon would take care of it itself, so no one had to worry. That was stone cold against the law—and for good reason. You don't want each oil company with their own little untested, seat-of-the-pants response system.

Seven months later, when the *Exxon Valdez* ran aground, Exxon dramatically took charge of the emergency. Exxon's seat-of-their-pants spill response didn't even have the pants: no equipment, no plan. While watching the *Exxon* oil hit the fan, BP-Alyeska was more than happy to slink away from its responsibility.

So, there I had Fraud #5: Concealed pass-off of the spill plan—and a count of conspiracy to boot.

* * *

How do I know what happened in closed meetings and conversations between honchos? It's on paper. The photocopier is the investigator's prayers come true. People like memos and copies of memos. Making paper is what most managers do.

Bless them. A paleontologist glues together bones to make a dinosaur. Likewise, I have to tape each piece of paper into a psycho-dramatic map of a conspiracy.

In my investigation of the nuclear industry, one exec routinely asked his secretary to shred incriminating files. She did so, and routinely made a copy of each to keep in a file marked "Shredded Documents."

Dumb, eh? Or not. Before you add this to the sexist blonde jokes in your head, think for a moment: What kind of salary does an executive secretary earn who can at any moment whip out a file called "shredded"?

Hail to the photocopier! The Small People's weapon of choice.

(And light a candle in thanks for cc's on e-mail.)

PRINCE WILLIAM SOUND

March 1989. Inspector Lawn, sleepless, yet methodical and calm, confronted the oil slick, now as wide, unrelenting, and merciless as the Russian front. BP, by law in charge of the response, didn't lift a finger; but their boobacious executives chattered away, jamming up the emergency radio channel, and chiming in with a brilliant suggestion: Can we send over a wave of bombers to drop tons of chemical dispersant, bombing a pathway through the oil slick so BP tankers can resume their business?

I didn't have to ask Inspector Lawn his response.

* * *

Beyond the fraud investigation, I was given a tougher job: talking to our own clients, the Chugach.

At trial, I would have to give the jury a number, my calculation of "hedonistic" damages. How much is it worth to be a Native, to hold fast as the last Americans to live on what they could hunt and catch and gather? And then— *ka-BAM!*—you lose it. What's that worth?

NEW CHENEGA, EVANS ISLAND

I couldn't easily keep my eyes off the half-dozen slash marks cutting a parallel pattern across Larry Evanoff's torso. He'd invited me to join him in his sweat lodge. I was killing time waiting for Chuck, the Chenega Corporation President, who was out somewhere doing his breakfast doobie, to show up at the busted-up trailer that constituted the Corporate Headquarters.

Not everyone in these villages is thrilled to have an outsider arrive with a notebook and questions—how would you feel about someone with a clipboard measuring the value of your life?—so when the pontoon plane dropped me off, I took it slow.

Larry was only alive because of the cruelty of the Bureau of Indian Affairs.

He was snatched away from home and sent to the Lower 48 to Indian school. They didn't teach much, but that was not their purpose. They were created to knock the Native out of their students. A word in a Native language was punished with a whack. Seal-hunting skills could not be easily passed on in Texas or Seattle or wherever the hell they were sent. Students had no sight of home or family for years. That would interfere with the task of melting Indians into the great American melting pot.

But the BIA's Kampf Amerikana saved Larry from the '64 tsunami; or, at least, it saved him from watching the wave grab his parents, grandparents, and little sister. The Evanoffs were gone, except for Larry.

Some time after Father Nicholas had tried to kill himself, Larry told the Father he was going back to Chenega even though there was no Chenega to go back to.

Larry had tried America. After the Service, he got a city job as an air traffic controller. Then Pappy Reagan fired every air traffic controller who joined in a strike over their insane working conditions. Reagan had been in the service too and, like Larry, flew combat missions. But Reagan could not remember that his flights were only on movie sets. Nevertheless, Americans loved Reagan because a fake warrior with a happy grin beats the hell out of a scarred-up Indian who doesn't smile when the camera's light goes on.

For Larry, that was it for the American Dream. Evanoff took off for his island in a barge, loaded with a generator and some power tools. In the dead middle of absolutely nowhere, he put together a house and then brought in his wife and two kids, ages eight and ten. The sub-Arctic winter closed in. There was no way out, no way in, no shortwave radio, and nothing but the meat he'd put up to skin and smoke, deer he shot standing at his front door, and seal taken from the rookery across the Sound at Montague Island. And salmon that wiggled right up to the cabin.

I couldn't imagine doing that. My own island. A life without a Whole Foods Market, without 7-Elevens with cop cars in front, without the friends we promise to get together with, without Disney World and parking tickets and meetings with publishers. *How could I ever give that up?*

After a couple of winters, the Chenega diaspora joined Larry. It was 1984. They put together about two dozen bungalows and a church with a steeple for Nicholas, whom they still called Father.

What about those stripes, Larry? Some kind of Native ritual scarification? "Yeah," Larry said. "The sacred Vietnam Ritual." He told me he got the stripes riding a helicopter when a burst of small-arms fire came close enough to sear his skin.

Larry had called it quits on the America of union-busting Presidents and their habit of stuffing the powerless into helicopters to be shot at. He had escaped to return to the Pleistocene life, isolated from the alien madness. Then, in 1989, Exxon crashed America right into his house: camera crews, oil company executives, and Vice President Dan Quayle standing on a plank of wood so his tasseled loafers wouldn't get smeared. Not to mention an over-zealous gumshoe from New York.

The leading edge of the oil moved south and it had to go somewhere. Since BP had failed to provide that rubber containment boom, something had to capture and hold the fast-swimming oil. That would be Chenega. Exxon designated Chenega's fisheries, clam beds and rookeries as "sacrifice" zones. Of course, it wasn't Exxon that would make the sacrifice.

The seal rookery was a death zone now. There was still a lot of salmon, in your choice of leaded or unleaded. Clams were declared deadly poisonous by the State. Chenega lived on food drops now, flown in by Exxon. Refugees in their own homes.

Father Nicholas's church, once the tallest structure on the island, was soon topped by a mountain of cans and crates and other garbage. Larry hadn't thought of building a dump on the island because, before the spill, he never had to take plastic wrap off his lunch.

Until March 24, 1989, you could say that Larry, in his office of forest and ocean, was God's employee. Now, once again, Larry was fired. That left him the only job oil offered. He was back in uniform: spending his workdays zipped into a head-to-toe yellow-orange Hazmat suit, wiping Exxon's crud off the rocks on his beaches. He was back on the clock.

Eight years after the spill, Gail and Larry invited me again to stay with them in their cabin. In the morning, I boated out with him and other islanders, to watch them pressure-blast the rancid oil still left at Sleepy Bay. To look at their spattered outfits after an hour, you'd think they'd hit a gusher.

* * *

During the investigation, I hung around Father Nicholas's kid brother, Paul, by then seventy-something. He was Uncle Paul to everyone. His conversations had more silence than words, thinking about what he had heard, then thinking through what he would say. For a New Yorker, this was physically painful.

Paul looked out his window at the water. What are you thinking about, Uncle Paul? "I think about their bones."

At the Old Chenega, Naked Island, junk captured by the tsunami, pots and pans and toys, would wash up on the beach. And so would the bones. Maybe they were his parents. Naked Island was also "sacrificed" and now the bones were soaked in crude oil. Chenegans complained and Exxon's chief kindly agreed to order clean-up crews to stop picking up bone "souvenirs."

Then the Exxon circus came to town. With camera crews at Exxon's call, the company CEO, Lee Raymond, showed up at Chenega to show his concern for the victims of that drunk-driving reprobate Hazelwood.

Uncle Paul told me, "I feel hungry all the time. They bring me your store food. I eat it. But I still feel hungry." He also told that to Mr. Exxon who, abracadabra, ordered a crate-load of seal meat for Chenega. It came in cans marked *NOT FOR HUMAN CONSUMPTION*. Zoo food.

Years later, when I met up with Chenega Corporation's president in Anchorage, I asked him if, like other Natives, he received "subsistence" food only Natives may legally capture, such as seal meat.

Chuck gave me a look. "Seal meat? You ever *smell* that shit? Give me a Big Mac anytime."

Well, *de gustabis non est disputandum*.

NANWALEK

"They flew in frozen pizza, satellite dishes, Hondas. Guys who were on sobriety drinking all night, beating up their wives. I mean, all that money. Man, people just went *berserk*."

Sally Ash Kvasnikoff, Chief Vince's sister, told me, "This place went *wild*. They gave us rags and buckets, at sixteen-something an hour to wipe off rocks, to *babysit our own children*."

The village of three dozen Native families at the end of the Kenai Fjord Glacier had survived on the sea and forest since the Russians marooned them there a century earlier. Now they survived on the Exxon payroll.

But it took two weeks before the party started. Nanwalek heard reports of the leading edge of the oil slick approaching and Exxon didn't do squat, despite the village's pleading. Sally's uncle Mack Kvasnikoff was chaining logs across the salmon-spawning rivers. His boots filled with gravel and tore away the skin.

It was Nanwalek's turn for a visit from the Exxon circus with the cash and the promises. Exxon even agreed to fly Mack to a hospital in Anchorage—but not until he signed a waiver promising he wouldn't sue Exxon. (BP took good notes about that waiver game, which BP would use in the Gulf of Mexico.) Mack's foot was amputated.

Then, after a couple of months, the industry's clean-up circus folded its tent. They left Nanwalek with dead salmon, a bankrupt cannery, and their food, Badarki snails and razor clams, designated off-limits for the next decade. Chief Kvasnikoff lost his fishing boat; five of the island's eight commercial boats were repossessed.

I didn't get there until 1991, two years after the spill. Some of the guys were sitting inside, watching an endlessly repeating Elvis in *Blue Hawaii.*

The Exxon clean-up left some of the villagers with a drug habit—and ten cases of HIV/AIDS, which took one child. For Sally, that was it. "I felt like my skin was peeling off. After the oil, I thought, *This is it. We're over, Sugestun,* we're gone unless something happens."

Something did happen. *Sugestun,* "Real People," is their tribe's traditional name. And in that Sugestun language—which only the women knew and passed on—Sally and the other women led an uprising against her brother, Chief Vince, and voted him out.

That's when the Cultural Revolution began: *No* alcohol, *no* junk food (Vince's little commissary was closed), and even the halibut in the smoke houses would be dried by electric fans, not smoke and molasses. (For me, *that* was a step too far.) When Uncle Mack flew home from a doctor visit, as soon as the four-seater landed on the beach, they threw his behind in jail for bringing in a six-pack. Not everyone supported the Revolution. Sally's *Sugestun* name, Aqniaqnaq, means "Leading Star," but not everyone thought she should lead. (The women tagged me with a *Sugestun* name meaning Calendar Boy; they'd say it and giggle.) Anyway, guns were oiled and loaded, and Leading Star found it prudent to stay away from the Christmas Masking Ceremony. I stayed close to neutral territory, playing the drum set in the dance hall.

Nanwalek rocked. Their band was famous all over the Sound. Their big hit was "World Upside Down." It began, Chief Vince said, when a guitar washed up on the beach, and by morning, he was playing "You Ain't Nuthin' But a Hound Dog." (Chenegan Don Kompkoff verified that you could learn any instrument in a day by turning your clothes inside out, hinting that a dark Raven-like spirit would help.)

Back in Chenega, Uncle Paul's silences grew longer as he watched the villagers go off the rails. I went along with him and his wife, Minnie, up a slope to the edge of a snow line, where we picked gallons of blueberries. He looked over at the little village a hundred miles from nowhere and said, "I think I have to find someplace else to live. It's just too crowded."

He was silent again. Then he added, "My home is now a strange place."

TATITLEK VILLAGE, BLIGH ISLAND

Gary Kompkoff, Chief and President of Tatitlek's village council, said he'd meet me at the airfield, the island's softball diamond. The Natives had cleared some rocks so I could land. Gary told me to look for his red truck. That was easy: It was the only vehicle on the entire island.

This was just after his warning to me about the village going crazy with the oil and oil money, and years before his daughter's murder.

Gary didn't say hello. He didn't say anything. That was OK: The Chugach tend not to speak unless they have to. Even then, they may not speak. Gary directed me with a nod into the truck cab and threw my bags on the pickup's back bed, next to a huge compressor motor.

He drove across the infield down to the end of the village's one road, about two hundred yards, killed the engine, and nodded for me to get out. The entire journey took ninety seconds. He parked next to the village cemetery in front of a trailer, where I could cook and sleep while I worked in the village. I got out of the cab into icy quiet, only the sound of his front tire hissing. I thanked Gary for the ride and added, "I think you got yourself a flat."

Gary didn't say anything and he didn't look at the tire. Instead, he jumped onto the back of the truck, fired up the compressor, uncoiled a ratty air hose, jumped down, and filled up the tire. The compressor howled and quaked and it looked like it might shake right off the truck and crush him flat.

I stared at Gary and he stared at me. Then he cut the compressor and spoke. "You don't want to talk to Bear."

I tried to contain my inner New York. I grinned and chewed on my tongue. Then I said, "Gary, I have just traveled seven *thousand* miles over *three days* to come to this very *remote* island. I have to speak to an Elder. I intend to speak to Mr. Gregorieff and I would *appreciate* you telling me *where I can find him.*"

Gary said nothing. He nodded toward an old mobile home between some rusted-out boats and broken engines near an unused dock. It looked abandoned.

He waited, then added, "So, are you staying?"

I said nothing. He threw down the bags, then hauled them into the "guest" trailer and drove the truck back across the ball field. I headed off through the weeds, holding a cantaloupe.

Ed Bear Gregorieff did not have a phone. He had no idea I was coming, but at the door, he greeted me like he had been waiting for my arrival. *"Cha-mai!"* Aluutiq for "welcome."

I maneuvered through the dark trailer home, with its damp, old carpeting and aluminum walls patched with duct tape. I walked through a tight maze of makeshift shelves jammed with large, dusty no-label cans, motor parts, dishes, and trophies. He'd placed the stuffed shelves to cover over the windows that faced his neighbors' stilt bungalows up the slope.

I put the cantaloupe on Bear's formica table. He saw me scan the cluttered shelves and old wedding photos in cheap metal frames. There were several of a bride.

"She's passed," he said. He popped open a couple of nonalcoholic beers.

Bear was in his seventies. It looked as if he'd let his white beard go unshaven for a week and that he'd been wearing his Joe Cool T-shirt just as long.

He didn't know who I was or why I had come, but he could guess. A white man would only come to talk about the Exxon tanker and its oil. I opened a notebook.

"Bear, I need to know what happened when the oil hit. You know, how things changed."

"I warned them," he said. "I told them, *'We're fishermen. We're no oilmen.'"*

He had drifted back to the sale of Valdez. I tried to steer him back to the spill. "Ed, I need to know what happened *that night.*"

He said, "This is what happened:

"There was a man once. A Native man. A fisherman, you know, a 'net seiner.' A subsistence man. He loved this woman. Then the woman's husband died. So then he married her. Then this Native man, he went away to the war. And when the war ended, he came back to the village and back to his home. And his son stayed up in his room. And he didn't see his son all day, the day he came back from the war. And then it got dark and his wife made supper. And his son came out of his room and his son was all dolled up. And his son didn't say anything; he just headed for the door. And the Native man said, 'Where are you going? I just got home and your mother's fixed us supper.'

"And this man's son looked right at him and said, *'Dad, while you were out at the war, I got a Alyeska job and I made twice as much money as you made in your entire life.'*

"And he went right out the door."

Bear looked through the filthy window at the rusted boats. He looked at the warning light turning around on the tower over the reef.

"Where's your son now?"

"Seattle," he said. "Pipeline engineer."

I left the cantaloupe on the kitchen table, closed the door softly, walked up through the weeds to the guest trailer, removed my bags, still packed, and called in a seaplane on the shortwave.

* * *

Not every native finds inner peace in a life of gill netting or skinning sea lions. Exxon's attorneys were having a good old time harpooning the idea of a "Native way of life." To them, the claim was a joke. The company deposed Chenega's Corporation President, Chuck Totemoff, about the last time he hunted seal. Evanoff said Chuck answered, "Oh, I don't know . . . years ago." Then he added, without prompting, "You know, that water IS REALLY COLD."

SAN DIEGO, CALIFORNIA

There are many ways for a corporation to say *Go fuck yourself*.

Here's one:

The Chugach of Prince William Sound pooled their money, borrowed some, and with good old American can-do spirit, set up a cannery for the salmon they caught.

The *Exxon Valdez* crack-up was not the best advertising for their canned salmon. Diners of the Lower 48 lost their appetite for "crude in a can." Plus, there was the cost of the lawsuit—the confabs with lawyers, the experts (and the investigator from New York). Exxon folded its arms and watched the Chugach Corporation go belly-up with the salmon.

The Sound had been the world's herring supplier; no one had more of it. A year after the spill—*shaZAMM*—the herring disappeared. From millions to zero.

BP looked down on the tragedy they caused and saw a cheap exit. With the Native-owned businesses up and down the coast going under, BP offered them a lifeline: the insurance fund.

BP and Exxon had a cute game going. Exxon would hold out, and the victims of the spill, looking into the chasm of bankruptcy would have no choice but to settle for peanuts from the BP consortium. BP offered the Natives, fishermen, oiled towns, and all the injured the amount already sitting in an industry insurance fund, $125 million. Even Exxon admitted that the damage would be in the billions.

My Native clients had a choice: Take it or die. It was the one-dollar deal all over again, but with a few zeros added on. A few added zeros were not enough to prevent the Chugach Alaska Corporation from sinking into bankruptcy court. (There went that investigator's bill.)

In other words, BP didn't pay a penny out of its own pocket.

Once BP was off the hook for free, the company's Alaska Chief, Bob Malone, was sent to run BP operations in the Gulf of Mexico

Here was Lesson #1 for BP to take to the Gulf:

If your lost oil destroys an economy, back up the truck and finish the job.

The devastation so weakened the company's victims, they had to take anything.

And there was Lesson #2:

It's a heck of a lot cheaper to pay off the victims than to prevent oil spills.

A by-the-book oil spill response operation requires over a billion dollars in equipment for Alaska, way more in the Gulf with ten times the traffic and drilling.

We can sum up Lessons #1 and #2 as DP-DP: *Don't Prevent, Don't Pay.* BP not only got away with it, they took this lesson to the Gulf.

* * *

There's yet another way for corporations to say *Screw you.* This is the one Exxon used on Uncle Paul.

All Uncle Paul wanted was a commercial fishing boat sturdy enough to carry him and his son beyond the oiled death zone. They were not very excited about their career opportunities in rock wiping. He asked me if I thought Chenega and the other Native villages could get enough funding for boats and licenses to get back into the business of being Native.

I knew not all the lawyers liked that idea (what's 20 percent of a herring?). When he asked me to go straight to the Exxon chiefs, I said that we'd get in trouble.

Uncle Paul said, "We're already in trouble." So I went to San Diego to confront The Man With The Checkbook.

Chuck, as Chenega's Corporation President, joined me on the four-seat float plane, along with Larry's wife, Gail. She was just brilliant with the technicalities of the case, and more important, it was her life on the line.

We were on a mission to San Diego, where we could track down Otto Harrison, the General Manager of Exxon USA, hosting a symposium on oil spills. On the last leg out of Seattle, Chuck's seat was empty. We pretended not to notice and flew on.

After three days' wait, Harrison agreed to meet, just in time for Chuck to show up. He called from the airport, the travel budget gone and therefore no cash for a cab. We retrieved him and headed for a cheap motel next to the San Diego Freeway, where Exxon's man had rented a conference room for our meeting.

Otto Harrison is a dead ringer for General Norman Schwartzkopf, who led U.S. troops in Gulf War I: the bearish frame, even the military buzz-cut hairdo above bulldog jowls. Harrison placed himself dead center between fifteen empty chairs on his side of the table, framed by heavy green curtains that blocked out the California sun. He faced us alone, without the usual scrimmage line of lawyers, PR operatives, and whispering consultants that other corporate chiefs typically employed as human shields in negotiations.

Otto smiled.

I handed Harrison one sheet of paper, the carefully honed list of repairs and economic aid needed to keep the five stricken villages alive. Enough for a boat for Paul and the other uncles in the Sound. Otto smiled again. He turned the paper over, facedown on the conference table, without looking at it. He smiled once more. "So, Gail, you have something to say?"

Before we left the village, Gail was an angry lion, announcing she would "tell that Otto Harrison. . . ." We had come to demand the cash, and *right this minute*! But now, a small Eskimo woman sat next to me, with a voice nearly inaudible. She asked only for sixty extra days of pay for the Chenegans to clean the oil out of their fishing grounds on Latouche Island.

Otto deliberately thickened his Texas drawl. "Now, Gail, ah cayn't be payin' a bunch o' Natives to go 'round picking up oil that ain't there, can I?"

I launched in, unasked. I cajoled, I wheedled, I told the Exxon chief I could "see it from your point of view," I threatened to put Paul Kompkoff on TV with a dead oil-covered eagle. Otto let me run on until I was winded.

"Are you done? Son, have you said everything you'd like to say?" Otto turned over my sheet, glanced, smiled, stood up, and handed it back to me. "Ah don't think I'll be needin' this."

Through the entire meeting, Chuck said not one word. Not *hello*, not *goodbye*. In a chair in the corner of the room, he gripped a pen and wrote nothing. You could see the hangover hammering at his temples. In his huge round head, through eyes closed down to sleepy slits, he watched Gail and me break up on the hard reef of Otto Harrison. Chuck knew it was a fool's errand, and, I surmised, he thought it best that we be the fools.

At the door, Harrison threw down a bone. "Well, Gail, ah think we can come up with thirty days' work for *your people*."

She took it. There is justice and there is survival, and Gail, more experienced in this world than me, understood the difference.

DISNEY WORLD, FLORIDA

In the meantime, Native leader Kathryn Anderson decided it was time to "put on the feathers." Maybe shame mixed with good PR would tame the Exxon tiger. She led a retinue of Alaska Natives to the corporation's annual stockholder meeting in Orlando.

At the Exxon Disney World meeting, Kathryn brought The Mask of Tears. It was a turquoise face carved on wood, garnished with eagle feathers, with tears made from something shiny I couldn't make out.

With support of sympathetic nuns who held Exxon stock (don't ask), Kathryn confronted Exxon's board with the mask. "We bring out our traditional Mask of Tears every time our people are endangered. He is crying for our ancient way of life. You must help us."

The executives pretended to be moved.

The Mask of Tears may have been a Chugach tradition, but it was one that had started only a few months before its Disney World appearance. It had been created by a Cordova artist inspired by ideas from some visiting professor from Seattle.

KAKTOVIK 2010; THE OLD VILLAGE 1969

While I was hanging in Kaktovik, I asked Etok about BP and Exxon maneuvering the Chugach of the Sound into selling Port Valdez for one dollar.

"Oh yeah," said Etok, "the One-Dollar Warriors. The Ahtna, too. The oil companies got them for a dollar, the cowardly assholes. They sold out for nothing; corrupt bullshit, they should all be in prison with the Americans and the British."

The young rebel from Harvard scolded them, "I told them to get a lawyer that wasn't controlled, wasn't in the pockets of oil, and you can't get one in Alaska." Etok himself had flown down to Seattle, where he retained his two Jews: first, former Supreme Court Justice Arthur Goldberg (my second cousin, really), and later, Goldberg's would-be replacement on the Court, Abe Fortis, personal counsel to the President of the United States.

Etok had zero sympathy for Father Nicholas and the One-Dollar Warriors. What could I have said to Etok to change his opinion?

Maybe this: No Chugach had come back to the land of ice because they'd grown tired of San Francisco and university life. The Chenega refugees and the other Chugach did not have a pot to piss in. When "Humble" Oil showed up, their Native Association had exactly $129 in the bank. I saw the old records. So, how were these Natives who spoke Aluutiq better than they spoke English supposed to get to Seattle? By kayak? They couldn't afford a used chicken sandwich, let alone airfare.

And besides, they were given legal help for free. A big-shot politician from Anchorage, Clifford Groh Sr., offered to bargain for them against the oil companies. How the hell were the Chugach to know he was about to become a highly paid lawyer for these same corporations?

I met Groh Sr. in 1997. In Alaska, apparent conflicts of interest are considered just smart business. In his Anchorage office hung a huge baleen, a sperm whale's "tongue," mounted on his wall. I assumed it was because it would not be appropriate to display the skin of a Chugach.

Today, it's not easy to imagine back four decades to the stilt house where, as dawn approached, the august Eyak elder, Cecil Barnes, told Father Nick, Henry Makarka ("Little Bird") of the Eyak Village and the Kvasnikoffs of Nanwalek to surrender. They must hand over Valdez for whatever they could get, mostly jobs clearing garbage from the port site.

Why did the Natives take the deal from the oil companies, the jive from Groh? Did they believe it? To develop my fraud theory, I dropped in on Agnes Nichols, Eyak Chief-for-Life, who had, as a young woman with stenographer's skills, kept notes of the Natives' deliberations. The cabin was a museum of Native and Indian artifacts she had gathered in her travels, including a porcelain sculpture of Pocahontas with a lampshade sticking out of her. The matriarch produced her verbatim notes of Barnes's words:

> "Have you been down to the mouth of Ship Creek in the summer? How many salmon were on the drying racks? Try the Cordova area, the Eyak village, Alganik. They moved it lock, stock, and barrel to make way for

the railroad. Where's Alganik now? Gone. Where are the Eyak? We're almost extinct. How many of us live to forty? How many of you have electricity? If we go to work for the canneries, our people are virtual indentured servants."

If they didn't hand over Valdez, it would be taken from them—and maybe the other villages seized and cleared as well.

"This has been our home as long any of us can remember. We must stay here until we die."

It was not lost on Barnes and the Natives that Exxon's logo is a man-eating tiger.

Surrender or be swallowed.

PENTHOUSE, CAPTAIN COOK HOTEL, ANCHORAGE, 1997

The Natives' last hope would be a plea to the Secretary of the Interior, whose department runs the Bureau of Indian Affairs and whose job it is to protect Native interests. There was no sense bothering. Richard Nixon had just taken office and installed a new Secretary of the Interior: Wally Hickel.

Governor Wally Hickel invented the State of Alaska. With his buddy Richard Nixon's help, in 1959, he won his star on the flag, statehood.

"That was a mistake," he told me. "We should have been our own nation." I pointed out that would make him President.

Hickel grinned and took me over to a globe. As he massaged and caressed the planet's crown, he told me of his plan to create a circumpolar resource cartel linking Siberia, Alaska, sub-polar Scandinavia, and northern Japan. He had already begun the engineering work on a railroad that would wind around the North Pole, connected by a tunnel under the Bering Straits to Russia. A Confederation of the North, an Arctic Empire, that circled the top of the planet benevolently ruled, he made clear, by Emperor Wally. Mad, yes, but all of Hickel's plans were nuts, and usually successful.

When I met with him in 1997, he had already prodded the Governor of Sakhalin Island, Alaska's twin in population and minerals, to declare its independence from Russia. (That didn't last.)

Hickel, elected Governor of Alaska twice, with two decades between his terms, was one strange Republican. "Capitalism," he told me, "is an artifact of the temperate zone; it just doesn't work for most of the planet." For a man averse to capital and private property, he sure had a lot of both.

He had a heck of a view from the top of the Captain Cook Hotel. He owned it. The view was kept clear because the Captain Cook, by law, must remain the tallest structure in Anchorage. You could see almost all of Anchorage—he owned most of that too—and beyond to the Kenai Peninsula, more Hickel holdings.

That wasn't enough. He was already the richest man in Alaska and that, too, wasn't enough.

Since Alaska attained statehood in 1959, he knew his Arctic dreams began with oil, gas, coal, and lumber. But extracting and shipping those resources required removing a large obstacle: the Natives who already owned it.

But where was their signed deed? "You can only claim land by conquest or purchase. Just because your granddaddy chased a moose across some tundra doesn't mean you own it."

So much for the claims of my reindeer-chasing Native clients.

But Native claims were a most powerful weapon in the hands of a most powerful governor. Hickel had worked himself into the White House as Nixon's Secretary of the Interior charged with protecting the nation's natural resources and environment. God help us.

He had a hell of an idea: With a wave of a legislative wand, he turned Alaska's Native tribes into Corporations. The chiefs would become CEOs and Presidents; the Council of Elders would become boards of directors; and each Native would become a shareholder in the corporation that would own the land.

Lots of land. Hickel told me he convinced Nixon to hand the Native corporations 100 million acres. Nixon signed the Alaska Native Claims Settlement Act in 1971. Natives could pick any land they wanted—except for Valdez. Valdez was for the BP group.

There was one other notable clause: the Natives could sell their shares after ten years. But who would buy up millions of acres of wilderness?

"I made them [Chenega] an offer for that property myself; but I wouldn't pay them anything like what they are getting from Exxon."

On Chenega, when I was staying at the Evanoffs, Gail told me, "They set us up to fail, to take it away. They gave it to us so they could steal it."

CHENEGA

Hickel may have coveted Chenega, but Exxon had jumped his claim stake. The day I met Hickel in his penthouse office, Exxon sealed the deal with Chenega's Chuck Totemoff to buy up 90 percent of the Native corporation's land.

They couldn't call it a "sale" because Hickel's successor as Secretary of the Interior erased Hickel's cute little codicil in the Claims Settlement Act that allowed non-Natives (named Hickel) to buy and sell Native corporation stock. Instead, the land's development rights were put in an Exxon "Trust." (The Exxon Trust would protect this lovely land. Exxon, BP, and Shell Oil also said they would protect the Arctic Wildlife Refuge—by drilling into it for oil and gas.)

I flew to Chenega, and Evanoff picked me up at the airport—a real honest-to-god airport with a runway that could land a C-17 cargo jet. On previous visits, I could only get there by sea plane. Now there was a satellite communications dish, a power plant for the sodium lights, and a huge docking facility for big ships in case of another spill, all of it paid for by the Exxon compensation fund. In other words, Exxon installed all the infrastructure needed for drilling for oil, using the funds for oil spill containment.

Would Exxon drill? The offshore oil lease sales are creeping closer, now near Nanwalek and heading north toward Chenega and Cordova. They've already got the airport; they've got the docks.

Larry was just back from directing the hose-and-rag operation at Sleepy Bay, still heavily oiled. It was eight years after the spill. The day before, cleanup work had stopped for the funeral of eighteen-year-old Frankie Gursky, who had killed himself at the airport after an argument with his grandmother.

I asked Larry about the land sale, and Gail jumped in, murder in her eyes. "This is *not real estate*."

Larry spoke to me later, quietly. "I don't think you can own land. All we can do is use it for a little while. That's all we ever did, my family. We just pass through for a while and the land remains here."

The Chief of the traditional council, Ed Kompkoff, was less philosophical. "Who the hell gave Chuck the right to put a For Sale sign on my back?"

But, then, who is the Chief? He's just a tenant on corporate property. Most of Chenega's shareholders have moved away: oil pollution, oil jobs, and the lit-up lure of the cities. Some who still live there in the village, like gill netter John Totemoff, Chuck's uncle, don't own a share. Lucky they let him stay at all.

That's the point of a corporation. It's not the Park Service. Chenega was just real estate to sell, and with a million bucks for each shareholder, you can buy one hell of a double-wide in Tempe, Arizona (the largest center of the Chugach diaspora), where icy water won't touch your feet until you drop a beer bucket on the patio. In fact, it will be the Chenega stockholders in Arizona who will *demand* that BP and Exxon drill there. Cash money beats Grandpa's story of a seal on a spit every time.

The Eyak Corporation went bankrupt, then had no choice but to sell. Exxon's gold ultimately lured Nanwalek and the rest of the village corporations to sell to the "Trust." Wally Hickel's vision was complete.

ANCHORAGE, ALASKA, 1991

I still had yet to measure the value of their way of life so they could sue Exxon and BP for its loss.

How do you measure the value of your kids never learning how to hunt a seal; how do you measure the despair that leads to alcoholism, and the sudden end of a three-thousand-year-old way of life?

The answer is: with a computer. I had developed a monstrously elaborate software algorithm, perfected for me by professors at the Wharton School of Economics, that could measure what we call in the econ biz "hedonic value." I can tell you with surprising and horrible accuracy the number of suicides to expect, wife beatings and early deaths caused by oil spills, defense plant closings and anti-Muslim riots. We like to say that not everything has a price. We like to say it because it's not true.

When the mayor of the fishing village of Cordova took his own life, leaving a note blaming Exxon, folks were shocked. I wasn't. There would be thirty-five more.

I admit, some hedonic damage defeated my abilities at quantification. I asked the lead guitarist of Nanwalek's village rock band, with the Susgestun nickname of Kwadl'k, or Stinking Anus, if he'd felt any changes in emotion since the spill. In a slow, thoughtful Native cadence he said, "Well, until we got in that satellite TV, we didn't know our women were ugly."

* * *

On March 23, 1994, Judge Russell Holland reached his decision. In compensation for the damage to Native culture and way of life, Exxon would pay nothing.

> All Alaskans have the right to lead subsistence lifestyles, not just Alaska Natives. . . . Neither the length of time in which Alaska Natives have practiced a subsistence lifestyle nor the manner in which it is practiced makes the Alaska Native lifestyle unique. . . . Quite simply, the choice to "engage in [subsistence] activities" is a lifestyle choice. . . . The lifestyle choice was made before the spill and was not caused by the spill.

Just a "lifestyle" choice, like Yves Saint Laurent shoes over Gucci. There was some consolation, however. In the Old Village, Agnes Nichols, the Eyak Chief-for-Life, told me, "At least those goddamn otters are dead."

CORDOVA, 2010

Moose was pissed off. Moose Hendricks is Chief of the Eyak, the tribe that lived just outside the commercial fishing port of Cordova, just south of Valdez. "Where the hell can you buy property like that for one hundred dollars an acre?"

But, Moose, I tell him, the land had *oil* on it. It *still* has oil on it, twenty years on.

At least admit that Exxon is brilliant: It slimes the property with oil, then buys it up cheap—*because there's oil on it.*

When the salmon were poisoned and the herring fled, it just about finished Cordova. There are no roads in or out. The only game in town is fishing and that was kaput. Exxon blamed Mother Nature for killing the herring; the mayor blamed Exxon in his suicide note. The only secure job in town was in repossessing fishing boats. Moose's was one of them.

As to the BP consortium buying Valdez for a buck, it wasn't just the price that bugged him. "Who was Cecil Barnes to sign away Valdez?" Well, he signed for the Chugach because he made them up. The Natives had lived there for thousands of years, but tying them into a neat little bow marked "Chugach" was a Barnes invention. Moose thought it was BS, not tradition.

So how did these indigenous folks get piled together and tagged "Chugach"? The answer begins with another question, *Qui bono?* Who benefits?

The oil companies needed someone to take their dollar and sign on the dotted line. They had to give Valdez to Cecil Barnes's crew so the oil companies could legally take it away from them. Moose notes that the deal involved only five villages. Where was Village #6, Valdez? Not one name from Valdez was on the document giving up their home. Of course not. They would never have given way to the oilmen, so the oilmen found those who were most weak and vulnerable, like Father Nicholas, desperate enough to accept nothing more than an offer of jobs, a bunch of jive about protecting the environment, and other shiny trinkets.

BP and the petroleum giants had played this same game before. In 1953, BP engineered the coup against the elected President of Iran, replacing him with a Shah ready to sign anything the company put in front of him. Later, they would play the same game in the Caspian to get their "Contract of the Century."

If Barnes didn't sign, the companies would find an Indian who would. Barnes took what he could get.

* * *

This nonfiction fable has a moral to it: "Power, Crime, Mystification, Mr. Palast," Etok said. "That's how they do it. Power, Crime, Mystification."

Etok walked me through the three steps on *"How to Take Oil That Isn't Yours."*

1. **POWER:** The expression of the conqueror's strength or, more often, the weakness of the conquered.

    It's not wild coincidence that Bob Malone, who headed BP's Alaska and Gulf operations, was simultaneously co-chair of the George W. Bush re-election campaign.
2. **CRIME:** Making promises you don't intend to keep is fraudulent inducement. Do it three times and it's racketeering.
3. **MYSTIFICATION:** The web of rituals, usually legalistic—including treaties, land deeds, and laws—imposed by conquerors to legitimize their crime. In the fog of legalismo, the victims often acquiesce to the terms imposed.

In Prince William Sound, the oil companies picked out an alcoholic priest, some pragmatists, and some desperate poor folks, labeled them the "Chugach," gave them a buck, took Valdez, and sealed the deal with the mystical authority of a "contract."

Power, Crime, Mystification. We saw it in Baku. War, poverty, and dictatorship imposed the Contract of the Century. This treaty of economic surrender is masked as an agreement among equal parties. "Contract," my ass.

Since the U.S. government screwed the Natives out of all this oil, *why don't we own it?* How come it now belongs to BP, Shell, and Exxon? Teddy Roosevelt asked that exact same question about the Arctic reserves—*Isn't this the public's oil?*—and it cost him reelection to the presidency.

Governor Hickel of Alaska once told me that he had proposed state ownership of North Slope oil fields. Hickel backed down, rare for him, but prudent in the face of oil company power—and the slice they left for him. (They got the oil; Hickel's company got the natural gas pipeline rights.)

But We the Sheeple of the United States have been three-stepped so successfully, we never even question why BP, Shell, and Exxon have our oil. If we had taken back our own oil as Venezuela and Saudi Arabia did, today we wouldn't have to beg China for a cup of capital.

Another example? Here's one. In Iraq, in 2003, before BP could sign new contracts for the giant Rumaila oil field near Basra, the old contracts signed by

Saddam Hussein with the Russians had to be modified. They were, from the air, by B-52s.

Power, Crime, Mystification. Again and again.

In 1991, on the second anniversary of the *Exxon Valdez* tanker spill, I was in Paul Kompkoff's house, watching TV. The oil was still all over his island beach, and America couldn't care less. We were distracted: Everyone, even the patriarch, was glued to CNN. The U.S. Air Force was bombing the bejesus out of Bagdad. Uncle Paul rarely shared his thoughts, rarely speaks at all. But now, Uncle Paul, talked to the soldiers loading into Humvees in the Arabian desert, heading out toward Iraq's oil fields, "I guess we're all some kind of Native now."

*   *   *

In 1918, Nuciiq Island, the largest Chugach settlement, was wiped out. Traders had brought in beads, knives, candy—and influenza. All the Chugach there, and almost all the rest in the Sound, died. How many? Some say eight thousand. I can't tell you for certain; who counted Indians in 1918? That seemed to settle the "Native Question."

When the epidemic first struck, some of the children were sent away while their parents died. The kids were planted at the Eyak Village on the Copper River. One was Moose's mom.

The Eyak village was miles from Cordova, the commercial fishing town. In 1948, quite ill, she walked to the hospital there. White people had to be served first. She was told to wait. She did, and died waiting, from a burst appendix.

Moose told me about his mother as he looked out the window of the tallest building in town from a top-floor office worthy of Hickel. A couple years back, Moose built the biggest, largest hospital within a hundred miles, the most expensive building in Cordova. Natives are served first.

Moose had taken the dollar from the sale of Valdez and jammed it right up the Company's law firm. It was more than a decade after the spill. BP decided it politically wise to live up to the forty-year-old deal and hire the Eyak-owned companies to man the oil spill response operation. Chief and CEO Moose demanded millions and he got it. And, he told me, he's going to get that herring boat back, too.

WASHINGTON, DC

In 1991, Exxon did offer to settle all Native claims for peanuts, probably from the same bag as BP. It was an "eat it or die" situation once again. The commercial fishermen, which included many Natives, were tired of swallowing whatever the oilmen tossed their way. They chose to fight it out in court. They won. The jury awarded them over $5 billion.

Justice done. Chapter closed.

Not quite. They offered even more peanuts now, but with an admonition. As one Exxon lawyer put it to me, you can take a few measly bucks now or wait twenty years for a judgment from the court.

A scare tactic, a ridiculous exaggeration.

On June 26, 2008, twenty-*one* years after the spill, the Supreme Court issued its final judgment. In black robes, they looked like a coven of ravens.

Justice David Souter said that Exxon's behavior was "profitless." The court cut the judgment by 90 percent.

I didn't know if that left enough for Uncle Paul to get his boat. It didn't matter. By then, Paul was dead and so were one-third of the other plaintiffs.

Lesson #3 for BP:

Wait them out. Corporations are immortal, humans die.

FLOAT PLANE TO KNIGHT ISLAND, 2010

If you want to get a laugh at a BP or Exxon board meeting, just read them this, from their 1969 statement to the Department of the Interior to get the OK on the Pipeline:

> "Most importantly, Alyeska believes that its Plan will have a positive effect on the unique environmental conditions of the Native communities."

What will make an oilman laugh 'til he cries is not that the statement is Grade A bullshit, but that *they used it again* forty years later, in 2009, forty years after the original snow job. They used the same pacifying line to sell Congress and the President on deepwater drilling in the Gulf. This from Shell's President, Martin Odum:

"We can operate as good stewards of the environment. We can drill safely and efficiently in ever greater water depths."

I picked up a color brochure at an Exxon gas station in New York. Two years after the tanker crack-up.

In it, an eagle soars over the deep blue Sound, and Exxon declares, "The waters of Alaska are pristine once more." All's well, dear, go back to sleep.

I brought it with me to show Uncle Paul. He pointed to a mile-long smear of oil behind the eagle, the "bathtub ring" of crude that stuck on the high-tide point. But that's a detail.

Now look at this photo.

Call it "Native Alaska Beach Party." James McAlpine of BBC snapped it when we flew into Chenega. That was six years *after* the spill. The Chenega Natives, decked out in yellow hazmat suits, look like firemen from outer space, wielding high-pressure hoses and pulling up the crude from the *Exxon Valdez*. It's six years after the spill, and you can see this black crap all over them, like they'd thrown grenades into an outhouse.

And here I am on Knight Island in 2010, two *decades* after the tanker spill.

I just have to stick my hand in the gravel, and the place will suddenly smell like a Bronx gas station.

In June 2010, the U.S. Department of the Interior said the Deepwater Horizon spill will be cleaned up by the fall. In the fall they revised that to "two years." What they meant was, it will take two years for you to forget all about it.

Remember the Tsunami of 2007 that killed a quarter million people? I don't: That is, I had to Google the date. The massacre of over three-quarters of a million people in Rwanda in . . . what was it, 1996? 1998?

The poet Wordsworth said, "Our birth is but a sleep and a forgetting." Exactly. In a couple of years, you'll forget all about the Gulf Coast, and BP will run ads that Nature has taken care of it all. And in two years or five, you'll chuck this book in your recycle bin or clean it out of your iPad's hard drive.

And we repeat the story again. The levees of New Orleans collapsed in 1925, and the nation was repulsed and angry. Then we slept and forgot. The United States of Amnesia.

I look at my file cabinets of stuff and yellowing junk, like the Exxon booklet from the gas station, and I think, *Why do I keep all this crap?* I don't have an answer.

ANCHORAGE

In 1997, I met again with Chuck Totemoff at the Chenega corporate office. This wasn't the busted trailer at the island's dock. It was a modern office complex that could fit the entire village on just two of its floors.

And Chuck wasn't Chuck. I met Charles Totemoff, President and CEO. A white shirt, subtle necktie, bespoke suit, with an MBA in business management and a computer flashing reports from his multi-continental subsidiaries. I caught up with him in the parking lot, getting out of his silver BMW. He was dead sober, which is more than I could say.

Exxon and BP shafted Chenega on its claims for the spill but, Charles explained, using the grubstake of the land sale, the Natives launched a corporation expanding faster than Microsoft. If the Petroleum Club worked Congress, so could he. Federal law gave Native-owned companies first crack at government service contracts. Charles understood that Native-owned didn't have to mean Native-"manned." Why not employ the white guys for a change? The rent-a-Native operations beat the heck out of casinos and cigarettes. Charles soon became the true commander of his operation with CHENEGA CORP signs from

Iraq to Florida, whose thousands of employees probably couldn't point to the village on a map.

The Corporation's Web site home page is divided between a photo of Prince William Sound and an aircraft carrier sending off helicopter gunships, touting its "base support" and military intelligence operations. Wally Hickel would have been proud.

Is Chuck/Charles a sellout or a seer? Does he have to stay in the village gathering razor clams to be Native? With some Romanian blood in me, have I insulted my heritage because I don't live in a gypsy wagon and carry a tambourine? Must Natives put on the feathers to fit into a museum's display case?

GROWLER ISLAND, 1993

After the Judge wiped our Native claims, Exxon President Lee Raymond could now retire a happy man. And later he would, with a $400 million retirement bonus. What's not to be happy about?

I quit.

Not just the case. The whole shebang. Closed the door and hung up my investigator-for-hire gumshoes. After years of investigation, I had the information to blow Exxon and BP from hell to breakfast. I was paid to dig it up. Now I was paid to bury it.

Exxon, always holding out the carrot of a big fat settlement payoff, made it clear that if the Natives used the "F word," *fraud*, they would take away the carrot. They did anyway.

And the Natives' lawyers didn't need my discoveries. Racketeering, fraud, and willful negligence are expensive, complex, difficult cases to bring. But that wasn't the lawyers' job, nor the Natives'.

It wasn't their job to warn the planet about the industry's systemic fraud, corruption, and penny-pinching la-di-da view of safety. It wasn't the Natives' role to tell the white folk that the oil industry will suck out your resources and leave you slimed and devastated.

Their job was to take the money and run and let the rest of the world go to hell. "DRUNK SKIPPER HITS REEF" worked for the jury, worked for the judge—and worked for Exxon. Human error. A one-time failure of a sad alcoholic.

A week after the *Exxon* tanker destroyed the coast, Exxon fired Hazelwood, the drunk. The world was now saved . . . from Captain Hazelwood. Hazelwood drove the boat drunk—there are 238,000 Google citations to prove it. But it wasn't human error, it was inhuman corporate miserliness, profit-boosting shekel-shaving and the fraud that covers it over.

I took a kayak out from Growler Island to Columbia Glacier, the ice floe that shed the icebergs that the radar-blind *Exxon Valdez* recklessly steered to avoid. The four volumes of evidence will make a nice campfire on the glacier. Unless I violate my contract and put it out for the world's lazy eyeballs.

Well, I wasn't hired to save the world, to be Paul Revere warning the planet about BP and its brethren. "The Greencoats are coming! The Greencoats are coming!"

Where the hell was I going? Didn't know.

American news media got the story of the *Exxon Valdez* dead wrong. Why not report it myself? Paul Revere was a journalist. Surely, there were newspapers and television outlets in the United States that would like to get out the real story, real investigations. This was not the first time I had fooled myself, and not the last.

I didn't realize then that quitting my job meant quitting my country. The only way I would be able to lay out the facts on Corporate America was via BBC's electronic beams from an island off the coast of Ireland.

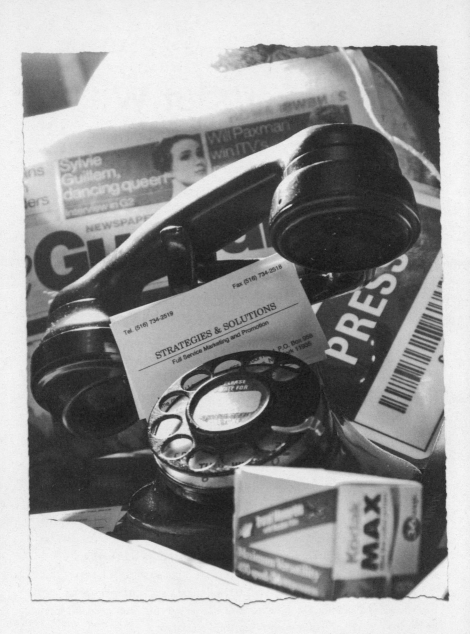

CHAPTER 8
We Figured Out Who Murdered Jake

BLACKPOOL, ENGLAND, 1998

Now, if this were a movie, you would hear the audience screaming, *DON'T TAKE THE KEY! DON'T GO UP THOSE STAIRS!*

The reporter part of my brain was screaming *THIS SMELLS BAD,* but I couldn't hear a thing because, while I was out for the story, the memory of Ms. Jamaica's hand in my pocket had drained the blood from my cerebrum.

So I took the key she left for me at the desk with the message to meet her up in her room. I went up the stairs. Knock-knock. No answer.

DON'T OPEN THAT DOOR!

I opened the door.

FOR GOD'S SAKE, DON'T TAKE OFF YOUR CLOTHES!

I took off my clothes. I needed to change my shirt and pants for the *New Statesman* party, though if she walked in, hey, we could start the party early.

The door opened. I smiled . . . at the desk clerk and Ms. Jamaica's husband.

Husband! This bitch has a HUSBAND? The poor pudgy schmuck had a face like the map of Liverpool, lost and pathetic and pugnacious at the same time.

The clerk, turning red, stuttered, "I explained the circumstance, sir. . . ." But I got the impression from the husband's look that this wasn't the first time Ms. Jamaica had handed some guy her hotel room key.

Thank god the Lord told me to pull up my pants a moment before the door opened. I babbled. *"How's the vote count looking for our gal?"* She was running for the Labour Party's leadership council, the hand-picked candidate of the

Prince of Darkness. To get the shit on the Prince was the reason I went "undercover" (so to speak.)

This was not a nice moment. I fell all over my own words. *"Been trying to,
to, trying to call her. Guess I'll meet up—say, are you coming?—catch up with
her at the* New Statesman *'do'. Guess I'll get going."*

Guess I will.

*   *   *

Look, this was not an easy investigation for me. My face had already been all
over the front page of every newspaper in England when I broke Part I of the
story that July.

In a nutshell, here's what happened. In the late 1990s, I was still going
through my withdrawal, legal and emotional, from the *Exxon Valdez* investigation. I was done with being an investigator, a fancy gumshoe. I was hunting
for a new job, a new life. OK, I'll be a poet. I took poetry lessons from Allen
Ginsberg, who was terminally sad because, by that time, he was too old to die
young. If that's how you end up, forget poetry.

Why not academe? There's me: sucking a pipe and pontificating to hormonal grad students. I lectured at Cambridge University, Oxford, University
of São Paulo. I could feel myself rusting.

OK, back to my roots, to labor unions, guys who do real stuff. To India,
Peru, to Brazil to meet Lula, to London, forming a flying fighting unit against
the international power pirates, targeting a company no one had heard of,
Enron. Now I was going in reverse. Bang: I'm forty-six—*this only happened to
other people! Old people!*

What could I do with my decomposing self? All over the world, I had
heard people scream, but no one was listening. Americans just turned up their
TVs. The victimized could scream through me. Journalism. If Clark Kent
could do it, why not me?

I sent a fax to *The Guardian* in London, dropping some tidbits from my
files about an operation called Southern Company; and at four the next morning, an editor rang to bring me over to Britain immediately. "Do you know how
explosive this is?"

I did, but America didn't. I would learn the cruel lesson that to report
the news about my homeland, I would have to leave it. So, I moved house to

England to work for *The Guardian* and its Sunday paper *The Observer*. I quickly formed a partnership with . . . a fifth of Felipe II. Our relationship began after more than a few rounds at the Coach & Horses, the pub near the *The Guardian*, also known as *The Guardian*'s second newsroom.

While still sober-ish, I got an assignment: American power companies— Southern Company, Reliant, CSW, Entergy—were buying up Britain's power systems left and right, sucking out the cash with big straws. It started with Maggie Thatcher but got worse under the new Labour Prime Minister, Tony Blair.

Oddly, Blair allowed the gigantic London Electricity system to be swallowed by a company from Little Rock, Arkansas. Entergy International of Arkansas had once hired the Governor's wife for legal work, but she didn't work too hard. Her billing records, which I reviewed, were phony as a three-dollar bill. The firm really hit the jackpot when the Governor, Bill Clinton, became President of the United States and Entergy's gal Hillary Rodham became a Lady.*

But that was nothing. American power giants were screwing with Britain's environmental laws, messing with regulations, and getting strange exemptions signed by Prime Minister Blair himself.

This game was up when N. Gregory Levy of Strategies & Solutions, consultants for the little-known Houston outfit Enron, blew the whistle. Levy had secretly recorded lobbyists tied to Trade Minister Peter Mandelson and Chancellor Gordon Brown. On the tapes, the lobbyists detailed how they got laws fixed, rules pushed aside, and were slipped confidential government budget information for their clients, U.S. banks, power companies, and others. For a fee of £5,000 a month, these lobbyists would let you in through the back door of Downing Street, literally. ("Levy" received an invitation to go right in. No kidding.) For what you got, it was damn cheap.

N. Gregory Levy was reporter Greg Palast. Strategies & Solutions was *The Guardian/Observer*'s elaborate front.

The upshot? My story pulled the political pants off Prince of Darkness Mandelson, the Prime Minister's claw hand, Tony Blair's Karl Rove.

---

* The full story would be a chapter by itself. If you want it, click *here* (enhanced edition) or go to GregPalast.com/VulturesPicnic.

Some of the U.S. energy giants and banks I'd exposed in the cash-for-access goo with Mandelson were not amused.

My most flamboyant connection was an icky little lobbyist named Derek Draper, "Dolly" to most. Dolly was only in his twenties, and Prince Mandelson, in his forties, liked boys. My editor, Will Hutton, wanted to know if Mandy and Dolly . . . "well, you know." I didn't know and didn't want to. What Mandelson shared with Dolly was a deep sense of Mephistophelian amorality. It was Rasputin and Rasputin-in-training. Or Lord Voldemort and his snake, Nagini. What they did with other men before they ate them, I don't care.

When my "Cash for Access—Lobbygate" story broke in *The Observer*, it splashed over the front pages of every British newspaper for a week. And so did I. In letters bigger than their "*Hitler Defeated*" headline, *The Mirror*'s front page screamed, "*THE LIAR*."

The photo of me was most unflattering, suggesting that because I had no hair, I was bald.

As you can imagine, it was difficult, then, to go back undercover. My face was known, and the list of those who wanted to see me die in pain was now long enough to cross the Atlantic.

I was only able to pull off my scam because I also played a third fake character, Greg Palast. Not the journalist, but Greg Palast who had been the American expert advising candidate Tony Blair in 1996 and 1997 on power and nuclear industry regulation. I pretended I was trying to secretly cash in on that connection, and the creeps who were cashing in on their own connection to Blair bought it.

In 1997, as Blair was on the cusp of being elected, and I was his advisor, not yet his accuser, I showed up at the Labour Party Conference gala with the (soon to be) Deputy Prime Minister, the rotund and confused John Prescott, and other political poo-bahs. The hotel dance hall was filled with pasty-faced Brits turning red from fattening ales. One gent had unbuttoned his shirt down to his bare chest and was rubbing his own nipples. And they make fun of *Americans!*

Across the room, alone and quiet, a slender woman. A woman who *sizzled*. How the hell did *she* sneak in here? And before I could avert my gawking eyes, she had knifed across the hall and asked me to dance. "So how did you get in with Prescott and Blair?" Power is an aphrodisiac, and combined with celebrity and opportunity, an orgasm in a bottle. She was *vibrating*. With ambition.

She slipped her hands in my pockets and asked how she could work her own way into the Labour Party leadership. For her, that would be easy. Half–Black Jamaican and all female. That made her a "two-fer" that the Prince of Darkness could surely use on a ballot somewhere. He did: The next year, Mandelson ran her for the Labour Party leadership council against another female, one of Mandy's enemies. Smart, that prince.

Jamaica gave me her coordinates, played some more in my pocket, and asked me to call her. My male idiot ego could never imagine that this sweet little muffin—and her husband—would, in a year or so, set me up like a bowling pin.

I don't think she started out with such a plan to set me up for the kill. I surmised that the lady just wanted to have fun, a little dance, a little tickle—and maybe make some politically advantageous connections. She would not be the first talented woman to climb up the political ladder panties first.

* * *

One year later, after I busted Mandelson and Blair, I see she's running for office as Mandelson's cat's-paw at another Party Conference. Their galas were coming up in September. I hunted for Jamaica's number. I left a message and she called back breathlessly telling me I was far more handsome than those terrible photos in *The Mirror* ("Trouble, Palast, trouble," a wise voice spoke before I smothered it). Mandy, I learned, had failed to get his star two-fer a ticket to the *New Statesman* party, the one that anyone who's anyone just *has* to attend. I called the magazine's editor and told him whom I would escort: My nemesis's little gal.

* * *

With my shirt on, I headed off to the *New Statesman* ball, without his wife. Or mine.

I hit the dance floor, looked around, but Ms. Jamaica wasn't there. Well, fuck her, the cheating bitch. (It didn't bother me that I was a cheating butch.) Not by my third gin and tonic. It was the only time since the age of fifteen that I made a decision to get drunk drunk drunk.

Then I saw her. Not Jamaica, but Sweden. That is, one of the two all-legs-and-long-blond-hair women that had stood next to Dolly at his Banqueting Room reception months before, cooing and rubbing him all evening. The Banqueting Room is where King James lost his head.

I was about to lose mine.

How we ended up dancing, I don't know. But Sweden was close, she was warm, it was going to be a good evening after all. The Son of God was Jewish and all was well, especially when she put her hands inside my suit jacket, rubbing up and down, and down the legs of my trousers. Oh my.

Then the rubbing got a little, it seemed, *violent*. She was patting me down, harshly, fury in her eyes.

"Where is it!? Where's the tape recorder! You have a tape recorder! You just wanted to get me to talk to you about Derek. I can't believe I was about to . . ."

No no no no, I wanted to tell her, but I had to step back to avoid a roundhouse slap to the head. I really truly just wanted your cool thighs crushing my ears. I just wanted to see an angel in underpants who would make me forget Dolly and forget Ms. Jamaica and forget Prince Poofy Mandy-kins AND HOW DARE YOU HIT A DRUNK!

I didn't want to be a reporter tonight. (Sure, I was recording her. Fake cigarette lighter. Blondie should have noticed I don't smoke. Asthma.)

* * *

Hangovers are not my thing. Don't like them. No, I don't. And here I was, made nauseous by the filthy carpet in the hotel lobby. The carpet was pulsing at me, threatening me. I didn't like it. The Labour Party press office had woken me at a criminally early hour and told me I had to, *had to,* get to Party Headquarters and right now or I'd lose my press credentials.

New Labour never got drunk. It sipped white wine and knew nothing of love lost. But I said with cheer, *"I'll be right over, mate!"* You scrotum-biting crud muncher. Mate.

Got there, waited in line, hating Blackpool and exile from the United States. Well, Palast, stop bellyaching and let's just get to work.

"Greg Palast? No, sir, no credentials, sir, for you."

Look, Princess Di or whatever your Limey name is, they told me to come in right now right away for the press pass.

"Been withdrawn, sir. Revoked."

Huh? What for?

"It says here, for 'moral violations.'"

MORAL VIOLATIONS?

"You must leave the Blackpool red zone directly."

I pushed out the door to the street, looking down at my shaking cell phone, when I was slammed hard by two guys standing outside the doors.

I began to apologize when they each slammed me again, even harder, with their shoulders, and pushed me back against a stone wall.

"Palast, we know what you're up to."

One then whipped out a camera and started clicking it in my face as the other prick held me pinned to the bricks.

Even hungover, I knew I must *not* run. *Never, ever run when there's a camera.* Every time a target of mine ran, they looked guilty guilty. The prick twins stayed on me, squeezing me from either side. We must have looked like quite a trio.

"We've got you in her room, Palast. We know what you were doing in her room, but why don't you tell us. Make something up, Palast."

Who the fuck *were* these guys? Later I would get their names: Will Woodward and Stephen White. If you see them, urinate on them, squeeze them against a wall, and take their photo.

Thank God I wore my fedora. In England, some folk would recognize it. The Lord sent me Paul Farrelly, now an Honorable Member of Parliament. About the *only* honorable member of Parliament.

"Get away from Palast or I'll have the cops on you." Paul's a little guy but built like a brick shithouse. He clearly was *not* going to wait for the cops to take care of these twats.

And Paul obviously knew them.

The gin and tonics had by now sweated out of me, and Paul, my guard, as they stalked behind us, said, "They're from *The Mirror*."

Oh shit oh shit oh shit.

The next morning, I was hungover from my hangover and grabbed a coffee and a newspaper, with the screaming headline

SEX SCANDAL ROCKS PARTY CONFERENCE

And: FROM THE LIAR TO THE LURKER

And: UNDERCOVER MAN'S SNEAKY NIGHT AT A LABOUR HOTEL

Well, at least they didn't use that ugly photo of me again. Instead, they had the hottie herself, Ms. Jamaica, and me with a "you've caught me!" guilty surprise on my face against the Party Headquarters wall.*

That was just page one. There were *five more pages of nothing but the Sex Maniac and poor damsel,* Prince Mandelson's lovely and innocent protégé. Well, at least I'd upstaged Tony Blair at his own convention.

The Mirror had dropped hundreds of free copies around the convention area so no one could miss it.

"He broke into my room! He's been stalking me for two years! I'm a married woman!"

Two days later, *The Guardian*'s political columnist, Simon Hoggart, wrote that he was standing right near Alastair Campbell, Tony Blair's press officer and feared political hit-man, who "thanked" *The Mirror*'s editor for "what you did for us." For Tony.

The Mirror's editor, the dirtball who had pulled this stunt, the man who makes vomit look like apple pie, the cockroach who would later be removed as editor of his shitty little tabloid for running a completely fabricated story *with faked photos,* the schemy little spider is named Piers Moron by *Private Eye.*

Yes, Piers Morgan. Who returned from the crypt as a judge on *America's Got Talent!* And now, Pus Moron has replaced Larry King as a big-time TV host for CNN.

This confirms my theory that when American television executives need a replacement for a news show, they simply wait for a toilet to overflow.

JACKSON, MISSISSIPPI

But this isn't about America's talent, journalism's celebrity turds, Mata Hari politicians, or Dolly's blondes.

This is about power. Nuclear, coal-fired, and oil-fired electric power. And political power.

Electric power and political power are two sides of the same doubloon. There is no way to separate the power you get through a wire so you can burn your morning toast, from the political power needed to overcharge you for it.

Prince Mandy, now the Right Honorable *Lord* Mandelson, Tony Blair,

---

* No, I won't give you her name, which you can look up. I won't give her the gift of notoriety, which, in our twisted times, is of some value.

Piers Morgan. Who are they, really? They are high-priced messenger boys, no more than that. The question is, *Whose message were they carrying?*

Piers didn't write *THE LIAR* headline story out of his own tiny head. I traced it back to the *consigliere* for a New York power company, a nuclear plant operator, Long Island Lighting Company. I'd taken the company down for racketeering. Guess they didn't like that.

Then there's Southern Company, the biggest power corporation in America. But that was not enough for them; they were going for biggest in the world.

In 1995, Southern, which operated in Mississippi, Georgia, Florida, and Alabama, made a move that was thought to be legally impossible: buying another company across the ocean. Their first cross-border raid was on England's Southwest Electricity Company. I had questions about how they could get around the law, the U.S. Public Utility Holding Company Act. But before I could get an answer, industry lobbyists had eliminated the law.

I had questions for Southern Company's executives. I put these questions in that article I faxed to *The Guardian,* the one that provoked their 4 A.M. call to me in New York. They splashed it across Britain's front pages, and that had turned me into a reporter in the space of thirty-six hours. My query to Southern was, *Who Killed Jake Horton? And where are the parts?*

Horton was the company's Senior Vice President who was taking the fall for breaking that Holding Company law. He had been caught making illegal payments to Florida state regulators for Southern. The company had the shit on Jake, all right, but Jake had more on them. The company, I learned, was charging its several million electricity customers for coal from its own mines, but the coal trains were loaded up with rocks. Really. There was more, lots more, and Jake borrowed the company plane to lay it all out to a state Attorney General.

A few minutes after the plane took off, it was blown to pieces.

The Chairman of the Board told our BBC team: "Poor Jake, I guess he saw no other way out."

And the other question: *Where are the parts?* Not the pieces of Jake sprinkled over the Southland, but the spare parts Southern used at Plant Vogtle, its Georgia nuclear station, and on the company's power lines. Southern charged its customers about a hundred million dollars for using the parts. But the parts were not in use. A group of law firms brought me down from New York to Georgia and Mississippi to try to figure out Southern's spare parts magic trick, the accounting legerdemain.

I began at the capitol building in Jackson, Mississippi, at the state regulator's document file storage room, a warehouse of haphazard folders and old carbon-paper copies. I jumped into the hopeless task of finding the spare parts accounting sheets for Southern's Mississippi unit. All the while, behind a desk covered by a mess that looked like it hadn't been touched in years, sat a gentleman in short sleeves whose entire conversation with me consisted of shrugging his shoulders and "Don't know 'bout that."

It was Delta hot, no air-conditioning and the fan above simply stirred the flies and humidity. I was hungry but couldn't bring myself to buy the pickled pigs' feet being sold from a huge jar in front of the Governor's office.

Then Jackson Ables walked in, straight from the pages of a John Grisham novel: a rotund and lively lawyer wearing a white seersucker suit, smart as a whip. In a drawl thick with Southern syrup, Ables told short-sleeves, "Jasper, this here young man, he's a good boy." *New York Jew-boy* need not be added.

Short-sleeves spoke. "Over there, right on top of the cabinet." And indeed, there it was: The Unholy Grail, a hundred pages of spare parts accounts, and they left in my briefcase.

Southern had charged for parts never used, a complex accounting game that violated several sections in the thick rule book used for setting the prices charged by the monopoly power company. I took two months to decode it and lay it out for Ables. His firm sued on behalf of the public: fraud, wire fraud, misrepresentation, conspiracy, racketeering.

Our racketeering and fraud complaint alleged that Southern overcharged its millions of electricity customers tens of millions of dollars for using spare parts it never used. Technically, the company had violated the accounting regulations set out by the Federal Energy Regulatory Commission under federal law.

Southern Company's view was *no problem*: The industry simply had Congress repeal the law and end the regulations. The company walked away waving its parts at me.

So, when you hear the word *deregulation* said with glowing praise, think Southern Company and poor Jake. Because when they say *deregulation*, they mean *de-criminalization*.

The judge said, case dismissed. But I kept that list of parts from Plant Vogtle.

* * *

Today, as I write this, I have taken time to reach out to two sources.

> **SOURCE 1:** "I was a Southern Company——. . . . I knew Jake. . . . It has taken some time, but we have figured out who murdered Jake, and the weapon used. . . ."

> **SOURCE 2:** "He clearly committed suicide and murdered the two pilots in the process. . . ."

You know, it would be nice if insiders could have just *one* story. Anyway, Southern Company didn't mention Jake in their application to take over a piece of the British market. But I did, in *The Guardian*. And, from my file cabinet, I pulled out the list of phantom parts. I was not making friends in the power industry.

HOUSTON, AMSTERDAM

Three other U.S. power companies swiftly joined Southern's corporate invasion force offering to buy the remainder of England's electric system.

First, there were the Arkansas boys, Hillary Clinton's former client,

Entergy. When the First Lady's old law partner was indicted for phony bill-ings, he accepted a short prison term rather than rat on her. On his way to the Big House, the felon was hired by Entergy as a "consultant." Then Entergy bought London Electricity with the helpful blessing of the White House. I'm not saying these things are connected. These are just dots, you draw the lines.

There were two other companies, Texans on the prowl for English utili-ties, CSW and Reliant Inc. Together, they owned two nuclear reactors, called the South Texas Project. Reliant makes that famous nuclear plant engineer, Homer Simpson, look like Leonardo da Vinci.

When Reliant and partners first proposed the South Texas nuclear plants, they were challenged on the gargantuan cost and sheer bone-headedness of building the twin reactors. But the companies got the state to order custom-ers to subsidize building the nukes by promising regulators they could build the reactors in just five years for $1.2 billion. That was the "definitive cost estimate." And they swore to it under oath. It took twelve years. Ultimate cost: $5.8 billion.

In an attempt to keep costs down, the companies had drilled holes in the workers' locker room, dropped in secret cameras, attempting to find out which employees were ratting them out to the Nuclear Regulatory Commission on their shortcuts to safety. The companies were busted, but got off with only a fine for their nuclear crime spree.

Reliant and its contractor, Halliburton's Brown & Root, ultimately ended up paying more than a billion dollars in fines and penalties when the state Public Service Commission ruled they were "imprudent" managers of the plant. *Imprudence* is the regulatory term for gross incompetence. Still, several billion dollars to cover those cost overruns on the plant were loaded on to the electric bills of Texas consumers, thanks to a deal Reliant cut with Governor George W. Bush.

And *"SEX SCANDAL ROCKS . . . "*? The business with Ms. Jamaica became a dum-dum bullet that the Texas boys used on me in Amsterdam. I'd tattled on the operators of the disastrous South Texas Nuclear plant in *The Guardian* just when Reliant wanted approval from Her Majesty's government to buy a hunk of the UK power system. When Reliant, the nuclear disaster-maker, made a move on Holland's power plants, my investigations were given a big play in *Handelsblad*, the *Wall Street Journal* of Europe. Reliant didn't like that, so they slipped *Handelsblad* the SEX SCANDAL files.

Reliant was the Rosemary's Baby of utility "deregulation." It had once been Houston Lighting & Power, then changed its name to Houston Industries and shifted its corporate shape. Houston morphed into Reliant for cross-ocean raiding and mergers, then took on the alias NRG Corporation (NRG = En-er-gy— get it?).

But more South Texas–type projects ultimately put NRG/Houston/Reliant/HLP, international power giant, into Chapter 11 bankruptcy.

I thought I'd seen the last of them and they assumed they'd seen the last of me.

We were both wrong.

NRG, this once-bankrupt financial ghoul, after blowing billions on the crime scene known as the South Texas Nuclear Project, has come out of its crypt to feast on the U.S. government's new loan guarantees for new nuclear plants. The Southern Company, Jake's former employer, also grabbed for the Treasury's guarantee. In 2010, NRG, and in 2011, Southern, were designated the winners of the U.S. Department of Energy's contest for our cash. That's the first hot load of cash from Obama's nuke 'em program.

It was NRG's internal files that had arrived in that big fat Radioactive Brick. Or I should say, "NINA's" internal files. NRG, as I've mentioned, has shifted shapes again. The Nuclear Regulatory Commission had considered pulling Reliant's license for lack of "moral integrity," yet in its latest mutation, NINA, "Nuclear Innovation North America," is getting Treasury loot.

(NINA's banks, the ultimate beneficiaries of the Treasury guarantee, must have had quite a laugh at the name used to get government loan backing. "NINA" is the finance industry's acronym for No Income No Assets, which pretty much summarizes the nuclear consortium's profile.)

Now, as soon as I show you the file I have on them, I assume they'll show you their file on me: so I've done it for them. You now know as much about my penis as NRG/NINA. I'm taking away their favorite trick: Discredit and destroy.

You want to know what's in the Radioactive Brick file? In a moment. What's more important is *why* I'm telling you this, and what brought me here tonight, a hundred miles from the kisses of my twins, to write this to you. And why I have been waiting many, many years to sit with you and tell you tales of polar bears and oil drills.

CHAPTER 9
The Sorcerer's Stone

LA, CHICAGO, GARY, AND ANCIENT ATHENS

et's say your daddy's rich. Let's say your name is Bush or Bin Ladin or Bloomberg.

　　You can screw up six ways against the middle, get caught snorting coke off a barroom counter, blow millions of your poppy's money on bone-headed schemes, remain illiterate even in moments when you're sober, and *still* get into Yale. And then, when you screw *that* up, Daddy has a place for you in his oil company. In one case I know of, this dumb kid's dad from Texas made him President of the United States because his parents knew he simply didn't have the competence to hold any other job.

　　I've told you I'm from The Valley, the Anus of Los Angeles. Not the people, the set-up. We only got what the rich released through their colons.

　　If I screwed up, my dad could get me a job in the furniture store ware-house, I suppose. I figured this out from the jump: If I was to stand a chance of escape, I could not wait for the outcome of school grades and SAT test scores or recommendations from important people because we didn't know impor-tant people. So, while I was still attending Dead End High School, I lied like a snake to get into Cal State University (age fourteen), then a year later, conned my way into UCLA (good), and another year later, boosted that into a spot at the University of California, Berkeley (better), then boosted the Berkeley con to get into the University of Chicago (best), fully paid with scholarships from god knows where.

Why stop? Rather than bother waiting to get my undergraduate degree, I flim-flammed my way straight into the University of Chicago's big-shot Graduate School of Business. (It is not worth explaining my trick, which you could not possibly get away with today.) And then (1973), when the leadership of Chicago's industrial unions and the Communist Party thought I should get into Milton Friedman's post-graduate circle, I figured *Why not? I can do that.*

I did, and simultaneously worked my way into a closed little circle called "The Workshop on Latin America," led by Arnold Harberger, the post-graduate seminar better known as the Chicago Boys, the crew then advising the dictator of Chile, Augusto Pinochet.

Milton Friedman was easy to charm. The charm I used on him was a theory I had about a new phenomenon: multinational corporations. These huge international corporations could, through their internal transfer pricing and accounting methods, work around the centuries-old laws that controlled, and pretty much prevented, speculators from shifting capital across borders. Once these capital controls were finally defeated and removed, I foresaw a dystopic world, with borders erased, with international corporations more powerful than any nation and above any one nation's laws or regulations, markets unchained, trade barriers demolished, and finance capital racing like a wild animal from continent to continent.

Few of my fellow travelers on the political Left understood what the hell I was ranting on about or thought it at all important. "Currency arbitrage" and "interest rate hedges" were not things you'd find in Karl Marx or the Little Red Book of Mao. Marx and Mao were all about "the means of production" and gargantuan factories with muscular, sweaty proletarians like the union guys I would soon work with at U.S. Steel Gary Works.

But Milton Friedman got it. *Boy, did he get it.* But whereas I saw a banker-incubus about to suck the life out of the laws that kept economies sane, Friedman saw something hotter than a porn flick: the *mechanism* for erasing financial borders. He thought we should publish a paper about it together. But that was too much for me. That would be like penning a laudatory ode to smallpox.

Nevertheless, Friedman invited me into his finance workshop (*ka-ching!*).

Milton Friedman was mesmeric. He could suck your intellectual soul out through your eyes with his true brilliance. It was like looking directly into the sun. The mostly dull grad students, divided between the avaricious and the careerist, left zombified, their own meager intellects ensorcelled by his venom, ready to fan out to the corners of the globe to inflict their master's heartless economics on our innocent planet.

For my own safety, I had to focus my eyes elsewhere.

But my brain was still hungry. David, my best friend, was sneakily sticking his thing into my girlfriend (redhead/insatiable). Relieved of the burden, I had time to quietly allow David's own true love to seduce me: I was secretly reading Aristotle.

Aristotle, the Greek philosopher, wasn't Greek. He was Macedonian, and the Greeks hated him for it. Of greater interest is that he was the first economist to write about the oil industry. (He had a head start because he was the first economist. He invented the word *economics—Οικονομικά*.) Anyway, the Father of Economics tells the story of the invention of commodities futures contracts—and the first time the oil market was cornered, monopolized.

It goes like this:

The philosopher Thales, getting a tip-off from an insider, knew that an oil shortage was just around the corner, so he bought all the future output of the olive oil trees in the city of Miles. When the season turned and the shortage of oil hit, he cranked the price of olives through the roof. But the public wasn't at all angry that Thales was skinning them for the oil they desperately needed to eat and to keep their lamplights on. Instead, people lauded him for his genius in making such a pile.

So Thales told them, YOU FUCKING IDIOTS. You despised me when I was a poor philosopher trying to give you invaluable wisdom for nothing. Now you're praising me for destroying the economy. You think that a good economy is one in which smart people with inside information make money off of money and get richer beyond their ability to even spend it. But making money from money *is against nature, schmucks!* A successful economy is one in which money and exchange of production results in a Good Life for all.

I got it. Friedman was more than wrong, he was a conspirator against nature itself. An economy's success should not be measured by the accretion of wealth by the wealthy, but by the ability of political leaders, like good fathers—Aristotle was obsessed with the idea of "the good father"—to insure the care of the citizens, that all may pursue happiness and attain the Good Life, not just a pile of goods.

And the Good Life certainly didn't require a redhead with hot pants. It would require the pursuit of a Maoist yoga instructor (brunette) and an Oxford graduate fashion model (blond).

. . . Meanwhile in a nearby classroom at the University of Chicago, the campus losers, Paul Wolfowitz and Richard Pearle, studied the "manly art" of war with Professor Leo Strauss and still couldn't get laid. The world would one day suffer mightily for that.

* * *

I bet your kids often ask, as mine do, *Daddy, where do hedge funds come from?* For your own protection, and the protection of your loved ones, you should know the answer.

Here it is.

In that strange period with Friedman at Chicago, furtively slinking through the economics laboratory that was inventing a new hell on Earth, I fell in love, intellectually, with a professor of statistics, Fischer Black. While the other students were bored and resentful of having to learn the *coefficients* and *r-squares*, to me this thin, tall man was a wizard with a magical numbers box. He took to me, while the others snoozed, and loved to explain his weird theorems, which came, literally, from outer space. Black was a failed physicist. Forced to look down, he theorized that the same mathematical forces that controlled the stars and the same probabilistic motion of sub-atomic particles ruled the behavior of the stock market.

Black saw the stock market, not as a hunt to pick the best stock, but rather as a solar system ruled by the laws of physics and probability. Stocks were like electrons, whirling and stumbling about randomly, like a drunk trying to walk away from a lamppost.

Black's Magic was the sorcerer's stone of finance. Hold it, know it, and you could virtually eliminate all financial risk in this risky world.

You could amalgamate groups of investments into "portfolios" in such a way that the risk of one offset the risk of the other. Gambling in the stock market by investment banks would be, necessarily, eliminated. No more picking stocks, a fool's errand. Financial rewards would be small, but risk would vanish. The world's financial panics would be left to history, and all economic booms and busts smoothed into calm waves.

I met Black not long after he'd put this Drunk's Random Walk into an academic paper with his friend Myron Scholes. They called it the Capital Asset Pricing Model.*

---

* If you want to write down the formula, here it is: $K_c = R_f + \beta x (Km - Rf)$. If you don't understand this arithmo-Greek, don't worry about it.

About the same time, a newly expanding investment bank, a small house on the edge of the financial universe, Goldman Sachs, also fell in love with Dr. Black's Magic Model, and hired all his best students and, eventually, Dr. Black himself.

Black's magic crew at Goldman looked at the stock market but, instead of seeing securities, saw simply a soup of financial molecules, which could be manipulated and sliced and rejoined in strange and wonderful combinations.

The Model and its correlatives could be used to find risk and offset it. If General Motors sold cars in Mexico, it could offset its risk by *betting that the peso would fall*. The currency risk had been "hedged," eliminated.

"Hedge funds" could be created for the buying and selling of financial "products" that would each incorporate one of these risks. It's just like hedging your big bet at the race track by placing a little one on the other ponies. Hedge funds, as their names imply, could reduce the risk of financial crisis for companies, for investors, for the planet.

It is not by coincidence that experiments in the first practical applications of atomic physics were conducted at the University of Chicago, the first splitting of an atom, showing that, indeed, $E=mc^2$. Under the bleachers of the university's football field, Enrico Fermi set off the first "controlled" chain reaction. Control it, and make enough heat to power all of a city's lights. Remove the control, and eliminate the city of Hiroshima.

Back at Goldman, and then at other investment banks, the experiments with financial molecules continued.

Then, the financial science turned weird. Turned dangerous. If you could extract the risk of currency fluctuations from GM stock, you could also derive from this currency-risk security another security that would extract the risk of the fluctuations in the first security and then a security that would fluctuate with the security that moved with that new security, and so on and so on.

Securities that were themselves "derived" from the movements of still other securities began to form in the financial universe. And metastasized. The "derivatives" market, through the meiosis and mitosis of securities fractioning, grew from a few billion dollars in trades centered on multinational companies to $83 trillion by 2008 on the balance sheet of a single bank, JP Morgan. That's $83 TRILLION. The chain reaction had begun.

Everything could be sliced and diced into risk-reducing derivative securities: You could eliminate the risk of sub-prime mortgages in Los Angeles by "securitizing" the risks of defaults and selling the derivative of it to a pension fund in Norway. And you could eliminate the cost of electricity risk to mortgage payees (that is, reduce your exposure to foreclosures caused by rising electricity bills) if you hedged the weather in Argentina by selling a derivative of its derivative in a "tranche" to . . . If you don't follow this, remember, *you're not supposed to.*

Then, Adam Smith's bony hand rose from a cold grave to wag his finger at us. "Beware," said the rector Smith, "of men who reap what they do not sow." Aristotle's cold voice followed: "Rentiers," those who made money from money, molest nature itself. The hurricane must follow. It did.

By 1994, "hedge funds" were no longer Dr. Black's dull mathematical machines for offsetting risk. Securities derived from securities derived from securities set off that feared chain reaction. While panicked regulators watched the explosion with fear, Clinton's Treasury Secretary, Robert Rubin, who'd come from Goldman Sachs, saw only one new world, a post-industrial America. The USA would "manufacture" and sell financial "products," while we would leave the dull manufacturing of objects to China.

In 1997, with the world's stock markets climbing through the clouds, Myron Scholes received the Nobel Prize for the Black-Scholes Model. The committee could not honor Black, my guide to the Brave New Numerology, who had died of throat cancer years earlier.

Then the rains came.

How could my master Black have gotten it so horrifically wrong? He had slipped on the banana peel dropped by Milton Friedman. Friedman had sold Black and the world the idea that markets are perfectly "efficient," from its pricing of French fries to derivatives and money itself, all set in a perfectly rational and fair way. The market's magical Invisible Hand needed no arm attached. Government would only get in the way of this wondrous self-regulating economy.

Crucial to the Friedman theory—and please pay attention to this—was that markets have "wisdom." That is, *prices in a free market communicate all information* about a product, securities included (and their derivatives). A free market is a fair market with all information available to all the players. No one could make $7 billion by an "arbitrage" of the flaws in the markets or take advantage of special information. Therefore, no investor could, in the long run, make a dime looking for better stocks. The Sack can't make the monkey jump. Steven Cohen's sack of billions simply can't exist.

Remember, the information is already incorporated in the price. No one can gain off the imperfections in markets because there are no imperfections. And no one can make a penny from secret, "inside" information because there is no such thing as inside information: It's all out there in the market price.

It's nonsense of course, and Friedman's Fantasy would bring the world to its knees.

In the meantime, Friedman's theories and Black's models became the way to *find* those imperfections, to *create* those imperfections, to evaluate the control of information and manipulate the suckers.

The quickest of the Chicago students, often armed with mighty computer algorithms that could make Einstein sweat, praised Friedman and the free market to the sky—and made billions proving Friedman wrong. The market could be fixed, fondled, fucked with, bent, and the suckers kept deaf, dumb, and blind, have their pockets slashed, lose their jobs, homes, and pensions to the arbs, the hedge fund operators, and Enron traders guided by their secret, well-proven theorem:

Just ask the Sack. Just ask the Vulture.

* * *

But I had their sorcerer's stone, the Capital Asset Pricing Model, right in my hand. The preppies and climbers around me knew exactly what to do with their little stones: Goldman and friends were paying a quarter million dollars a year starting salary for Chicago B-School trainees. (Chicago was the hot place, and unlike Harvard grads, Chicago kids weren't afraid of arithmetic.) Some of my classmates earned millions, but most earned tens of millions, some billions.

To me, working as a glorified clerk at some bank just to buy a Ferrari seemed brain-murderingly dull, an inglorious waste of this one life. I simply got nauseous thinking I'd have to take one of these horror-show jobs where life waited for "casual Fridays" and quickies with interns in the lunchroom. Offices filled with vultures and dicks. God save me.

He didn't. The United Electrical Workers did. I was guided there by a dark, delicious Italian, Ann Lonigro, my only intimate ever who actually believed in God, that is, a real Lord high in a cloud.

I picked that up when she said she wanted to introduce me to her younger brother and parents. Sure, I'll fly to Italy. "No, they're in Heaven. You'll really like them."

And she was a committed Maoist, just returned from Peru, where she got herself tangled up with guerilla assassins.

It didn't have to make sense, only that Lonigro ("The Black One") had connections to the labor union leadership in Chicago, especially the brilliant chief of the United Electrical Workers, Frank Rosen. Rosen had worked his way up through the union ranks from a job on the factory shop floor at General Electric, where he worked as an assembly-line mechanic after getting his degree in physics from U Chicago. (This Aristotelian choice was echoed in his son Carl, who took work as a subway electrician after graduating Harvard.)

So there we were, me and The Black One, two Maoists (who had no idea what "Maoism" was) who studied the Chicago models and numbers night and day.

We had this idea: What if some skinny long-haired kids figured out a way to use the Capital Asset Pricing Model not to make a killing but to *stop the killers?*

In her llama-wool poncho at the business school, Lonigro was so strangely out of place that I stopped her and told her that I didn't know what she was doing but I wanted to do it with her. She walked me to her Southside apartment, picking up weeds from between the sidewalk cracks to make us a luncheon salad.

Inside, spread across a fifteen-foot wall, floor to ceiling, were huge sheets of butcher paper with a rough-drawn map of the planet. It was covered with crazy arrows and numbers and names in Spanish and Dutch and English and Italian of the subsidiaries, shells, covers, and mutations of Deltec Corporation, one of the earliest of the multinational mega-conglomerates, that mixed finance, raw-resource extraction, and manufacturing. Canned beef from Argentina became insurance from Switzerland, then widgets in Australia, with capital funds and cash flow moving from peso to gilders to dollars and back, whirling and whirling into a corporate vortex without a center. And everywhere, on every continent, its workers got screwed.

Lonigro had created this money map for a transnational labor union based in Geneva, Switzerland, that was attempting, somehow, to organize and protect the workers under each of Deltec's far-flung tentacles. Lonigro's task was to investigate the movements of this shape-shifting octopus's capital from zone to zone.

The wall of arrows and names and numbers seized me. And I knew, instantly, that I wanted to do *that*. As a career, for the rest of my life. Whatever "that" was. I wanted to make arrows! I wanted to ride them in my head across continents.

> And the light became so bright and so blindin'
> in this layer of paradise
> that the mind of man was bewildered.

I nearly tore off a piece of Africa grinding Lonigro against it.

And as the arrows whirled round and round, pretty soon the products they rode upon meant nothing. It was money making money making money. The oil moved out, but the petrodollars came back in. Around and around. Argentina's rich hid their money in New York banks, and their desperate government borrowed it back at usurious rates. In out in out in out.

Here, in a world pierced and bitten by moving arrows and snakes, was Ezra Pound's Canto XXXVIII.

> A factory
> has also another aspect, which we call the financial aspect
> add into the prices caused by that factory, any damn factory and there is
> and must be therefore a clog and the power to purchase can never catch up

It was this map, this billion-dollar game of shoots and ladders, reduced to words, that I gave to Milton Friedman. Aristotle and Ezra Pound and Lonigro.

* * *

More important than showing Friedman, I put The Model in front of Electrical Workers leader Rosen and offered him my new skills in finance and my connections to the new right wing Storm Troopers. Rosen, a math whiz and street-fighting man, understood the value of it all. "Get rid of the Mao button" was his first advice, wear their uniform, and quietly learn to work their tools. Stay low and stay inside the Friedman circle. So, I bought a shirt, tie, a used brief-case, and sunglasses. (All the Chicago Boys from Brazil and Chile, dictators in training, wore sunglasses just like in the movie Z.)

While Lonigro continued to track Deltec, Rosen gave me my own corporations to dissect, two that I lived inside: Commonwealth Edison Corporation (that's Exelon today) and Peoples Gas Co. These were Chicago's electric and gas companies. Com Ed was shutting off lights as it tripled its electric rates. "People's" Co. was cutting off heating gas to poor Hispanics, Blacks, and Polish families on Chicago's Northwest side. That was where my parents grew up. The gas monopoly had quintupled its rates, and if you didn't pay up, they would send out trucks to shut off the heating pipes, even in the middle of ice storms. Freezing families abandoned their homes; several lit kerosene lamps, which burnt their decrepit houses; kids died; some old folk just froze in their beds. Well, that's the free market for you, Milton.

UE President Rosen saw an opportunity to expose the whole machinery of the system. He figured that electricity and gas monopolies that held life-and-death power over captive customers were capitalism's flesh-ripping wolf teeth, despised, indefensible, and therefore most politically vulnerable.

Rosen called a meeting and introduced me to a rare set of birds: people who gave a shit (in the Aristotelian sense). There was Charley Hayes from out of the stockyards, then President of the Meatpackers union. We shook hands and my hand was swallowed in his huge butcher's fist. (Later, when the stock-yards were shut down, Congressman Hayes would found the Congressional Black Caucus.) There was Teddy Smolarek, President of the Ironworkers local; Norm Roth, head of the UAW's huge Caterpillar tractor manufacturing local union (before the company fired all union workers); and Jack Spiegel of the Shoeworkers union (shoes were still sewn in the USA then). And Fred Gaboury, a not-so-secret executive of the Communist Party.

Meanwhile, Rosen sent Lonigro into a wire-making factory to grab a job on the assembly line and, in Spanish, which the management couldn't understand, organize a union.

These were the days when power companies and gas companies were still regulated by little-known government agencies. Citizens had a right to appear before them when they set the prices for heating gas and household electricity, but the rulers of Chicago made sure no one showed up except the companies. . . .

. . . Until, to the city elite's surprise, the entire labor leadership of the state of Illinois, twenty-six unions in all, at a time when unions meant something, entered the courtroom where the regulators heard their evidence and shoved me forward, and had me lay down my papers: two hundred pages of calculations, accounting minutiae, and statistical analysis showing that the gas company's charges were grossly bloated by outrageous profits.

For the first time ever, the Chicago Model, instead of sucking in millions for Goldman, was used in defense of the system's victims.

Every TV station in the city and the dailies covered the moment. The gas company executives and lawyers were chuckling and nudging each other, looking at this badly typed pile of numbers handed over by some long-haired kid in sandals. (I wore a suit but forgot the shoes.)

The commissioners, every one of whom would soon work for the companies they regulated, looked at their winking future employer, at the cameras, and at the political battleship of the labor leadership . . . and ordered a full trial on my calculations.

The gas company executives couldn't believe it, and perplexed by my mathematics based on the Capital Asset Model, hired a Chicago professor to translate the magic stone's coded thoughts. The most expensive lawyers in Chicago cross-examined me almost every day for a month, challenging every "beta" formula and data point. It was like taking the SAT, but with a hundred million bucks at stake.

Then, with articles nearly daily in the press reporting creepy stuff I had found crawling out of the company's account books, the regulators, despite the desires of every bone in their bodies, had no choice. They voted unanimously to end the company's out-of-control profiteering. Heating gas prices were cut.

Who would have guessed that accounting could be such a revolutionary tool, could be so much fun, or, as Jake found out, could get you killed.

The gas company was stunned, livid, and far from finished with me. The industry's huge lobbying power, revolving-door bribery, and more lawyers than O. J. Simpson couldn't help them. But there is always a way to slither under the law.

I discovered how when I got a call from a dean at the university. He was very excited for me: A really big corporation was offering me a really big job. So I asked him, "Was this big corporation by any chance People's Gas?"

"Yes! It's all supposed to be secret. I'm not supposed to tell you."

"And did they ask for my confidential files?"

He got it immediately. And he was horrified. Through this low-rent "job offer" deception, they suckered the Dean into a violation of federal law, the Buckley Amendment, which kept these records sealed. Trying to help me, he had given my enemies the ammunition—and now he would lose his job once I went public. I couldn't do that to him because he'd saved my ass when the university found out I conned my way into the graduate school without having graduated and he told them to go fly. Besides, we shared a secret: the Dean also knew Milton Friedman was full of shit. So, I said, "Just forget it. Let them look. Let them keep it."

There was another file I'm sure the company stooges got. Lonigro and I let some guy from some Lefty group crash with us for a few days. The ACLU, via a civil suit, got me a copy of the lengthy report he wrote about us for the Chicago police red squad. (In one file, they said a doctor friend of mine dynamited a hot dog stand. Really!) Well, fuck 'em.

I decided it would be great fun to go after more of these bastards—and they decided to go after me. Well, it beats waiting for the office Christmas party. But no Ferrari. I proudly became the first (and I'm sure the only) Chicago Business School graduate to get a gold-plated MBA and, the same week, sign up for food stamps. I had work, but I didn't have a job. Didn't want one, either.*

* * *

The Chicago Boys creeped me out. I certainly did not want any job that would require my working close enough to smell them. Frank Rosen came to the rescue. While I picked up what I needed from the Boys and Friedman and nailed my parchment, Rosen tutored me in the mathematics of wages, benefits, and the kabbalistic actuarial prognosticating for pension funds. He then sent me off, a young punk, to negotiate contracts for steelworkers at the coke ovens at Interlake Steel and for the power plant workers in Gary, Indiana. Rosen hooked me up with the Steelworkers union where I was assigned to investigate the pricing tricks of U.S. Steel, and arranged for me to get an adjunct professorship at the University of Indiana. Rosen did this while founding an organization for universal health care and another for a shorter workweek, all while fighting the mobsters moving in on his union. Maybe this practically minded revolutionary couldn't change the direction of history's train, but at least he could unionized the conductors.

His wife, Lois, and I worked together lobbing info-grenades at the power companies from desks in the union's windowless basement. This was *living.* And I had found the father my father was supposed to be.

Eddie Sadlowski was a mechanic at U.S. Steel Southworks. In 1976, he led a workers' rebellion to take control of the million-person United Steelworkers of America. (Back then, workers were united and America made steel.) Oil-

---

* The fun hasn't stopped. While typing the last paragraph, I was interrupted by a FedEx delivery of a package weighing about three pounds: another manila folder from a power company's files. I sent a message to the sender: "Got your gift. Just my size! Hugs to mom!"

And you can join the fun. Send me your "burn this" files to DeathThreat@GregPalast.com. I'm serious.

can Eddie was America's working-class hero, back then, when America was working. He'd been profiled on *60 Minutes*. The Business School thought it cute to bring him to the university to lecture, with his rough hands and Local 1110 windbreaker, so the yuppies-in-training could make fun of the workers' monkey trying to speak English.

Sadlowski stunned them, his brain racing beyond them. But it was their decade, with Reagan rising, and they would close Southworks, then bury both Eddie and his union. I didn't know that then and I'm glad I didn't.

Sadlowski ended his performance by looking out over the packed auditorium, saying, "Is Greg Palast here?"

Heads turned. Mine, too. Huh?

"Yeah, you. You Greg Palast? Meet me downstairs."

OK. In the basement coffee shop, I got us two Styrofoam cups and lots of sugar, and without even a hello, Sadlowski said, "Rosen told me where I could find you. Teddy Smolarek says you're a genius."

He said it like "You're the guy who has the tire size I'm looking for."

Sadlowski told me that this big-shot politician, a Boss Daley Machine hack on the South Side, was running against a decent lady who cared about steelworkers. The union needed info on the Machine's candidate. Sadlowski said, "He's a crook."

I asked how he knew the guy was a crook.

The entire 240 pounds of Polish steelworker leaned in to me.

"*You're* the genius. You tell *me!*"

Two weeks later, through some BS story I used about a research paper, I got my hands on the bids for county emergency roadwork. There it was: the Machine's boy was the costliest bidder for the job. He still got the contract. And he still got elected.

Whatever, that was my first real investigation. I didn't know it, but this side of beef of a mechanic was handing me my life across a plastic folding table.

Elated with this assignment, I must have been giving off pheromones left and right, because an astonishing long blonde in an elegant dress (odd for a student) came up and said, "You *know* Sadlowski?"

Carol was in the B-School, but she had quietly joined the Union of Radical Political Economists. She'd leave that off her résumé for Morgan Bank. But she, too, was trying to marry the derivatives model to the proletarian revolution.

I explained how I was working with Actual Working People and Actual Poor People—and described the quest on which I was sent by Sadlowski. "That's so . . ." I'm glad she didn't say "cool." I'm gladder that she pressed her lips so violently against mine that I slammed into the school's ivied wall.

That's when I first got the inkling that by doing work that assholes would shun, I might not get a Ferrari but I could get a Carol Overby.

Up in her apartment, the Oxford graduate said, "I promise I won't do anything that will hurt you." She was nearly six feet tall. How bad could it be? Ropes? Blindfolds? Was it worth it? *Yes, yes, YES!*

I said, "OK, but please nothing that leaves a visible mark."

Carol pulled away. "I meant *emotional* harm!"

Note to female readers: Have mercy. We men are idiots. We don't know shit about love, about Eros's dance with Artemis and Cupid. Half of us don't even *know* we are ignorant savages, and the other half are desperately looking into your eyes, hoping to find the instruction manual.

It was the first time I heard the word *knickers* or *teddy* or seen anything made entirely of silk and lace. I grew up in a working-class world of white underpants bought for girls and boys in discount packs of eight.

Slowly, cautiously, tenderly, I swam toward England's shore, a land I could never afford to see except through Carol's silky intimacy. I was so astonished by it all that I could pretend for a moment that I wasn't cheating on Lonigro.

Life got weird and hectic because I've always been attracted to weird and hectic. Each night before a Friedman seminar or Chicago Boys meet-up, I'd leave Lonigro and travel guiltily from her Italy to visit Carol's England.

I let Carol take my job interviews; it wasn't a trade for time with her knickers off, but why take a chance? I really didn't want to go to interviews—what if Goldman really came through with that big-ass offer? You know, I was a working-class kid, and it would have been brutally difficult to turn down a fat six-figure salary. Instinctively, I knew that no one ever escapes from a prison made of gold.

Sorry to keep bringing up the ladies. But I was in my twenties, and anyone with unclouded memory knows that's the time your genitals and your soul and the hum of the planet are all tangled up together in some magical way. It's only later, in your fifties, when the delicious season is only memory, that such sack-hopping activities seem just sick and piteous. *Post coitum omnia animalia tristia sunt.* After making love, all animals are sad. Many, many years after.

* * *

That winter of 1976, the gas company continued to cut off the poor when the wind off Lake Michigan brought the temperature to -10°F. Cruelty and greed dancing cheek to cheek. A group of pissed-off Latino, Black, and poor Polish folks from the Northwest side marched into the corporation's headquarters building, somehow slid past security, and on the penthouse floor of People's Gas Co., seized the office of the Chairman of the Board. In a radio broadcast from their occupied hold-out, they vowed to live or die there unless the corporate jackals agreed to stop the heating gas cut-offs and until the Governor agreed to fire the head of the utility commission.

They got both.

In the middle of this militant cadre, with cops going nuts, stood their "community organizer," with *legs up to here*. Across the crowded room, she looked at me with green eyes lit up by a brain I correctly guessed was way quicker than mine. In black high-heeled boots. I didn't catch her name then, but in bed she told me, "The moment I saw you, I knew I would marry you."

It was a hasty decision that, thirty years and a pair of twins later, Linda says she regrets.

But I have not, not for one minute.

It was a marriage for the record books. From the basement of that union hall, where she joined me to rip the lungs out of the gas company, to that high pass in the Himalayas, we took big bites out of the world and spit out the horrid bits at the makers of the horror.

CHAPTER 10
Fukushima, Texas

TOKYO BY TELEVISION, MARCH 12, 2010

Badpenny is watching Japan drown on CNN. It's one A.M. but she won't let me quit for the night just because I told the TV, "It's bullshit."

At the nuclear plant at Fukushima, north of Tokyo, three reactors are committing suicide. The CNN guys are saying that the huge earthquake and tsunami from the night before knocked out the plant's generators, the engines that pump water to keep the fuel from melting; but don't worry.

They're lying, and what's sick is, they don't even *know* they're lying.

First, the earthquake didn't take out those diesels. Second, the tsunami didn't take out those diesels. Third, you should worry.

You should worry because every nuclear plant in operation today, and the ones they want to build, all depend on this same emergency diesel engine set-up to save your behind from a nuclear meltdown. Good luck.

How do I know the Japanese reactor should have stood, but didn't; that its back-up diesels busted all by themselves? I'm not telepathic. I can't see inside the minds of distant diesel motors. I can't see into next Thursday.

All I have are files.

Badpenny's on my ass. "Well, if you know all this, why aren't you writing about it? Why aren't you calling *Newsnight*?"

Here's why: I'm about finished with *Vultures' Picnic* and I'm not going to expand the nuclear chapter, and I'm up against a deadline that I can't extend, dearest lady, because my publisher has a heart of gold. No blood, just yellow metal. And the kids have to be up for school at six forty-five A.M.

"You promised Harvey!"

The Angel. That was a low blow. The Radioactive Brick from Houston was throbbing and glowing at the end of my desk.

OK, then, *get me the fucking files!* We're in the basement office and I start throwing around huge plastic containers of old papers, screaming, *"Why the hell are all these papers out of order dammit dammit dammit!"* The answer is that I made a mess of the old files, dumping them into giant plastic tubs despite Badpenny's best efforts to sort them in case we had to pull them quickly.

Now we have to pull them quickly. It's late, now nearly two A.M., and I'm cranky and didn't need this. I'm screaming (why am I always screaming?) that I want "every fucking file or report or binder that says *RICO*," especially anything marked *EDG* or *SQ*.

I give up. It's totally impossible. I've plopped down on the sofa and watch smoke rise from the Fukushima reactors. Sometimes there are black plumes, sometimes white, like when they're voting on a new Pope.

In twenty minutes, Badpenny organizes two two-foot stacks of papers, binders, tape transcripts, reports, and printouts, and sets them out on her desk. I inhale some asthma medicine to get through the dusty stuff. *I'll never find the evidence in this pile of crap.*

I've found it. The Notebook. Here was the handwritten log kept by a senior engineer at the nuclear plant.

Wiesel was very upset. He seemed very nervous. Very agitated. . . . In fact, the plant was riddled with problems that, no way on earth, could stand an earthquake. The team of engineers sent in to inspect found that most of these components could "completely and utterly fail" during an earthquake.

"Utterly fail during an earthquake." And here was the quake and here was the failure. The warning was in The Notebook, which I wasn't supposed to have. Good thing I kept a copy anyway, because the file cabinets went down with the building.

WORLD TRADE CENTER TOWER 1, FIFTY-SECOND FLOOR, NEW YORK, 1986

I'd seen a lot of sick stuff in my career, but this was sick on a new level of sick.

Two senior nuclear plant engineers were spilling out their souls and files on our huge conference table, blowing away my government investigations team with the inside stuff about the construction of the Shoreham power station.

The meeting was secret. Very secret. Their courage could destroy their careers: No engineering firm wants to hire a snitch, even one who has saved thousands of lives. They could lose their jobs; they could lose everything. They did. That's what happens. Have a nice day.

All field engineers keep a diary. Gordon Dick, a superviser, wasn't supposed to show his to us. I asked him to show it to us and, reluctantly, he directed me to these notes about the "SQ" tests.

SQ is nuclear-speak for "Seismic Qualification." A seismically qualified nuclear plant won't melt down if you shake it. A "seismic event" can be an earthquake or a Christmas present from Al Qaeda. You can't run a nuclear reactor in the USA or Europe or Japan without certified SQ.

This much is clear from his notebook: This nuclear plant will melt down in an earthquake. The plant dismally failed to meet the Seismic I (shaking) standards required by U.S. and international rules.

Here's what we learned: Dick's subordinate at the nuclear plant, Robert Wiesel, conducted the standard seismic review. Wiesel flunked his company. No good. Dick then ordered Wiesel to change his report to the Nuclear Regulatory Commission, change it from failed to passed. Dick didn't want to make Wiesel do it, but Dick was under the gun himself, acting on direct command from corporate chiefs. From The Notebook:

> Wiesel was very upset. He seemed very nervous. Very agitated. [He said,] "I believe these are bad results and I believe it's reportable," and then he took the volume of federal regulations from the shelf and went to section 50.55(e), which describes reportable deficiencies at a nuclear plant and [they] read the section together, with Wiesel pointing to the appropriate paragraphs that federal law clearly required [them and the company] to report the Category II, Seismic I deficiencies.
>
> Wiesel then expressed his concern that he was afraid that if he [Wiesel] reported the deficiencies, he would be fired, but that if he didn't report the deficiencies, he would be breaking a federal law. . . .

The law is clear. It is a crime not to report a safety failure. I could imagine Wiesel standing there with that big, thick rule book in his hands, The Law. It must have been heavy. So was his paycheck. He weighed the choices: Break the law, possibly a jail-time crime, or keep his job.

What did Wiesel do? What would *you* do?

Why the hell would his company make this man walk the line? Why did they put the gun to his head, to make him conceal mortal danger? It was the money. It's always the money. Fixing the seismic problem would have cost the plant's owner half a billion dollars easy. A guy from corporate told Dick, *"Bob is a good man. He'll do what's right. Don't worry about Bob."*

That is, they thought Bob would save his job and career rather than rat out the company to the feds.

But I think we *should all* worry about Bob. The company he worked for, Stone & Webster Engineering, built or designed about a third of the nuclear plants in the United States.

From the fifty-second floor we could look at the Statue of Liberty. She didn't look back.

My Southern blond alligator, Lenora Stewart, barefoot under the conference table, took down the info in shorthand. Did the corporation actually file the fake report? Our whistleblower engineer said he was sure of it. But how could we find it, prove it? There were over two million pages of documents at the nuclear plant's file room at the NRC. It took Stewart four months, but she got it. I gave her a sketch of a nose, and she painted the *Mona Lisa*. (You think that's easy? You've seen a page from The Notebook. That's what she had to work with. If you can do better, you're hired.)

OK, so we know the U.S. nuclear industry can play Russian roulette with earthquake safety. But is that what happened in Japan?

DOWNTOWN, MANHATTAN, 2011

Badpenny says, "So, you're not going to include Fukushima in the book?"

You know I'm not. I'm not going to fight my publisher to get this into a book they think is done and they want it *now*. They paid cash money for it and I can't afford to give it back. But she wants to pretend I'm something other than a craven hack. Penny wants me to pretend to be a Prophet, a Man for All Seasons, a Napoleon of Truth.

Besides, there's no need for me to investigate the Fukushima meltdown. They have the answer already. The experts on the TV, supplied by the nuclear industry, are telling us the plant was only designed to withstand an 8.0 earthquake; but it was hit by a quake way bigger than anyone could expect, a monster 9.0 on the Richter scale. They just said that on CNN, so it must be true. And it's also true that the Easter Bunny is going to reduce unemployment and Reagan was a great president.

There was no 9.0 earthquake at the plant. Nothing close to that number.

The industry story, the 9.0 fable, is a wet bag of horseshit. Sure, there was a 9.0 earthquake—*a hundred miles out in the Pacific Ocean*. The shake *at the plant* was only about 7.0–8.0 on the Richter scale. The Richter scale is logarithmic. That means the tremor was only about a *tenth* of the force of the 9.0 at the epicenter in the Pacific Ocean.

Something nasty was going on and I was trying hard not to investigate it.

MANHATTAN OFFICE, 2011

But I couldn't resist. Somehow, Tokyo Electric had, I suspected, played a game with the plant's Seismic Qualification and, once again, Mother Nature had given a corporation a perfect cover: an earthquake worse than their supposed SQ requirement.

Matty Pass sent me the "shake map" of Japan made by the U.S. Geological Survey, the technical photo of the quake. I stared at the station-by-station ground acceleration readings and after an hour found location "FKSH05, Lat:37," which had a maximum acceleration of "62.3241 N." From what I learned in my self-taught *Earthquakes for Idiots* crash course, that looks bad but not bad enough to shake the diesels so hard they can't operate.

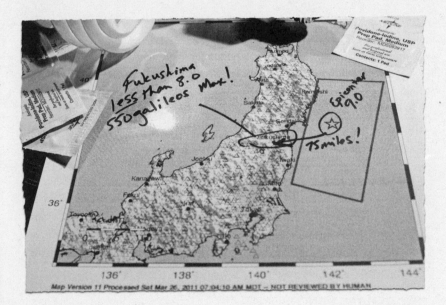

But I'm a confused man at times, and maybe my cynicism is showing me felonies when I'm looking at flowers. I wait until it's morning in Colorado and work the phones until I get a live USGS seismologist, an earthquake expert, to translate this "Max Vel %g PSA" lingo for me.

But as soon as he hears I'm the press, the government man gets nervous and simply won't tell me what's going on. He suggests I call Japan. *Arigato,* jack-off.

Then I log into some nuclear expert and engineering chats on the Net and there's lots of griping about the missing seismics, photos, and details on the diesel bunkers. Like me, the industry guys smell the bullshit. I just need to find the bull.

They lead me to it. The company, Tokyo Electric, said that the earthquake hit hardest at Reactor #2, a slam of 550 gals (*galileos* measure ground movement). What a shame, because the reactor had been designed to withstand only 436 gals. According to the company and *The New York Times,* the earthquake exceeded the safety requirement by 20 percent. But I don't buy that.

I dig further into the technical papers, and get this: The plant was not supposed to be designed for a 436-gal quake. Tokyo Electric *knew* that 436 would not make it. In dusty old technical papers, the company promised government regulators they would raise the seismic protection to 600. They promised. That was five years ago.

So there you have it. If TEPCO had not played the regulators, Japan would not be suffering a slow-motion Hiroshima.

It was the Shoreham plant all over again. TEPCO toyed with the plant's Seismic Qualification. But techno-talk and complex regulations are way too mystifying for the media, which prefers the Unexpectedly Big Earthquake tale. For all we know, the Fukushima plant would have melted down if a couple of Chihuahuas had danced on the roof.

TEPCO broke the rules, muscled the regulators into silence, and cowed the press with BS. You should recognize the pattern by now:

犯罪、消費電力、神秘

Hanzai, shōhi denryoku, shinpi. Crime, Power, Mystification.

SHOREHAM, LONG ISLAND

So now we know Tokyo Electric was pinching pennies on earthquake proofing the plant. Still, the emergency diesel generators should have kept Fukushima's reactor core from melting. They failed. And I suspected it was neither the earthquake nor even the tsunami that knocked them out. My suspicious mind was stoked by something else I found in my asthma-provoking files of yesteryear.

Here it is.

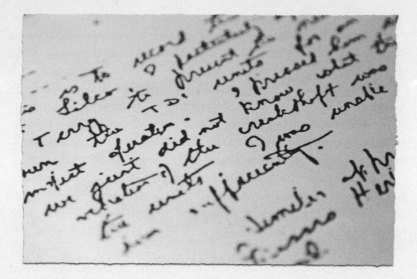

A page from the notebook of an Emergency Diesel Generator expert, R. D. Jacobs, hired to monitor a test for a nuclear reactor's back-up cooling system.

> *This is to record that on my last visit, . . . I pressed [a company executive] saying we just did not know what the axial vibration of the crankshaft was doing to the [diesel] units. I was unable to impress him sufficiently.*

The diesels were "tested" by turning them on for a few minutes at low power. They worked fine. But R.D., a straight shooter, suspected problems. He wanted the motors opened and inspected. He was told by power company management to go to hell.

Suffolk County, New York, the wealthiest county in the United States, had the cash, the legal team, the experts, and the power of the privileged to question what was going on. Power companies aren't used to being questioned. When we forced the plant builder to test the three Emergency Diesel Generators in emergency conditions, one failed almost immediately (the crankshaft snapped, as R.D. predicted), then the second, then the third. We named the three diesels "Snap, Crackle, and Pop."

So, I was not surprised to see, and it was no trick to predict, that the Japanese diesels, roughly of the same type, would go *gyoshi, makka, pop* ("snap, crackle, and pop" in Japanese).

My suspicions then took me to a darker hypothesis. In my gut, I believed that the diesels *were never* expected to work, *can't* work. Not anywhere: not in Japan, not in the United States, not in Russia, nowhere. That means every nuclear plant built or about to be built doesn't stand a chance in a power outage emergency.

Cynicism is not proof. Even if my horror-show appraisal is correct, I'd need an expert to back it up, someone from the inside willing to rat out their own industry and put their livelihood on the line.

Within three days of the quake, Badpenny got a note from the West Coast from the man I needed.

SOMEWHERE, CALIFORNIA

God bless the notes and the little fairies who tug at someone's conscience and tell them to send it. This one, from a Jonathan Sellars, came via the *Contact Greg* button at www.GregPalast.com. (Keep that address in your wallet.)

Sellars is an expert with hands-on work on nuclear plant emergency diesels. His long message contained some techno-chat about "in-line 8 cylinder engines making 450 revs, 17 inch bore and 21 inch stroke, turbocharged and inter-cooled"—Sellars seemed to know his stuff.

I called the phone number he included and asked for Mr. Sellars.

"Sellars: That's not my real name." Well, no kidding. It's not an industry that turns the other cheek. I got his true moniker and locked it away.

Apparently, "Sellars" was watching Fukushima melt and had that I-told-those-fools feeling that strikes honest engineers, which is most of them, when stuff goes bad. He had worked for General Electric, which built most of Fukushima's reactors.

The issue was the water on the diesels. He told me, "It was obvious to the entire crew of skilled millwright-mechanics and engineers that the one very large vulnerability that the system had was a flood."

He issued the warning in 1985. Fukushima was built in the 1970s so a retrofit would have cost a mint. The warning was ignored.

Sellars checked out the photos of the Fukushima plant on cryptome.org (an excellent source), and saw the diesel buildings were standing up just fine. The earthquake didn't knock them down. They simply did not have them sealed against water.

"They have them hardened against a terrorist shooting the louvers with a bazooka," he told me, "but a simple flood, that's going to trip them."

Well, there goes baloney cover #1, that a larger-than-expected tsunami "destroyed" the generators. The ones that didn't simply crack apart got wet. Like when you leave your cell phone near an open window and then a storm soaks it and it shorts out. It doesn't take a tsunami.

So big deal. The Japanese are schmucks. How could they be so dumb? Water and electricity don't mix, just like they warned you in school not to take your radio into a bathtub.

My insider worked on the diesels at a California nuke, but it's the same story almost everywhere, from Fukushima to Florida. Diesels open to water remain standard industry practice worldwide (except Germany). The engineers shrug and say, "Those are the specs." Meltdowns and cancer? That's handled by the office down the hall.

Then I threw a curveball at this expert, a question he didn't expect. I knew that all these diesels were basically designed, or even taken from, cruise ship engine rooms or old locomotives. I'm not an engineer, but I suspect a motor designed for a leisurely float to Bermuda is not fit for a life-and-death scramble. So I asked him, "They really can't work *at all*, the diesels, can they?"

That's when he introduced me to the phrase "crash start."

On a ship, he explained, you would take half an hour to warm up the bearings, and then slowly build up to "critical" crankshaft speed, and only then add the "load," the propeller. Kind of like warming up your car before putting it in gear.

That's for sailing. But in a nuclear emergency, "the diesels have to go from stationary to taking a full load in less than ten seconds." That's like jumping in my cold Honda and roaring out of the garage at 120 mph.

Worse, to avoid having to buy additional diesels, the nuclear operators turbo-charge them, revving them to 4,000 horsepower in ten seconds when they are designed for half that output.

The result: snap, crackle, pop.

I learned that, at Fukushima, at least two of the diesels failed *before* the tsunami hit. What destroyed those diesels was *turning them on*. In other words, the diesels are junk, are crap, are not capable of getting up to full power in seconds, then run continuously for days. They're decorations attached to nuclear plants so people will think these radioactive tea kettles are safe.

Just testing them can damage them. There are alternatives to snap, crackle, pop diesels, but they can cost a billion dollars per station. And the operators have decided you're just not worth it.

Sometimes the diesels work, sometimes they don't. It's meltdown roulette.

"So, you're saying emergency diesels can't work in an emergency?"

"Actually, they're just not designed for it."

Failure is in the design, the design of the political system, the corporate system. Instead of diesels, they might as well surround the plant with tin foil and Christmas wrapping. They are decorative, there to reassure a snoozy public that all is well. Much like BP's Clean-up Theater, this is the nuclear industry's Safety Showtime.

THE REAGAN WHITE HOUSE

Well, wait. After Snap, Crackle, and Pop were exposed as worse than useless, why didn't the Nuclear Regulatory Commission check the diesels all over America?

It did. The NRC found several plants with no-damn-good diesels, especially those made by a company called Transamerica Delaval Inc. (TDI).

Then that brilliant nuclear engineer, Ronald Reagan, took over. Within the White House, as Ollie North set up the secret Iran-Contra crew, another group, led by political hyena Lyn Nofziger, secretly set up a crew to manipulate the Nuclear Regulatory Commission, although it is a quasi-judicial entity. (A White House that would give guns to the Ayatollah and Central American drug lords certainly won't have qualms about snapping diesel engines.)

Reagan's nuclear warlocks used manipulation and raw power to stymie the NRC's attempt to fix the diesel problem. Nuclear operators learned a lesson: Fixing the regulators is cheaper than fixing the problem.*

---

* How do I know about the White House extra-legal finagling on emergency diesels? It was uncovered by the greatest investigative journalist of the twentieth century, Ron Ridenhour of New Orleans. Ridenhour's the guy who uncovered the My Lai massacre in Vietnam, a story typically credited to Seymour Hersh. Hersh is truly brilliant and deserves credit for expanding on Ron's discovery and getting it into the U.S. press, but I've waited for years to make sure Ridenhour gets his credit.

It was my friend Ron, not me, who had the contract to write this book when, in 1996, I thought these stories needed telling. But Ron died young and I took up the pen he dropped. I apologize that I'm no Ron Ridenhour. But then, no one is.

BROOKLYN, NEW YORK

In 1985, I was sitting at my desk in a basement I rented in Brooklyn, where I could work and play my drums without disturbing anyone with any authority to stop me. I began a kind of aimless and endless coffee-break romp through a few thousand pages of confidential memos sent between Stone & Webster Engineering (now Shaw) and Long Island Lighting Company (LILCO). The memos were about the building of the Shoreham nuclear plant, on which LILCO had already blown $5 billion over eighteen years—and it still wasn't done.

Beginning in 1973, the power company's Chairman and its President swore under oath the plant was only "a year" or so from completion. Because the plant was nearly done, the government allowed the company to charge up to half a billion a year for the nearly finished plant.

Year after year, the same thing. The plant will be done in a year, the public gets charged another half billion dollars, then the plant isn't done. Repeat. For *twelve more years*. The public thought the managers of this company and its builder were real stupid.

Call me crazy but it struck me that maybe they weren't so stupid, or maybe, stupid like a fox, like a jackal, like a raven. What if "stupid" was a cover for lying, for perjury, for scamming? Could these white-haired members of the North Shore country clubs simply be well-coifed scumbag fraudsters, racketeers, just like the Mafia but with a more dangerous weapon: a nuclear plant?

Sho' nuff: The confidential memos revealed to me that completion dates were *never* just a year away. Their testimony was bullshit just to take in billions from the public.

Here's an example.

In December 1975, a power company executive testified under oath that the plant would be complete for "load fuel" by "the end of 1977."

Then I found this: a confidential memo from Stone & Webster two months earlier saying that the two companies had secretly agreed on "a Fuel Load date of 2/79 plus a five-month contingency." By my calendar, there's a two-year difference at minimum. I say "agreed," but the courtroom term is *conspired*.

> lgnificant events occurring at Shoreham during
> period pertain to a complete reschedule of the jo..
> schedule now demonstrates a 3 to 5 month slip. The
> is being done without a given fuel load date until a..
> .. been gathered from construction enat..
> .. approach which ..

The con never stopped. In June 1983, Stone & Webster *still* hadn't finished building Shoreham. The Chairman of the Board personally begged for money from the government, swearing, under oath, that "the Shoreham Unit is complete as far as construction is concerned except for the diesel engines," and would load fuel in two months.

In fact, the Chairman had already received a confidential report that said they'd be lucky to complete the plant within a year.

And then we get to those emergency diesels, Snap, Crackle, and Pop, similar to the set-up that would fail in Japan. Another power company executive swore under oath, "There was no indication in any of the problems with the Shoreham diesels that the catastrophic crankshaft failure would occur."

Which was bullshit. The company already had the memo from R. D. Jacobs that he'd recorded "axial vibration of the crankshaft" in the diesels and wanted them shut down and taken apart. They hid his demands from the government.

I knew that some government officials thought I'm completely mad—and were willing to pay extra for that. So I called the Attorney General of New York and his unit chief who was in charge of bird-dogging these companies. Deputy AG Jerry Oppenheim told me that my findings sounded completely insane. I was alleging that upstanding executives of a multi-billion dollar corporation had committed perjury to suck up billions of dollars from the public. He couldn't wait to file the case.

But. *But* meaning "no money." It's easy to bring a case against some kid who steals a bike. Cuff 'em, impound the bike, impound the kid. Cheap. But governments simply can't afford to enforce the laws on billion-dollar operators. That's one way the big guys get away with it.

This case would require millions in legal fees for expert lawyers, for engineers up the wazoo, and for years of litigation against resistance from the Governor and political establishment.

But the power company executives had made a big, big mistake. Power plants are supposed to be located in places like the Coon-Ass Riviera (e.g., the Grand Gulf nuclear plant), or Waynesboro, Georgia (63 percent Black, for Southern Company's proposed Plant Vogtle), or in The Valley (where LA Water and Power put its filthy residual-oil-burning plant, the one that gave me asthma).

LILCO, foolishly, decided to put its nuke right in between the country clubs on the North Shore. Land that should have been a golf course! Even Republicans were upset. The exceptionally wealthy county government said, "Investigate it, shut it down, whatever the cost. Just send the bill."

It took two years to compile a million pages of evidence. In 1988, we schlepped it all to federal court in Brooklyn, where I showed a jury the documents I'm showing you here (plus several hundred more), and suggested they require the company to pay $13 billion to its customers.

The conspirators' lawyers pounded me for fifteen days on the witness stand. They didn't like me. And the power company *consigliere* warned the jury that the Governor of New York had called me an astrologer! Oh my.

The jury didn't care about the Governor's horoscope. They unanimously voted that the power company pay $4.3 billion. They found the company LILCO and its Chairman had violated the anti-Mafia racketeering law in a conspiracy with Stone & Webster. The nuclear plant itself, after operating just one single day, was dismantled. No one cried. Certainly not Stone & Webster, which made a billion dollars on the plant-building scam and, despite the verdict, walked away with that $50,000 settlement payment.

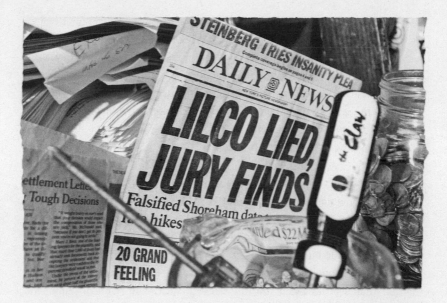

I have to say that on the Liar-Liar-Pants-on-Fire scale, the power company LILCO, now out of business, was far from the worst. I have investigated dozens of nuclear operators, and in every single case, no exceptions, I found this: Fraud is as much a part of the structure of a nuclear plant as the cement and steel.

TEXAS AND TOKYO

In June 2010, Obama addressed the nation, casting hellfire and brimstone upon damnable BP. He pulled out his crying towel to weep over our national addiction to petroleum, and prescribed the energy methadone that would cure our need for an oil fix. The President laid out a vision of windmills o'er purple mountains' majesty and solar panels from sea to shining sea.

That was bullshit, of course. The money would go to nuclear power.

By the beginning of 2011, the newly Republicanized U.S. Congress, which could not bring itself to spend twenty cents to keep a million families from foreclosure, was about to lend $56 billion to nuclear plant builders, and Obama loved it.

There are hundreds of power companies in the United States, but only four were chosen to climb the U.S. Treasury's candy cane: UniStar Nuclear, Scana Corp., NRG, and Southern Company, poor Jake's employer.

How could a benevolent God allow this? I'm a cynical bastard, but this was a new level of weird. After NRG went tits up into Chapter 11 bankruptcy years back and paid me a fee for libeling me in Europe, I thought we'd seen the last of them. I also thought common sense had put a stake through the heart of nuclear power twenty years ago. Now the nuclear ghoul is rising from the crypt, come back from the dead the moment they heard the words *government guarantee*.

NRG's Chapter 11 bankruptcy, 500 percent cost overruns, and fines for nuclear safety violations hardly add up to a winning profile for a competitive loan application. What must have won the government guarantee for them, despite their creepy background, was their spectacularly low bid. They claimed they could build a new reactor for $5.709 billion. In the economically berserk world of nuclear power, that's a bargain.

But then I broke open the Radioactive Brick. The ream of paper was another one of those fraud investigator's Valentine's Day chocolate boxes: so many sweets to gorge on, it's hard to choose. But this one stood out, this one here.*

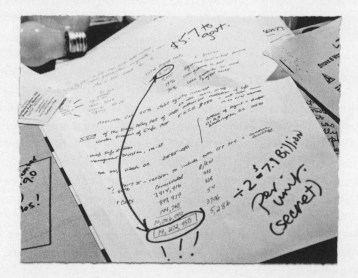

---

* Several pages of the "Radioactive Brick" are at GregPalast.com/VulturesPicnic.

Note the scribble in the left margin. It says, "submitted in confidence; trade secrets or proprietary"—which suggests the writer couldn't figure out which legal BS the companies would use to conceal it. The winning number for the Department of Energy is there, $5.709 billion. But below, I see a different number, $14.272 billion. That's for two reactors. Now wait a minute: That's $7.1 billion for each of two reactors.

In other words, $5.7 billion is the number they appear to have submitted in their bid, but $7.1 billion is the companies' own internal estimate for construction. A $1.4 billion discrepancy. Where I grew up, we'd call that real money.

Or you could call it fraud.

When you give one number to the government and one number is kept in your pocket, secret, that's fibbing. *Fraud* is the term we use.

Warning, warning, warning: We don't know who wrote these numbers, except they are on the inside of the deal with NRG. So we can't call the mystery source and say, "Hey, there are, like, $1.4 billion out of whack. What can you tell me about that?"

And there's probably a good explanation. There always is. I told you that.

There are a lot of other documents with a lot of other numbers that don't match these, that don't match each other, that don't match the official statements, that don't match reality.

The $5.7 billion number was ginned up in Houston, NRG's headquarters. The higher number, $14 billion ($7 billion per reactor), was calculated by the corporation that will actually build the plants: Westinghouse, you know, the old American stalwart that made refrigerators. They don't make refrigerators anymore and the name Westinghouse was sold to Toshiba of Japan. The Japanese will actually build the reactor core. (So much for American jobs promised.)

The $5.7 billion from Houston was used to sell this hot dog to the public and the President. They swallowed it whole, no mustard. The $7 billion was used by the guys who will make the thing and will bill the Texans and the U.S. taxpayers for it.

So Toshiba and NRG, it appears, are in on the concealment. Who else?

It's quite difficult to conceal a multi-billion-dollar cost overrun unless the construction company building it helps. The designated builder is Shaw Construction, the King Milling funders, Governor Jindal's buddies from Baton Rouge who piled up the wash-away sand berm in the Gulf.

Well, sand castles aren't dangerous. But this is: Shaw's nuclear unit is none other than our diesel popping and seismic test-faking friends, Stone & Webster, which Shaw absorbed some time after the racketeering trial exposed them.

Stone & Webster as Shaw is doing all right for itself. Besides the reactors at South Texas, S&W will construct the nation's first new reactors to go up, for Southern Company, using $3.46 billion in U.S. Treasury guarantees. They should be able to do it cheaply: Southern has a lot of unused spare parts.

And the two other nuclear stations backed by the U.S. Treasury? They're all Shaw.

And new nuclear plants in the UK? Shaw again.

And recently, Japan announced the winner of the big contract to clean up their busted plant with the busted diesels. It goes to . . . Shaw. Maybe they felt a special kinship with the company that faked earthquake tests.

Westinghouse is Toshiba, but who is Toshiba? Its big stockholder: Shaw Construction.

I know what the corporate group will say: Stone & Webster isn't Stone & Webster anymore. By becoming Shaw, the Radioactive Raven is now clean, green, and honest as the day is long. Fair enough. But, if you get caught driving drunk, you'll never get to drive a school bus for the rest of your life. Get caught faking nuclear safety tests, get a mile-long rap sheet for nuclear safety violations, and you get another nuclear license so long as you change your corporate costume—and, if you're lucky enough, or mendacious enough, a few billion dollars from the government to boot.

* * *

Given their unsavory history, NRG was unlikely, on its own, to win the sweepstakes for free money from the federal government. For the South Texas Project, NRG/Reliant/Houston has masked itself with yet another name: Nuclear Innovation North America. NINA. NINA, while led by NRG, is another consortium with all kinds of operators underneath its blankets. But the one that impressed the U.S. Department of Energy most is the operator with the best reputation in nuclear power on the planet: TEPCO, Tokyo Electric Power Company.

TEPCO will get a 20 percent piece of the South Texas Project action. I feel safer already.

In all fairness to NINA, the group did inform the Department of Energy on

September 6, 2008, that the price of the plants had risen to $7 billion for *both* reactors. But according to the Radioactive Brick, at a meeting just one month later, Toshiba kicked up the real cost to $12 billion. And it's not clear that NRG ever mentioned to the DOE that Toshiba was not only building the reactors, it held a 12 percent ownership slice, presumably allowing the foreign company to benefit from 12 percent of the U.S. Treasury booty.

Am I looking at another billion-dollar fraud or just something lost in translation? And does the Department of Energy know about this? Do they care? And what about David Axelrod, campaign manager for Barack Obama. What does he have to do with this? I knew him from Chicago, and that he was once under contract with Exelon, the biggest nuclear operator in America. Axelrod's dead in the middle of this, undoubtedly. But even when I say "undoubtedly," I have my doubts.

Then, as if the nightmarish info in the The Brick and the warning from "Sellars" weren't enough, I received a call and another package from a nuclear "fire suppression" specialist who worked on setting international standards to fight fires at nuclear stations. To protect his identity, let's call him, "The Fireman." The Fireman directed the tests for fire safety standards used at every reactor worldwide. But the standards issued by the International Atomic Energy Agency were based on data he did not provide. Someone had switched the real data with false data that made fires appear less dangerous, easier to control. By setting safety standards based on the faked data, the industry did not have to improve its designs, saving operators a bundle. But the public will pay the price, especially the Japanese. The fire suppression systems at Fukushima failed, worsening the disaster.

"The Fireman" sent me the faked data. His accusations are solid. Notably, he sent me the info on the compromised fire-fighting systems in July 2010, eight months before Fukushima burned.

So, now what? What do you want me to do with this? What I have here are extraordinary shards of evidence. The Geiger counter needle is jumping, but it's a long way from the appearance of fraud to the proof of it.

Jones calls from London and wants me to saddle up and get on the nuclear hunt for BBC.

But haven't I been here before, at Shoreham, with Southern Company, with Reliant/NRG? How many times can we tell the same story before the few who listen become the none who listen? What for?

Am I my Texans' keeper?

NOWHERE, LOUISIANA

In 1997, the Ku Klux Klan rode into Forest Grove, suggesting that residents welcome a nuclear fuel reprocessing plant. Or else.

"Forest Grove" is too poor to incorporate as a real town, so officially, it's invisible, just not there. And because it is legally nowhere, British Nuclear Fuels (BNFL) chose it as a place to dump a nuclear-waste recycling plant.

BNFL chose this spot after the company concluded the place must be partly abandoned because the houses they saw from the highway were boarded up. But, as 40 percent of the folk there have no heat, they board up their windows in winter to keep out the cold.

I spoke to Juanita Hamilton, the non-town's seventy-seven-year-old matriarch, who was wondering how the British picked Forest Grove, out of the entire vastness of the United States, to place their hot waste plant.

The company did a scientific narrowing of the potential sites for its fuel plant, in fifteen steps (really), and at each step, the target zones got Blacker and Blacker and Blacker. Other Louisiana Delta towns had "scenic views" and "pretty churches," and therefore the cash to fight a poisonous industry.

Juanita told me, "If it was so good, why'd they come all the way from Europe to this little Black town in Claiborne Parish? Why wouldn't they keep it for themselves?"

Local folk were worried about Claiborne Pond. Since a third of the houses didn't have any plumbing, this was all they had for drinking and cooking.

Juanita told me, "Not many folk around here know a lot about uranium enrichment."

BNFL counted on that. At a community meeting, the shill for the nuclear operation held up a chunk of what the company called "uranium hexafluoride," and there was nothing to fear from this handful of dirt.

It was an impressive display. However, Forest Grove residents may be Black and poor, but they know when a magic show is jive. The township residents called a local university, and found a physicist who explained that uranium hexafluoride UF6 would vaporize on contact with the humid air and, possibly, vaporize the BNFL spokeswoman as well.

GERMANY 1942; WASHINGTON, DC, 2009

Hermann Goering never visited a concentration camp.

Hitler's happiest Nazi could order the firebombing of a couple or three million people and then put on a toga to party hearty. But Heinrich Himmler paid a visit to one camp and watched a hundred Jews, women and kids too, shot in the head one by one. He nearly fainted, vomited.

We don't like to look our kill in the face. And we certainly don't like them looking back at us.

That's why civilized man invented masks and corporations.

When I look back over a life of exposing real nasty, crazy, dangerous ill-making behavior, the big question that stares in my face is: How could they do it?

How could BP honchos fail to mention that their rig blew out its cement in the Caspian, how could Stone & Webster engineers deliberately fake nuclear plant safety reports to cover over a potentially lethal dosing of radiation—then go home and read bedtime stories to their kids?

Maybe I'm giving evil jack-offs too much credit. Maybe they couldn't care less if Chief Criollo's son, or yours, gets leukemia. But I think they're more like Goering, average guys blind behind a corporate veil, unable to see the consequences of their actions. And not wanting to.

The human animal will do things behind a corporate shield we would never dream of doing if we were face-to-face with our victims. Imagine how BP and Chevron would act if Chief Criollo were a member of the Petroleum Club, or if Lord Browne had to spend the night in prison with Mirvari, or if BP big shot Tony Hayward had to live on a deepwater platform.

What marks the difference between the white sheets of the Ku Klux Klan and the Brooks Brothers suits at Southern Company? Distance and responsibility. If a hooded Klansman poisons a Black family in Forest Grove, he goes to prison and must pay the victim's damages. But if the poisoning is done by the Senior Vice President for Gulf operations of BNFL's URENCO affiliate, well, then, *hey, stuff happens.*

The guys at the top don't see that far down from the pyramid's pinnacle.

Not that they want to. The Corporate Mask provides the distance necessary to commit profitable cruelties.

From Louisiana, I called up a media flak at BNFL in London, who said no one at the company could say anything about Forest Grove. They were part of URENCO group, which was part of the LES group. Between the poor folk getting the poisoned droppings of nuclear plants and the executives planting the poisons is a complex set of corporate shells nested like Russian dolls.

The BNFL man told me, "We have nothing to do with the decisions. We just collect the dividends."

And that's the motto of BP and Shaw and the entire corporate planet: We just collect the dividends. BP told me that, so far as saving money by not having safety equipment out in Prince William Sound, it was not their responsibility, it was left to that thing called Alyeska. BP just collects the dividends. Read their note to me and see if you still like these people.*

British Petroleum and the entire tribe of multi-continental oil companies have their own masking rituals, and they're damn useful. Exxon was dumb enough, arrogant enough, to put its name on the *Valdez*, so when it hit the rocks, the villain was naked to the eyeball. Of course, the real dark lord of the spill, British Petroleum, was a clever little Raven, hiding itself behind the upbeat and local sounding corporate name, *Al-YES-ka*. BP knew Rule One for banditos: cover your face.

But in the Gulf, BP, puffed up with itself, forgot the mask, so that when the oil hit the Delta, even the President knew who to point at.

Still, who is this thing "BP"? Who will burn in Hell? The problem is, corporations have "neither bodies to be kicked nor souls to be damned." Andrew Jackson said that. The populist President tried to ban these artificial creatures from our new republic.

The sole purpose of a corporation is to limit the liability of its owners, its stockholders. Transocean Corporation, which operated the Deepwater Horizon for BP as well as the Caspian rig, provides a complete legal shield protecting the identity of its stockholders. Like me. I discovered $600 in Transocean stock in my little IRA pension. Hey, I just collect the dividends.

In France, corporations are legally designated *société anonyme,* "anony-

---

* The entirety of BP's response to accusations here in my films are found in the enhanced edition or at GregPalast.com/VulturesPicnic.

mous society." The irresponsibility of anonymity is at the degenerate core of corporatism. Rob a bank and you've made a personal decision. Fake the seismic tests at the nuclear plant and the decision has been made for you—by the corporation.

On the Orthodox Christmas, Nanwalek Natives perform their pre-Christian "masking ceremony." In times past, it could get violent, scores settled, the perpetrators well hidden, like Raven painting himself black. Father Benjamin, the priest ministering to the village, said he let the pagan ritual meld into Christmas, but on one condition. At midnight, the masks must be removed or destroyed.

We've seen an awful lot of masks in this book, from the Mardi Gras Rex, King Milling, whose America's Wetland is the grinning environmental mask on Shaw and its shovels, and Big Oil and its drills. And the Hamsah, the eyeball without a face.

(And there's Lady Baba's surgically frozen face, the mask most frightening because it can't be removed.)

On January 2, 2006, an explosion at the Sago Mine in West Virginia killed twelve miners. John Nelson Boni, the mine's fire-boss, and William Lee Chisolm, a dispatcher, had sent the men, whom they knew well, down to their deaths. Boni and Chisolm both committed suicide.

But not Wilbur Ross. I knew Wilbur; he helped me on the Shoreham case. Nice guy. Billionaire. Owns the Sago Mine and the International Coal Group through his vulture fund. Every time I open up *Hamptons Magazine*, he has another wife younger and blonder than the one before. After the Sago Mine exploded, it was found that communications lines that might have saved the miners, required by law, were missing. That made Wilbur feel terrible, so he went on TV and asked the American public to send donations for the dead miners' families. He didn't say whether to send the donations to his home in the Hamptons, or to the one in Palm Beach or to the New York condo.

* * *

In September 2009, the U.S. Supreme Court ruled that corporations have the same rights as "natural" citizens. These "unnatural" citizens could donate to political campaigns (and, I assume, will soon be allowed to vote).

British Petroleum may now rent their own Congressman as long as it's done through their BP USA unit. The Mexican Zetas gang, Baby Baba, Charles

Manson's disciples, the Taliban, the Chinese Peoples Liberation Army can now pour unlimited cash into U.S. politicians' hands so long as they first pay $100 to incorporate in Delaware. What to do?

I don't have a gun and, being unincorporated, cannot shoot with impunity, not that bullets mean anything to these headless, heartless creatures.

All we have to protect us during this corporate crime spree is Inspector Lawn's big fat rule book. When Pig Man took a stand, he cited CFR §192.3 regarding the PHMSA MAOP for the HCA, which, if ignored, he says, "means people get blown up." And when Bob Wiesel attempted to save the population of Long Island from incineration, he pulled down the thick Nuclear Regulatory Commission code book, reciting section 50.55(e). It didn't stop the fraud but ultimately gave Wiesel's boss, Gordon Dick, the legal hammer that helped us win the case and close the plant.

Regulation, the rules they tell you to hate, are the way we apply democracy to the economy. Votes versus dollars. I think you can understand that.

Yes, I know, the government is deeply fucked up. That's the U.S. government, the UK government, and let's not even talk about the Chinese, Malaysian, and Tanzanian governments. People have been belly-aching about rules and regulations ever since Moses schlepped the first ten down from Mount Sinai.

But the Big Problem with government is that we don't have enough of it; the rules aren't tough enough to stop BP from blowing Cajuns to Kingdom Come. Or the rules are corrupted, made by politicians who are greased to make Steve Cohen's monkey jump.

If you're screaming for the "*guvmint to git off*" your back, I see your point. But you're still a loser, a cheap mark, a decoy duck, a dim, unwitting stooge for forces even more powerful than that ugly guvmint, a toy for powers who are shitting on you while telling you it's raining chocolate.

But then, who regulates the regulators? Well, Shaw Construction for one. Shaw is now constructing a plant that will turn plutonium from old atomic bombs into nuclear plant fuel. The Nuclear Regulatory Commission exempted Shaw's bombs-to-nukes plant from anti-terrorist security measures. A commissioner who voted for this take-a-terrorist-to-tea exemption, Jeffrey Merrifield, now works for Shaw. And the Secretary of Energy who promoted the plan, Spencer Abraham, is now Chairman of Areva USA, partner in Shaw Areva MOX Services.

Heinrich Himmler's solution to the problem of having to look into the eyes of your kill was to industrialize the process, using gas from I.G. Farben Corporation and ovens from Siemens AG. They just took the orders.

But there's a regulator of regulators we must rely on. The Fourth Estate. Me. And Matty Pass and Badpenny. That's our job as journalists, to rip away masks. It's what we do in that cheap downtown office as the sirens scream by. And I'll get back to it as soon as I drink some courage and stop feeling sorry for myself. . . .

DOWNTOWN, NEW YORK

It's all bullshit, you know. I'm pretending that I'm doing Something Important here, all this running around the globe and snooping in files with all this Drama and demanding that you pay attention to it. Pay attention to me. It's fake, vainglorious, and a joke and I'm terrified you'll figure that out before the end of this book, and then what?

In other words, I feel like crap. God has every right to smush me under His shoe like a cigarette butt.

Badpenny orders me to call a doctor.

I dial the Reverend Thayer Greene, doctor of psychology. Dr. Greene, well into his eighties, once liberated a concentration camp, or what there was left to liberate. It turned him to God and Carl Jung.

I tell him about my failure, my failure to liberate anyone, but making a movie about it anyway, a big empty noise no one will listen to and no one should and then I'm dead.

The silence was short while he consulted—whom?—Jung or the Lord?

Then the doctor says, in a surprisingly aggressive and irrefutable voice, "YOU'RE NOT YOUR FATHER."

He asks for an address to send the bill. Immediately, I feel better.

Into the toilet bowl goes the last of a grape's golden blood . . .

. . . Trinken Sanftmut Kannibalen
Die Verzweiflung Heldenmut!

Is that Badpenny singing? Is that me?

So, God damn, Palast, spede the plough.

CHAPTER 11
Mr. Fairness

FEDERAL COURT, SOUTHERN DISTRICT
OF NEW YORK (BROOKLYN)

When the Energy-Finance Combine needs to screw the public, they hire a screwdriver. And they call him Mr. Fairness.

On June 15, 2010, the fifty-sixth day of the BP blowout, the Obama presidency was floating facedown in the Gulf of Mexico. The President gave a Big Speech about BP from the Oval Office. And it was a disaster.

Even his allies were fed up. They didn't even like the standard, hokey closing shtick, "And may God Bless America." TV host Keith Olbermann said, "We're looking for action and he tells us the best we can do is *pray*?"

The President promised he would make BP pay $20 billion to the blowout victims *at a minimum*. If BP refused to pony up, Obama was screwed, political roadkill.

Within a week, the President got his $20 billion. See, Virginia, there is a Santa Claus.

Unfortunately, it's my job to look up Santa's chimney.

BP knew it would have to pay out $20 billion, or at least pretend to—no big deal for a company that sucks in a third of a trillion dollars in revenue a year. But the oil company would not budge from its single condition: the $20 billion, said BP, must be *it*. Basta. No more.

Obama, a constitutional lawyer, knows even the President can't promise that. The White House can't order courts to dismiss lawsuits of the injured, the poisoned, the dead. Besides, a cap on BP payments would be political suicide. The negotiators and oil company lawyers, locked in the White House, stared at each other for two days.

Then the President asked Carl-Henric Svanberg, BP's Chairman, to come into the Oval Office, just the two of them. Half an hour later, they emerged. Obama got his $20 billion from Carl-Henric, and no cap.

What happened in there? Did the President pull a Dirty Harry, take out a lit cigarette he'd hidden from Michelle, and say, *"Feeling lucky, Carl?"*

The real story is the *second* announcement the two of them made.

How could Obama secretly, and legally, agree to cap BP's liability but not announce it? To lock in a limit, the President would need to throw a reptile into the scrum of lawyers bringing class action suits. The snake would have to paralyze the litigants and force them, through threats, payoffs, and manipulation, to accept less than $20 billion for BP's victims. Obviously, the gentlemen in the Oval Office agreed on the snake.

The President came out and announced, "There will be no cap." And then, subtly, the President unleashed the reptile: Every single claim by every victim, and there are more than 100,000 of them, would, Obama said, be settled by a single man, Kenneth Feinberg. Or, as *The Wall Street Journal* dubbed him, "Mr. Fairness." No panel, no rules, no experts, no anyone except Feinberg.

The New York Times, on hearing the name Feinberg, nearly jizzed in its underpants.

> The unusual degree of discretion granted to him, which BP and President Obama agreed to last week, is hard to imagine being given to anyone without the experience and respect Mr. Feinberg has gained after years of mediating mass injury claims.

I know Ken. He's an incredibly talented man, the Babe Ruth of mediators. Babe Ruth was tops in his field, but then, so was Dracula.

But I wanted an independent opinion. So I called another Babe Ruth, Victor Yannacone. You'll remember, Yannacone is the guy who invented environmental law. He founded the Environmental Defense Fund (though, at a pro-industry donor's request, EDF fired him). And Yannacone brought the granddaddy of all public interest lawsuits against Dow Chemical for poisoning American soldiers in Vietnam with Agent Orange.

Yannacone said to me, "I told my clients, the Vietnam War Veterans: Ken [Feinberg] is a slimy sack of shit who lies like a rock. But over the years, I've come to realize that that's his good side."

I have to say, Ken Feinberg never lied to me. As to whether there's a whiff of packaged fecal matter about him, well, yes, there's that.

Here's Yannacone's story, the Vets' story. The lawyer, after several years of work without a dime in compensation, had wrapped up a settlement with Dow Chemical's lawyers to create a fund of $2.5 billion for injured veterans. But when Yannacone got on the phone to the company Chairman for pro forma approval, the Dow honcho said, "No." What the hell happened? Another deal had been worked out by the "special master," Mr. Feinberg. The Vets would get less than 1 percent of the sum Dow originally agreed to pay, though the government would pick up Vets' medical bills.

Yannacone said, "No way, no deal." The court then fired Yannacone as the Veterans' lawyer, but not before Mr. Fairness met with him. He wanted Yannacone not to challenge the 1 percent deal publicly. Maybe Yannacone could administer the fund, a lucrative job.

Yannacone said, "Ken, are you trying to bribe me?"

Ken, Mr. Fairness, said no, but he hinted at something that sounded an awful lot like blackmail. If Yannacone refused to go along, he wouldn't get a dime in fees, not even expenses. That would mean bankruptcy for the public interest lawyer: He had paid all the expenses of the case out of his own pocket.

Yannacone refused. And it came to pass that, as Mr. Fairness predicted, the judge granted big fees to other lawyers who had done nothing compared to Yannacone, but for the lawyer who had brought and fought the case: zero. Not even expenses. In the courtroom, Yannacone slammed his fist into the counsel table and told the judge, "This is fucking unjust." But the record reads only, "This is unjust." Yannacone silently mouthed the adjective to the judge's face so it would not *appear* in the transcript.

Some veterans, stuck with the 1 percent deal and seeing their man shafted, offered to take care of the matter as they would have in 'Nam. Yannacone chilled them out.

Now wait a minute. How do I know this happened? How do I know what Mr. Fairness told Yannacone? I mean, we have the zero fee the judge gave the lawyer; we have the 1 percent deal that Feinberg recommended as fair (about $10 per affected veteran). But I can't possibly know if Mr. Fairness said those threatening things to Yannacone.

But I know he said them to me, in 1988. Same Brooklyn courtroom. Same judge. Same "Master" Ken, who was appointed after we won the gigantic verdict against LILCO, the power company, for its conspiracy with Stone & Webster. The verdict for the County government (Suffolk, New York), applied to all customers, would cost the power company $4.3 billion. They didn't have $4.3 billion—they would go bankrupt.

Fine with me, the dirt bags.

The judge ordered settlement negotiations, which Feinberg would master. The Governor of New York jumped in, hidden from public view—he's entitled. Ken liked to walk into the room with the phrase, "I just got off the phone with the Governor," as if we gave a shit. Then Ken would chew on a big cigar.

The Governor's "experts" told the court to cut the judgment by 95 percent. They're entitled: Power company executives and the state regulators are consenting adults and have the right to do what they want in bed.

Ken was hoping I would go along. I was negotiating for the County government and the company's three million customers. Nope, I wouldn't. Mr. Fairness then told me that the judge might just *throw out the verdict* if my clients didn't go along. He'd do an Agent Orange on my case.

I like Ken. I don't like blackmail. And because I like him, I said, "Go fuck yourself," with a convivial smile. And it came to pass that the judge indeed threw out the verdict, removed the lawyers who had brought the case. A lawyer who hadn't been in the courtroom a single minute of the trial was paid over a million dollars and signed the 5 percent deal.

One local newspaper reacted with an unkind—dare I say "unfair"?—cartoon of Mr. Fairness, the judge and the Governor as reptiles bailing out the power company.

Sell-out of the Ratepayer

Now, I didn't have a tape recorder. And I sure as hell don't know what motivated the judge. He could well have decided on his ruling and never ever spoke to Mr. Fairness about it in advance. I will never know.

I do know that when Feinberg reaches across the table to twist, you don't forget it. My nipples hurt to this day.

Mr. Fairness also handled the 9/11 Fund for the families of the World Trade terrorist murders. Ken recommended that lawyers who "cooperated" in taking quick money for their clients get a reward (over $100 million in fees were passed out); those lawyers who held out got creamed. But that judge threw out the lawyer-enrichment plan and told Mr. Fairness to make it fairer.

Still, there's a pattern. The big boys put up a fund of cash, and miraculously, Mr. Fairness keeps the payments within it.

And now the President of the United States and the Chairman of BP PLC have put the lives of the Gulf Coast shrimpers, roustabouts, fry cooks, croupiers, and Raphael Gill, the BP clean-up man with the pooper scooper, in the judicious hands of Mr. Fairness, the Spill Fund Trustee.

But what's there to trust? A "trustee," under the law, is only and solely a fiduciary for the beneficiaries. That is, Feinberg is supposed to act only for Mr. Gill and other victims—BP and Obama be damned. But Feinberg immediately did something quite odd for a fiduciary. He required all the victims in his trust, if they took payment, to sign away their right to sue *other* wrongdoers at fault in the Deepwater Horizon explosion.

There's Halliburton, the company that pumped in that dodgy nitrogen cement, and Transocean, the Swiss rig owner of the Deepwater Horizon that fled from responsibility. Should they make a contribution? A trustee usually tries to "increase the estate," a fancy term for getting in more money for the beneficiaries. Not Mr. Fairness.

Why? "I want the lawsuits to end," he says.

That sounds reasonable. Except for one thing: It's not true. He does not require *BP* to waive its right to sue Halliburton and Transocean. BP has sued. The result is that any money BP gets from Transocean or other negligent parties goes right into BP's bottom line, not a dime to the victims taking Ken's take-it-or-leave-it checks.

As I write this, Feinberg has already announced that he might need only *half* the $20 billion. As an economist who has calculated damages in mass tort cases, I'm gob-smacked astonished. Did his dog eat his calculator? By the way, the leftover $10 billion would go right back to BP.

Write this down: I guarantee you this. Mr. Fairness will not pay out two cents beyond the fund, even if every fisherman in Louisiana vomits blood. So, my Creole comrades, you may get screwed but remember, *you're getting screwed by the best in America.*

Is Mr. Fairness an evil man? Wrong question. This is not about Feinberg. If he didn't do it, they'd find some other law firm to take the million-a-month fee. I'm trying to explain how the *system* works. How you get worked on. He's their tool, you're their fool.

And my own racketeering case? An appeals court threw out the trial judge's goofball ruling but then overturned our case on a technicality. Nevertheless, we did shut down and dismantled the Shoreham nuclear plant. So New York can sleep at night. Mr. Fairness's 5 percent deal was rammed down our gullets (still, $200 million for consumers). And then, in private, after Feinberg quietly took care of my fee, Ken and I kissed and made up. I took antibiotics for two weeks.

CHAPTER 12

The Generalissimo of Globalization

CHICAGO

You know what the perfect crime is?

It's the one that's not illegal.

Uncle Maxxie told me that.

My great-uncle Maxxie Eisen had his disagreements with Al Capone over who ran the numbers game and speakeasy casinos on the North Side of Chicago. When Capone's West Side organization moved into Maxxie's neighborhood without a formal invitation, Uncle Max's boys threw Capone's slot machines into the Lincoln Park lagoon. It was settled amicably. Maxxie was left with two quarters in his pocket and both legs intact.

But Uncle Max, who used to give me five-dollar bills (that he borrowed), told me, "Capone was a schmuck."

Capone, who made his big money off the illegal numbers racket—the Italians called it "lotto"—ended up behind bars.

Guy Snowden is way smarter than Capone. In 1980, Snowden created GTECH Corporation, and turned ghetto "lotto" into respectable "State Lottery." GTECH promoted the government-blessed numbers gambling as a way to fund education. After thirty years of the lottery, America remains uneducated and GTECH is doing just fine, running the numbers racket under lucrative monopoly contracts with several states and the British crown. Capone made millions, then went to jail. Snowden stayed on this side of the prison walls, miraculously, while his corporation made billions.

Snowden's big trick was to unleash a lavishly paid lobby, an army ranging from used politicians from Texas to Dolly Draper in London, who turned the crime—lotto—into a legal business. He muscled out competitors, not by employing knuckle-dusters like his predecessor Capone, but by deftly changing laws and rules before he would break them.*

Another example. Take John Dillinger, the big-time bank robber. He broke into banks and took the cash. Dillinger bought fancy suits but ended up in a Chicago alley with bullets in his belly.

Sanford "Sandy" Weill must have thought Dillinger was another schmuck. Weill didn't bother with a few greenbacks in the bank vault. Weill stole *the whole fucking bank. I mean bricks, bonds, parking lots, and assistant managers included.*

In April 1998, Weill's company, Travelers Group, an agglomeration of investment banks and other hot financial operations, took over CitiBank. Weill picked up about half a trillion dollars in Citibank assets. Brilliant—and against the law.

While Dillinger, the fool, used fast getaway cars and Tommy guns to avoid the law, Weill simply had the law repealed.

The law was the Glass-Steagall Act, signed by President Roosevelt in 1933. Glass-Steagall prohibited banks that take deposits ("commercial" banks) from merging with "investment" banks. Investment banks, despite the upright name, are financial casinos, which can make high-stakes, high-risk bets on stocks, bonds, currencies, derivatives, weather, whatever.

Glass-Steagall was based on a deal FDR made with banks during the Great Depression: The government would guarantee savings accounts, but the banks could not then use those government-backed deposits to finance loading up a poker table with chips to play a two-pair bluff.

Of course, the world would be a much happier place today, and Greece would not have burned, if Weill and his fellow banksters had simply taken a trillion dollars and blown it on a bad-ass weekend in Vegas.

I've done a quick calc on Weill's deal that broke the law (I mean, literally shattered it). The stock of the combined Weill companies popped up by $24 billion on the day of the announcement. Nice. The fools and the fleeced were

---

* Part of GTECH's success could be attributed to the lucky charm Snowden kept in his pocket: George W. Bush's draft record. That's a story by itself. Click *here* for it in the interactive editions, or go to GregPalast.com/VulturesPicnic.

told the combine "created value." The hell it did. It created a government guarantee for Sandy's casinos. The American public, in effect, put up insurance valued at $24 billion.

Weill's bank heist was an inside job. Removing the law that formed the rock-solid foundation of America's financial structure would require a lot of demolition work by U.S. Secretary of the Treasury Robert Rubin.

Bob Rubin's jackhammer on Glass-Steagall was effective—the law's demolition was signed on November 12, 1999, just four months after Rubin left Treasury and just two weeks after he joined Sandy Weill as a co-chairman of Citigroup.

Rubin picked up $126 million in payments from Sandy's now-legal operation. That was not a *payoff.* That was *compensation.* There's a difference: six letters. Count'em.

(After Citibank's collapse and bail-out by the U.S. taxpayers, Rubin escaped with his $126 million and is now Co-Chairman of the Council on Foreign Relations. Well, you expected that.)

In between stopping at Citibank to pick up his pay and taking control of the Council, Rubin became Presidential candidate Barack Obama's chief advisor (on bailing out Citibank and Goldman Sachs. Note: Rubin had been Co-Chairman of Goldman when he was appointed U.S. Treasury Secretary in 1992).

When Rubin left the Treasury for Citi, he put his protégés Larry Summers and Tim Geithner in charge; Summers to take Rubin's post, and Geithner sent to Geneva on a very special assignment.

There's no sense de-criminalizing betting with government-guaranteed deposits at the derivatives casino if there are no games to play. My old classmates from Chicago who moved on to Goldman solved that. They were cranking out new derivatives "products" faster than bedsheets from a whorehouse laundry. Some gray-hairs worried about the risk. Risk, shmisk. With explicit and implicit government guarantees, the bankers were ready to go double-or-nothing on insecure securities. Secretaries Rubin and Summers body-blocked all attempts to regulate the derivatives market.

Unless you've been in Guantanamo for a decade, you probably know most of this—Rubin, Goldman, Summers, Citibank—but I can't kick off an investigation without first looking through the old clippings.

We are investigating arson. Who lit the fires in Greece in 2010 and 2011, and before that, Indonesia (1998), Ecuador (1999), Argentina (2000), Ecuador again (2005), Hungary (2006), and Latvia (2009)? (The list is not exhaustive.)

Luckily, some birdies flew over our office and dropped several papers through the transom, one written by Tim Geithner to Larry Summers. I shouldn't read their mail—it was confidential—but, you know. It was dated November 1997.

No document except maybe the Bible and *Mein Kampf* has caused so much harm and tears and terror. It would shudder through the world finance system and engender there the broken walls of Detroit, the burning roofs of Ecuador, and the Greek dead.

> "As we enter the end-game of the WTO financial services negotiations, I believe it would be a good idea for you to touch base with the CEOs. . . ."

"End-game"? Let's piece together how the game began. In 1997, there were two burning questions for Summers, Geithner, Rubin, Weill, and the gang.

The first was, *What if shit happens?* What if, that is, when, the de-criminalized trade in weird securities goes bad, where can the United States dump its toxic assets?

Rubin's Deputy Secretary, Summers, would apply the same solution he had suggested earlier, in 1991, regarding chemical toxins. Then Chief Econo-mist of the World Bank, Summers wrote a memo stating that poor nations are "UNDER-polluted" (his own caps), so the West should dump more toxins there. When the memo leaked, Summers said it was a joke. It was certainly a joke, but it was also, under Summers, World Bank policy.

In 1997, Summers would make the rest of the planet swallow toxic *finan-cial* assets. Let Ireland, Brazil, and Portugal pay cash money to take on the U.S. bankers' risk.

The second question for the bankers was, *How do we bust down financial rules across the planet?*

America is a big sandbox, but these guys want to play anywhere in the school yard. It was not enough to erase the laws against speculating with bank deposits in the United States if it was still a crime to do so in Brazil, India, Spain, and Greece. In most nations, betting government-guaranteed savings accounts on funky securities remained *verboten*. Moreover, national laws barred Sandy Weill's Citigroup from buying up local banks.

What to do? You can't engineer enough coup d'états and install General Pinochets everywhere. So then, how to change the laws of 152 nations with a single coup? Treasury called a meeting.

From the memos, it appears there were little gatherings of Treasury with The Boys (David Coulter from Bank of America, John Reed from Citibank, Walter Shipley from Chase, Jon Corzine from Goldman, David Kaminski from Merrill Lynch), CEOs all. How could they make 152 nations bust apart their banking laws and allow purchases of U.S. toxic assets?

The answer was to take a minor trade treaty, the Financial Services Agree-ment (FSA), and turn it into the new finance law of the planet. In their closed little gatherings, this bankers roundtable (please don't say, "cabal") rewrote the FSA, with protocols forcing every nation to remove restrictions and old-fashioned safe-banking regulations. The rewritten agreement would require every nation to allow trade in new financial products, whether magical or toxic. It would blow apart any nation's laws restricting foreign bankers.

The Agreement, once signed, would trump any attempt by any Congress or Parliament to restore protections. The Agreement also dictated that, once demolished, the barriers could not be rebuilt. Return to regulation, called *claw-back*, would be severely punished. Any resisting nation would be put on the economic wheel and broken.

In 1997, Assistant Treasury Secretary Geithner was sent to Geneva, to the headquarters of the World Trade Organization (WTO), with this new Law in his diplomatic bag. He was assigned to inform the ambassadors of all 152 nations, no exceptions allowed, that they would have to sign it. *Or else.*

Or else *what?*

Sometimes, people—and nations—have to eat shit. But no one orders it from the menu. The waiter has to hold a gun to your head.

The bankers' gun was a banana, at least in the case of Ecuador.

If Ecuador wanted to sell its bananas to the United States, it would have to buy the bankers' financial "products." If not, Ecuador could sell its bananas to the monkeys. Ecuador understood that resistance would be economic sui-cide and signed. More than one hundred other nations got the Ecuador treat-ment, fell to their knees, and also signed the Agreement.

The brilliance of the bankers was in using trade as the weapon. It worked like a military embargo. Ships could pass only if the papers were signed. If a nation wanted to sell America goods, they would have to swallow American *bads*, the derivatives, swaps, and all the other exotica coming out of the mad bankers' laboratories. Furthermore, Citibank, JP Morgan, and other banks would be allowed to jump into these nations' markets and suck out capital at will. Local banks would be deregulated and freed as well. Freed to be eaten by Citigroup.

Geithner was given the trade terror gun, and when I got a copy, it was still smoking.

That's what I took with me while following Geithner's trail to Geneva to the citadel of the WTO, designated as the bank treaty's bare-knuckle enforcer.

GENEVA

World Trade Organization Director-General Lamy offered me the deep leather chair. It felt like I was sinking into a big, soft hand.

Maybe Geithner sat in it when he wrote to Summers about the end-game when he was ready to light the fuse on the dynamite, that bankers' rewrite of the Financial Services Agreement. Geithner was ready for it. But he wouldn't take a pee-pee, let alone blow up the world financial system, until he was sure that at least five bankers had mobilized their lobbyist armies. Thus his message to Summers.

Director-General Lamy looked at the "end-game" and other confidential memos I'd fanned out across the boardroom table. Lamy is too smart to ask how I got them, too smart to defend them, and excellent at explaining why they don't actually exist:

> "No, no, no, no, no, no. In WTO we don't have cigar-smoking, rich, crazy bankers negotiating."

Well, then, did he recognize the names and phone numbers of this group of puffers:

> Coulter, Bank of America: (415) 622-2255
> Reed, Citibank: (212) 559-2732
> Shipley, Chase Manhattan: (212) 270-1380
> Corzine, Goldman Sachs: (212) 902-8281
> Kaminski, Merrill Lynch: (212) 449-6868

They were on the "end-game" note.
The Frenchman grinned so hard I thought his face would crack.
He knew what it meant.

> "The WTO was not created as some dark cabal of multinationals secretly cooking plots against the people."

I hadn't used the word *cabal* even once, General.

> "We do things in the open! Look at our Web site!"

I had. I didn't see the memos with these phone numbers. Maybe I wasn't looking hard enough.

Then Lamy went on to paint a picture of the WTO not as Citibank's enforcer but rather as a kind of Oxfam or ACLU for trade. "It's about freedom, about human rights, about technology, about media, about political civil liberties!"

My God! I was in the presence of another Jefferson, not Thug's progeny. I meekly suggested that, outside the WTO's gated compound, few people associated fourth-order derivatives and worthless mortgage securities with human rights and freedom.

"They should!" Lamy said. *"They should!"*

*   *   *

Geithner wrote about an end-game, but what game were they playing? World Trade negotiations used to be about trade in goods: you know, my computers for your bananas. But the bankers, through the mucked-with Financial Services Agreement, had switched the gameboard.

The juiciest target of the new FSA would be China. China wanted to sell us everything we used to make ourselves. The United States would agree to let their stuff in, but in return, China would have to join the WTO, sign the Treaties, and buy what America makes now, banking "products." China would have to let Citi and JP Morgan set up shop in Shanghai.

In effect, U.S. manufacturing jobs would be sold for the bankers' right to gamble in the new market.

To capture the China queen, the worker-pawns had been sacrificed—yet they had no idea they were even on the chessboard, that they were being played.

The score? In the last decade of the last century, U.S. multinationals shed 2.9 million employees in America while increasing their foreign workforces by 2.7 million. China signed the World Trade treaty in 2006, ending the OPM War, letting foreign bankers into the Forbidden City.

Did it concern the Director-General that U.S. banks are calling the shots from the shadows?

That wasn't his department.

"[It's] not for me to judge the democratic credentials of members. There's a place in the UN, not far from here, which is called the Council on Human Rights where this sort of debate can take place."

If an unelected junta of bankers drafts America's trade position, well, here's the number to call.

And so the law of international finance became Lawlessness.

ATHENS

In May 2010, the end-game ended for Greece.

The new financial products were packaged, polished to a shine, and sold to government pension funds all over the planet. The bankers sold blind sacks of sub-prime mortgages, sliced and mixed up, as Collateralized Debt Obligations (CDOs) and other fetid concoctions. The Financial Services Agreement was rockin'!

But when opened, buyers found the bags were filled with financial feces. Government pensions and sovereign funds, from Finland to Qatar, lost trillions. The bags were toxic to bank balance sheets and several failed. However, in most cases, bankers could get a refill of capital juice from governments fearful of full-bore financial collapse. Re-funding banks meant de-funding economies: pension cuts, salary cuts, all the things that bring an economy to its knees. And sets it on fire.

When Bankers Gone Wild slammed the planet into recession, Greece's main industry, tourism, lost two million visitors who were too broke, too panicked, for beach party vacations and ouzo.

And the more Greece lost, the greater "the spread."

In May 2010, after the banks burned, Greece's Prime Minister George Papandreou said, "Everyone in Greece, whether three years old or ninety-eight years old, now knows what a spread is."

If you're not a Greek three-year-old, I'll let you in on it. A *spread* is the extra interest demanded by speculators and banks to insure against a nation's bankruptcy and default. When sold as a derivative, the bankruptcy insurance is called a *credit default swap* (CDS).*

How much does this insurance cost? If you have to ask, you can't afford it. In 2010 and 2011, the "spread" for Greece hit as much as 10 percent versus German debt. That is, Germany could borrow at 5 percent while Greece paid 15 percent. (At the same time, U.S. banks had the right to borrow for next to nothing, less than 1 percent, from the U.S. Federal Reserve.) On Greece's roughly $100 billion debt, the extra vigorish demanded by lenders raised the interest payments to $14,000 a year *per family,* over half a year's salary for the average Greek worker. And that's just the interest.

---

* Yes, I'm over-simplifying. But I can't turn this book into *Derivatives for Idiots*. Go to my Facebook page for discussion of subtleties and details. And put in your two drachmas' worth.

How could that happen?

Greece is a crime victim. Its banks, burnt and un-burnt, a crime scene.

In 2002, investment bank Goldman Sachs secretly bought up $2.3 billion in Greek government debt, converted it into yen and dollars, and sold it back to Greece at a big loss. Goldman isn't stupid. The deal was a con, with Goldman making up a phony-baloney exchange rate for the transaction, hiding the Greek debt as an exchange rate loss, and working a scam to get repayment of the "loss" from the government over time at loan-shark rates. Through this crazy and costly legerdemain, Greece's right-wing free-market government was able to pretend its deficits never exceeded 3 percent of GDP.

Cool. Fraudulent but cool. Fraudulent but legal. Read your Financial Services Agreement.

Flim-flam isn't cheap these days: On top of murderous interest, Goldman charged the Greeks over a quarter billion dollars in fees.

And those rotting bags of CDOs sold by Goldman and others? Did they know they were handing their customers gold-painted turds? Well, in 2007, at the same time banks like Goldman were selling sub-prime mortgage securities to Europeans, the firm itself was betting that the securities they created were crap. Goldman held a "net short" position against the securities they themselves sold. Goldman picked up half a billion dollars on the bet. Now, if General Motors built a car they knew would fall apart, would the company be praised, as Goldman has been, for the brilliance of offloading the junkers to unsophisticated rubes?

So Greece went down. It was the spread itself, the premium for the bankruptcy insurance that put Greece into bankruptcy. It's as if a fire insurance company set fire to your house and then charged you higher premiums because you had a fire.

Not everyone runs from a burning building or a burning nation. Riots have their fans. One riot tourist couldn't wait to get to Greece and, to savor it fresh, invited Greece's President to lunch.

So, while the streets erupted, while the bank burned, while in the midst of his sleepless, humiliating begging sessions with the IMF and the German Chancellor, Greece's new Prime Minister George Papandreou was called away to a luncheon with a stout man with a combed-down mustache. Others in the Athens restaurant could be forgiven for mistaking him for a misplaced Bavarian Burgermeister. The mustache belongs to Thomas Friedman, the world's most influential writer on economics. He is not actually an economist, but he plays one in the pages of *The New York Times*.

Friedman had flown business class and had already visited the burnt bank, a "shrine," as he called it, to globalization.

Friedman then arrived at the restaurant beaming with delight and, by his own account, dug into his fish with gusto. Greece had been "profligate" but now faced the wonderful opportunity for "regeneration." The bubbly pundit was so excited by the prospect that Greece would now have to "cut public sector pay, freeze benefits, slash jobs, abolish a range of welfare entitlements, and take the ax to programs such as school building and road maintenance" that you feared he would soil his underpants before the courier delivered his fresh ones.*

Friedman ticked off with relish: 20 percent wage cuts, social security slashed by 10 percent, retirement age increased by four years, and massive cuts in government spending. While incomes fell, the national value-added sales tax would rise by four percentage points. Friedman was thrilled. A follower of the proto-fascist philosopher Schumpeter, who coined the phrase "creative destruction," Friedman applauded this creative demolition of the Greek economy.

The flames and mass unemployment, the permanent reduction of wages, said Friedman, would bring about a "revolution," a "regeneration" of Greece. And, of course, the post-fire fire sale of national assets.

Prime Minister Papandreou did not throw his feta in Friedman's face.

Profligate?! Papandreou had just signed an accord to cut budgets that would increase unemployment by half, from 9 percent to 14 percent. The real cause of the crisis was the $14,000 per family "risk premium" on funds owed to speculators, the spread. Even the chief of Britain's central bank, Mervyn King, said, "The price of this financial crisis is being borne by people who absolutely did not cause it."

But you can't make the innocent pay unless they accept that they are to blame.

---

* Mr. Friedman's briefs were a topic of an intense discussion between myself and an actual economist, Paul Krugman, in 2006. The question was how one dealt with a sudden shortage of clean boxers when a book tour is unexpectedly extended. In a pinch, I turn mine inside out. Krugman said that washing them in the shower would do it; and in the morning they'd be nearly dry, and one can comfortably wear them slightly damp. The Nobelist then noted, without having to name the name, that a "certain columnist, I've heard, had fresh boxers FedEx'd to himself every day."

Papandreou understood the role of the two Friedmans (Thomas, and before him, Milton). Globalization's implosion needed apologists, much like the professors and pundits who, a century ago, blithely sang praises of the Bolsheviks while ignoring the rotting bodies. Lenin had a name for them: *useful idiots.*

The Friedmans are very useful to the bankers: to take the spotlight off the perpetrators, and blame financial ruin on the victims. The U.S. press especially is always ready to blame the victims of financial crime, whether it be home foreclosures or auto plant closings. Teachers and street cleaners who lose their jobs, factory workers who lose their pensions, especially if they belong to unions, are lazy, greedy, and guilty. And these sniveling workers are always grasping for their "entitlements," as if collecting your social security is an avaricious crime, whereas selling bogus bonds to pension funds is simply smart business.

Papandreou looked at the Bavarian mustache and understood the terms of surrender. He had to eat shit with his spanakopita, kiss the whip that beats him, announce that he loves swallowing the job-cut medicine, even if it tastes suspiciously like cyanide.

Greece will cut pensions until grandma has to live on dog food and fire departments sell their hoses, so long as the creditor bankers, supposedly the "risk takers," get their interest and principal, in cash and in full, all to pay off the debts created by fraud. Greece was now a sub-prime mortgagee to the IMF and the holders of the swaps—Detroit with beaches.

It could be worse. What if Papandreou were Spanish? As Spain's "spread" widened for no damn reason except that Spaniards look kind of Greek, its socialist Prime Minister had to cancel the €2,500 ($3,170) payment to parents of newborn babies.

An IMF insider said that Greece would have to return to its status as "a low-wage nation." Greeks must accept that they are again the Jamaicans of Europe, condemned forever to wait tables and bring piña coladas to overweight Germans on cruise ships for low wages when wages can be found at all.

And so, Aristotle finally got even with the Greeks for dicking him around.

The fires of Greece had spread to Spain and Portugal and savaged employment throughout the Euro Zone. Thailand imploded into riots, but when the poor were gunned down and chased out of Bangkok, it was no longer news. Italy and the UK were next. Foreclosures in California melted Iceland's banks. And now the economic infection had already returned to its source in Detroit, in Los Angeles, in Miami, in Las Vegas.

So here it is: Lonigro's giant map of arrows slithering across continents. And now I know they were fuses, and these bastards were crazy enough to light them.

NEW YORK

That whole scam with Goldman that knifed Greece in the gut was a goofball attempt by the right-wing government of Greece to cover up a government deficit exceeding 3 percent of its GDP. For the United States, a 3 percent deficit would be frugal. Frankly, in hard times, no nation can keep to a 3 percent limit. No nation should.

So why the deadly fraud to adhere to a plain stupid rule?

The answer is that the 3 percent rule is the price Greece had to pay for replacing its ancient currency, the drachma, with the Euro.

Odd that. There are a lot of cool things a nation can do with its own currency. If you need more, you print it. That's what the Federal Reserve does when America needs a few trillion. (I imagine Reserve Chairman Ben Bernanke down in the basement blowing on the bills until they are dry enough to send to Citibank.)

Greece does not even have a central bank anymore, or one that means anything. There's no one to print and blow on the bills. Worse, Greece can't change its currency's exchange rate, which could solve some of its woes, because it no longer has a currency of its own.

The 3 percent rule is not about being frugal, it's about fiscal policy. Greece can't have one. Join the Euro and you give that up. Have a recession or depression? Well, you are not permitted to spend for jobs for recovery. In fact, the Euro treaty requires governments to cut budgets in the middle of a depression, which is like having a rule that makes you drink water while drowning.

It's cruel, and it's *supposed* to be cruel, which no government may reverse. It works like a strict gold standard, which, as Mr. "Creative Destruction" Schumpeter put it, "imposes restrictions upon governments or bureaucracies that are much more powerful than is parliamentary criticism. It is both the badge and the guarantee of bourgeois freedom, of freedom not simply of the bourgeois interest, but of freedom in the bourgeois *sense*."

I don't know what that means, but I know I don't like the sound of it. Especially coming from an Austrian. But this I can gather from it: You can choose the Euro or you can choose democracy.

Given the flames and cries of pain from Greece to Spain to Ireland caused by joining the Euro, you wonder why there are nations that mutilate themselves to join this currency leper colony. Yet, Latvia deliberately threw itself into a depression with 25 percent unemployment to qualify for Euro membership.

Who spawned this cruel little bastard coin?

I called its parent, Professor Robert Mundell. Mundell is known as the Father of the Euro.

The Euro is often spoken of as a means to unite post-war Europeans together emotionally and politically and to give this united Europe the economic power to compete with the U.S. economy. That's horseshit.

The Euro was invented in New York, New York, at Columbia University.

Professor Mundell invented both the Euro and the guiding light of Thatcher-Reagan government: "Supply Side Economics" or, as George Bush Sr. accurately called it, "Voodoo Economics." Reagan-Thatcher voodoo and the Euro are two sides of the same coin. (Ouch! Some puns hurt.)

Like the Iron Lady and President Gaga, the Euro is inflexible. That is, once you join the Euro, your nation cannot fight recession by using fiscal or monetary policy. That leaves "wage reduction, fiscal constraints (cutting government jobs and benefits) as the only recourse in crisis," *The Wall Street Journal* explains with joy—and sell-offs of government property (privatizations).

Why the Euro, Professor? Dr. Mundell told me he was upset at zoning rules in Italy that did not allow him to put his commode where he wanted to in his villa there. "They've got rules that tell me I can't have a toilet in this room. Can you imagine?"

I couldn't really. I don't have an Italian villa, so I cannot really imagine the burden of commode placement restriction.

The Euro will eventually allow you to put your toilet any damn place you want.

He meant that the only way the government can create jobs is to fire people, cut benefits, and, crucially, cut the rules and regulations that restrict business.

He told me: "Without fiscal policy, the only way nations can keep jobs is by the competitive reduction of rules on business." Besides bowl location, he was talking about the labor laws, which raise the price of plumbers, environmental regulations, and, of course, taxes.

No, I am *not* making this up. And I am *not* saying the Euro was imposed on the Old Country just so the professor could place his toilet at a place of maximum pleasure. The Euro is fashioned as an anti-regulation straitjacket that would eliminate gallons-per-flush laws, flush away restrictive banking regulation, and all other government controls.

I didn't hold up the Nobel laureate for long, figuring that, due to his unresolved bowl placement problems, he seemed to be uncomfortably full of shit.

LONDON

The drachma was good enough for Plato and Socrates. Why give it up for the Euro *diktat*? Why remove regulations on banking that kept your pensions and pennies safe for decades?

In most nations, a fifth column of domestic financiers were ready to open the gates to the Trojan Derivative.

In Europe, the group hungering for deregulation called itself The Unnamables. Don't laugh.

This group of select leaders of banking and insurance was chaired by Leon Brittan, Baron of Spennithorne, during the reign of Rubin. Despite his lordship's title, he was chairing the group in his post as Chairman of UBS Ltd., the Swiss bankers.

The unfortunate name for the secretive group was changed so it would not sound so . . . secretive. Besides, most of their meetings were not conducted in secret. That is, someone boosted most of their meeting notes and, through a circuitous route, they landed in Jones's office at BBC Television.

The new name of The Unnameables is the LOTIS Committee, Liberalization of Trade in Services committee. Trade in services, as D-G Lamy pointed out to me, includes my own profession of international journalism, as well as art, music, poetry. And, of course, investment banking and contract killing. (I added those.)

According to the lifted minutes of the LOTIS meetings, there were no poets (though there was, among the bankers and insurance big shots, a Reuters executive advising the wealthy gentlemen on how to parry harsh questions from reporters about their goals).

One of the most powerful members was, according to the meeting notes, Peter Sutherland. Sutherland holds the title of Consultor of the Extraordinary Section of the Administration of the Patrimony of the Apostolic See (i.e., the

Pope's stock broker), but his real powers rest on lower authority: Sutherland is Chairman of Goldman Sachs International.

(Sutherland was dubbed "the father of globalization" by Mickey Kanter, a former U.S. Trade chief, now a lobbyist, who has been dubbed "the little bastard of globalization," and thus a relation.)

The question for the group was how to influence the World Trade Organization to make banking and financial services a *trade* issue. Thereby they could use the WTO as the battering ram for deregulation.

Certainly, Sutherland had some helpful clues: he was the founding Director-General of the WTO.

Sutherland is a busy man. Besides Goldman, he was, at the same time, Chairman of BP. Sutherland is the Energy-Finance Combine in one bespoke suit.

And the man has impeccable timing. He left the Generalship of the WTO just before the spam hit the fan—and left his post as Chairman of BP just a few months before the Deepwater Horizon blew out.

It is quite unusual for one man to hold the chairmanship of two giant multinational corporations like Goldman and BP at the same time. Few men are so flexible they can kiss their own ass.

And only one little bearded man had the courage to kick it.

ELECTRICAL WORKERS' UNION BEACH HOSTEL, NEAR SÃO PAULO

In 1998, after killing a little cask of Zeb's homemade *pinga* and a couple *caipirinhas* (a mixture of three parts lime and seven parts brain solvent) at the Synergia electrical workers' union beach hostel outside São Paolo, I felt the need to tell a young Brazilian, even if she couldn't understand English, that she was the most beautiful woman I'd ever seen in my life; and, that accomplished, I gently fell face forward into the sand.

The next morning I realized that she may not have been all that beautiful or young or even a woman, and given my condition, I was in no shape to meet with a little bearded guy named Lula.

Luiz Inácio Lula da Silva is an unschooled, rough-hewn union leader and head of Brazil's Socialist Workers' Party. At the time, Brazil was heading into economic meltdown, Greece before Greece, and had accepted an IMF bail-out. Its collapse occurred in the nineties after a World Bank economist named Larry Summers demanded Brazil deregulate its banking sector. After the banking bubble popped, the economy dropped into the flames. In return for bail-out funds from the International Monetary Fund, Brazil's President, the pontificating but well-dressed Fernando Henrique Cardoso, had agreed, in secret, to fire sales of national assets, beginning with "opening" Brazil's oil reserves to Shell and other foreign operators. Next on the auction block was the electrical system, sold off cheap to American, French, and British Corporations, notably our boys from Georgia, Southern Company, and my Texans, Houston/Reliant/NRG. When Houston took over the Rio de Janeiro Light Company, the Texans decided to fire a bunch of the workers and pocket their salaries. Then Houston found there was no map or diagram of the Rio Light system; it was known only by the guys they had fired. Locals renamed the company Rio Dark.

Now Brazil's Gas and Electric workers, either jobless or waiting for the pink slip, were plying me with caipirinhas and playing *choros* on their guitars, including songs about their "beautiful generators." They assumed I would be sober enough within a week to help them.

Lula, the union's party leader, wanted solutions, so he had my academic writing on regulating the energy industry translated for him into Portuguese. Lula's advisor, economist Ildo Sauer, wanted my ideas for when Lula took over the country. They would kick the U.S power pirates out on their keisters. Sure. I assumed it was the caipirinha talking. I skipped Lula. I didn't want to waste time on meetings with a guy who was forever running laughable fringe campaigns for President.

A decade later, when the financial planet fell face forward into the dirt, one nation stood up unharmed. Bestride the wreckage of the Western world like a colossus stood Brazil's President Lula.

The bankers would not tolerate it.

Under Lula, elected in 2002, Brazil ended the "liberalization" mania in banking and unhooked itself from the brave new world's free-for-all finance system. Brazil survived and thrived while the Great Recession knocked the West on its ass. From behind a border barricaded against the contamination of derivatives-crazed bankers, Brazil's economy rocketed up by nearly 70 percent while Lula held office.

And that drove the banks crazier still. That Brazil thumbed its nose at the bankers' plan and saved its economy will never be forgiven.

———

It was in 1998 when Brazil was Greece'd. And that's why I've dragged you back to Latin America and my pinga-fuzzed memory cells. Brazil, like Greece, had opened up its banks to ravishing by New York, London, and Swiss financiers. The moment that happens, money floods in to buy up a nation's assets quickly and cheaply. It looks like an economic boom, but you'd look rich too if you sold your house and threw a party. But when the party's over, you can't go home.

When the party ended for Brazil in 1998, the "hot" foreign money fled and the panicked rich of the nation sent their money with them. Brazil's foreign currency reserves dropped from $70 billion to $26 billion. The hot money hadn't stayed long enough to burn toast.

To pay for the demands of investors and the local rich to take their money out of the country, Brazil had to raise the funds by selling its electric companies cheaply as well as the cell phone system and more. That wasn't enough. To keep the money from leaving, the International Monetary Fund told Brazil to raise interest rates to 70 percent—*seventy percent*—and that meant credit cards and business loans would cost consumers up to 200 percent interest. The economy was dying.

The result: insta-depression, the whole disaster a result of the deregulation of the banking system.

Suddenly, Lula was no longer a joke but a serious candidate for President. The foreign financiers nearly shit themselves.

The threat of a Lula Presidency drove all the globalizers mad, but not Peter Mandelson. He'd already arrived. And on the way, taking a vacation from corruption, the Prince of Darkness stopped in Brazil to endorse Lula's opponent, quite odd for a subject of the Queen, but not if you see Brazil as a financial colony. His attacks on Lula were squeezed in between bargain hunting state assets for British multinationals and samba dancing in the sand with Reinaldo.

Robert Rubin doesn't samba, but the U.S. Treasury Secretary knew the Brazilian dance and was more effective than Mandelson. He and his successor, Summers, helped arrange a $41 billion bail-out loan to Brazil just before the election, so that Cardoso could eke back into office.

Cardoso defeated Lula, then, just fifteen days after the election, the U.S. Treasury let Brazil's currency crash, interest rates rise again, and its economy go to hell.

The IMF's loan money came in and shot out. Cardoso's solution: more privatizations and a giant cut in pensions—Lula's greedy union workers were the real cause of the disaster, the IMF and Cardoso agreed.

Fire-sale privatizations, cuts in pensions, mass lay-offs of government workers . . . are you smelling the Greece yet? There is nothing new under the sun. Except that in Brazil, the IMF and vultures went after the crude oil, not the olive oil. These old dogs don't need new tricks so long as our amnesiac press gets its periodic brain scrubbings.

There is no shame: The bankers tried to pull the same trick in 2002, when Lula and Cardoso faced off again. This time, another IMF line of credit was offered. But the secret terms were harsher: Brazil would have to turn over its state government banks to private financiers. I'm not guessing about this, either. A sixty-some-page agreement marked CONFIDENTIAL AND DOCUMENT OF THE INTERNATIONAL MONETARY FUND AND NOT FOR PUBLIC USE* is an agreement signed by Cardoso's Finance Minister just three weeks before Lula was about to take office. (Brazilians, unlike Americans and Britons, are rarely fooled twice.) The Banco Do Brasil had already been sold off, but now Cardoso's man agreed to sell off the five state banks. From the confidential document:

> A court has delayed the privatization of the Bank of Santa Catarina, the largest of the four federalized state banks. The privatization of one other federalized state bank is on track for end-2002, while that of the two remaining federal banks is now expected to be completed by January 2003.

These public sources of funding had kept Brazil breathing when the international bankers were choking the country. But they had to go . . . to the international bankers. Like Sandy Weill, the lenders had learned the easiest way to rob a bank is to steal it from halls to walls.

---

* Take a look for yourself. This document and others at GregPalast.com/VulturesPicnic. Warning: An IMF spokesman says, "Palast is the master of disinformation." I didn't write the documents.

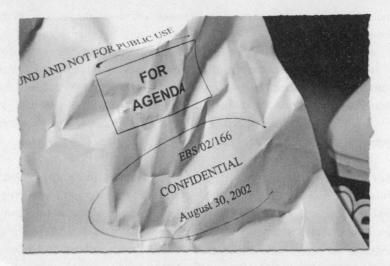

The new President, Lula, resisted, despite the gun of bankruptcy threats in his face and the deals Brazil signed before he was sworn in. But Lula told the IMF to jam it and body-blocked privatizations, especially of the state-owned banks. Instead of begging international financiers for scraps, he opened the vaults of the state bank and lent out over half a trillion dollars for factories, farms, infrastructure—but not for one *real* for derivatives, hostile takeovers or collateralized debt obligations. During his two terms in office, Lula's state banks gave their citizen-owners more credit than the IMF gave to over hundered nations. And Brazil's economy went from the swamp to the stars.

Then Brazil struck oil, lots of it, in deep Atlantic waters. In the old days, that is, a decade ago, Chevron, Shell, and BP would have been onto those reservoirs like ticks, sucking up Brazil's oil. And, of course, giving up state ownership of Brazil's vast oil supply was one of the IMF bail-out conditions.

But Lula's Director of Oil and Gas, my drinking comrade Ildo Sauer, told the oil majors to go fly. Via Brazil's once-small state oil company, Petrobras, Ildo and Lula planned to keep ownership of the oil in public hands. How was Lula, the guy telling Big Oil to kiss off, going to raise the capital to get to his mid-Atlantic reserves? With flippers and a snorkel?

Ildo and Lula had another problem: Brazil has to sell the oil. Brazil itself doesn't need much; electricity is water-powered and Lula has forced Brazil to go cold turkey on its gasoline addiction. Most cars run mainly on biomass ethanol. That means Brazil must sell its oil (and its excess ethanol) to the petro-leum junkies of the United States and Europe.

But now, Lula was told, let the U.S. and European banks in or drink your oil and ethanol yourself, and your orange juice too. Uncle Sam hit Lula where it hurt, right in the biomass, slapping a 54-cent tariff on each gallon of the clean fuel imported to the United States.

This was meant to be a lesson to Brazil, to Greece, to Spain, and any other weakened nations that might dream of resisting.

The lesson wasn't sticking. In September 2010, Brazil's Petrobras success-fully raised $70 billion in the largest share offering in world history. Appar-ently, a whole lot of capitalists felt more secure with their own money in the hands of socialists, even though each mid-ocean oil derrick is a floating mid-dle finger to Summers and Rubin.

Most important, Lula sealed the borders against new financial "products" from foreign banks. Guards were ordered to shoot derivatives on sight.

Brazil dodged the bullet in the 2008–11 worldwide Recession by reject-ing credit default swap bingo and sub-prime blind-man's bluff. Foreign banks are particularly incensed that they couldn't open shop in Brazil without a "presidential decree," that is, Lula's personal approval. And he approved of very little.

It saved his nation's life.

Such conduct would not be indulged. Lula must be spanked, his allowance taken away, and his banks and his ass-kicking economy. Matty Pass scored a copy of the plan for punishment, the confidential "EC Request to Brazil." The EC, the European Commission, does not make requests, it makes demands. This demand, still on the table, was whipped up by the EC's Trade Commis-sioner at the time, Lord Peter Mandelson.

GENEVA

"Brazil has not yet accepted the Fifth Protocol," the "Request" begins in a huff. Brazil sure as hell hasn't.

"The Fifth Protocol" sounds like some Satanic torture ritual. It is. The Fifth Protocol of the Financial Services Agreement, that new law of lawless-ness, requires nations to allow foreign banks to open shop and sell almost anything they want at the teller window (CDOs, CDSs, whatever). The signing nation may not restrict the "form" of the bank, i.e., no Glass-Steagall-type laws may keep savings accounts out of the hands of speculators.

Just about every nation had signed up to at least part of this FSA protocol. But not Lula, not Brazil, virtually alone out of 153 nations.

And this drives the bankers nuts. They can't stand it. This behavior must end.

So the European negotiators, with the blessing of the United States, are still, as I write this, planning to squeeze Brazil until its coconuts scream unless Brazil agrees to spread wide open for the Royal Bank of Scotland. The U.S. banks will ride in right after.

I brought the confidential Mandelson/EC/U.S. demand with me into the baroque WTO conference room to show Director-General Lamy.

Wasn't it plain psycho, I asked, after all that just went down with the collapse of banks, to demand Brazil invite the lepers in? To force derivatives trade down Brazil's throat? The EC document called it "progressive liberalization." The WTO chief began,

> "All depends on what you mean by 'liberalization' which, by the way, is a very ambiguous English word that can mean two things which are different in other languages. . . ."

We were entering a multi-lingual vortex. Lamy went on,

> "Sharing derivatives across borders is about interdependence. . . ."

Sharing? I don't remember Goldman "sharing."

* * *

Badpenny and I left Geneva late and got lost, distracted by the moon-tinted Alps.

I was thinking about General Lamy's pale, bloodless lips. They never lost their smile. He knew and I knew: The WTO survived the Battle of Seattle, Greece in flames, and a Depression it had a hand in creating. It would certainly survive Greg Palast. Thug wins. Biggest rock and all that.

But the Frenchman had given me what I needed: authentication of the documents. Now, the gods, the BBC, and budget willing, I could take them back to South America, where they might be of some use.

So pretty, the Swiss chalets, even the modern towns. But pretty in a violent way, imposed, intolerant of any suspected deviance. And safe. The Swiss have fitted out thousands of caves like armed shopping malls, where the entire population can live for a century in case of attack. But no one is attacking. Penny said, "Terrorists don't bomb their own bank."

We were starving and lucked upon a lone rustic eatery serving, to our dismay, fondue only. Worse, by local custom, every time a fondue is served, they dim the bar lights and, with a special flashlight, project the Swiss flag, a white cross on red, on the melted cheese. Everyone clapped to some national military anthem. Except Penny. The stultifying order that drove her into exile from her homeland of carnivorous financiers remained stuck in her spleen.

The clapping burghers shoved a huge Swiss flag in her hand and she smiled while looking for a hole to crawl into and die.

Here was Switzerland's "industry": regimentation and a commitment to secrets and complicit silence, a nation restrained by the trusteeship of Other People's Money, that highly addictive OPM, guardians of the neutral ground for the World Trade police and dictators' shoe shops.

The guilt that comes with this *geld* has a psychic price she will not pay.

QUITO, ECUADOR

On May 6, 2010, the day after the Greek riot, *The Wall Street Journal* quoted a finance analyst on its government's imposition of the draconian IMF cuts to jobs, pensions, and pay. "There is no doubt that the deaths ease some of the political pressure" on the Greek government. On May 21, the *Journal* headline read, "In Greece, Anarchists Fear They've Given Austerity a Helping Hand." They had. The bank burning had pulled the moral steam out of the protests of the desperate citizenry, and now the whip could come down.

I'd seen this story before, but not in Greek.

The first riot I remember came quickly after Geithner had lit the FSA fuse in Geneva. In 1999, Ecuador's banks, deregulated, ran wild, and the nation's hard currency ran off to party in Miami. Ecuador's banks were quickly bankrupted by their owners freed of old-fashioned rules. The IMF then forced the government to take over the failed banks' debts. According to an IMF document that was slid onto my desk, Ecuadorans would pay for this through a 66 percent to 92 percent hike in the price of gasoline, a 50 percent hike in electricity charges, pension cuts, and, most painfully, an increase in the price of bottled gas used for cooking, which would rise by up to 333 percent.

Quechua-speaking women who had to pay off the banks' debts disagreed with the IMF's policy suggestions. They came down from the Andes Mountains to Quito, the capital, banging pots and pans—then began to burn the city.

The whip came down, the tanks moved into the street. The armor defeated the women and the IMF *diktats* were imposed. Ecuador, like Greece, lost its own currency as part of the deal. Ecuador agreed to pay the United States to use dollars, an annual penalty that Rubin and Summers collected with joy.

Then in 2000, Argentina blew, also following the collapse of banks after deregulation. And again, there were women banging empty pots and pans, school teachers hunting for food in garbage cans. Riots, whips, then IMF "reform." And so on, from Indonesia to Hungary. Bank deregulation, collapse, riot, whip, IMF reform. You could mark your calendar in advance.

It was so regular, so predictable, you'd think it was the plan.

It is, and I have a copy. It is called the "Poverty Reduction Plan" for Ecuador, a World Bank document with the usual *confidential, not for public distribution*, and all those warnings that give me such pleasure to ignore.

"Poverty reduction?" Who comes up with these titles? Who do they think is fooled? Well, when your memos are taped to the front of a tank, you can call it just about anything you like.

In 2005, Ecuador blew again when the IMF squeezed harder. While phone land lines were down, I was able to get Ecuador's incoming President on his cell phone (how is a story too crazy to believe).* The new President invited me

---

* That story and others, just too weird for print, are included in the interactive editions "extras" and at GregPalast.com/VulturesPicnic.com.

down. (The outgoing President left via helicopter from the balcony of his office.)

In Quito, working my way through chanting women (I liked their style—they wore fedoras), then through rings of armed and nervous military guards, I made it into the Presidential palace for my appointment—but immediately was shooed away.

Apparently, the U.S. Ambassador had seen *Palast* on President Alfredo Palacio's calendar and told him to forget it. The President knew that the Ambassador, who held his nation by the currency, had to be obeyed, and sent me off. Then President Palacio told his son, Alfredo Jr., to let me in through a back door into the Ecuadoran Oval Office.

I had those World Bank/IMF agreements that required horrific budget cuts of Ecuador and the sale of state assets. Though his predecessor as President had agreed to the terms, the new President had never seen a copy.

Well, I like to share.

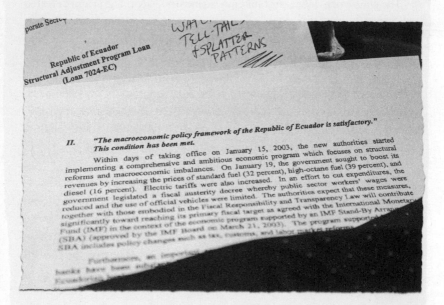

Palacio told me he was sure George Bush, then President, would listen to "reason" and get the World Bank to back off. Palacio reasoned, Bush listened, grinned, then left Palacio and his country to die.

LONDON SCHOOL OF ECONOMICS

Sometimes it's helpful to have your paranoia justified by an expert.

Joe Stiglitz is an expert, a big-shot economist. He made a big splash by analyzing the First Catechism of Free Market economics: that The Market has "wisdom," that The Market is always right. That's why we should be happy to designate The Market as the modern Thug, the Invisible Hand with a big rock to keep us in line with its wisdom. But Stiglitz proved, mathematically, that sometimes The Market can be just crazy, cruel, insane, ignorant, especially when some of the players in the market are keeping secrets.

Now, you and I and Lonigro and most of the planet know that already, but to economists, the discovery that The Market could be wrong was so astonishing that they gave Stiglitz the Nobel Prize.

In 2000, he and I were lecturing at the London School of Economics on the same night, and I figured I'd learn more by listening to him than by listening to myself. So I wrapped up early and went over.

The man is wicked smart, an academic with enough real-world scars to let you know that numbers on the chalkboard can save or destroy nations. Stiglitz agreed to chat with me the next day up at Cambridge, where he was visiting his son. We spoke for what must have been three hours. He stayed cheerful except when I used the words *Larry Summers*. He'd turn purple and the academic guard would go down. I used *Larry Summers* a lot.

I came to Stiglitz not just because he was an expert, but because he was an eye-witness to a crime. He had been inside, a member of President Clinton's cabinet, head of the Council of Economic Advisors from 1995 to 1997. Clinton didn't take his counsel, but he did let Stiglitz sit in the room with Summers and Rubin while they convinced the good ol' boy President to decriminalize banking. Stiglitz sat through it somehow, without making gagging sounds or rolling his eyes. He did finally intervene, he told me, when Summers asked Rubin, one too many times, "What will Goldman think of this?"

Apparently, Summers and Rubin never made a major economic policy decision without measuring the implications for Rubin's former bank. They thought of it as a fine way to test their policies against The Market's expected reaction. Stiglitz thought it sick, bad governance, and a blatant conflict of interest. He pointed that out and got no more than a look one would give a child that doesn't understand the ways of the adult world.

In regard to letting banks run wild worldwide, Stiglitz raised some questions and got more tolerant "you'll see when you grow up" looks.

In 2008, when Barack Obama was elected by a nation in deep economic recession, the President-Elect waited barely a week before picking his economic cabinet: Larry Summers to the new post of Economics Czar and Tim Geithner as Czarina, Secretary of the Treasury.

Stiglitz and others who successfully warned of the fires that would erupt from bank de-control were passed over. Instead of the economic firefighters, Obama chose the arsonists.

Maybe Stiglitz was just sore at Summers over getting fired by the World Bank. Like Summers, Stiglitz had also held the post of World Bank chief economist. He took the job seriously and, word has it, Summers had him taken out.

Stiglitz had seen it all while at the Bank, including despots turning World Bank privatization programs into bribery free-for-alls ("briberization," Stiglitz called it), cruel demands on nations begging for food (Ethiopia still bothers him), and the Bank's pathological desire to tear down finance regulations in nations that barely had finances.

But crucial to me was his authentication of the "Poverty Reduction Strategies" and other inside documents from the Bank that had come to our BBC offices. And they needed translating from Bureaucratic Esperanto.

One in particular disturbed me, regarding Ecuador. The World Bank, after ordering the thirty-fold increase in the cost of cooking gas, warned the government to expect "social unrest," which, the Bank said, should be met with "political resolve."

What? It seems to me the Bank and its partner, the IMF, were saying in euphemistic fashion that the harsh austerity program would lead to mayhem in the streets and the government should get the police readied for the crackdown. Was this just Palast paranoia?

Stiglitz's answer nearly knocked me out of my chair.

"We had a name for it: the IMF riot." It was cold strategy. And you thought banking was dull. Stiglitz said that when the IMF has nations "down and out, it takes advantage and squeezes the last pound of blood out of them. They turn up the heat until, finally, the whole cauldron blows up."

———

Just as I thought, the riots were in the plan.

And we could see the squeeze, explosion, and crackdown repeated from Greece to Thailand.

I suggested we rename the IMF and World Bank "Riots R Us."

MANHATTAN, DOWNTOWN

On July 18, 2006, President George Bush gave German Chancellor Angela Merkel a shoulder massage. On May 9, 2010, President Obama twisted her arm off, or, as the White House said in its official statement, the President and Chancellor "discussed the importance of resolute action by Greece and timely support from the IMF and Europe to address Greece's economic difficulties."

Germany would have to pony up. Or else. Or else *what*? Or else this, Angela: In 2008, in a truly strange and wondrous accounting maneuver, the Federal Reserve, for the first time in its history, transferred wads of U.S. currency, totaling half a trillion dollars, to the European Central Bank (and the Central Banks of Switzerland and Japan). Now, Obama signalled the wincing German Chancellor, unless Greece (and Spain) got "resolute" on their citizens—whips, truncheons, and wage cuts—and Germany put money into the pot, the United States would not throw in the additional half trillion the Fed had promised.

Why did our nice President put a half-nelson on the lady Chancellor? Because Barack Obama is not just President of the United States, he was also chief executive of AIG Insurance, which the U.S. Treasury had just bought for $170 billion in bail-out funds.

One single corporation, AIG, not a bank even, was given this $170 billion (six times California's deficit) because it was the "counter-party" that had sold the world's banks these crap Credit Default Swaps, thereby promising insurance against the underlying loans going bust.

The U.S. taxpayers had it up to *here* with bank bail-outs, so slipping the money to AIG was a way for the U.S. Treasury to back-door a hundred billion to The Boys indirectly. Goldman got $12.9 billion via the AIG bail-out fund, but so did the Swiss ($5 billion to UBS); and, Angela, your Deutsche Bank got $11.8 billion, all of it hidden from Americans' jingoistic eyes. (The German bank immediately ran off with the U.S. Treasury money to Las Vegas and bet it all on a casino, literally. The Germans bought The Cosmopolitan casino-hotel, now bankrupt, and their $4 billion bet with our money is *kaput*.)

The United States had bailed out Deutsche Bank, and now Obama wanted Merkel's skin in the game too. To bail out "Greece," though Greece would get none of it. The German money would go to the speculators, banks holding the credit default bag, including AIG.

And that's their big joke, isn't it? That the Greeks don't get a dime. Germany, France and the European Union gave Greece a €110 billion ($160 billion) bail-out loan in 2010, while investment banks and speculators dumped about €110 billion in Greek debt. In other words, the money went to the bankers, not one Euro to Greece's Treasury.

But at least AIG would not go down again. And for its CEO, Obama, that was enough.

But not enough for the German banks and Greece's ruling class, the we-don't-pay-no-stinkin'-taxes grifters that helped drain Greece's treasury. In July 2011, the Association of Greek Industries and the German Chancellor demanded that the Greek government sell off €50 billion in state assets, including the water system, to pay the "spread." (I'd seen this movie before: in 1988, when Argentina, to pay off interest on loans at rates that would reach 101 percent, was ordered to sell off the Buenos Aires water system to Enron. Rates quadrupled, pipes broke, and Enron left the Argentines thirsty and busted.) And Greece's state bank has to go as well. The EU is not going to let Greece do what Lula's Brazil did, keep its own bank as a financial life buoy. The arsonists demanded their fire sale. German speculators topped the list of buyers hungry for the nation's assets. The fabled ports of Piraeus and Thessaloniki were taken, obtaining with just a little financial finagling what Hitler couldn't obtain with Panzers.

Badpenny could hate in a clean and pure manner: Vultures chewing Zambia, speculators igniting Greece, bankers scamming the Swiss railway retirement fund, which then cut pensions. And when she went after them, it was personal, physical, hormonal. Sometimes she was on it for twenty, thirty hours, non-stop. She was fixated, she was crazed: There must be a connection between Greece, AIG, the bail-outs, and the Goldman currency swap scam. It was dawn in Europe, midnight in America, and I was on the office mattress, safe in dreamland.

Until five A.M.

Suddenly, there was the investigatrix, standing over me, crazy, excited.

Badpenny was reading, actually she was *shouting*, "*Hedge-Fonds im Oktober...*" and then lots and lots of German.

"ARE YOU FUCKING CRAZY? IT'S—WHAT TIME IS IT?—OH MY GOD, IT'S LIKE FIVE A.M.!"

"It's from the—*Are you listening to me?*—the *Frankfurter Allgemeine....*"

I was helpless, on my back, trying to claw my way back to sleep while getting machine-gunned with multi-lingual shrapnel *at five fucking A.M.*

"LISTEN TO ME LISTEN '*Die Wette...*'" then some more German. OK, Jesus. What? WHAT?

"I found it! ARE YOU LISTENING TO ME? You wanted me to find it! I found—see, it means— '*... the question now is, who sold the credit default swap?*' LOOK AT THIS, I GOT IT, THE CONNECTION BACK TO GOLDMAN!"

The room was hellish hot and she unzipped that little tight jacket she wore on top of the leathers.

"Look! You told me to find it. I've got it—you're not looking! Here *Le Figaro* picks it up"—she threw off the little top—"*La banque*"—then lots of blah blah in French words and—"*de 300 millions de dollars.* That means *the bank pocketed $300 million,* which matches—I DID ALL THIS FOR YOU AND YOU'RE NOT PAYING ATTENTION"—snap! the black motorcycle pants zipped open— "it matches *exactly...*"

I paid attention.

"... *exactly* the spread ..."—she pulled away the leather, switching to Italian—"Look. *Borsa Plus—migliori tassi sul mercato...*"

Then next to me, white lace, heartbreakingly girlish, that had hidden under the tough leather.

And I could not speak.

High above the office ceiling, I could hear idiot angels hooting and whistling like cowboys, touching themselves under their robes.

And then they fell silent, as she looked down into my eyes and through them, while their wings beat slowly, rhythmically.

She whispered. "It's just a technicality by now, isn't it?"

Those were her last words in English in that warm hour before dawn.

* * *

Badpenny's sleeping breath purred in my ear. But breaking through it, the sound of glass shattering on Second Avenue. Some drunk probably.

Now sleep was impossible. I got up, got dressed, wrote a note, a line from Rilke—*Ein jeder Engel ist schrecklich*—tore it up and left to go home to the woman I had loved for so long, for the last time.

Every angel is terrifying.

RETURN TO ECUADOR

All my investigations—of global finance, of oil, of the vultures—seem to weave their way through this land at the center of the Earth. Now, I was back in Quito with World Bank memos marked *confidential* and a lot of questions for a new President, Raphael Correa.

Correa and Ecuador were under attack on three fronts, by the World Bank/IMF combine, by Chevron, Occidental, and the oil industry, and by the finance Vultures.

His predecessor, Palacio, had refused to cut the health budget to pay off the debts of Ecuador's long-gone scoundrel bankers. The World Bank was not amused. Its President, Paul Wolfowitz, who, in his own mind, had just won the war in Iraq, and was thus filled with the testosterone of self-delusion, dropped the hammer on Ecuador, cutting off the country's access to the world's capital markets. It was a banking embargo that could lead to Ecuador's starvation. The appeal to George Bush failed and that's when Ecuador was left to die.

Ecuador didn't die.

Palacio despaired, but his Finance Minister, Rafael Correa, on his own, secretly went to the President of Venezuela, Hugo Chavez, and got loan guarantees and other help from Chavez worth up to a quarter billion dollars.

Correa saved his nation—and was fired. Palacio really had no choice: ministers can't run off on their own ponies cutting deals, even life-saving deals.

In Ecuador's December 2006 election, the IMF and international banks were counting on the owner of the biggest banana plantation in this banana republic to be returned to the presidency. But Correa, which means "The Belt" in Spanish, whipped him. The country's credit rating, in bad shape, fell apart. Correa grinned.

Ecuador's agreement to pay off the losses of banks run by straight-out crooks had been coerced out of Palacio's and Correa's psychotic predecessors. (There are more psycho presidents in history than I can count, from Iran to the USA. But Ecuador's Abdala Bucaram, removed in 1997, had an official medical diagnosis.)

Correa's presidential campaign anthem was Twisted Sister's "We're Not Gonna Take It." Sure. I'd heard that before, from his predecessors. Once in office, once under the World Bank gun, they changed their tune.

Correa didn't. He told me, "We are not going to pay bonds with the hunger of our people." Food first, interest payments later, vulture payments never. Big talk. I'd just met with his compadre, Hugo Chavez, Venezuela's President who could back up big talk with big oil reserves. But tiny Ecuador?

And there was more heat on Correa. George Bush demanded that Ecuador maintain a U.S. military base on its coast. Correa told Bush, forget it—unless Bush allowed Ecuador to put a military base in Miami.

Clearly, Correa was asking for it. Indeed, he once asked for it, literally, when some angry cops mobbed him. He ripped open his shirt and told them, *"Dispara a mí!!"—Shoot me!*

I showed the President agreements made by an Ecuador finance minister with the World Bank in 2005. The March 10 meeting minutes I had in my hand were marked *for OFFICIAL USE ONLY*. The President was official enough for me, if not for the World Bank.

He was disgusted, but not surprised, that the World Bank required Ecuador to sell off the nation's oil fields. It read,

> ". . . Despite political opposition the government was moving ahead with
> an ambitious package of structural reform, including an opening to pri-
> vate partnership in the oil sector. . . ."

Opening to private—as in, sell us your oil reserves. *Partnership*—like with Chevron.

Correa had been a Finance Minister, but he'd never been shown these documents. He asked me if he could make a copy. Since they were, presumably, stolen from his office, I didn't see how I could object.

While he'd never been shown the deals, the attacks on him from banks and diplomats let him know he'd certainly violated terms secretly made before his time.

As to the required sell-offs of the oil fields and privatization of power companies, Correa told me, simply, "Ecuador is no longer for sale." Good luck with *that.*

Much of the power of the WTO, IMF, and World Bank is not just in their brute ability to choke off a nation's money supply, but the gallons of greasy highfalutin techno-economic-theoretical jive that covers up their cold threats. But they were trying to blow their complex economics smoke in the face of *Professor* Dr. Correa, European-trained economist, fluent in five languages. Until he was tapped for the Finance post by Palacio, Dr. Correa taught economics at the University of Illinois, where his doctorate and publications included *"Destabilizing Speculation in the Exchange Market: The Ecuadorian Case," "The Washington Consensus in Latin America: A Quantitative Evaluation,"* and so on. In other words, he had Larry Summers's number. When the World Bank spoke in macroeconomic bullshit, Correa knew exactly what they really meant.

Correa knows that Ecuador's only hope, other than begging, is to take back control of its own oil. Ecuador was once a member of OPEC. Correa rejoined it.

He had already taken the first difficult step of taking back the public's oil, while Palacio's Finance Minister. The two of them threw Occidental Petroleum out on its ass for not living up to its contracts. Occidental was shocked. Oxy must have confused Ecuador with Azerbaijan and thought it could treat contract terms like baby-bottom wipes.

While President "Belt" laid out his demand that the rules must be enforced on Occidental and Chevron, I couldn't help but compare him to my own President's somewhat supine pose. Just as Chevron and Occidental broke their contracts with Ecuador, BP violated its contract with the U.S. government by BP's negligent (and deadly) drilling of the deepwater property. Why didn't Obama take away BP's lease? If I spill oil all over my apartment in New York, you bet your ass that my landlord will cancel my lease. Obama did the opposite: He publicly stated that BP was welcome to stay, even after poisoning the coastline of the Gulf and, before that, the coast of Alaska. I suspect BP would have kept its leases even if, during their meeting, Chairman Svengard had taken a big dump on the Oval Office rug.

Unlike Obama, Correa wouldn't take shit from an oil company, nor its pollution.

But what about the Chevron trial?

The oil giant was none too happy about the lawsuit filed by Chief Criollo and the Cofan Indians. Correa himself had gone to the Amazon, seen the toxic pits, met with the grieving parents. His integrity required him to tell me that his own state oil company had to accept its share of responsibility and he wouldn't shirk it. But Chevron must as well, depending on what the court ruled.

Of the carcinogens and poisons Chevron's Texaco operation left near the farms and villages, Correa said, "America wouldn't do this to its own people." *Oh yes it would,* I was thinking to myself, remembering Alaska's Natives.

But no one messes with Chevron. The corporation, after all, had put a U.S. Secretary of State on its Board and her name on its tanker. You'd think Correa would get the hint.

Correa's eat-no-crap approach is about to get a hell of a test. The Ecuadorian judge dismissed Chevron's claim that crude oil pollution does not cause childhood cancer. The court's independently appointed scientists have determined that some, but not all, of the old crude oil pits I saw were left by Chevron's Texaco slobs. The decision was reached carefully: The trial and scientific review took seventeen years.

On February 15, 2011, Ecuador's courts ruled that Chevron must pay $8.6 billion for clean-up and compensation—cheap, from my experience with these cases. What I saw in the rain forest, the deadly exposure, was far, far, *far* worse than anything I saw in the Gulf of Mexico or in Alaska.

Chevron once promised to abide by the ruling of Ecuador's court. Now, their lawyers told me, "We will not pay. We will never pay. They will never be able to collect." The company lawyers told me that Chevron took the opportunity of the long trial to move every asset out of Ecuador. The attorneys giggled like bad little boys who'd hidden candy from the teacher. What about the desks in their law office? Jaime Varela, the one with the bouffant hairdo and yellow golf slacks said, "Not even the desk. It's not in [Chevron's] name." He grinned some more.

What will Ecuador do, Mr. President, now that Chevron says it won't pay?

Before Correa was elected, the answer would have been known in advance. The Indians could take their judgment and shove it. Courts were for Vultures, not for cancer-ridden Natives in war-paint.

That's how it is in Nigeria, in Indonesia, in Azerbaijan.

As a nation, Correa is taking a page from the Vultures: he threatens to seize Chevron's assets anywhere in the world he can grab them.

No nation has had the balls to do that before.

Chevron is now claiming that the farmers and the Indians and the President and the scientists and the journalists and the judge and Sting's wife (yes) are in on the "biggest fraud in history." The oil company has taken the unprecedented step of suing the Natives' lawyers for racketeering and conspiracy. The company that still has not given me an explanation for their own executives' order to destroy evidence is accusing the rain forest lawyers of destroying evidence. Pablo Fajardo is the farmer who grew up in the poisoned zone and put himself through law school just so he could fight for his town. They've sued this guy, who doesn't have a pot to piss in, for millions.

And in an attempt to stop the Ecuadorians from collecting their judgment in America, Chevron is also suing the U.S. lawyer who had advised the Natives, without pay, for the whole seventeen years, Steve Donziger. Donziger graduated from Harvard Law school, but unlike his classmates, he didn't cash in big-time. The sharp Harvard grad could have gone to work for Gibson Dunn & Crutcher. He could bill $600 an hour (I know, I've paid their bills). They represent Chevron and are billing up a storm to prevent the oil company from having to pay for Ecuadorians' cancer treatments. Hey, Steve, that's a million bucks a year. *Are you crazy?*

I've met Steve and his wife and kid. He *is* crazy. Good crazy. The one thing going for him is that, while Chevron is suing him for everything he has, he doesn't have much.

But Correa is not crazy. It's one thing for a public interest lawyer to bet his career on a cause, another for a president to bet his nation.

I wanted to know why he wasn't crapping in his presidential pants? Ecuador is tiny. Why wasn't he scared shitless of the financial chiefs and petroleum powers, especially as they were backed by the not-insubstantial authority of the American State? Where did he get those *cojones gigantes?* And where can I get some too?

I had to ask: What about your father?

His staffers, looking on, froze. It's not a topic he would speak about nor did they want him to speak.

Correa's doctorate and bespoke blue suits can mislead. Correa is from the streets of Quito, a kid as poor as they get. Only through grit, wit, and luck did he end up in the Presidential Palace instead of a Wendy's in Baltimore cleaning the grease traps. That was his dad's job—or what he thought was his dad's job.

When Ecuador's currency collapsed, while Correa was a boy, maybe a million desperate Ecuadorians left the country any way they could. Most went to the United States to find work. His dad followed, a trip paid for the only way it could be.

"My father was a *mula,* a mule."

He paused, then added, "He brought one hundred sixty grams of cocaine to the United States and went to prison. For four years."

"My mother told me he was away at work."

His father, released from prison, was deported back to Ecuador. Humiliated, poor, broken, his father died; I heard it was suicide.

When I was in Venezuela, the blond leaders of the old order referred to themselves as "Spaniards"—and to President Hugo Chavez as "the monkey." Chavez told me proudly, "I am *negro e indio*"—Black and Indian, like most Venezuelans. Now, all over Latin America, the "monkeys" had taken charge for the first time in four centuries: Correa, Lula, Chavez, Evo Morales in Bolivia, and they are unlocking the economic cages. Washington be warned: Humiliation is history.

I know this is an incredibly simple story: Indians in white hats with their dead kids, and oil millionaires in black hats laughing at kiddy cancer and playing musical chairs with oil assets.

But maybe it's just that simple. Maybe in this world there really is Good and Evil.

Maybe Santa will sort it out for us, tell us who's been good and who's been bad. Maybe Lawyer Yellow Pants will wake up on Christmas Eve staring at the ghost of Christmas Future and promise to get the oil sludge out of the Cofan's drinking water.

Do you think so?

I had one more question for Correa. What about The Vultures? Just as in Zambia and Liberia, finance vultures had swooped in, found old Ecuadorian debts (Henry Kissinger's clients found half-century-old railroad bonds), and paid a fragment of their face value for them. Records suggest FH International, the hedge fund of Dr. Hermann, the Vulture from our stakeout, was one of them. Now the Vultures are demanding payment on the face value of the bonds and then some, expecting the 1,000 percent returns they squeezed out of neighboring Peru.

But unlike the leaders of Liberia and Peru, Correa has no interest in sitting with feathered predators and begging. (See "Humiliation is history," above.)

The "Doctor Professor," as he is sometimes called, had a better idea.

In 2006, Correa announced Ecuador would not pay debt created by fraud or bribery. Imitating the Vultures' own strategy, he filed a series of lawsuits worldwide to prevent collection. As my father would say, The Vultures didn't know whether to shit or go blind.

You could see the steam coming out of Goldman Sachs's ears. Goldman announced that Ecuador was heading straight into default.

That's exactly what Correa *wanted* them to say.

Goldman's hysteria and cries sent the value of Ecuador's debt plummeting from low to ridiculously low.

Then, Correa did something quite naughty: He did exactly what the Vultures do, and arranged for Ecuador to buy up some of its own bonds at a super-deep discount, thereby cheating the Vultures out of their pay-day.

Correa had out-vultured the Vultures.

COAL COUNTRY, PENNSYLVANIA

Matthew Pascarella—Matty Pass—scored the confidential *"EC Request"* and that stack of World Bank documents stamped "not for public distribution." How did this kid get so good at digging? His dad wasn't a coal miner, but Matty would have been, if the coal mines hadn't gone bust.

Pascarella's dad has a Caddy *and* a Mercedes, and Matty's never gotten a ride in either of them. His parents split when Matty was five, leaving his mom with nowhere to go but the Army Recruitment Center to join up. His militarized mom took him on a gypsy shuffle through fifteen Army bases in fourteen years, which sucks for a kid. High school was above the dead coal mines in rural Pennsylvania. They call it Coal Country but it should be called Foreclosure Country. Of course, that was the best place for Mom, now an Army recruiter, to harvest kids for wars in various foreign oil and opium fields.

Matty Pass is wise enough not to blame her, even when he learned some coal miners' kids didn't return. Realistically, someone is going to get shrapnel through a helmet, so a single mother who really needs it might as well get the sign-up bonus for it; but that kind of shit can screw with a kid's head. Not Matty's. He had enough sense to panic and run screaming to New York, get a scholarship, do enough bar-tending until three A.M. to get by and get laid and get to class in the morning. Though he's very much a one-gal kind of guy. Anyway, Matty Pass read a book of mine handed him by some professor—*Palast assigned? You could knock me over with a feather when I heard that!*—and he liked the story about my dad and about doing journalism without bleached teeth. Somehow he had been working for nothing in our office for weeks before I knew he was there.

After a year of torturing him with unpaid and unthanked junk work, I saw smoke and flames coming out of the dark back room in our Second Avenue office; and sure enough, the kid was on fire, writing, researching, filming. OK, he's just twenty-two, but why not make him the boss film Producer on our BBC investigation of the President? U.S. newsman Dan Rather once said, "George Bush is my President and I'll line up where he tells me to line up." I figured a kid who'd been hauled to more military bases than a POW would never line up. And if he found the line, he'd erase it.

There was no way my little op could keep such a wunderkind, and Matty Pass took off to launch a multimillion dollar fashion and politics magazine. *TAR* magazine was the arbiter of international cool for at least ten minutes. Note that he got to the top at an age younger than Tina Brown when she was launch editor of *Vanity Fair,* and Matty did it without marrying a connected old fart. But he knew: Success in publishing and a six-figure salary would only weaken him, so he came back home to Second Avenue to work for cookies and milk. He had just been chosen for a big-time graduate fellowship at the London School of Economics, but he made the crazy decision to turn it down just so he could help me finish this investigation. I am ashamed to say, I let him go crazy.

And he's got his own gumshoe work going now as well, more dangerous than he realizes, inside Cuba, hunting for Fidel's lost soul. What he found there was a mother who clawed her way through graveyard dirt to see, one last time, the face of her child whom Castro had executed that morning.

Secretly, on his Canon 5D Mark II, he gathered up the story of mother and son and a revolution eating its young, and, as I've mentioned, got the film chips out in ways I cannot tell you.

What I don't want to tell him is that no one gives a damn about the mother and her kid buried in the dirt. It's sad, it's the world, but it's no one else's kid. Just like the kids Matty's mom signed up for Iraq, it's personal tragedy, not momentous history. It's a snore for most editors and TV producers. At twenty-seven, you want to wake up the world. At fifty-seven, you wonder if it's better to let it sleep.

INSANE VORTEX, NEW YORK

A note on my desk:

Wrong, Papa Palast!

I moved TWENTY-SIX times before graduating high school. I was five; my brother eight when my mom joined up.

I think my mother was the one who left my father, but it's a moot point; I don't want him to be vilified—it really isn't fair to him. I'm quite confident that the man has spent much of his life having his soul devoured by guilt.

You've said it about your own father: "He was wounded to the center of his soul . . . so I could do the work he could only watch from a distance." Your dad sold furniture, mine sold groceries.

Both my mom and dad have suffered enough for their sins and sins of others. And they have brought a lot that's good into this dark world. I thank them even if I don't tell them that I thank them.

You may want to make the point that I've now worked with you, ENDURED YOU and your crotchety ways, for nearly a fucking decade! I keep getting sucked further and further into your insane vortex . . .

And you—you cynical old SOB hiding under your fedora—you are WRONG! People will give a damn once I finish my novel and film. And I can't wait to prove that to you!

Neither can I.

CHAPTER 13
Vultures' Picnic

FBI HEADQUARTERS, WASHINGTON, DC

The FBI told us to come in. Jones and me.

It was a big-shot G-man and a top gun from the Department of Justice. You don't need their names and I'm not allowed to give them.

It was 2008. Jones and I had done a story about one of their bosses, Federal Prosecutor Tim Griffin. You wouldn't confuse Griffin with Elliot Ness the Untouchable, the gangbuster. Griffin had gotten his post as Prosecutor by running a secret "caging" operation out of the Republican National Committee. "Caging" is a way to throw out the ballots of legal voters. Griffin's op targeted the votes of soldiers of color, and the homeless living in shelters. Nice guy. Civil rights attorney Robert F. Kennedy Jr. looked over the evidence for us and said, "What [Griffin] did was absolutely illegal and he should be in jail. So should Karl Rove."

Rove was Griffin's boss at the time. Rove wasn't in jail. He was in the White House as Senior Counsel to the President of the United States. He was known as "Bush's Brain." He made sure Griffin was made United States Attorney for Arkansas: What better way to cover up an alleged crime than to do it wearing a badge? I say "alleged" crime because there's been no prosecution.

Griffin, a real schlemiel on a computer, had sent caging lists and evidence of the Republic National Committee plan to fix the vote in the 2004 election to campaign chiefs at GeorgeWBush.com and GeorgeWBush.org. That was

Tim's big mistake: The "dot-org" address was, in fact, an e-trap set by my bud John Wooden, who passed the smoking guns on to me.*

Politically, Griffin was Rove's little go-fer, which should have made him invulnerable. But the Bush crew dumped him when we exposed his caging game on BBC. Griffin called a press conference the next morning. He complained, he cried, and he turned in his badge. Here's a hanky, Tim. I should say "Congressman Tim." The Honorable Tim Griffin was elected to Congress in November 2010 (Rove wasn't going to let them keep his boy down).

So, here at Justice, Griffin's old department in the FBI building, I didn't expect a lot of love. They put us in a small windowless room, dark as an overpriced restaurant. The FBI and DOJ, they told us, wanted Jones and me to turn over our info on one Michael Francis Sheehan.

Goldfinger! Wake me from this dream! George W. Bush was suddenly concerned about bribery. And you, cynical reader, thought Bush put Justice in a coma. I felt like Elvis must have felt when he got that Bureau of Narcotics and Dangerous Drugs badge from Richard Nixon.

---

* To cover their tracks on the election steal, Rove and Griffin fired United States Attorney (Captain) David Iglesias, who then gave me some of the skinny on the scheme. A student at the University of Florida asked Senator John Kerry if the Senator had read the caging list story (he was holding up a copy of my book, *Armed Madhouse*). The answer came from local cops who shocked him with a Taser, despite his plea, "Don't Tase me, bro!" Senator Kerry did, indeed, dig into my "caging" evidence and then sponsored a bill to outlaw the practice. That's not surprising. If caging had been stopped in 2004, he'd be *President* Kerry. If you want to see the caging lists and get the whole story, click *here* on your interactive edition, or go to GregPalast.com/PalastInvestigates and to GregPalast.com/VulturesPicnic.com.

Here they were, the Feds going after a bad guy. Well, hot damn.

Goldfinger was the guy who lubricated the President of Zambia, the short autocrat whom Badpenny tracked to the Geneva boutique where he bought the elevated shoes.

The FBI wanted our evidence on what looked like Goldfinger's violation of the Foreign Corrupt Practices Act, that is, bribery. Jones and I don't give out sources, but we did pass them the goods we had already flashed on TV.

"Bribery" can be a bit slippery. We had that e-mail written by Sheehan/Goldfinger himself, that in return for a contribution to the Zambian President's "favorite charity," Sheehan's British Virgin Islands corporation would receive $15 million from the Zambian Treasury in payment for bonds worth less than $3 million.

Zambia would bleed, literally. The payment would come out of donations given to the dead-broke nation for AIDS medicine and education.

Can a "charity" contribution be a bribe? Sure smelled like it. Sure paid off like it. Just so we felt comfortable about tagging it an apparent payoff, we thought we'd ask experts: Sheehan's own law firm. It was a cheap trick but, given our budget, all our tricks are cheap. We went to the law offices of Greenberg Traurig in Washington. Goldfinger's offshore company had hired this hot-shot firm as lobbyists. He picked a good one. From the firm's swank offices and balcony, you looked straight across at the White House.

Greenberg Traurig not only looked onto the White House, it had a pipeline right to it. Most of it was legit. But one of the firm's top rainmakers, Jack Abramoff, had just been sent to prison for paying several million dollars cash to a Republican Congressman and others.

Not surprisingly, the firm also housed one of the nation's top bribery defense attorneys who represented some of the nation's biggest convicted bribers like Lockheed Corporation, now sworn to the straight path. On the deck overlooking the White House, I showed the Traurig partner the "charity" e-mail written by Goldfinger. But I didn't say it was written by his firm's own client. My bad.

The lawyer didn't use the word *bribery* but said that such a charitable contribution looked like "a violation of the law." "If" this were his client, he said, he'd be very worried. Jail time? "Hopefully not," said the counselor.

For the FBI, this would be a turkey shoot. Goldfinger would go down.

I'll have to call Congressman John Conyers and thank him. Conyers had heard our Vulture report on that Amy Goodman show, *Democracy Now!*

Immediately after the broadcast, the Congressmen went right to the White House and confronted Bush in the Oval Office. Conyers was then Chairman of the House Judiciary Committee and in the middle of drafting a subpoena for Rove and Griffin. Bush had no choice but to pretend he gave a shit about Conyers's concerns.

The President claimed not to know a thing about the debt vultures (a defense Bush used often with success). Conyers, a lawyer, wanted to know why the FBI wasn't on these birds. Bush mumbled some promises.

Now here we were with the FBI and Justice. They were telling us about their big plans for the bust.

While we waited for the FBI to make the arrest, a British court ruled that Goldfinger/Sheehan was "deliberately evasive and even dishonest," that he had "deliberately" given "false evidence." Still, the UK court gave him his pound of flesh and then some. Seeing no U.S. objection, the judge felt compelled to order Zambia to pay Sheehan's company $44 million, eleven times his $4 million "investment."

Zambia's new government arrested no-longer-President Chiluba and seized his shoes; but that's not enough to pay for the AIDS medicine lost to Michael Francis Sheehan.

President Bush had taken up the cause. He lunched with Bono, the eighties rocker with the *Star Trek* glasses, who then joined Bush in a press conference announcing hundreds of millions of U.S. tax dollars for debt relief for poor, poor nations.

The Vultures, circling overhead, must have been grinning. Unless the debt law is changed, the relief funds will, in the end, feed the predators. It was something else for Bush not to know about.

Jones and I waited for the G-men to make their move.

Then, on November 4, 2008, history was made. The United States elected Barack Obama. The new President had been sired by an ill-tempered shepherd from Africa turned Harvard professor who had abandoned the future leader Barack when he was just two years old. As President, Obama, during a visit to Europe, took the opportunity to buzz into the continent of his forefathers, using his few hours in sub-Sahara Africa to lecture its leaders about their corruption.

It doesn't take a graduate degree in psychology to see that the most powerful man on the planet had seized his moment for PAYBACK. And it must have been particularly satisfying for Obama that he could watch the entire continent cheer the tint of his skin (several African saloons are now named Obama) while he gave them the lashing his father much deserved. Obama jetted away in the smoke of Air Force One, abandoning Africa as quickly as his father had abandoned him.

The New York Times ate it up, jumping at the chance to repeat the stereotypical story about those crazy, corrupt Africans. The *Times* even regurgitated our BBC story of Zambia's President's shoe-shopping spree in Geneva. But the *Times* left out the core of our report: The elevator shoes were paid for with bribes like the *shopka* the dinky dictator Chiluba picked up from Goldfinger.

Africa is way too poor to bribe itself. So, Mr. Obama, who is doing the corrupting? Bribes are one of the few things still Made in the USA. Bribery is also a major export product of Britain, Switzerland, Germany, and France.

"No person wants to live in a society where the rule of law gives way to the rule of brutality and bribery," Obama admonished. You're absolutely right, Mr. President—too bad the Constitution requires you to live in the United States.

Today, I can report that Michael "Goldfinger" Sheehan is not in prison. Well, at least he's not in Congress. Yet.

PARK AVENUE, NEW YORK

The ex-Mrs. Steven Cohen had the shit on The Sack all right—names, dates, documents about the grandee of SAC Capital, billionaire arbitrageur—and wanted me to help her hit the fan with the feces. The crime: insider trading.

"You'll get a Pulitzer Prize for this." Sure, lady. I've done a half dozen stories that deserved a Pulitzer or at least a night with Halle Berry. Unfortunately, all my "Pulitzer" stories ever earned me were two lawsuits, a dozen cranky editors, and enough money for a set of shoelaces to hang myself with.

I calculated: What the hell, *Vanity Fair* would pay $4 a word for this: a story of billions, blondes, and stock-market buggery. Five-thousand words @$4/wd = $20K.

"Start from the beginning. Spell the names."

Wife #1, Patrician Cohen, walked me through the shoots and ladders of ex-hubby's first miracle stock-market success. The Sack, then a small biter at some investment bank, she said, learned through his employer that General Electric was about to buy RCA. RCA's share price would go through the roof once the offer was announced. Through a cut-out, she said, The Sack purchased the RCA shares about to turn to gold.

Trading on inside info like that is a jail-time crime.

This was one hell of an accusation. It meant one of two things. One, Steven Cohen, hot-shot billionaire hedge-fund maven, is nothing but a felon, like some crack-head who holds up a 7-Eleven except that the amount of money involved is like holding up two thousand 7-Elevens. Or, two, Steven Cohen can see into the future and Patricia was a con artist of exceptional talent.

The Sack was disturbed for weeks, she said, acting like a crazy-man. Until, finally, she made him confess. "Is it worth it to do it?" she said, hoping to talk him into telling the truth to his boss.

He looked at her. "Is *nine million* worth it?"

I took more notes. Sack and Mrs. Sack split after that, before she knew he was on his way from millions to billions. She had folded on a winning hand. And now she was furious and ready to smear the man who made so much money he could be called a "philanthropist."

Mrs. Cohen (Patricia keeps his name to haunt him) divorced The Sack and his "money makes the monkey jump" mommy. Mr. Cohen then found a nice Bronx girl on an online dating service who is now spending his billions and having her photo taken by Annie Leibovitz.

Apparently the new Mrs. Cohen doesn't mind a little sobbing after dinners with Mom nor little pudgy hands on a little pudgy guy. Maybe she doesn't notice. "It's amazing how tall he is," my bud Donna Litowitz says, "when he's standing on his money."

I got up from the kitchen table, thanked ex-Cohen for the astonishing information, promised to follow up, and promised myself I wouldn't.

I'd regret that. But what *don't* I regret?

Someone else could have this Pulitzer. The Sack has more lawyers than his shark has teeth (Cohen owns a shark). I calculated: Once his attorneys finish with my carcass, and the political heavies have leaned on my editors, I'd have blown six months of my life and life's savings and I'd end up with a story locked in the magazine's legal department, just a little jar of shredded galleys.

And all because Mrs. Cohen just wanted a hammer to chisel off a bit of those billions *she deserved*. Let's see: 1 percent of six billion is sixty million, I calculated: Once she had that, once The Sack gave her one last golden kiss, she would deny everything she told me; she'd stand by her man; and I'd be standing there holding my *putz* and looking for shelter.

Momma Cohen was right. Money makes the monkey jump. And I wasn't going to be Patty's monkey.

* * *

Then, on May 7, 2011, Badpenny shoots me a wire headline,

SAC'S 'COHEN ACCOUNT' EXAMINED BY U.S. IN INSIDER TRADING PROBE

There goes my Pulitzer.

The billionaire arbitrageur/philanthropist/mamma's-boy is in hot water. Or maybe not. I read the story again, then hurriedly got a copy of ex–Mrs. Cohen's lawsuit (you expected that one).

Hmm. It seems that Patricia's story had gone through the laundromat. According to her attorney, the ex-Mrs. heard *nothing* across that pillow that she could understand. It was fancy arb-y talk, way over her blond little head.

Her official statement was well-crafted to make herself as innocent as a long-legged nun and make The Sack a *ganiff,* a crook.

Think about it: Patricia likely spent her share of the $9 million that was gained from the alleged insider trade on RCA. And if you believe her story, she knew damn well how The Sack got it. And remember, when he said, "Is nine million worth it," she must have nodded *yes!!*

In other words, from what she told me herself, she was a *co-conspirator,* not a whistleblower. The smoking gun she had shown me had her fingerprints on it as well as his.

Patricia must have realized at some point that $9 million was *not* worth it, but a share of Sack's $7 billion certainly was.

The issue for me is not whether The Sack trades on inside information, though that would not be nice. The problem is that he "trades" at all.

What I mean is, there is no such thing as a victimless billionaire. Cohen is Thales cornering the (olive) oil market. What Sack gets praised for was a crime when I was an economics schoolboy. Still should be.

Economics is called "The Dismal Science." Do you know why? There's only so much stuff in this world. It gets divided up. Thug and Ug, remember?

The Chairman of Goldman Sachs was called "farsighted" and "brilliant" for unloading his bank's sub-prime mortgage securities before they were exposed as cow pie. But his brilliant sales means that some fireman in Alabama loses his job because the state just lost a bundle on Goldman's toxic securities. It means a train driver in Switzerland dependent on his railroad retirement fund sees his monthly pension turn from steak to hot dogs.

Don't complain about the rich eating your slice of the pie, says Thomas Friedman. Just grow a bigger pie. Pies don't grow, they get devoured. Eat or be eaten. The Dismalest Science.

But the billionaire boys club has better things to do with your money than you do, I suppose. In 2006, Steven Cohen needed a new shark. He bought a dead one in a fish tank from a middling British artist and paid $6 million for it. Then the shark began to get . . . fishy. It wasn't properly preserved, so the artist told The Sack he had to put in a new dead shark. That cost well over $100,000, an "inconsequential" sum, said Cohen.

"I like the fear factor," says the roly-poly little man. Grrrr, says Patricia.

Adam Smith and Karl Marx agreed on one fact: All value is created by labor. Value is created by Mr. Mamonov making shoes in Sangachal, farmers making pumpkins for Halloween, and economists making more economists in classrooms. If nobody makes it, it has NO value. That's the law carved into the Ten Commandments of Economics. Therefore, when you hear some New York "arb" makes a billion bucks by "researching" the future movements of a stock, a hundred thousand poor schmucks not in on the game lost that billion, sold their stock too cheaply to The Sack.

Creating new financial products does not create something of value, economically speaking. When new financial products are spun out of thin air, then sold to marks like us, the value we've created is boosted, hijacked, removed, and buys the shark. If you pocket a twenty from a cash register, it's a crime. Pocket $2 billion by snaking a pension fund into buying bottle caps they think are diamonds, it's "arbitrage."

Remember your Adam Smith, "Beware the man who reaps what he does not sow."

(Good advice, Adam, I should have passed it to Patricia. A judge threw her, her lawsuit, and her monkey down the courthouse steps, dismissed.)

Though maybe there *is* a way to create value without (too much) labor. I think I could convince the folks in Terminal Town that for $6 million they all draw straws and stuff the loser into a fish tank and sell it to The Sack.

*   *   *

Anyway, I couldn't stop my real work to investigate The Sack family's dysfunction nor worry about whether Cohen could pull off an arbitrage between his wives. I couldn't because the Vulture, Dr. Hermann was lurking out there—unless Hermann was still cowering under his desk with the other millionaires at FH International. And because Hamsah, whatever that is, *whoever* that is, was holding a knife to Liberia's throat.

Badpenny has just asked me to explain how some guy hiding in the dark under his desk could "own" the debt of an African nation. In this case, Hermann purchased the right to collect a debt supposedly owed by Liberia to Chemical Bank, later a unit of JP Morgan. It was then left to Vulture Hermann and his lawyer Straus, as repo men, to get the money from Liberia by any means possible, as long as they did it in a way that did not visibly connect back to the Morgan Bank. (Morgan had signed an international pledge never to turn over debt to Vulture funds.)

So then why would a trillion-dollar banking colossus like Morgan bring in knuckle-draggers like Straus to break Liberia's bones over a couple of shekels? Answer: for the same reason Morgan units foreclose on worthless homes in Detroit. First, a few bucks is always better than no bucks. And second, to make a visible and bloody example: When you don't pay up, we'll stick the raptors on you. And on your kids and on your grandma.

MIDTOWN, MANHATTAN

There is a bigger game being played here, the political protection of the Vulture system, and I wanted to get to the Big Bird behind it. Dr. Hermann, despite his Coliseum-size home, and Goldfinger with his mag wheels, are relatively small biters. Deadly, yes, to weak nations like Liberia and Zambia, but mere chicks compared to the Über-Vulture, the granddaddy of the flock, Paul Singer.

Jesus may have turned water into wine, but Singer can turn shit into silver. For instance, in the midst of the Congo's civil wars, Singer picked up bonds with a face value printed on them of $100 million. He paid, reportedly, about $10 million for them but now has a judgment to collect $400 million from the Congo. Not bad for a $10 million flutter.

Vultures don't feed only on hungry Africans. Indeed, Singer's first big score was his hit on America's asbestos victims. The executives of a few companies, WR Grace, USG, and Owens Corning, knew that their asbestos manufacturing plants were killing their workers, but didn't bother to tell them. When caught and sued, the companies filed for bankruptcy, agreeing to pay all they could to those dying and injured by their asbestos.

But Singer had a better idea. Grace, USG, and Owens Corning, as you can imagine, were worth next to nothing, and Singer bought Corning for a song. Simply by cutting the amount paid to the victims, he could boost the company's value.

You don't want to die from asbestosis. Your lungs turn to mush and you suffocate, slowly. A campaign was begun attacking the dying workers. They were faking it. One attacker was a guy named George W. Bush. In January 2005, the President held a televised meeting with an "expert" who said over half a million workers suing were liars. If workers couldn't breath, it wasn't the fault of asbestos. The "expert" was not a doctor, but notably, his "research" was partly funded by Paul Singer. And so was Bush. Since the death of Enron's Ken Lay, Singer and his hedge fund crew at Elliott International have become the top contributors to the Republican National Committee. It's hard to measure their largesse exactly, because some of that help comes in through the side door. For example, in 2004, Singer put money behind the "Swift Boat" smear on Bush's opponent for the presidency, John Kerry.

The legal, political, and PR attacks on the dying workers chiseled away the compensation expected to be paid by the asbestos companies, boosting the firms' net worth. Singer then flipped Corning, selling it for a neat billion-dollar profit.

It's legal, it's brilliant, it's sick, it's Singer.

That's why Congressman Conyers didn't believe that President Bush knew nothing about the Vultures. Even if Bush didn't remember Singer's business, the President could hardly have forgotten the name of his party's Number One sugar daddy, the man who floated Bush into the White House on the swift boat.

So I thought I'd talk with Singer about his Congo jackpot—and what he might know about his former lawyer: Michael Straus Vulture Hermann's secret partner. Camera in hand, Ricardo and I walked through midtown Manhattan looking for a thirty-four-story building with a skull and crossbones on it. We located Singer's headquarters, but we didn't find a Dead Man's Chest guarded by a guy with an eye patch. Instead, we found George Gershwin, that is, a Gershwin look-alike in tuxedo tails, playing *Rhapsody in Blue* on a grand piano in the lobby of the office tower housing Elliott International, roost of the Vulture-in-Chief.

More than a decade ago, Straus, smelling a bird of his own feather, approached Singer with an idea: Buy up some bonds from the impoverished nation of Peru; buy dirt cheap, then sue for the "face" value. The prize: a 1,000 percent profit.

There was only one problem with Straus's method. It was against the law. The law is called "champerty." In New York, as in all states, you can't buy stuff for the sole purpose of filing a lawsuit. For example, you can't buy a wrecked car for $100 and then sue for $10,000, claiming, "Hey, this car is a wreck!"

Singer took Straus under his dark wing. They bought Peru's junk bonds and sued. A judge ruled "champerty" and threw Singer's suit in the garbage can, but an appeals court backed Straus and Singer.

Legal ping-pong can drag on for decades. But Singer got lucky. Peru's President decided it might be prudent to flee his country. Something about murder charges on the way. President Alberto Fujimori's cover for escape would be an official state visit to Japan, using the presidential plane.

That's when Singer, the billionaire repo-man, struck, and seized Peru's equivalent of Air Force One. Champerty, shamperty—Fujimori had to *get the hell out*. Peru's stunned U.S. lawyer told me that the President ordered Peru's treasury to pay everything Singer asked for ($58 million). Then the fugitive Fujimori, the locks off the wheels of his getaway vehicle, high-tailed it to Japan and renounced his citizenship in the country in which he remained, oddly, President.

So Singer still soars. What next? What does a man want who already has everything, or eaten everyone?

Congress. Gift-wrapped.

The day Congress passed Obama's weak but good-intentioned law to return some semblance of reason to the finance markets, Singer invited the Republicans who voted against it to come by his Central Park West apartment for some coffee, tea, and a million dollars that passed to them. Campaign contributions. Legal. Of course it is: The recipients of the million wrote the law that made it legal.

Singer, a generous man, had lent his own jet to Rudy Giuliani for Rudy's run for President.

But it's lonely at the top, atop the pile of carcasses. So Singer invited two other billionaires to join his picnic: Steve Schwartzman, the speculator known as Mr. Blackrock (after his "hedge" fund)—and The Sack.

The three together—Singer, Schwartzman, and Cohen—have agreed to make the Republican monkey jump, to fund a fearsome cash battleship to prevent the return of the rule of law to their finance playing field. They understand quite well that regulation is the expression of democracy in the marketplace. So, Singer is taking democracy head-on. Singer funded a referendum to change the way California allocates the nation's biggest pile of electoral votes for President.

Let's admit it: These guys are good at what they do. To us.

There is one instance in which the Elliott International corporate mask dropped from Singer's face, when a victim of cruel prejudice sat down to dinner with him. His son. His son wanted to get married—to another man. Suddenly, Singer's heart and checkbook opened to every gay rights political action campaign in the United States. It's just too bad that his son didn't fall in love with a sickly boy from the Congo with asbestos.

I had a lot of questions for Mr. Singer, but his gendarmes stopped us at the door. Even Gershwin looked at us with menace. I called up to his PR flack, who told me I could meet with Mr. Singer "never."

"Never ever?"

"Never *ever*."

I called Jones at BBC London. He had a new lead inside Elliott International. Singer didn't know it yet, but never ever is shorter than he thinks.

PARK AVENUE, DOWNTOWN, NEW YORK

Not quite raining. New York City just wet enough to be greasy, just red tail-lights and some depressed cop ready to shoot a Puerto Rican kid. "I thought he had a gun." That kind of day.

Singer won't talk but a buddy of his will. I'm not up for this. Maybe it was the second Presidente last night before I went to sleep. Or maybe the fourth at 4 A.M. when I couldn't sleep. I'm not a drinker anymore, but I'll have a few drinks now and . . . whatever. You don't care. *Sólo mi mamá llora para mí.*

On Park Avenue, the cabs whip by, carrying our betters and splashing us with gutter slop. So Ricardo and I hoof it to the grim stone building housing Greylock Capital. The name is not exactly a ray of sunshine.

Greylock's principal is Hans Humes. Hans has a surfboard in his office. Hans is way cool. There are photos of his Peace Corps buddies on the wall. There's a letter from a priest from a slum in Ecuador thanking him for helping the little people there to get pipes for water.

For the interview, Hans has put on a ripped sweater from a flea market. Brilliant: He knows exactly how to jack the camera image of a millionaire hedge fund speculator.

Rick is getting all this camouflage on the Digicam and whispers, "He's still a Vulture."

Actually, Ricardo's wrong. It takes more than feathers—collecting on the debts of busted nations—to make a predator. Doesn't matter. I don't care if Hans is Saint Francis or lower than a spider's testicles. He has information on Hermann and Straus and I think I can nudge him to wade into the dangerous waters of ratting on his compadres and sometime rivals.

It doesn't start so well. The remnants of the Presidente led me to bring up Presidente Correa—who, I'd forgotten, had checkmated Greylock on its Ecuador bonds. However, Hans admits to a kind of admiration for Correa's brilliant cheating in his nation's public interest.

Greylock has a market niche: The Nice Vultures. Instead of holding up a nation for big ransom, Hans holds up nations like Nicaragua or Liberia for *small* ransom. In fact, he has lots of friends in Liberia because he facilitates deals to let the poorest countries settle debts cheaply. He'll buy debts for a penny on the dollar. Liberia's bonds he found in a forgotten box in a bank's storage room.

Mr. Nice Vulture had worked a deal for Liberia. He took his box of old, dusty, forgotten Liberia bonds and offered them up on the cheap to the government: only three cents on the dollar (which would still leave a fat profit for Greylock). But Liberia couldn't afford a meat loaf sandwich, let alone 3 percent of the face value of all its old debts. However, the World Bank, IMF, and donor nations—in this case, Norway, Switzerland, Britain, and the United States—agreed to pay the small sum on Liberia's behalf, but on one condition: *Every* bondholder, everyone owed money by Liberia, must agree to take the same terms. If Nice Vulture got 3 percent, everyone had to take 3 percent.

And everyone else did. Almost.

Here's where the story turns sick and sad. (I'll have to finish this tale of Liberia's debt from what I can piece together from documents and the words of Hans and two more insiders, plus others spread over three continents. I would have liked to get the viewpoint of Dr. Hermann, but he'd gone into hiding, or skiing, or both.)

In 2007, all Liberia's debt holders met in New York. That included French banks, Mr. Nice Vulture, Dr. Hermann, Straus, and others. The United States, Britain, Norway, and Switzerland cut the deal behind closed doors and wrote checks for everyone at 3.1 percent of the amount "owed" by Liberia. (I put "owed" in quotation marks because in some cases Liberia never saw the money.)

Nice Vulture and everyone else mailed in their bonds and took their 3.1 percent—except Straus. Some of Straus's bonds were missing. He'd *sold* a big stack of them. These bonds were now in the hands of the Evil Eye in an open hand: Hamsah.

Straus didn't have Hamsah's phone number, didn't know how to find them. Sorry.

This was a real crisis—for the donor nations, and the nice-guy speculators who were willing to take the 3 percent and run, but especially for Liberia. Hamsah could now foreclose on its bonds, $26 million worth, and legally seize anything donated to or invested in the struggling nation.

Hamsah could name its price. Hamsah had no address, but it did have lawyers, and they had the price: *fifty times* what everyone else accepted.

Notably, this was the same trick Straus, as Singer's lawyer, had pulled on Peru years earlier. In Peru, it was creepy, smart but creepy. This was creepier.

Why? Answer: inside information. All the debt holders had gone into the negotiating room on the condition they would put up all their bonds, not to sue, and not to trade on the information learned in the negotiations. Straus walked in knowing something none of the others knew: The bonds held by

Hamsah were missing from the deal. If—and I emphasize *if*—Straus had prof-
ited from that, then he had scammed his fellow bondholders into giving up
their claims cheap, getting their competing claims out of the way.

Hamsah now held Liberia hostage: As the last standing creditor, everything
the country had was theirs. And the millions of dollars paid out by the taxpayers of the United States and Britain to help Liberia's poor went for nothing: The
donor governments would now have to put up a pile more to pay off Hamsah.

Mr. Nice Vulture had let me in on the game because he thought I could
find out if Straus kept a connection with Hamsah; or, if he *is* Hamsah. If Hamsah is in fact the hand of Straus, he'd suckered Greylock and every other holder
into taking short money.

And the ultimate suckers? The people of the United States and Europe
who had responded to the heart-grabbing pleas of Bono and Nelson Mandela
to pay off the murderous debt burden crushing Africans. Instead, the budgets
for "debt relief" would be snatched by this hand called Hamsah.

But what the heck does this have to do with Dr. Hermann? Hermann, said
Hans, was a good guy, no Vulture at all. Oddly, though, Hermann seemed to
defend the creep Straus, taking Straus's side on details of the division of the
spoils. That led Hans to ask Dr. Hermann—twice—whether Hermann had some
deal with Straus. Hermann said, "No!" And Nice took Hermann at his word.
Now, when a gentleman gives his word of honor—twice—I assume that it's a
complete load of horseshit. Gentlemen and their honorable words have started
more wars, killed more Jews and Serbs and Africans, stolen more Indian land,
and turned more little girls into sex slaves than your average mercenary.

Matty Pass deftly procured paperwork showing Straus had acted as Hermann's
lawyer in suing Liberia during the nation's civil war. That didn't smell nice,
but BBC lawyers said that Straus being Hermann's lawyer did not make him
Hermann's partner.

Then I remembered the hand-to-hand combat between me and Badpenny
and Felipe II. Through the cloudy memory of my bloody lip, my booze, and
my extreme pain, I remembered her saying that she'd found the connection
between Straus and Dr. Hermann: a hedge fund called Montreux.

Badpenny was fanatic, fevered over finding this connection. The investigatrix went through every SEC filing in the history of Montreux Capital. The
task is inhuman, brain freezing. This is what she was trying to show her hungover boss at five A.M., this document here.

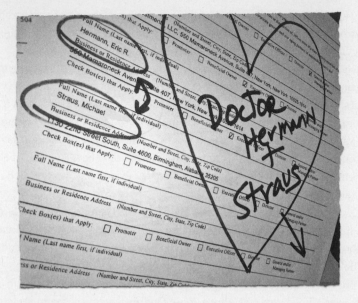

Here was proof: For more than a decade, Straus's partner in Montreux was the upright Dr. Eric Hermann.

When we told Hans what we'd found, he freaked out. He'd been had, snaked, bamboozled, fleeced, greased, then taken to the cleaners. For millions. That's when he told me, "It looks like Eric's gone over to the Dark Side."

A COURTROOM IN LONDON

Dr. Hermann does not want to be known as a Vulture. The Hollywood luvvies would toss him right out of the Sundance Film Festival soirées. But the Doctor wants to have it both ways: to eat carrion with the speculators and drink wine with the stars. So his game is subtle and, like all marathon runners, he is patient. The ownership of the Liberia debt, the right to seize Liberia's assets, was obscured in a crazy maze of transactions, passed back and forth between companies named Red Barn, Montrose, Red Mountain, and Wall Capital in a head-spinning dance before it ended up with Hamsah.

Hamsah's lawyers swore to a British court that they have no idea who or what Hamsah is, but they were instructed to rip out Liberia's heart unless Hamsah got its pound of flesh, 5,000 percent more than the sum accepted by other creditors.

This was no joke. Liberia was barely breathing. A mad civil war had killed a tenth of the population. Now, with the war over, after its first democratic election, Liberia was hoping to feed itself again. However, no one could give Liberia a dime, invest a penny, because Hamsah had the right to seize it. They owned the country.

Once all the Liberian debt except Hamsah's was settled under the 3 percent deal, a British court ruled that Hamsah could get every dollar it demanded. But the court had delayed for a short time the right of this mysterious outfit to begin seizing Liberia's assets.

What if I could hunt down this eyeball-with-five-fingers company, and connect it back to inside info known to Straus and Hermann? If Hamsah had any connection back to Straus or Hermann, then Liberia could have Hamsah's claim voided by the British court because the transfer of bonds would have been fraudulent.

Jones was horrified at the cost to BBC's skimpy budget, but I knew Rick and I had to get to Africa immediately.

MONROVIA, LIBERIA

In 1980, after Colonel Sam Doe had all of Liberia's cabinet ministers tied to stakes and shot, his men mutilated and killed the President in his bedroom. That was pretty much it for a hundred years of Africa's oldest democracy.

Doe, half insane with power, named himself President. The incoming U.S. President, Ronald Reagan, *fully* insane with power, was overjoyed with the opportunity to have Doe, a self-declared ally of Reagan's in the war against Godless Communism, seize this Western edge of Africa. Reagan dumped millions of U.S. dollars for weapons on the new despot, Mr. Doe, whom Reagan called "Mr. Moe."

It didn't take long for other warlords to try to get a piece of the U.S. pie. as well as Liberias' gold mines. They formed Africa's first armies of children, some ordered to shoot their own parents.

In Monrovia, the lights went off, then the water was shut off—it would stay off for nearly a decade. In 1990, Prince Johnson named himself President, that is, he hacked up Doe into unappetizing pieces, all filmed for television. The nation fell into howling anarchy.

Then things turned bad.

Somewhere in darkest Massachusetts, a convicted embezzler, during a prison transfer, jumped from the armored van, shed his captors in the tangled rust jungle of the industrial wastes outside Boston, and made his way, by God knows what means, to Goma, Liberia, where in 1989, he too declared himself President.

The escapee, Charles Taylor, is another psychopathic killer, a con man and a credentialed economist, an all-too-frequent combination. Taylor had studied Liberia for his thesis at Bentley University in Massachusetts, so he knew that to make good his rise to high office he would need lots of drugs, diamonds, guns, child soldiers, and the help of someone as profoundly disturbed as himself. And for that purpose, the Good Lord made Jimmy Carter.

Carter's endorsement of Taylor's "candidacy" was crucial to the ultimate success of Taylor's homicidal campaign, which was notable for its winning slogan, "He killed my ma, he killed my pa. I'm voting for Charles Taylor!"

In 1993, Deputy Secretary-General of the United Nations Winston Tubman, for God knows what reason, asked me to help sell the U.S. State Department on a plan to save the bleeding nation where he was born. My assistant Jim Ciment volunteered to go into Monrovia to get the story (which he did, from General Butt Naked). With Ciment's info, I pitched my plan to an Undersecretary of State: *"Liberia: A Success Waiting to Happen!"* I knew that the happy-talk-good-old-boy Clinton crew would prefer that to *"Liberia: A Totally Fucked-Up Hell That the USA Had Better Accept Some Responsibility For."*

Success would have to wait a decade for real elections and for Hamsah to release its creditor grip.

Diamonds were President Taylor's best friend and he allegedly fomented civil war in Sierra Leone to get some.

It's only fair to mention that President Taylor (from his current prison home) has sworn to the International Justice Tribunal that he never even held a diamond. Mia Farrow, however, testified in 2010 that he gave a pouch full of rough stones to supermodel Naomi Campbell, who, seeing just a bunch of dull rocks, gave them away. (There are others who think of Ms. Campbell as a dull rock who should be thrown away, but that's another matter.)

It was in 2002, in the middle of civil war madness, with a tenth of the citizen population dead or dying, that Messrs. Straus and Hermann sued the Liberian government in federal court in New York demanding millions for the junk bonds held by their hedge fund, Montreux. Of course, it's not clear there was a government in Liberia to sue. Straus and Hermann liked it that way.

Not surprisingly, neither the cannibals who had roamed the presidential palace (really) nor the escaped convict Taylor nor anyone else showed up in the New York court to defend Liberia. And so Hermann and Straus's Vulture fund, Montreux, won a big judgment by default.

It was Montreux's right to collect that judgment that somehow got from Straus's hands to Hamsah. A U.S. court might have given Liberia's new elected government a second trial, but Hamsah sued the nation in London, whose courts were notoriously welcoming to Vulture claims.

Hamsah: An All-Seeing Eye in a mystical hand. Who the hell would enjoy such a game of names and symbols? I'd say a Moriarty with a wide and classical education, who thinks much of their own mind's twists and bends. Notably, we could not locate Michael Straus because, it turns out, he was brushing up on his Latin at Oxford. He is already proficient in ancient Greek languages. A Renaissance Man, Straus was also the Chairman of the Andy Warhol Foundation. (It's a shame the Foundation was caught selling fake Warhols.)

Here's what we know: *Hamsah* = Arabic for "Five."

Investigation starts with speculation. Here's my shot:

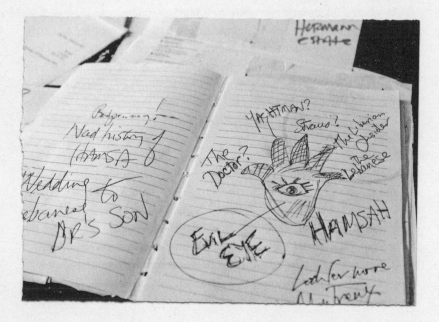

1. Thumb—Doctor Hermann
2. Ring finger—Landis
3. Middle Finger—Straus, the Singer man

Steven Landis is Hermann's stealthy partner. We were never able to find him. But we found his yacht slip. We drove by the marina and filmed Liberia's money floating there. (Does that fill me with resentment? Am I jealous, angry at the gross unfairness of a world in which a complete hyena like Landis has a big fat yacht while I have an old red Honda with BRAKE flashing at me, and fishermen in Liberia have dysentery and will die by forty-seven? *Yes.* Do I want to drop smart bombs on some poor Taliban loser in Tora Bora? *No.* Do I want a Predator missile to take out Landis's yacht? *You bet.* Does that make me a bad man? Do I care?)

4. Pinky Finger—The Liberian Insider

There's *always* an insider. Information and hidden influence is key in this game. Someone has to convince the President to pay the questionable bond, or tip off the Vultures to deals to be had.

So who could identify the Liberian insider sabotaging the nation? I discreetly put in a call to meet with Tubman, the UN man who originally sucked me into this Liberia maze. Erudite and formal, Tubman dined with me and Rick on kabobs and dolma in the well-appointed dining room of the only real hotel in Monrovia. He passed me a name of someone within the President's circle.

The best way to smoke out this insider would be to alert the President herself; maybe she could nail the Pinky Finger.

* * *

President Ellen Sirleaf-Johnson, the first woman ever elected head of state in Africa, greeted me at her modest home in the capital, wearing a colorful, simple African wrap and head scarf. She wore simple black slippers. Of course I checked.

I came to her home because her "Oval Office" had burnt down, although the fire station was just across the street. The country did not have enough money to put gas in the fire truck.

I told her of my suspicions about an insider revealing government confidences, the Evil Eye in Hamsah's palm, but she was too wise to let me know what she would do with the info. However, she asked me if she might make a personal plea, on camera, to the shadow called Hamsah. "Please! Have a heart," she said. *"Have a heart."*

Sure.

* * *

And Number Five? The forefinger?

Pointing to the kabobs, Ricardo said, "Lebanese."

The hotel is owned by a Lebanese. *All* the hotels are owned by Lebanese. There is nowhere in the entire nation where you can use a credit card. You must get cash from a Lebanese. In a nation simply blown to bits, all finance was handled by Lebanese who had their own independent cash transit system running back through Beirut.

In New York, Badpenny went to work on the hand with the Evil Eye. A Hamsah is a Kabbala symbol, the Hebraic benediction symbol you'd see at Jewish weddings, but also, Badpenny discovered, something you'd find at a Lebanese wedding. Then she snagged this: an old *New York Times* clip, a cute story about a Lebanese Maronite priest and a rabbi together conducting a wedding ceremony in Beverly Hills. The young lady, from a powerful Lebanese family, was marrying a Mr. Fredston-Hermann. As in "FH" International. The Doctor's son.

Time to head to London to find Straus and talk some straight Latin.

On the way to Monrovia's airport, Rick wanted to pick up "GVs," local atmosphere shots. Kids were all over the street, jerking around like kids. But with a difference: a missing leg, a missing arm. Lots of kids without four limbs.

So we stopped and I called over a kid selling chewing gum, missing his right arm. His name is Peter Tah. Peter, what happened to you? When? Who?

When the rebel come capture our community, they catch us and say, why don't you join us? At time I were nine years old.

No food, my family, everybody was crying, was starving.

So they give out the gun and how to use a gun, for training on the gun only two days and from that they took us on the front line.

And then when the rebels started shooting I was so confused, I knew nothing about gun, so confused. And they shot me in the arm.

So my little brother ran for me; came, pick me up, and brought me all the way back to the hospital. But the doctor say he couldn't fix my hand because there were no good treatment, no drugs, so they were forced to cut my arm. My whole arm.

Peter is fighting tears, so his little brother, Fan Foley, picked up the story. He was then eight years old.

After I brought to the hospital a lot of guy, even two our friend die in hospital, because there were no good treatment. . . .

Why did you join the warlord?

He said, if we did not join him, he would kill our father. So we were forced.

You saved your dad by joining the warlord's army?

They KILL him. They brought him outside and hack on him. And I'm trapped. And they wanted to kill me and my brother too.

It is my wicked duty as a reporter never to pay someone for an interview, a strangely righteous (and wonderfully budget-sensitive) rule in an industry of whores. But that's another matter. At the moment, here was Peter with his one arm and his one brother, and all their goods had been taken by the police because they were running an illegal street stand selling chewing gum. I had a plastic bag of this red Liberian currency on the car floor, worth toilet paper. But in this wounded city, that's not nothing. I handed Peter and his brother each a big fistful of the red currency and they beamed at me like it was Christmas.

I'm a prince.

* * *

So who are the real predators? And I don't mean the five-fingered hidden jackal, Hamsah.

I mean, *Qui bono?* Who really benefits from this system of mayhem and tragedy? Who turned Ecuador's riots, Azerbaijan's terror, Liberia's hunger into a profit center?

Vultures ate the carcass, but who made the killing?

Let's start with those kind nations that generously offered to pay off Liberia's vultures: Switzerland, Norway, Britain, and the United States.

Switzerland? I mentioned to Badpenny that the Swiss were doing something that really seemed selfless to me, paying off Liberia's debts. She gave me McEnroe's you-cannot-be-serious look. "The Swiss? *Selfless?*"

It turns out that, while Switzerland's biggest business is counting Other Peoples Money and hiding Nazi gold, the landlocked little nation owns four out of five of the world's deepwater drilling rigs, including the one at the bottom of the Gulf of Mexico owned by the Swiss firm Transocean.

Britain? As in British Petroleum. BP has learned that Americans get really, really upset about billion-gallon blow-outs. But in Liberia, no one can hear the screams.

Norway? Owner of Statoil, the world's number one deepwater oil driller.

You've guessed by now, Liberia had just discovered a big bunch of deep-sea oil.

USA? After the oil discovery, America's petro-President George W. Bush made an unusual visit to Liberia, where he samba'd with Mrs. Sirleaf (really). You could imagine the SS *Condoleeza Rice* right behind him, steaming across the Atlantic.

It's the old two-step. First, a country is crippled by super-state war games. Vultures race to the carcass. Step Two: The big "donor" nations offer themselves as saviors with loans—payable in crude.

The Vultures, therefore, are welcome scavengers to the oil elite, a critical part of the carnivorous food cycle of the Energy-Finance Combine, where debt collection arm-twisting and resource confiscation go hand in hand, claw in claw.

Think about it: What terms can Liberia demand of oil companies when it must beg them for a bit of gasoline for the nation's one fire truck?

And the winner is . . . Chevron Corp. Announced by President Sirleaf in November 2010.

Score? Energy-Finance Combine: 1. Liberia: 0.

LONDON

And then: it was over. Liberia . . . won.

On the night of February 25, 2010, BBC televised our story. There was Dr. Hermann's snowy lair, the office sign ripped off his building wall, the millionaire speculators hiding behind the door, President Sirleaf's plea and the wounded children.

The public wretched and roared. And the very next day, Parliament voted to bar Vultures from collecting their pound of flesh in British courts. Hamsah's court order for $26 million was now worthless.

I admit, I don't expect happy endings. I don't expect anyone to *watch* my reports, let alone change the law, especially change the law to prevent millionaires from making more millions.

This is a terrible test of my cynicism.

* * *

Badpenny and Jones want to kick my ass. "We've just saved a goddamn African nation and you're *unhappy*."

"Saved"? Liberia doesn't look "saved" to me. Has Peter Tah been saved?

And besides, I'm not "unhappy." I'm grumpy. Stopping Hamsah's Vulture act on Liberia was a Good Thing. But it was a little like winning a date with a beauty queen who turns out to be your cousin. It's just not fulfilling.

Because they're still out there, whoever "they" are. I was writing a book about finding the Hamsah, the Five. And I know less about Hamsah now than the day we started. Kind of a bust, no?

The only fact I feel confident about is that Lukasz, the wannabe journalist and computer hijacker, now has his own news broadcast in Poland.

In detective stories, the clues are supposed to come together in the final chapter with a *ta-DAH!* The butler did it in the library with the candlestick. The mobster was innocent because the crooked mayor had him set up to take the fall for the power company chief's girlfriend.

That's fine for pulp fiction, but what about pulp *non*-fiction? You'll close this book and I'll still be wondering if the Japanese diesel generators snapped before or after the tsunami, whether my network will pay me to find out, and whether Singer's lawyers will wait until after my son's bar mitzvah to ruin me financially. *Thanks for listening.**

Badpenny is not listening. While I'm singing "Palast Feeling Sorry for Himself," she's trying on her new Soda Effect-S black-strapped wedge platforms (FoureverFunky.com, $28) and I get a tent. She grins, "I can see your cock is a lot smarter than you are, Palast."

* You can keep track of the progress of these investigations by subscribing to our periodic updates at GregPalast.com.

CHAPTER 14
Lots of Fish

IN THE AIR, NEW YORK TO LONDON

Maybe BP will give me an explanation about the Baku blow-out. There's always an explanation.

Britain's *Dispatches* has broadcast my BP film on prime-time. It has everything: birds covered in black crap, herring gone, whales in a bad mood.

And, somewhere over the Atlantic, I realize, *I don't care about herring.*

I'm not even sure I care about raging oil plumes that drown fish. I mean, look down, it's a big ocean. There are a lot of fish.

I listened to myself say this and I thought, *You're either a terrible, terrible man, Palast, or a great philosopher.* I didn't know which and I wasn't quite sure it mattered.

But there's a story I still have to tell. Not about the fish, but about the fight.

I don't know if I like whales, but I know I like Etok. I like the way when his people were jerked around, he jerked back.

It was this realization that made me feel very lonely and very happy, a rare momentary burst of gratitude that the world had given me a quest, a vocation and fat targets, and a place on this planet where my job is to punch these guys in the face.

It was the job my father wanted, but quietly sacrificed his life to furniture, wounded to the center of his soul, so I could do the work he could only watch from a distance.

I think that even in Hell, there are some enchanted evenings. Satan hates it, but he can't stop it. The fires of damnation throw embers against the underside of Heaven and we, the condemned, believe we see the stars.

I have to quit here. I see no more to write that you don't know.

I thought this would be a book about oil and nuclear reactors and bad guys and dictators' boots on our backs. I'm not so sure anymore.

If, years from now, D-Man and Peanut ever read this, what have I told them?

I look around and I don't see a shortage of oil. I see a shortage of courage. I leaf back through these pages and it just hits me in the head that what I've written are biographies of the courageous.

Mirvari
Larry & Gail Evanoff
Inspector Lawn
Kadija and her dad
Caspian Man and Pig Man
Professors van Heerden and Steiner
Tundu Lissu
Jack Grynberg
Paul Kompkoff and Father Nichols
Chaim Ajzen
Chief Criollo
Steve Donziger
Lonigro
Etok
Party Blogger
President Correa
Victor Yannacone
PFC Manning
Frank Rosen

Embers against the ceiling of Hell.

Maybe I'll add *Gil Palast*.

My father thought you had to have a lion's heart and a steeled soul to face a world too terrible for words. He was wrong. Mirvari, van Heerden, all them, showed me you can face down a dragon *and* be a coward. Just don't let the dragon know.

IN THE WOODS

On August 8, 2011, President Obama approved Shell Oil's permit to drill in the Beaufort Sea off the shore of the Village of Kaktonic.

And now, it's my birthday. Linda called. A moonless eve, especially dark, came over the woods and other, older regrets also called.

At Steven Schwartzman's sixtieth birthday party, Rod Stewart sang "Happy Birthday." The Sack and Paul Singer and Donald Trump sang along. Blackrock's trophy wife, Christine Hearst, paid the aging rocker $1 million to sing it ($40,000 per note). Maybe it was love. Maybe it was fear that she'll end up like the previous four Mrs. Schwartzmans.

Life is choices. I suppose I fucked up when I gave away my interview with Goldman Sachs. I could have been invited to Blackrock's party. I could be feasting at the Vultures' picnic.

I can still go—as the food. I have a better idea. Jones called from Television Centre London. He's got the shit on FG Hemispheres, another Vulture. I'll have to fly to the Isle of Man, the tax haven in the middle of the English Channel, then the Congo.

Jones is making me hungry. I hear vulture tastes like chicken.

The twins and Badpenny have just surprised me right as I'm typing this. They're marching over here to this picnic table with a birthday cake burning enough candles to make it look like an oil well on fire. Rod Stewart hasn't shown up. I don't miss him.

THE ALPS

We carried Badpenny's mother's ashes in the back of the sedan almost to the border toward Milan, high up through the vapor-breathing ice. Her dad, the train driver, was behind the wheel, of course. A few prayers, a walk toward Roveredo's little chapel, but only as far as the curved bridge over a rivulet, covered with vines waiting for spring, a fairy tale grotto.

I asked Badpenny if she ever thought of getting married there? She said, yes.

To me?

Penny was cold, shivering even in the brilliant sun, silent.

It was just a technicality by now.

So this is the happy ending.

Is it? Are you happy? Am I? It's impossible for me to forget that deep underneath all our wedding cakes, BP still pumps satanic chemicals into the aquifers; a donkey-headed blogger is going mad in Baba's jail cell; the VLCC *Raven*, loaded by industrial vampires sucking at Mama Nature, still plies Arctic waters. And Chief Criollo's son won't ever come back, nor my father nor Linda. So, why continue? What for?

BUDAPEST, HUNGARY

For this.

When I was at Francis Polytechnic High in LA, we were required to take wood shop class. We took drafting. Drafting like in "blueprint drawing." We took metal shop. They made me make an ID bracelet out of an aluminum can. I wrote DAD on it because it was the shortest thing I could write.

If you went to Bevvie—Beverly Hills High—or Hollywood High or Pallie—Pacific Palisades—you didn't take metal shop. You took Advanced Placement French classes. We didn't have Advanced Placement French. We didn't have French anything. We weren't Placed and we didn't Advance.

We sat at those drafting tables with these triangular rulers so we could get jobs at Lockheed as draftsmen drawing blueprints of fighter jets. Or do tool-and-dye cutting for refrigerator handle presses at the General Motors plant where they assembled Chevys and Frigidaire fridges.

But we weren't going to fly the fighter jets. Somewhere at Phillips Andover Academy, a dumbbell drunk was going to go to Yale and then fly our fighter jets over Texas. We weren't going to Yale. We were going to Vietnam.

In the meantime, we scratched away with our pencils and the triangle rulers and learned about tool-and-dye making so we could get union scale at GM. Vietnam, GM plant. That was their plan for us.

What we didn't know was that the Chevy plant would close. We didn't know and we didn't care. We just wanted to see Christie Hernandez's panties.

Christie wore short, short dresses and so did Rikki Gross, and sitting between the two of them I nearly flunked Spanish class. But then I took Christie up to the platform under the HOLLYWOOD sign and she let me touch her.

I thought I had touched the face of God. But God had his face turned away. He was smiling on some nitwit from Texas with an oil well for a daddy. God used the guys from the Poly High drafting class to wipe His ass.

I shouldn't be ungrateful. I didn't go to 'Nam. I didn't have to work on the Chevy line and spend my paycheck at the stripper club across the railroad tracks from the plant. And thank God I didn't get Christie pregnant. Not that I got closer than groping some thin white cloth.

I'm writing this from the Presidential Suite at a five-star hotel in Budapest. (Why? I'm sure I'll find out soon enough.) This is where I began: down the road, where my Hungarian grandma, on my mother's side, was born. But I don't know a word of Hungarian. So some things worked out OK.

Maybe Christie is dead; maybe Louie Hernandez died in Vietnam in my place. Maybe they turned their backs on those rail tracks that sent the Chevy tool-and-dye equipment to Mexico after NAFTA was signed. Maybe they're Republicans in a Las Vegas suburb, grateful they are watched over by the Department of Homeland Security.

God wipes and flushes. And we're gone.

There is nothing new under the sun. But I'm going to write about it anyway.

Mudqnò.

CONTACT THE PALAST INVESTIGATIVE TEAM

THE FAT LADY HASN'T SUNG . . .

Vultures' Picnic isn't over yet.

Sign up right now at GregPalast.com to follow Matty Pass, Jones, Greg Palast, Ms. Badpenny and the investigations team as we continue our hunt for The Hamsah, nuclear industry insiders, and BP's next blowout.

And follow us on facebook.com/gregpalast.

For more inside documents and videos from the investigations, go to VulturesPicnic.com, updated continuously.

IF YOU KNOW WHO MURDERED JAKE . . .
OR HAVE A DOCUMENT MARKED "CONFIDENTIAL."

Don't shred it! Send it to us at the Palast Investigative Fund. Caspian Man, Pig Man, and the Chief of Intelligence of the Free Arctic Republic were all readers of our reports who became our sources. We really do need your eyes, your ears, your secrets. *www.GregPalast.com/contact*

Our investigations for BBC and *Democracy Now!* are supported by the not-for-profit Palast Investigative Fund, a 501(c)(3) charitable trust funded by our readers and viewers. *www.PalastInvestigativeFund.com*

NEW FROM GREG PALAST
WITH A FREE COLOR COMIC BOOK BY TED RALL
TALES FROM THE CRYPT OF DEMOCRACY
HERE'S HOW THE BASTARDS COULD STEAL THE ELECTION.
AVAILABLE SEPT 18th, 2012
EVERYWHERE BOOKS AND COMICS ARE SOLD
AND FROM
SEVENSTORIES.COM
FULL COLOR ART AVAILABLE
IN THE E-BOOK VERSION ONLY.
TO FIND OUT MORE ABOUT THE CAMPAIGN
TO BEAT THE BALLOT BANDITS, GO TO
Ballotbandits.org
BILLIONAIRES & BALLOT BANDITS
HOW TO STEAL AN ELECTION IN 9 EASY STEPS
CLOSED
BOARD OF ELECTIONS
LIVE
GREG PALAST
INVESTIGATES THE KOCH GANG, KARL ROVE, AND THEIR BUCK-BUDDIES
WITH COMICS BY TED RALL
INTRODUCTION BY ROBERT F. KENNEDY, JR.
SEVEN STORIES

READ, LISTEN, INTERACT . . .

Vultures' Picnic **Interactive**

» The video-enhanced edition is available for download and includes documents you're not supposed to see.

Armed Madhouse

» Sordid secrets and strange tales of a White House gone wild
» From Iraq to New Orleans, the *New York Times* bestseller *(Penguin 2007)*

"*Armed Madhouse* is great fun. Palast, detective style, provides . . . pieces of the secret puzzle." —*The New Yorker*

The Best Democracy Money Can Buy

» The international bestseller *(Penguin 2004)*

"Up there with Woodward and Bernstein." —*The Guardian*

Steal Back Your Vote **by Greg Palast & Robert F. Kennedy Jr.**

» The comic book of the *Rolling Stone* and *Guardian* reports, illustrated by Ted Rall with Lloyd Dangle *(Top Shelf 2008)*

Regulation and Democracy

» With Jerrold Oppenheim and Theo MacGregor, the original United Nations Guide to Regulation of Public Services *(Pluto 2002)*

The Joker's Wild

» A wicked little pack of Tarot cards, illustrated by Richard Grossman *(Seven Stories 2007)*

Vultures' Picnic

An Investigative Comic Book Series

by Darick Robertson and Greg Palast

WATCH THIS . . .

Vultures' Picnic: The Film

This is pulp non-fiction, the investigation live as it happened from Africa to the Arctic to the Back Alleys of Baku. The video companion for the book.

The Original Investigative Reports for BBC and *Democracy Now!*

» *Palast Investigates: From 8-Mile to the Amazon*
» *Big Easy to Big Empty: The Untold Story of the Drowning of New Orleans*
» *The Assassination of Hugo Chavez*
» *Bush Family Fortunes: The Best Democracy Money Could Buy*
   (BBC documentary)
» *The Elections Files: The Theft of 2008*

"Greg Palast is Jack Kerouac meets Seymour Hersh."   —BuzzFlash.com

"Twisted and maniacal!"   —Katherine Harris

ACKNOWLEDGMENTS

Greg
allyn
Palast

Thank You!

I didn't write this book. I just wrote it down. This work, like all my work, is the creation of folks with more soul and dedication than I can muster even sober. They include my sources, too many who'd be endangered if I named them, though most are in danger anyway.

This work is dedicated first to The Two-Thousand: the donors to the Palast Investigative Fund. It's because of you that I'm not picking cotton on Mr. Murdoch's plantation: You allow us to hunt for news, not dollars. And I would thank our corporate sponsors: but there are none, and that's plenty.

My gratitude cannot be measured for those who pull the oars in the dark hold of the Palast Investigations galley ship, who get the unpaid overtime while I get the credit: Matthew "Matty Pass" Pascarella, who must promise to write my obituary with more forgiveness than I deserve. Donald Roberts, whose *other* real name is Zach ZD Roberts, intrepid investigative photo journalist; Richard "Rickie Ricardo" Rowley, whose camera invented cinema Semtex, and his Big Noise Film compadres, Jacquie Soohen and David Rowley. Kat L'Estrange, bodyguard and operations maven: no, your resignation is not accepted; The Blonde Alligator, detective and co-writer Lenora Stewart, who says, "It's not worth saving people who don't want to be saved." I wish it were that simple. Oliver Shykles, researcher, "fairy, peace-nik tree-hugging asshole," as one jealous reader called him and we love him for it. Yuriy Kushnir, webmaster extraordinaire; Ray Romano, Creative Director and on-switch for my brain; Tom D'Adamo, who translates me into English; Zane Groshelle for breaking the media's truth-hymen; Angelo Staeldi, camera and caffeine; Christine Speicher for Art and Life Direction; Dave Ambrose, film editing and "Palast Noir;" Tikonaut Ana Chen; Santiago Juarez, consciousness; Victoria Crawford, archivist; Liz Mescall for the *español con corazon*; Marianne Dickinson; Keri Melshenker; and portrait film ultra-artist Lili Wilde for social nutworking and keeping other boys off my baby's motorcycle.

And an up to my homey "Jones in London," Meirion Jones, my producer at BBC Television *Newsnight*, and patient film director, "NO NO NO WRONG WRONG WRONG YOU'RE FUCKING MAD." Nothing is true until Jones says it's true.

To Benno Friedman, who conceived of the idea of *Vultures' Picnic*, but who deserves none of the blame. To Donna Litowitz, my *Yiddishe momme* who introduced me to Nanook. You're right, I say *fuck* too much.

To the Rosenstein Family and Puffin Foundation because the Truth is brutally expensive. To Michael and Sheila Wilkins, Sharon Duignan, Norman Lear, Bill Perkins, Andrea Friedell, Steve Bing, and the Michaan Family for investing in my fact mine. To Doris Reed, my favorite felon. To Working Assets, Caipirinha Foundation, the Threshold Foundation and Lori Grace, Sara McCay, Dr. Alice Tang, Jeff Barden, Danila Oder, James Yedor, Robert and Chandra Friese, Frank Kovacs, trampolinearian Barbara Kramer, Hope Morrissett, Alison "AL" Kennedy, Bill Perk, Bonnie Raitt and Jackson Browne, Pat Morrison, Timothy Finn, John B. Gilpin, Amy-Grace Shrack, James Schamus, Barbara Gummere *and* her mom, and David Johnson for help, which kept us breathing. To Joey Kaempfer and Andy Tobias for e-mails and a lifeline. And Theron Horton for investigative number crunching. And giant thanks to wave maven Kelly Slater.

And to the funders of the Arctic-to-Amazon investigation of BP: Joy and Jeff Vidheecharoen-Glatz, Brian Joiner, Erik Sjoberg (and for your research), Steve Kelem, Michael Finn, Helen Shoup (supporter from the beginning),

James Fadiman and truth-hunter producer Dorothy Fadiman, Stuart Pollock, Tony Shanahan, Ian Graham, Cindy Moeckel, Betty Dobson, Elena Anzalone, Brandon Gant, Stephen Church, William Veale, M. L. McGaughran, Janette Rainwater, Todd Diehl, Anne Posel and Pat Thurston and the triplets, David Johnson, Elliot and Nick Kralj, Anthony Spanovic, Bob "On the Front-lines" Fitrakis, Dale Pollekoff, David Riley, Annie and Willie Nelson, Ann and Mike Chickey, David Kahn, Kenneth Green, Keith Fuchslocher, Paul Mann, CF Beck, Janis Weisbrot, Doris Selz and Erwin Springbrunn, Steven G. Owens, Victoria Ward, Frank Reid, Gale Georgalas, William Schneider, Suzanne Irwin-Wells, Dan Beach, Fritz Schenk, Kenneth Fingeret, David Pelleg, Dick Shorter, John Wetherhold, Charles Turk, Edward Farmilant, Donald Duryee, Gilbert Williams, Sam Cowan, Tina Rhoades, Jack Chester, David Thomas, David Griggs, Barbara Sher, John Pearce, Peter Stubbs, and Charles and Candia Varni. And to NetOneMedia, our electronic postmen.

To Alan Rusbridger and David Leigh at *The Guardian* and *The Observer* and to John Pilger for saving my sorry job there; to Air Americans Randi Rhodes, Richard Greene, Janeane Garofalo, San Seder, Cenk Uygur, Mark Riley, Nicole Sandler, Marc Maron, Laura Flanders, Stacy Taylor, Mike Malloy, Cynthia Black, Al Sharpton, Shelly and Anita Drobny, John Manzo, Stephanie Miller, and especially Thom Hartmann for the happy side of ADD (our plane may have crashed but we still fly), and especially my supporter-megaphone Mike Papantonio and his co-host and my co-penman Bobby Kennedy (and their *Ring of Fire* wingmen Scott Millican and Farron Cousins).

To Kevin Sutcliffe and Dorothy Byrne of Channel 4 for paying for the whale meat. To Jann Wenner for sucking me into *Rolling Stone;* to Rabbi Michael Lerner at *Tikkun* and the Network of Spiritual Progressives; and Graydon Carter, Cullen Murphy, and Doug Stumpf for a welcome at *Vanity Fair;* Joe Conason at *The National Memo*; and at The Nation Institute, Katrina vanden Heuvel, John Nichols, Victor Navasky, and Esther Kaplan; Rick MacArthur at *Harper's;* and Matt Rothschild of *The Progressive* and Joel Bleifuss of *In These Times;* Bob Fitrakis and Harvey Wasserman at *The Cleveland Press;* and Larry Flynt and Bruce David at *Hustler,* not afraid to reveal it all.

To Chavala Madlena and Maggie O'Kane at Guardian Films for insisting we continue the Vulture hunt.

To Gail Ross, Anna Sproul, and Diana Finch for representation without taxation. To Jessica Horvath, Carrie Thornton, Penguin USA editors, for their impossible patience and Dan Simon and *Seven Stories*. To Andreas Campomar and Dan Hind, for publication under the Queen's nose.

And to the radio, TV, and print hosts, producers, editors who first aired and printed my samizdat reports: Pacifica Radio aeronauts Dennis Bernstein of *Flashpoints* and Amy Goodman and the *Democracy Now!* crew, Brad Friedman and the revitalizing Gary Null, Harry Allen, Verna Avery Brown, Heather Gray Radio Free Georgia, Allison Cooper, Jim Lafferty, Deepa Fernandez, Rob Lorei, Ree Blake, Kris Welsh, Daphne Wysham (*Here's lookin' at you, kid*), Dread Scott Keyes, Esther Armah, Indra Hardat, Tony Bates, Hugh Hamilton and Sharan Harper, Blase Bonpane, Sam Husseini, Fernando Velasquez, Sonali Sohatkar, Mark Babawi, Dave Mazza and the KBOO folks in Portland, Otis MacLay, Rob Lorei, Sam Fuqua, Tiffany Jordan, Jennifer Kiser, and the abnormally brilliant Norman Stockwell; Mark Babawi, radio newbies Martin Eder and Activist San Diego; and to the stand-up giant Jerry Quickley. And to the columnists who sneak Greg Palast into their big-shot papers: Bob Herbert, Paul Krugman, and EJ Dionne.

And to air pirates Louie Free (guilty of committing truth), Chuck "This Is Hell" Mertz, Scott "Between the Lines" Harris, Alan Chartock, Bob Lebensold, Alex Jones (who will outlive the IMF), Jim Hightower for the hat, Mike Feder, Leon Wilmer, Christiane Brown, Bob McChesney, Mark Crispin Miller, Jeff Cohen, Peter Werbe, Duke Skorich, Chris Cook, Bev Smith, Meria Heller, Joyce Riley and Mike De Rosa, Harry Osibin, Phil Donahue, GritTV, Link TV, Linda Starr and Santita Jackson and the Reverend Jesse Jackson for graceful Sunday mornings. And my best to Ed Garvey and Fighting Bob.

To the electronic publishers who've busted through the media's blackprint Berlin Wall, including Mark Karlin and *BuzzFlash,* Marc Ash and Jason Leopold at *Truthout,* Arianna Huffington, Michael Moore, Scott Thill at *Morphizm,* Bob Krall at *Op-Ed News,* and Nicole Power at *SuicideGirls.*

Huge thanks to: Darick Robertson for re-creating the Super Anti-Heroes of *Vultures' Picnic,* the comic book; to Mark Swedlund for no bullshit; to Uncle Ollie Kaufman (alev shalom) for showing me that geniuses must be hacks; for Marcia Levy because we love grandma; and for D. Neil Levy for the Lobbygate front op and the inside on Morgan (in memoriam). And to Jello Biafra for help with the un-Dead and Winston Smith for the *Armed Madhouse* and *Best Democracy Money Can Buy* posters and illustrations of the inside of my skull; and pens-mightier-than-swords Bob Grossman (*Jokers Wild*); and Ted Rall,

Lloyd Dangle and Lukas Ketner (*Steal Back Your Vote*); and Stephen Kling and his Avenging Angels.

To Stereophonic Space Sound Unlimited, Willie Nelson (*Democracy*), Chris Shiflett (*Palast Investigates theme*), Boots Riley & The Coup (*5 Million Ways to Kill a CEO*), Funkspace (*Mr. Beale, Meet Mr. Palast*), Moby (*Bush Family Fortunes*), Brod Bagert (*Jambalaya*)—and Miss Badpenny and The Bad Actors (*Human Condition, She's A Man*) with the genius of Tony Fabel—for giving me the rights to the soundtrack of my confused life (available on the interactive edition and at GregPalast/VulturesPicnic.com).

And to the entire Rosen Family who carry it on.

And, finally, thanks to all the jack-offs who send me death threats and thereby give me a reason to live.

And to Linda, the co-author of my life. If we could do it again, my love, I know you wouldn't. But I would. Most definitely.

Dedicated to The Peanuts, that one day you may read this book and understand your father—then explain him to me.

And to *mein schrecklicher Punk Engel,* our Investigatrix, the quadrilingual truth-a-licious Leni Badpenny von Eckardt. No, I *don't* know shit about love.

TREASURE HUNT: Like all gumshoes, I fancy myself a cultured man with a knowledge of the classics good enough to fake it at a Soho cocktail party. I've thrown in two plagiarized lines each from Dante, T. S. Eliot, Ezra Pound, Shakespeare, Raymond Chandler, Charles Bukowski, the Torah, and Oscar Hammerstein, and one each from Yeats, Melville, Schiller, Douglas Adams, and Saint Augustine. The first 100 readers to find just one unattributed reference from six of these authors and saints will get a free film, book, or deck of marked cards from our foundation. (Send to: GregPalast.com/contact.) Note: The prize remains unclaimed for the line in *Armed Madhouse* stolen from Hunter Thompson.

Also available from *New York Times* bestselling author Greg Palast

978-0-452-28831-7

978-0-452-28567-5

Plume
A member of Penguin Group (USA)
www.penguin.com